NORWAY'S WAR

ROBERT FERGUSON is an award-winning writer, translator and radio dramatist. He is the author of numerous books, including *Scandinavians: In Search of the Soul of the North*, *The Vikings: A History*, *Henrik Ibsen: A New Biography*, and *Enigma: The Life of Knut Hamsun*, which was nominated for the *Los Angeles Times* Best Biography Award and won the University of London J.G. Robertson Award. His translation of Lars Mytting's *Norwegian Wood* won Non-Fiction Book of the Year in 2016. Born in the UK in 1948, he emigrated to Norway in 1983 and has made his home there since.

Also by Robert Ferguson

Enigma: The Life of Knut Hamsun

Henrik Ibsen: A New Biography

The Hammer and the Cross: A New History of the Vikings

Scandinavians: In Search of the Soul of the North

Kierkegaard: Great Thinkers on Modern Life

The Cabin in the Mountains: A Norwegian Odyssey

ROBERT FERGUSON
NORWAY'S WAR

A People's Struggle Against Nazi Tyranny

1940–45

An Apollo Book

First published in the UK in 2025 by Head of Zeus Ltd,
part of Bloomsbury Publishing Plc

Copyright © Robert Ferguson, 2025

The moral right of Robert Ferguson to be identified as the author
of this work has been asserted in accordance with the Copyright,
Designs and Patents Act of 1988.

All rights reserved. No part of this publication may be: i) reproduced or transmitted
in any form, electronic or mechanical, including photocopying, recording or by means
of any information storage or retrieval system without prior permission in writing from the
publishers; or ii) used or reproduced in any way for the training, development or operation
of artificial intelligence (AI) technologies, including generative AI technologies. The rights
holders expressly reserve this publication from the text and data mining exception
as per Article 4(3) of the Digital Single Market Directive (EU) 2019/790.

9 7 5 3 1 2 4 6 8

A catalogue record for this book is available from the British Library.

ISBN (HB): 9781801104821
ISBN (eBook): 9781801104845

Typeset by Silicon Chips
Maps by Jeff Edwards

Printed and bound in Great Britain by
CPI Group (UK) Ltd, Croydon CR0 4YY

Bloomsbury Publishing Plc
50 Bedford Square, London, WC1B 3DP, UK
Bloomsbury Publishing Ireland Limited,
29 Earlsfort Terrace, Dublin 2, D02 AY28, Ireland

HEAD OF ZEUS LTD
5–8 Hardwick Street
London EC1R 4RG

To find out more about our authors and books
visit www.headofzeus.com

For product safety related questions contact productsafety@bloomsbury.com

Contents

Maps   *vii*

Prologue – Sognefjord, 12 April 1934   1

Part 1
From Independence to Occupation   3

1. The Pursuit of Neutrality, 1905–40   5
2. Occupation: The First Six Months,
   9 April – 25 September 1940   19

Part 2
The State Versus the People   37

3. Aryan Dreams, Norwegian Nightmares, 1941   39
4. Legislation for a National Socialist Revolution, 1942   67
5. The Conscience Struggle, 1942   91
6. The Norwegian Holocaust,
   14 March 1942 – 26 November 1942   105

Part 3
Violence and Culture   129

7. 'Osvald', 'Yellow Cheese' and the Violent
   Resistance, 1941–4   131
8. Revolution as Reaction: Culture Under
   Quisling, 1940–5   164

Part 4
Gunnar Waaler's War   **183**

9. Waaler's Work   185
10. The Execution of Inspector Gunnar Eilifsen,
    August 1943   203
11. Waaler's Arrest, 1944   215
12. Waaler Meets Albert Weiner   232

Part 5
Liberation and Aftermath   **247**

13. The Beginning of the End   249
14. Skallum   267
15. The Legal Reckoning   300

Epilogue: Requiem for a Border Guide   329
Echoes and Afterlives   397

Chronology   411
Endnotes   421
Bibliography   426
Image Credits   434
Acknowledgements   436
Index   438

Norway, 9 April – 7 June 1940

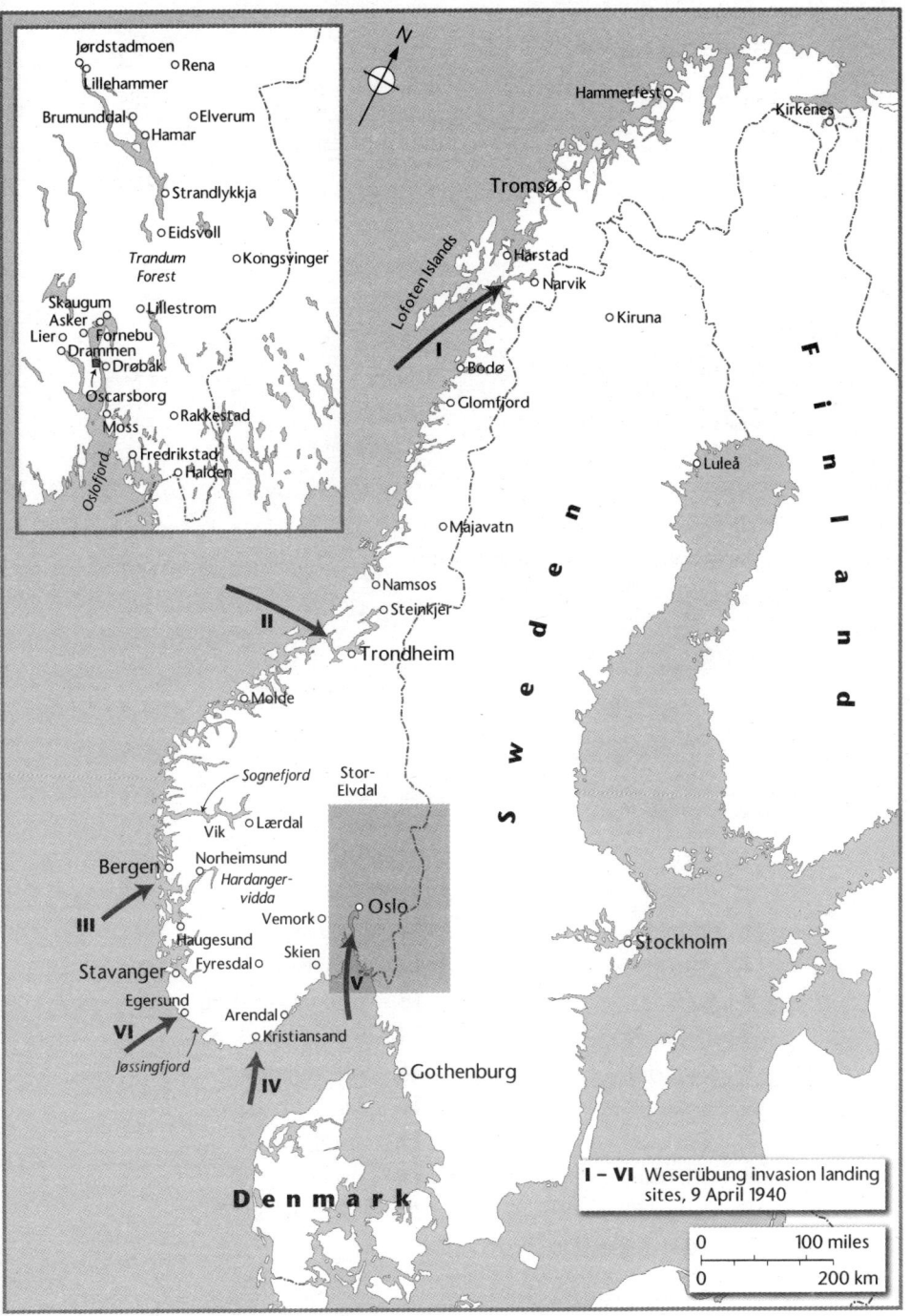

The Counties of Norway

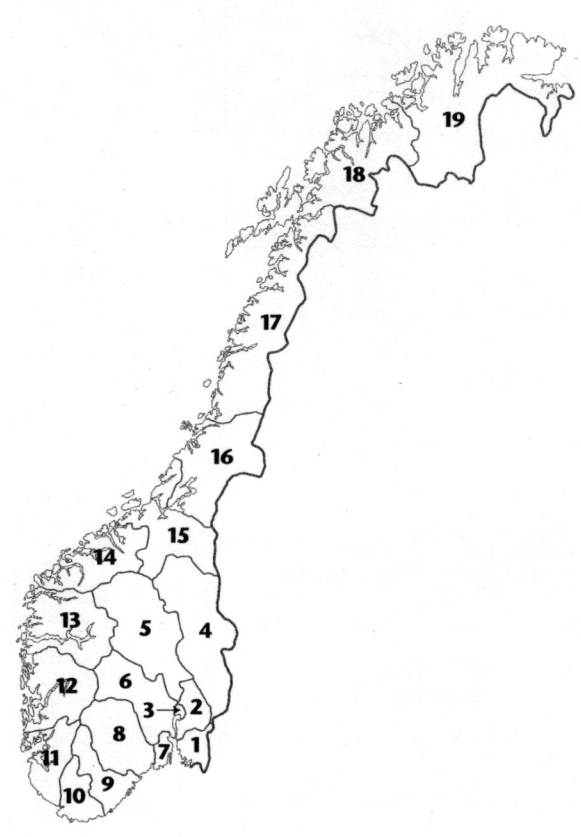

1	Østfold	**11**	Rogaland
2	Akershus	**12**	Hordaland
3	Oslo	**13**	Sogn og Fjordane
4	Hedmark	**14**	Møre og Romsdal
5	Oppland	**15**	Sør-Trøndelag
6	Buskerud	**16**	Nord-Trøndelag
7	Vestfold	**17**	Nordland
8	Telemark	**18**	Troms
9	Aust-Agder	**19**	Finnmark
10	Vest-Agder		

Oslo

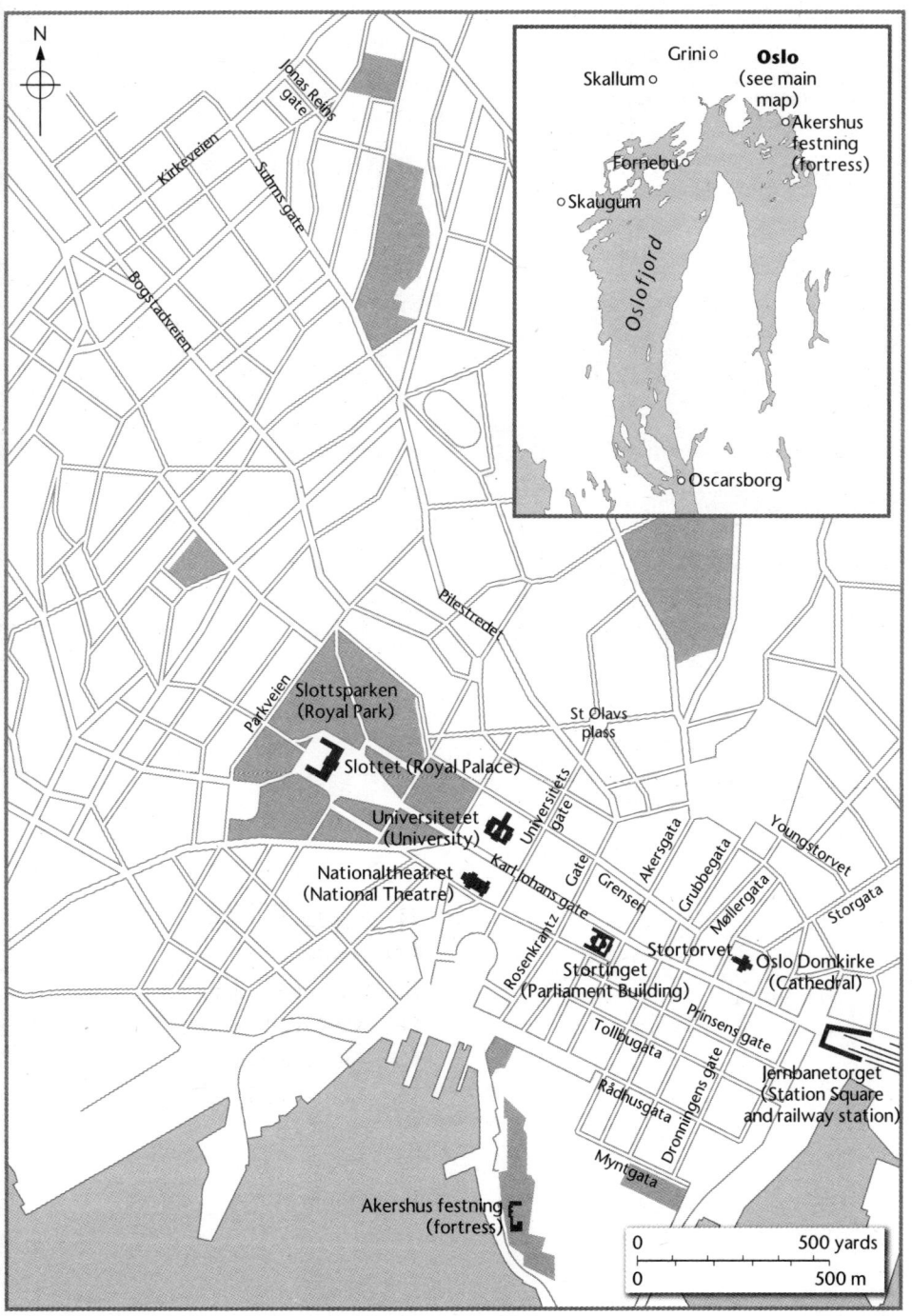

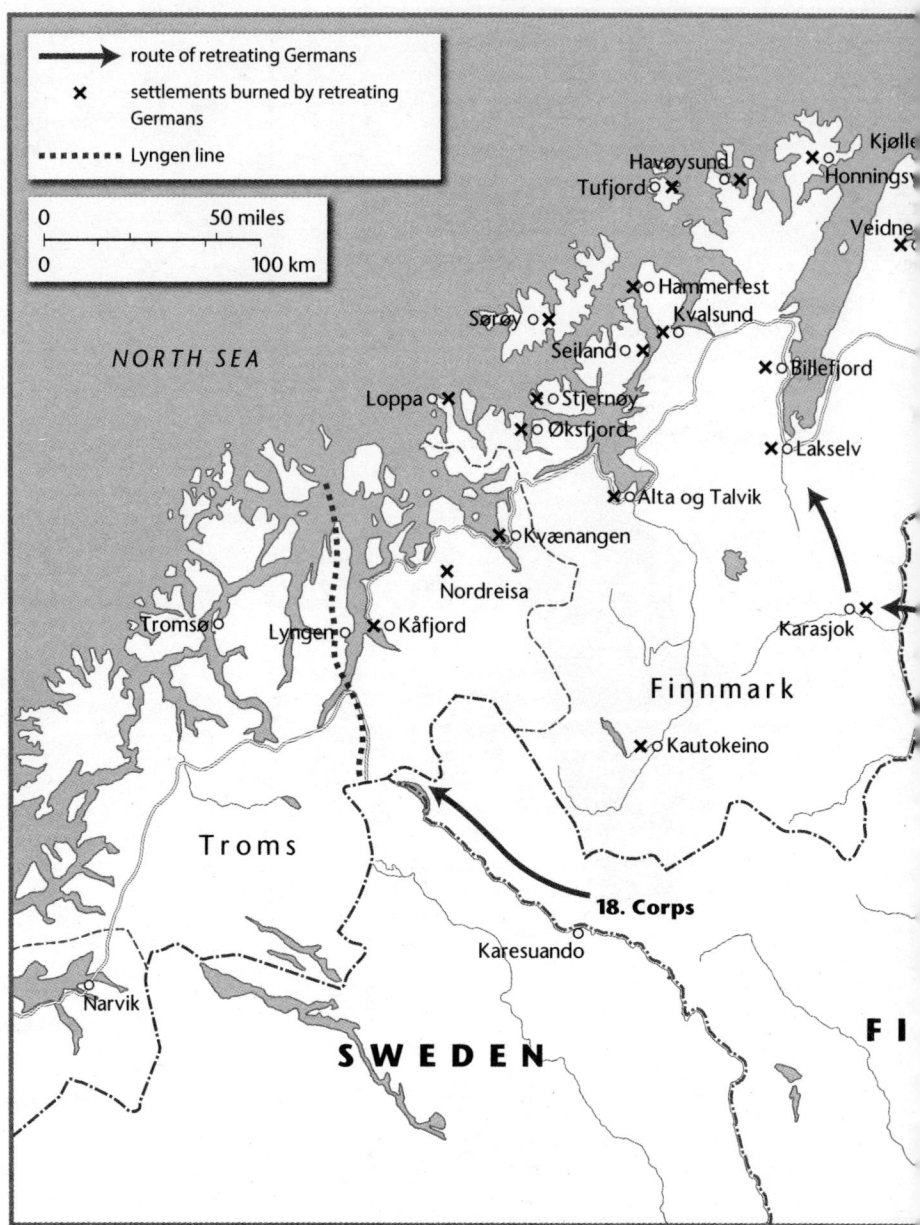

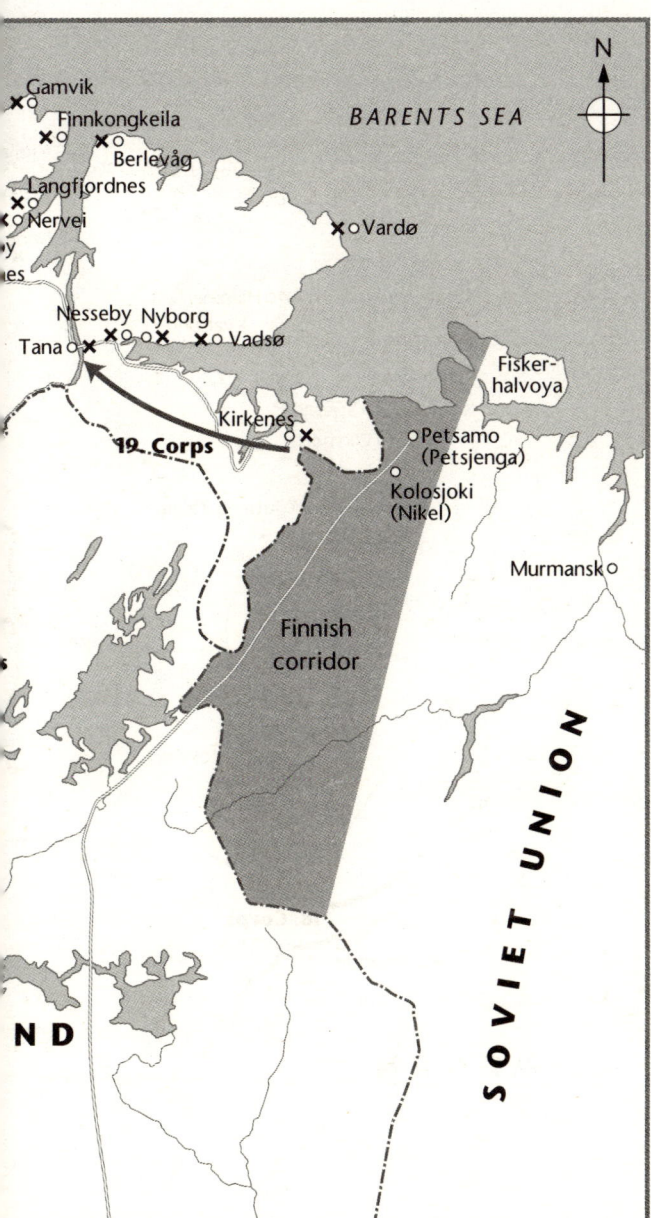

Prologue
Sognefjord, 12 April 1934

Each year for twenty-three years, between 1888 and 1914, the German emperor Kaiser Wilhelm II spent the summer cruising the Norwegian fjords in his royal yacht, the *Hohenzollern*. These annual trips of his prefigure in a curious way a brief journey made by Adolf Hitler to Sognefjord in 1934, in what was the new German chancellor's first trip abroad since taking office the previous year. On 11 April the *Deutschland* left Kiel to take part in spring manoeuvres in East Prussia. The following day the cruiser appeared in the waters of the Sognefjord. The local newspaper carried a brief report of the visit:

> On board the Deutschland, which paid a lengthy visit to Sogn last Thursday, was none other than the German chancellor, Adolf Hitler. The ship sailed to the mouth of the Nærøyfjord before turning and sailing on to Hardanger and from there back to Hamburg.

Bergens Tidende was one of several newspapers that carried an interview with Martin Karlsen, the young Norwegian who had piloted the *Deutschland* into the fjord. No, he hadn't actually

conversed with Hitler, but they had exchanged greetings several times. The chancellor spent almost the whole time on the bridge and was 'as excited as a boy by the fjords and the beautiful weather'. He spoke to everyone, Karlsen said, sailors as well as officers, in the same informal and friendly way, and appeared to be very well liked by all. Karlsen's overall impression was of 'a good-natured and pleasant man'. Underlining the fact that it was Hitler's first trip abroad, the paper added that it was 'worth noting it was to the Norwegian fjords'. They were all sure the chancellor would be back one day.[1]

The local pride was pardonable, the prophetic irony unintentional. Adolf Hitler never returned, but the *Deutschland* did. Almost six years later to the day she sailed up the Oslofjord under cover of darkness, without lights and showing no flag, on her way to capture Oslo as part of Hitler's *Weserübung* plan to occupy Norway. Group V consisted of another cruiser, the *Blücher*; a light cruiser, the *Emden*; three torpedo boats; and the *Deutschland*, cannily renamed the *Lützow* just weeks previously.[2] Confident as he was of success, Hitler wasn't willing to risk the possibility of losing a ship called the *Deutschland* in the attack on Norway.

PART 1

FROM INDEPENDENCE TO OCCUPATION

1
The Pursuit of Neutrality, 1905–40

When Norway unilaterally declared its independence from Sweden on 7 June 1905 it brought to an end 500 years of dependence on its two more powerful and populous neighbours, Denmark and Sweden. A hundred years as part of a double kingdom known as Sweden-Norway that came into existence as a result of the Napoleonic Wars had done little to displace the preceding four centuries of close association with Denmark. Norwegian culture remained largely Danish culture, its written language was Danish, and the Danish capital Copenhagen was its main regional access to higher education. So loyal were the Norwegians to the Danish crown that when the Treaty of Kiel awarded Norway to Sweden as compensation for the loss of Finland to the Russians, a group of prominent Norwegians, meeting at Eidsvoll in 1814, drafted a constitution and on 17 May invited their Danish regent Prince Christian Fredrik to be their king. After brief but fierce fighting the Swedes gained control of their new prize and Karl XIII became ruler of the double kingdom of Sweden-Norway. As a gesture of good faith, he promised to abide by the terms of the Eidsvoll constitution. Yet so extensive were the powers of devolution claimed by the constitution that full independence seemed an inevitable goal, and the history of Norway in the nineteenth century is, above all, a history of the pursuit of this goal, to its achievement in 1905.

A *sine qua non* of the pursuit was the creation of a distinct Norwegian national identity. Who, during the 400 years of Danish rule, might best have preserved this elusive quantity? The conclusion that emerged was that it had best been preserved by those living in the mountains and remote valleys of the country, unspoiled by the corruptions of contact with city life and by travel. As the century advanced and a Norwegian national identity began to take shape, in music, literature, architecture and the visual arts, it did so on and around the theme of the rural way of life and the beliefs, stories, clothing, songs, music and way of speaking of the country people as representing what it really meant to be Norwegian.

As a result of this unspoken but ever-present imperative the final decades of the nineteenth century became a golden age of Norwegian culture. The theatre produced Henrik Ibsen, literature the novelist Knut Hamsun, music the highly influential composer Edvard Grieg, who pioneered the use of native folk music as a basis for many of his compositions, and art Edvard Munch. Without exception, all these names first came to European prominence through the enthusiasm of Germany.[3] A host of names less well known in the anglophone world also enjoyed the pleasures of a European reputation as a result of German admiration, including Norway's greatest *dikterhøvding* (poet chieftain) Bjørnstjerne Bjørnson and the novelists Alexander Kielland and Jonas Lie Snr.* Every great painter of Norway's school of national romanticism received his training at the academy in Dresden, where the father of the school, the Norwegian master J. C. Dahl, was professor. Duke Georg of Saxe-Meiningen's private theatre group was producing plays written by the young Henrik Ibsen long before Ibsen

---

* Not to be confused with his grandson, the politician, police officer and novelist Jonas Lie.

came to the attention of English theatregoers through the work of his translator, William Archer.[4] The great playwright himself lived for lengthy periods in Dresden during his lifetime of self-imposed exile. Albert Langen, a young German who was married to one of Bjørnson's daughters, was so enthusiastic about Knut Hamsun's 1892 novel *Mysteries* that he started a publishing company in Munich in order to translate and publish it.[5] He followed this up with translations of many other books by Norwegian writers. Edvard Munch's journey to worldwide fame began in Berlin in the autumn of 1892 as a result of the opening and sensational closure of his exhibition at the Verein Berliner Künstler. Edvard Grieg took his formal musical training at Leipzig.

Probably as a result of these close cultural ties with Germany, a doctrine of Pan-Scandinavian brotherhood that had been popular among Norwegian artists and intellectuals in the middle years of the century gave way, following the unification of Germany in 1871, to the broader vision of Pan-Germanism. This followed the scientific fashion of the times in dividing humans into genetically distinct tribes, each with its own set of characteristics, each with a fixed place within a hierarchy of tribes. As the end of the century approached, the work of these cultural giants, complemented by Fridtjof Nansen's worldwide fame for achievements that included crossing Greenland on skis in 1888 and leading the *Fram* expedition of 1893–96 closer to the North Pole than anyone before him, seemed to guarantee a prominent place for the small country within this hierarchy of tribes. For a small country struggling to free itself of the heritage of four centuries of Danish rule followed by a century of unwanted union with Sweden, one of Pan-Germanism's greatest attractions was the negative virtue of not being Pan-Scandinavianism. As the nineteenth century drew to a close, all these factors had combined to form a Norwegian national identity so distinct that the country's right to independence was never seriously questioned by impartial observers following the *Storting*'s unilateral declaration of independence on 7 June 1905. The Swedes rattled their sabres, but with the threat of a British warship at anchor off Kristiania, the Norwegian declaration was accepted with a reasonably good grace.

While German enthusiasm for Norwegian culture was respectful and admiring, for contemporary Britons it hardly even existed. Norway was regarded as essentially a vast national park that could be used for their own pleasure and recreation. Between 1872 and 1921 a Yorkshireman named William Cecil Slingsby visited Norway twenty-one times and in the process introduced Norwegians to the novel idea of climbing mountains not in pursuit of financial gain, nor even to hunt, but for the sheer challenge of it. The title of Slingsby's classic memoir of his adventurous life, *Norway, the Northern Playground: Sketches of Climbing and Mountain Exploration in Norway between 1872 and 1903*, first published in 1904, illustrates well the difference in attitudes in the tripartite Germany–Norway–Great Britain relationship.[6] The Britons most familiar to Norwegians of the late nineteenth and early twentieth centuries were the so-called *lakselords* (salmon lords), wealthy industrialists from northern England and Scotland rather than genuine aristocrats, who built themselves second homes close to salmon rivers and arrived each year to spend the summer months fishing. Socially close if asymmetrical relationships developed between these *lakselords* and the Norwegians with whom they came into contact during their summer sojourns and whom they employed as domestics, guides and gillies.

As representatives of the dominant world power of the time, the British visitors enjoyed a respectful and distanced admiration. But it was a lopsided admiration, and in the older sense of the word as denoting the painters, poets, writers and composers who form a country's outward image, the British remained indifferent to Norwegian culture. Yet the overwhelming majority of Norwegians were anglophile to a fault. That the British acted as guarantors for Norway's declaration of independence from Sweden in 1905 played some part in this. So did the fact that Maud, wife of the Norwegians' new king Haakon VII, was the youngest daughter of the reigning

British monarch, Edward VII.* Norway was a declared neutral in the 1914–18 war, but that did not prevent the great majority of Norwegians from hoping for a British victory. One result of this Anglophilia was to leave Norway's intellectual and cultural elites marooned in their preference for Germany over Britain.

The Russian Revolution of 1917 had repercussions in Norway that were probably more extreme than in any other European country. In March 1918, *Den norske arbeiderpartiet* (the Norwegian Labour Party) passed a conference resolution reserving for itself 'the right to resort to revolutionary mass action in the struggle for the economic emancipation of the working class'. Uniquely among pre-war socialist parties outside the Soviet Union, the Norwegian Labour Party joined the Comintern, the international union of communist and socialist parties, placing itself under direct ideological supervision of Moscow. When party members voted to end the affiliation in 1923, revolutionary hard-liners resigned and formed *Norges Kommunistiske Parti* (the Norwegian Communist Party).

The first organised reaction from conservatives to the rise of communism was the creation of the *Fedrelandslaget* (Fatherland League) in 1925, on the initiative of Fridtjof Nansen, still Norway's most famous name and an influential figure in the diplomatic canvassing that preceded the declaration of independence in 1905. Independent Norway's first prime minister, Christian Michelsen, was a co-founder. The aim of the league was to rally 'national' elements against the threat from 'international' elements, by which was meant communism. The different factions of the Labour Party, now joined by the moderate socialists of *Norges Socialdemokratiske Arbeiderparti* (the Norwegian Social Democratic Labour Party), responded by offering the electorate a policy that, while committed to democracy, was still sufficiently left-wing for socialists to be able to support it with a good conscience, and in the election of 1927

---

* Haakon was a Danish prince. Christened Carl Fredrik, he adopted the Norwegian name and number to create a link to 1380 and the death of the last king of an independent Norway, Haakon VI.

the Norwegian Labour Party secured fifty-nine seats in the Storting, enough to enable it to form a minority government in January 1928.

This lasted just four weeks, its brief life only an extreme example of the outstanding characteristic of Norwegian political life during the period between 1920 and 1940 which saw altogether twelve different minority governments. Even in that short time, however, it managed to further alarm the conservative elements in Norwegian society when the new government's prime minister, Christopher Hornsrud, announced in his inaugural statement that the goal of the new government would be 'to prepare the country for the introduction of socialism'.

The polarisation of political opinion between left and right in the country reached a climax in the early years of the 1930s. In 1931 a strike at the Norsk Hydro plant at Menstad, in Telemark, turned violent when 120 policemen were sent in to disperse workers picketing the plant and preventing strike-breakers from reporting for work. In a pitched battle the heavily outnumbered police were routed by the pickets. The violence reached such a pitch that under Vidkun Quisling, the Defence Minister in Peder Kolstad's new *Bondepartiet* (Farmers Party)* government, troops and naval vessels were sent in to restore order. Many conservatives gave Quisling the credit for this decision. Yet it appears he had little to do with it. The Minister of Justice, Asbjørn Lindboe, who was present at the cabinet meeting when the decision was taken, recorded in his diary that Quisling played no part in it. It was the restoration of order at Menstad that gained Quisling a reputation as a strong, silent leader that he would attempt to exploit following the German invasion in 1940, although it seems clear the reputation owed more to his silence than his strength.

Vidkun Abraham Lauritz Quisling, who would play such an important part in the administration of occupied Norway between 1940 and 1945, was the son of a priest from Fyresdal. Born in 1887, in 1906 he studied at the Norwegian Military College where he

---

* In 1959 the party changed its name to *Senterpartiet* (the Centre Party).

proved a brilliant scholar, graduating with the best exam marks ever achieved since the college opened in 1817. Between 1918 and 1921 he worked as Fridtjof Nansen's assistant in famine relief efforts in Russia, where together they helped to save the lives of thousands. Quisling emerged from the chaotic experience with some sympathy for the goals of the communist revolution and in the 1920s flirted briefly with one of Norway's leading socialists, Martin Tranmæl. His advances included an offer to strengthen the Labour Party by forming a group of 'Red Guards'. He also advocated Norwegian recognition of the Soviet Union and was critical of the negative attitude shown towards the Soviet Union by the major European powers.

By 1929, however, Quisling's attitude had changed. In that year he published *Russland og vi* (Russia and Us), a book in which he articulated his fears of a communist revolution in Norway and the political takeover of the country by its powerful neighbour in the north in the name of international socialism. His tenure as Defence Minister in Kolstad's *Bondepartiet* government between 1931 and 1933, and on Kolstad's death under Jens Hundseid, coincided with a period when tensions between communists and the authorities were at their height. Matters looked to be heading towards a crisis of unmanageable proportions between left and right. One month after Hitler came to power in Germany in January 1933, Quisling was proposing a dictatorship as the only solution to the problem, in the Farmers Party's organ *Nationen*.*

His first move was to try to encourage the two main parties of the right, *Høyre* (Right/the Conservatives) and the Farmers Party, to put aside their differences and unite in the face of the communist threat. When this idea foundered, encouraged by the success of Hitler's Nazi Party (*Nationalsozialistische Deutsche Arbeiterpartei* or NSDAP) in Germany and Mussolini's triumphs

---

* Despite occasional protests, Quisling's period as a minister in a democratically elected government means that, to this day, his portrait hangs in the Storting gallery of ministers.

in Italy, in May 1933 he formed his own Norwegian fascist party, to which he gave the name *Nasjonal Samling* (National Unity).

From the start Quisling was concerned to identify his party as a Norwegian, national, cultural manifestation quite distinct from the Italian fascism of Mussolini, and he did so largely by requisitioning Norway's Viking past to create the public image of National Unity. All the symbols and terminologies introduced for the new party were self-conscious revivals from a 'golden age' of the previous millennium. The party's first annual rally was held in 1934 at Stiklestad in Trøndelag, the site of the battle in which Quisling's greatest hero and exemplar, Olav Haraldsson, the saint-king who unified Norway and established Christianity in the country, lost his life in 1030. Quisling further reinforced the identification by adopting the *Olavskors* (St Olav Cross) as the party's symbol and venerating the date of Olav's death on 29 July as a holy day.* A similarly symbolic thought lay behind the choice for the second rally in 1935 of Hafrsfjorden, where Harald Hårfagre (Finehair), attempting an earlier unification of Norway in the 890s, had triumphed in battle over an alliance of regional chieftains. On the model of Hitler's Brownshirts, Quisling also created a uniformed personal guard of 'stormtroopers' to which he gave the name of *hird*, as the retinue of personal followers of kings and earls in the Viking Age were collectively known. The principal task of this *Rikshird* (National Hird) was to maintain law and order at the party's rallies and meetings, as these were often the target of violent attempts to disrupt them by communists and others opposed to its anti-democratic policies. An *ungdomsfylking* (Youth Movement) was created to appeal to schoolchildren and students.

In another conscious invocation of Norway's lost golden age, the party adopted the use of runic letters and lettering styles in its iconography and literature. An early member, Harald Damsleth, son of a German mother and Norwegian father and a commercial artist talented enough to have been offered work by the Walt

---

* In due course the party image was simplified to a *solkors* (Sun Cross).

Disney Studios (he refused, citing family reasons), produced stunning examples of propagandic poster art for National Unity that made regular use of imagery from the Viking Age. A sustained attempt was made to reintroduce a formal greeting found in the Old Norse sagas, *Heil og sæl* ('health and happiness'), for use between members.

Over time, as the party's sense of itself and its purpose developed, other ingredients were added. These often tended in the direction of greater uniformity in conduct, greater exactitude in ritual. *Hirdboken*, a handbook for members written by Orvar Sæther, one of the *hird*'s more influential leaders in the late 1930s and into the war years, contained among other things precise instructions on how to give the straight-armed party salute in a variety of differing circumstances, including how to do so while riding a bicycle and unexpectedly encountering a comrade. A series of photographs helped to make the tricky manoeuvre easier to master.

Yet neither in 1933, when the party polled 2.2 per cent of the vote, nor in the election of 1936, when its share fell to 1.8 per cent, did National Unity succeed in persuading people that it had the answers to the social problems and tensions of the times. In fact, the Labour Party had taken much of the sting out of a potential class-based civil war by restoring the democratic pledge to its programme for the 1933 election, and with the election in 1936 of a Labour majority government pursuing social democratic policies under its prime minister Johan Nygaardsvold, fifteen years of political turmoil in the country had effectively come to an end.

In its foreign policy Nygaardsvold's government tried to marry two separate but related strains of political and social ideology. By some margin the smallest of the three Scandinavian countries, Norway's socialist rulers pursued the same policy of neutrality as Sweden had since the end of the Napoleonic Wars, and the Danes since defeat in the war of 1864 against the Prussians which had led to the loss of a quarter of Denmark's territory and a third of its population. It was a policy that had served Norway tolerably well during the 1914–18 war, with the country's anglophile instincts encouraged by the British blockade of Germany that left Norway largely dependent on the countries of the triple *entente* (Britain, France and Russia) for its import needs.

Aware that the tensions following the end of the war had not by any means been resolved, it nevertheless seemed to the Nygaardsvold government that an invasion by land was unlikely, and by sea equally so, since the British navy still controlled the North Sea. Its defence of its neutrality therefore rested on a distinctly abstract resolution to pursue a foreign policy based on what the Foreign Minister Halvdan Koht described as *en forutseende utenriksledelse* ('a prescient leadership in foreign policy').

As socialists, the Labour Party's leaders felt a natural reluctance to any thought of militarising the realm against the threat of an invasion, fearing the ways in which military power could be used to break strikes, as had happened at Menstad. Instead, the party preferred a model in which a military national defence was replaced by a civilian coastguard and a civilian *landsvakt* (National Guard). The result was that through most of the 1930s, Norwegian national defence was deliberately neglected and downplayed and the increasingly urgent expressions of alarm from the commander-in-chief of the armed forces were ignored or dismissed. The budget allocation to the armed forces was cut drastically. The Liberal Party government of Johan Ludwig Mowinckel that preceded Nygaardsvold's had argued that war appeared to be losing ground as the favoured means of solving international conflicts and institutions like the League of Nations now existed as the preferred option, and that for these reasons the danger of war had decreased. Quisling's reiterated argument that a strong military was necessary both to defend the country against invasion by a foreign power with no ideological purpose other than to gain territory or power and to counter 'powerful forces' within Norway itself, which were 'active in transforming every expression of discontent into social discontent, and transforming war from a struggle between states into a struggle between international classes', went unheeded.

By 1935, with Nygaardsvold's Labour government in place, Norway was committed to pursuing the ideals of social democracy. The most striking expression of pacifism as its preferred position in both domestic and foreign contexts lay in the party's persistent use of a symbol known as *det brukne gevær* (the broken rifle). Used for the first time in 1912, it depicted a rifle being broken in two at the shaft and it remained a popular visual slogan well into the 1930s.

Nygaardsvold's socialist government inherited the results of this long tradition of pacifism. The most notable effect of this lay in the severe reduction in defence spending agreed upon in the budget of 1933 to a level (30 million kroner) which, in the view of the leaders of Norway's armed forces, made effective military and naval defence of the country impossible. Nygaardsvold and his cabinet were aware that the assumption of office in 1935 called for a realistic accommodation between the idealism of opposition and the responsibilities of political office, but the tradition of idealistic pacifism proved tenacious. The viability of the young country's commitment to neutrality would be tested to breaking point following the German invasion of Poland on 1 September 1939 and the British and French declarations of war on Germany two days later on 3 September.

★

In mid-February 1940 a German supply ship, the *Altmark*, was returning to Germany from an assignment to supply oil to the pocket battleship the *Admiral Graf Spee* in the South Atlantic. It carried some 300 British prisoners of war, seamen picked up from merchant ships attacked by the *Graf Spee* before the *Graf Spee* itself was badly damaged in the Battle of the River Plate on 13 December 1939 and scuttled. The *Altmark* managed to get away and on 14 February entered Norwegian waters north of the Trondheim Fjord. With a Norwegian naval escort it continued south along the Norwegian coast. Under international law it had the right to use neutral waters for peaceful passage, even when carrying prisoners of war. The *Altmark*'s captain declined to allow the port authorities in Bergen to inspect his ship, at which point the Norwegians refused to allow the ship to pass through Bergen port war zone. When the Germans expressed concern that the British would seize the ship if it had to take the outer route outside the port war zone, the order was rescinded on higher Norwegian authority and the *Altmark* passed through the zone with a Norwegian escort. It was the first of several contentious breaches of neutrality involved in the incident.

RAF planes spotted the *Altmark* on 15 February and reported the sighting to a flotilla of six British destroyers. In attempting to get away from them the *Altmark* took refuge in the partially frozen waters of the Jøssingfjord in southern Norway, between Egersund and Flekkefjord. At 10.20 p.m., HMS *Cossack* followed, entering the fjord with floodlights on. The *Altmark* reversed towards the *Cossack* in an attempt to force it against the shore but ran aground herself. There was gunfire from the British which was not, according to Norwegian witnesses, answered. Six Germans were killed in the initial shelling, and when the British boarded the *Altmark* the 300 prisoners were freed. The Norwegian government delivered a sharp protest to the British, who claimed in reply that the breach was a mere technicality and that the action was morally justified. The engagement polarised public opinion in Norway. Supporters of the German cause referred to their opponents as *jøssing*, an intended mockery that was presently adopted as a badge of pride by loyal Norwegians.

The episode was the most dramatic in a spate of incidents that put Norway's declared policy of neutrality under severe pressure. In most important respects all were dictated by a single major consideration in the context of the war that had broken out between Great Britain and Germany following the German invasion of Poland in 1939. This was the issue of who could control the supply of iron ore mined at Kiruna, in northern Sweden, that was so essential to the German armaments industry. The summer route for exporting the ore to Germany was via a rail link to the Swedish Baltic port of Luleå and then southwards by sea to Germany. In winter Luleå was ice-bound and could remain unusable for up to six months. The option then was to use the direct rail link west to the Norwegian port of Narvik. Despite being over a hundred miles north of the Arctic circle, Narvik remained ice-free all year round thanks to the warming currents of the Gulf Stream. From Narvik the ore could be shipped down the coast of Norway to Hamburg. If the British could take control of the route, it would enable them to almost completely cut off the supply of iron ore to Germany.

An initial plan to accomplish this took advantage of the unexpected outbreak of war in the north, the so-called Winter War between the Soviet Union and Finland, in which the Russians invaded Finland at the end of November 1939 in a territorial dispute over the Karelian peninsula. In a gesture of Nordic solidarity, a number of young Norwegians travelled north to fight alongside the Finns against the Russians. The British plan involved landing at Narvik and marching inland to cross the border into Sweden and occupy the mines at Kiruna under the pretext of offering military assistance to the Finns. By 11 March 1940, a joint British and French force was ready to embark for Narvik on an operation codenamed Avonmouth. Norway and Sweden had both refused permission for their territorial neutrality to be compromised in this way, but with their eye still on the goal of stopping the export of iron ore to Germany, the British intended to make the landing in Narvik in secrecy and only then to inform the Norwegian government of their presence. For the Allies there was never any question of a full-scale occupation of Norway; the aim was simply to strike what would potentially be a fatal blow against the German arms industry. But two days later, on 13 March 1940, the conflict between Finland and Russia was temporarily resolved by the Treaty of Moscow, which imposed territorial losses on Finland in the north-east and south-east of the country. Hostilities would shortly be resumed and continue for the next five years in what was called the Continuation War, but with the pretext for a British landing gone, Operation Avonmouth had to be abandoned.

The British then came up with an alternative plan to sabotage the export of iron ore, which involved mining Norwegian coastal waters in order to disrupt the transport of the ore between Narvik and Germany. The tactic would force German ships transporting the ore from Narvik out into international waters, where they could legitimately be attacked. The joint British-French operation was planned to start on 8 April. Hitler, however, concerned by what must have seemed to him Norway's less than rigorous pursuit of its claimed neutrality, now decided to go ahead with a long-mooted contingency plan for the invasion of Norway, codenamed Weserübung (the Weser Exercise), after the river Weser. On 21 February, just five days after the *Altmark* incident, he had given General Nikolaus von Falkenhorst the task of leading the invasion of Norway. The German fear of losing control of the supply of iron ore from Kiruna was compounded by concerns that a British occupation of western Scandinavia, including Denmark, would leave Germany particularly vulnerable to air attack. Weserübung would therefore also involve the invasion and occupation of Denmark. The wholly unexpected nature of the attack, allied to the ease of military access, meant that this latter part of the operation was successfully completed within half a day. Norway, however, with a total coastline of just over 100,000 kilometres and a capital city protected by the long and narrow Oslofjord, presented the invaders with a much greater problem.

2

Occupation
The First Six Months,
9 April – 25 September 1940

Finished and launched in 1939, the German heavy cruiser the *Blücher* displaced 12,200 metric tons. She was 193 metres long and her forty cannons and twelve torpedo ramps made her one of the best-equipped warships in the world. She even had her own calculating machine, a forerunner of the modern computer, for the convenience of her artillery and torpedo handlers. The *Blücher* entered the Oslofjord through a misty drizzle on the night of 8 April at about 11.15 p.m. at the head of a small flotilla of blacked-out ships that included the *Deutschland*, under its new name the *Lützow*; the *Emden*, a light cruiser; and three torpedo boats as well as a number of supply vessels. Together they made up Group Five of the six groups involved in Weserübung. Group Five's mission was the capture and occupation of Oslo. To this end the ships carried some 1,600 infantry. Once the main airport at Fornebu just outside Oslo had been secured, paratroopers would land to exert further control over towns in the immediate vicinity of the capital.

As the ships made their way up the fjord they were seen by the captain of a coastal patrol boat, who radioed the information ahead to his colleagues further up the fjord. They were showing no lights and flying no flags, and he was unable to give positive identification of their nationality. Britain and Germany had been at war for the past seven months and these could conceivably be ships seeking shelter after a nearby naval engagement.

By the time the ships reached the narrow sound at Drøbak, the three cannon on the Oscarsborg island fortress that split the fjord in two at that point had been manned and primed for action. So had the artillery and torpedo batteries on the eastern side of the fjord. The commander of the torpedo batteries at the northern end of Oscarsborg had been ordered to load his torpedo ramps with the detonators in place. He recalled having to pinch himself to make sure he wasn't dreaming, then calling the fortress commander, Birger Eriksen, to ask whether he should actually *use* the torpedoes once the ships were in sight.

'Yes,' Eriksen replied. 'Once they pass the fortress security line, you fire.'

At this point, as Eriksen noted later, the identity of the intruders was still uncertain. And when the *Blücher* did cross the line, the first shell from one of the three Oscarsborg cannon toppled its state-of-the-art gun-control tower into the water and left the ship incapable of returning directed fire. A second shell took out the ship's electrical system and destroyed a hangar and the planes inside it. The fire spread to the large quantities of ammunition and fuel on board and within minutes the *Blücher* was out of control, drifting helplessly up the fjord, guns firing wildly in all directions. On land a sixteen-year-old maid at Reenskaugs hotel near the centre of Drøbak was hit and killed as she ran for the shelter of the trees behind the hotel. In the settlement of Gylte, just north of Drøbak, two young children investigating the sudden loud noises found their mother dead in the kitchen, her body almost divided at the waist by a stray shell from the fjord two kilometres away.

On board the *Blücher* the order was given to abandon ship. Watchers who had gathered on the shore, those who didn't simply turn and go back to bed on the assumption that it was all a dream, could see figures rushing about the deck and hear the ghastly cries of the wounded and dying as they struggled in the icy waters surreally ablaze with burning oil. Two torpedoes completed the damage. Just over two hours after the first shell hit her, the *Blücher*'s stern reared sharply up and she slid beneath the waves. Over a thousand men drowned or were burned to death in the debacle, and Oslo gained the briefest of respites from occupation.[7]

The five other groups involved in the Weserübung operation achieved their goals rapidly and without drama. The aim of the surprise attack was to take possession of all important cities and towns on the Norwegian coastline, and do it so quickly that the British would have no chance of coming to Norway's assistance. On the south coast the 150 men of Group Four landed in Arendal on the morning of 9 April and by 9 a.m. the town was in German hands. Kristiansand surrendered shortly afterwards. Group Six landed men at Egersund, some 80 kilometres south of Stavanger, charged with the strategically important mission of severing the North Sea telecommunications cable between Egersund and Peterhead in Scotland. Twenty-two minutes after the first soldiers landed the connection was cut. Sola, the Stavanger airport, was taken shortly afterwards and secured for the landing of paratroopers, marking one of the first examples of the use of this tactic in twentieth-century warfare. Stavanger was occupied later the same day. Bergen, the objective of Group Three, surrendered after a brief exchange of fire. Nor did Group Two experience any difficulties in taking Trondheim. The significance of the port of Narvik for the German war effort was reflected in the much greater resources allotted to Group One, charged with its capture. Parting company with the Group Two ships that made for Trondheim, a fleet of ten destroyers sailed further north, docked and set ashore a force of 2,000 men. Here they met some of the fiercest resistance of the whole operation so far, but again the fighting came to an end before sundown when the Norwegian commander, Konrad Sundlo, surrendered. Sundlo was an active member of Quisling's National Unity and in surrendering he was defying the orders of his regional commanding officer, General Gustav Fleicher.* Owing to its importance in the shipment of iron ore from the mines at Kiruna in Sweden to Germany, however, Narvik remained for several weeks the focus of persistent attempts to retake it by British, French, Polish and Norwegian troops.

The almost freakish success of the attack on the *Blücher* could only delay the inevitable, but the delay was sufficient to buy the king and his government time to evade capture and flee the capital. The decision to flee would turn out to have significant consequences for the nature of the occupation Norwegians would have to endure over the next five years. In the early hours of 9 April, with the prime minister Johan Nygaardsvold and his government frozen in disbelief at the night's events, the president of the Storting, C.J. Hambro, took command. Given his Jewish background it is easy to sympathise with Hambro's heightened sense of the threat posed by the German invasion. An intelligent and literary man, he had translated into Norwegian Sinclair Lewis's novel *It Can't Happen Here*, about the rise to power of an American fascist dictator clearly modelled on Adolf Hitler, soon after its original publication in 1935.

Hambro ordered the immediate evacuation of as many Storting members as could be contacted to a place of safety outside Oslo, and at 07.30 in the morning a train bound for Hamar pulled out of the main Østbanen railway station carrying the government, the king, Crown Prince Olav and members of his family, and a hundred or so Storting representatives. So crowded was the train that Hambro and Nygaardsvold made the journey by car instead. Shortly before their departure, the Foreign Minister Halvdan Koht, in an interview with NTB (*Norsk Telegrambura*, the Norwegian News Agency), unwisely revealed the government's intended

---

* Sundlo later became head of Vidkun Quisling's *hird*. At his trial after the war he was sentenced to life imprisonment with forced labour, but released in 1952.

destination. The announcement was subsequently picked up by Reuters and broadcast seven more times in the course of the day on *Norsk rikskringkasting* (Norwegian State Radio, NRK).

The abrupt disappearance of every significant figure or body of authority in the city and country left Oslo's inhabitants to fend for themselves, and within a matter of hours the capital fell to the invaders. German warplanes circled the city, dropping fliers that fluttered down like dark confetti. A nine-year-old boy, Ole Røthe, picked one up in his garden in Økernveien. There was nothing to worry about, he read, the Germans had come to look after them. Much relieved, he ran inside the house to tell his mother. She advised him not to believe it.[8] Another nine-year-old living in Økernveien, Finn Viksjold, ran out onto the grassy slope opposite Tøyen hospital to watch two neighbours with rifles who were lying on the roof of a yellow wooden house and taking potshots at the planes that swooped so low he could even see the soldiers sitting inside them, smiling and waving at him as they flew by.[9] In the west Oslo suburb of Bærum, Ingrid Bjerkås, a thirty-nine-year-old housewife and mother of two, mounted her bicycle and rode out to Lysaker to check that her parents were alright.

On the ride back, at the Snarøyveien and Drammensveien crossroad, she saw the invaders for the first time. A small group of men marching in tight formation, hunched forward, the barrels of their long rifles held out in front of them in both hands. The faces beneath the helmets were stiff, grey masks as they advanced, scouring the ditches on either side of the road. As they marched past one turned and looked straight at her. On Drammensveien she saw them stop a lorry, order the driver out and within minutes mount a machine gun on the cab roof. The soldiers split into small groups and hijacked other passing lorries, arming them in the same way and then driving on towards the city centre. *We don't have a country anymore*, she thought as she cycled back home. *We've lost it. We can't go berry-picking in the* marka, *can't go fishing in the lakes around Totenåsen, can't sail out to the skerries and islands in the Oslofjord.*[10]

Back home she watched from her kitchen window as a young Norwegian conscript stumbled through a neighbour's garden with a rifle slung over his shoulder. As though in illustration of the wretched state of the country's defences, she saw him jump up and clamber over a neighbour's tall wooden fence, seemingly oblivious to the fact that not two metres away from him a gate stood wide open.

She unlatched the kitchen window: 'The Germans are down by Lysaker!' she called out to him.

Spreadeagled across the top of the fence, he half-turned.

'They're closer than that,' he shouted back.

He dropped to the other side of the fence, tripped over his rifle as he got to his feet, then ran off. An annihilating sense of impotence overcame her. Boys like him could be no match for the grim automatons she had seen on Drammensveien. They looked different. Like men possessed.

That evening she, like thousands of other Norwegians, switched on her radio at 7 p.m. Two minutes later, preceded by a rustling of papers, she heard the voice of Vidkun Quisling, speaking from NRK's studio in central Oslo, next to the Continental Hotel where he had spent the previous night:

> Norwegian men and women! When England breached Norway's neutrality, laying mines in Norwegian territorial waters without encountering anything other than the usual meaningless protests from the Nygaardsvold government, the German government extended a peaceful offer of help to the Norwegian government, offering also its assurance that Norwegian national sovereignty as well as Norwegian lives and properties would be respected. In response to this offer of a solution to what is, for our country, an intolerable situation, the Nygaardsvold government has called a general mobilisation and given the futile order to Norwegian military forces to oppose the German offer of help by the use of arms. The government itself, having in this thoughtless manner

put the fate of this country and its inhabitants at risk, has now fled. In these circumstances it is both the duty and the right of the National Unity movement to assume the powers of government in order to preserve the interests and lives of the Norwegian people and Norway's security and independence. We are the only ones who, in virtue of the circumstances and of the goals of our national movement, are in a position to be able to do this, and in doing so save our country from the desperate plight into which it has been plunged by the activities of the party politicians.

Quisling went on to say that the Nygaardsvold cabinet was no longer in power and that National Unity had assumed the responsibilities of government. He declared himself the country's new prime minister as well as its Foreign Secretary, and announced the names of the eight members of his 'cabinet'. It seems only three had been consulted beforehand and, of the remaining five, two at once declared they would have nothing to do with any of it. One, so alarmed at the evident treason of Quisling's broadcast, went so far as to deposit a copy of his telegram of refusal at the Rogaland sheriff's office. It was an extremely inauspicious start for the leader of National Unity, and not improved by the reaction he encountered later in the evening at the Continental when he introduced himself using his new title to General Erwin Engelbrecht, a survivor of the sinking of the *Blücher* who had just arrived from Drøbak. Engelbrecht had never heard of him and telephoned the German legation, informing his superiors that he was in the company of a man who claimed to be the prime minister of Norway and asking for permission to arrest him.[11] He was told not to.

Given Koht's naïve indiscretion, it was no surprise that the first assembly of the political and monarchical refugees at Hamar was summarily interrupted by news of the impending approach of a group of about a hundred German paratroopers who had landed at Fornebu Airport. The group fled once more, this time east to nearby Elverum.* There the government resumed its interrupted deliberations and obtained parliamentary consent for an important emergency measure known as the *Elverumsfullmakten* (the Elverum Decree). This gave Nygaardsvold and his cabinet power to pass decrees and laws without the formal permission of parliament and ensured that they would remain, for the duration of the war, the legally constituted government of Norway.

The Elverum Decree gave them powers to influence affairs in occupied Norway that would prove highly controversial once the war ended and the judicial reckoning began. It also enabled them, without further discussion, to nationalise ships of the merchant marine that had been at sea when the invasion occurred, and whose crews must now remain stranded for the next five years. The new nationalised fleet was given the name Nortraship and numbered over 800 ships and 30,000 men. About a quarter of the ships were tankers. In the war years to come they would provide an invaluable life-line to the British, first in the months following the French surrender in June 1940, when for a period Nortraship's tankers delivered half of Great Britain's petrol and oil needs, and again in 1943, when German U-boats succeeded in almost completely cutting off the supply of fuel to the British. As what was now the biggest shipping company in the world, Nortraship would soon become the legitimate government's largest source of income, financing 90 per cent of its activities throughout the years of the occupation.[12]

Following his broadcast, Quisling sent a telegram to Adolf Hitler in which he thanked the *Führer* for his help and support in forming a national government to protect Norway's neutrality and integrity, and expressed the hope that, 'together with our Germanic brethren', the two of them would go on to create a safe

---

* At Hamar Crown Prince Olav said goodbye to his wife, Märtha, and their three children, making this little group the first to leave Norway for the safety of neutral Sweden as refugees.

and magnificent future in 'undying friendship and co-operation'.[13] On 10 April Curt Bräuer, Hitler's civilian negotiator in Norway, travelled to Elverum to obtain royal assent for Quisling as the country's new leader. Bräuer was a career diplomat who had been sent to Oslo in November 1939 with instructions to monitor and encourage Norway's neutrality, a project he seems to have believed in implicitly right up until the night of the invasion. In the course of his ten-minute meeting with Haakon at Elverum Bräuer found the king unwilling to discuss even the possibility of recognising Quisling. Once the king's refusal became known, it heralded the commencement of a search-and-bomb campaign as the Germans hunted him and the Nygaardsvold government as they fled ever further northward, first to Molde and then by sea to the temporary safety of Tromsø.

Bräuer returned to Oslo to ponder his next move. He did not have to wait long. On the initiative of Paal Berg, a member of the Supreme Court, which was now the only recognised Norwegian authority left in the capital, a group of prominent figures, including Eivind Berggrav, Bishop of Oslo and Primate of the Norwegian Church, came together to offer themselves as an alternative to Quisling's illegal government. Bräuer was not an admirer of Quisling and he welcomed the creation of this *Administrasjonsråd* (Administrative Council) on 15 April. Its function was to liaise with the Germans in administering daily life within the territory already occupied by the German military. Oslo may have surrendered without a struggle, but fierce fighting continued elsewhere as the Germans advanced north and westward through country.

Already aware of Quisling's unpopularity among the population in general, and that his presumption of office was more likely to provoke than to quell resistance to the occupation, Bräuer promoted Berg's council idea to Hitler, presenting it as a quasi-legal alternative government to Nygaardsvold's cabinet and assuring Hitler that Quisling would have a prominent place in it. On this basis Hitler agreed to accept the Administrative Council as an alternative government and informed Quisling that he must resign. Bitterly disappointed at what he regarded as an act of betrayal, Quisling nevertheless conceded and resigned 'office' on 15 April. Brief as they were, Quisling's six days in power had been enough for his name to be adopted as a synonym for 'traitor'. The bleak neologism appeared for the first time in an editorial in *The Times* on the morning of 19 April 1940.

As had always been its intention, the Administrative Council would have nothing to do with Quisling and for the next two months handled the Norwegian side of civil administration within the ever-expanding circle of the occupied territories without any interference from him. And did so with a new German negotiating partner; disappointed by Bräuer's failure to back Quisling, Hitler had recalled his emissary and on 21 April 1940 Josef Terboven arrived to take over as Norway's *Reichskommissar*. Born in Essen in 1898, Terboven had served with distinction as a lieutenant in the First World War and been decorated with both classes of the Iron Cross. He joined the NSDAP in 1923 and took part in Hitler's attempted coup in Munich that same year. In 1928 he was appointed *Gauleiter* of Essen and became a member of parliament in 1935 and *Oberpräsident der Rheinprovinz* in 1935. He was one of Hitler's closest and most trusted associates. He initially believed – and hoped – that the posting was only temporary until a more satisfactory solution to the problem of civil administration in Norway was found; but the changing fortunes of war militated against this and Hitler retained him as Norway's dictator for the duration of the war.

Terboven's brief was to find a way to administer civilian life with at least a semblance of legality in the occupied regions of Norway, an area that was expanding on an almost daily basis. The surprise tactic of simultaneously attacking and occupying several of the most important towns and cities on the Norwegian coastline was consolidated over the following weeks by advances through the interior of the country aimed at linking the forces in Oslo with those in Trondheim and Bergen. This was achieved by a series of rapid advances through the Gudbrandsdal and Østerdal valleys, the speed, professionalism and discipline of the *Wehrmacht* soldiers enhanced by the military-issue amphetamines that reduced their need for sleep and increased their willingness to take risks while decreasing sensitivity to pain and hunger.[14] On 29 April 1940 a bridgehead was established between Oslo and Trondheim, and on 1 May Oslo and Bergen were linked.

In practical terms this left only the fate of Narvik undecided. Here a joint force of 24,000 Poles, French, British and Norwegians faced the numerically inferior Germans, who nevertheless managed to hold out until the second week of May before abandoning the port. But there would be no consolidating the victory for the Allies.

On 10 May, the German attack on France and the Low Countries changed the situation dramatically. Three hundred and thirty-eight thousand members of the British Expeditionary Force had to be evacuated from Belgium and a major operation to rescue British army soldiers from the beaches of Dunkirk got under way. Instructions were wired to Admiral Boyle, in charge of the British fleet at Narvik, ordering him to arrange an evacuation from northern Norway as soon as possible: 'Reason for this is that the troops, ships, guns and certain equipment are urgently required for defence of United Kingdom.'[15]

Their departure took place between 26 May and 4 June and left the Norwegians, who had hoped for so much from the Allies, devastated and defenceless. On 7 June the king and the members of the Nygaardsvold government boarded the *Devonshire* at Tromsø and sailed for England as refugees, carrying little more than the legislative powers they had awarded themselves under the terms of the Elverum Decree of 10 April.

The following day the Germans were able to return to Narvik to take possession of what was now a ghost town. Most of the population of 10,000 had fled, leaving only a couple of hundred inhabitants. Three days later, at the Britannia Hotel in Trondheim, at 5 p.m. on 10 June, thirty-five years after declaring its independence from Sweden, Norway formally surrendered it to Germany.

Following the surrender, and with the distraction of the king and legal government out of the way, and Narvik and the transport route from Kiruna to Narvik now securely under German control, Terboven was finally able to give the problem of a viable, Norwegian civilian administration his full attention. In this he could feel secure in the backing of a Wehrmacht presence in the country that was never less than 300,000 men and at times as high as 450,000. From the beginning this abrupt increase in a population that numbered just under 3 million at the time of the invasion put an enormous strain on Norway's food-chain and its infrastructure. It also brought the enigmatic benefit of full employment to a Norwegian working class that had suffered the recession of the 1930s but now found itself offered well-paid and regular employment building an entire infrastructure of roads, bridges, barracks, airports and runways for the use of the men and machines that had invaded their country. Norwegian men and women were also in demand to serve the needs of a new and dramatically expanded bureaucracy.

From his first meeting with Quisling, on 23 April 1940, Terboven had been disappointed in the Norwegian *fører*-in-waiting.* On one occasion he was moved to describe him as *dum i potens* ('fathomlessly stupid'). It meant that part of his plan throughout the summer and autumn of negotiations that now got under way with the Administrative Council was to keep Quisling as far from them as possible. He realised quickly how deeply hated the NS leader was by most of his fellow countrymen, and that any attempt to involve him in government would provoke a backlash that would make his own task as Reichskommissar that much more difficult. The man tasked with putting forward the German demands for a revised Norwegian government and administration on behalf of Hitler and Terboven was a lawyer and SS general named Dr Hans Dellbrügge.

Dellbrügge soon made it clear to members of the Administrative

---

* *Fører* is the Norwegian form of *Führer*.

Council that they would have little or no say in how the constitutional crisis brought on by the departure of the king and government for London on 7 June was to be solved. He advanced the German demands for the first time on 13 June, and for most of the summer these would remain unchanged. Members of the Storting still in the country were to assemble at the historically important town of Eidsvoll, site of the creation of the Norwegian constitution in 1814, and there agree to discuss and approve a series of demands that included a formal declaration that the Nygaardsvold government no longer represented the country; that King Haakon VII be deposed; that mandates for members of the Storting currently outside the occupied territory be declared invalid; and that a new organ of central government to be known as the *Riksråd* (National Council) be introduced and include a significant number of members from National Unity. The reward for the Norwegians, if all this was agreed to, was that Hitler would recall the Reichskommissar and replace Terboven's *kommissariat* administration with one composed of Norwegians, free to administer the country under the watchful eye of a German ombudsman. The arrangement would bring it in line with the situation in Denmark, where the king and government had not had the opportunity to flee the German occupation and continued in office.

The Administrative Council rejected Dellbrügge's proposals and handed the poisoned chalice of negotiation to members of the Storting's *Presidentskap** (Presidential Council). Dellbrügge resubmitted his proposals to them, able to use news of the French surrender on 23 June to further turn the screw. The hapless members of the Presidential Council gave their assent to all of the proposals save the abdication of the king, offering instead a counter-proposal, that Haakon's status remain unresolved until

---

* A cross-party group consisting of five men normally responsible for arranging daily business in the Storting under the leadership of the Storting's president. All were vice-presidents; the president himself, C.J. Hambro, was no longer in the country.

the war was over. The Germans rejected this and countered with their preferred alternative: that the Presidential Council ask the king to abdicate voluntarily.

Feeling they had little choice in the matter, a letter to this effect signed by the members of the Presidential Council was duly sent on 27 June via a courier to Stockholm, and from there to London. On 6 July the king's reply reached Oslo by courier: on constitutional grounds he must decline the request. His refusal was repeated in a BBC broadcast from London on 8 July and was soon mimeographed and distributed illegally across Norway. It was widely regarded as a welcome first sign of principled leadership and for the great majority of Norwegians it turned Haakon into the symbol of resistance to the occupation that he remained throughout the war. It was from this time onwards that his monogram H7 began to appear on walls and roadways as a symbol of hope.

But the Germans would not be denied. Twice in the course of September 1940 the *Presidentskap* put the demand for a declaration of the king's abdication *in absentia* before the Storting. On both occasions members voted by a solid majority to accept the German proposals to depose Haakon, and to remove the mandate

from members of the Storting no longer in the country, rescind the Nygaardsvold government's Elverum Decree and establish as Norway's new government a National Council that included representatives from Quisling's National Unity. Negotiations continued but broke down irretrievably on 18 September, when Dr Dellbrügge put forward a demand for five seats for National Unity members on the new National Council which would have given National Unity a majority in the proposed new body. The following week, on 25 September, Terboven put an end to what had become a mockery in a broadcast statement announcing that the Administrative Council was now formally dissolved, and that with immediate effect all political parties in Norway were banned except National Unity.* From this point onwards, listeners were told, the party was 'the Norwegian people's only path to freedom and independence'. He announced the names of thirteen men who would run the country under his leadership and be known as *kommisariske statsråder* (temporary ministers).

Ten of Terboven's new ministers were members of National Unity. Two in particular were men whose field of activity would impinge most directly on the freedoms and peace of mind of the average *jøssing* Norwegian over the five years the occupation lasted. One was a man named Jonas Lie, whom he appointed head of a new Department of Policing at the special request of Hitler's second-in-command, Heinrich Himmler.† Lie had joined the Norwegian police in 1930 and by the following year been appointed Deputy Police Chief of Oslo. As the grandson of one of Norway's most famous novelists, Jonas Lie Snr., as well as a successful crime writer himself, he was already a celebrity twice over by the time the Germans arrived. A chain-smoker, a heavy drinker and a ruggedly handsome man of abrupt and unpredictable charm, the dedication Lie brought to his new job would presently make him, after Quisling, the most hated man in the country.

---

* NKP, the Norwegian Communist Party, had already been declared illegal on 16 August 1940.
† The two appear to have met when Lie visited Germany in 1935.

The other notable appointment was that of Lie's friend Sverre Riisnæs as the new Minister of Justice. Forty-three years old at the time of the invasion, Riisnæs was a jurist and a leading public prosecutor who had appeared in several widely reported cases in the 1930s. Like almost all Terboven's other appointees, Riisnæs came from a family with a long tradition of interest in and admiration for German culture. He liked to recall the almost mystical pleasure he had experienced one day as a small boy when the German emperor, Kaiser Wilhelm II, taking a stroll ashore during one of his annual cruises to Sognefjord before the First World War, stopped to greet him as he passed by the front gate of the Riisnæs family home in Vik, on the south shore of the fjord. Like Lie, Riisnæs favoured a Pan-Germanist future for Norway within the coming Germanic empire. In this respect he differed from the vision of a national socialist but fully independent Norway favoured by Vidkun Quisling and by Albert Hagelin, Terboven's new Minister of the Interior. Hagelin was one of Quisling's oldest and staunchest friends, so staunch he would sometimes describe himself as National Unity's *nestfører* (Vice-Führer). Gulbrand Lunde, head of the newly created Ministry for Culture and Propaganda, was of the same persuasion.

As a result of the party's tiny following in the country none of these men had previous experience of government. They were political amateurs. Terboven had no intention of leaving the running of the important economic departments to such individuals and appointed professionals from outside the ranks of National Unity to run the ministries of Finance, Trade and Industry, and Supply. Terboven held a protecting hand over these men, aware that many of the policies they would need to introduce to keep the economy going would run contrary to National Unity's interests. His protection was undoubtedly necessary; in his autobiography, Per Jahr, Quisling's private secretary during the war years, recalls how Hagelin once urged him to plague Øystein Ravner at the Ministry of Supply with anonymous midnight telephone calls, uttering dire threats of what would happen to Ravner if he did not stop 'making difficulties for the party'.[16]

There was no official post for Vidkun Quisling in Terboven's ministry, but as party leader in a dictatorial system he led weekly meetings of National Unity ministers and remained a visible and significant presence in Norwegian public life. His true status at the time was complex and controversial, among Germans as well as Norwegians. In a gesture of apparent goodwill towards his negotiating partners on the Administrative Council, Terboven had sent him to Germany on 5 July, and the National Unity leader remained there until 20 August. Adding insult to injury, before he left Terboven had asked him to agree to appoint Jonas Lie as temporary head of the party in his absence. In Terboven's eyes, Lie would have made a much more suitable *fører* than the clumsy, unworldly and shy Quisling.

But what Quisling had, and Jonas Lie didn't, was a special relationship with Hitler. With the help of this, and of a few influential German supporters like Alfred Rosenberg, one of national socialism's leading ideologists, he had been able to turn the humiliation of exile to his own advantage. The special relationship was based on gratitude. At meetings with Hitler in Berlin in December 1939 the military tactician in Quisling had warned the Führer of the danger posed to his plans by the outbreak of the Winter War between Finland and the Soviet Union on 30 November of that year. As Quisling correctly guessed, it gave the British an excuse to land troops in Norway as a preliminary to what he was certain would be a full-scale occupation. It seems that Hitler had not quite made the connection himself, and on several subsequent occasions expressed his gratitude to Quisling for the insight. With gratitude came a sense of loyalty that translated into an unwavering support for Quisling as the right man to head the national socialist revolution in Norway.

Throughout the summer and autumn negotiations of 1940, Hitler continued to reject Terboven's negative assessment of

Quisling's qualities, preferring instead to believe that the NS leader simply needed time in which to prepare Norwegians for the coming national socialist revolution. Alfred Rosenberg was of the same opinion. So too were Quisling's other main supporters in the German hierarchy, notably Gross Admiral Erich Ræder and Admiral Boehm. During his enforced exile in the summer and autumn of 1940, Quisling met Hitler three times, and on each occasion Quisling voiced his disappointment at the way he had been sidelined, first by Bräuer, on the occasion of the coup of 9 April, and then by Terboven.

Hitler promised to continue to back Quisling and National Unity as national socialism's best bet in Norway. A tentative timetable was even advanced. Following the 25 September announcement, Terboven's new administration would operate for a finite period only. Quisling and National Unity would use the time to expand and consolidate National Unity's standing among ordinary Norwegians. In this they would be aided by *Einsatzstab Wegener*, a unit named for its head, Paul Wegener, who was Terboven's deputy in Norway. *Einsatzstab Wegener* represented the NSDAP in Norway and had offices in the same building as National Unity's party headquarters at Rådhusgaten 19. The *ad hoc* unit's brief was to advise National Unity on how better to organise and recommend itself to the Norwegian people, and on specifics of Nazi health and education policies. If all went well then in six months' time, on 1 March 1941, a Norwegian government under Quisling's leadership would take over the administration of the country. Six months for Quisling to wait. Five, by the time of Terboven's speech. The war, however, proved an unpredictable horizon against which to hatch plans, and circumstances in the larger theatre of conflict outside Norway meant that Quisling had to wait a lot longer than that for his dream of imposing a national socialist revolution on Norway to be realised. But a crucial first step in that direction had been taken.

PART 2

THE STATE VERSUS THE PEOPLE

3

Aryan Dreams, Norwegian Nightmares, 1941

The Norwegians might look with slight envy at the Danes, invaded and occupied as part of the Weserübung operation of 9 April but still with their own king, their democratically elected government and a civil administration in Danish hands, for the flight and exile of the Norwegian authorities and the chaotic improvisation of Quisling's brief coup had left the country's democratic institutions in tatters. It gave Reichskommissar Terboven the time he needed to create an administrative structure that would, he hoped, presently enable him to hand matters over to the Norwegian national socialists, under the protecting arm of the Wehrmacht, and free him to return to his wife and young daughter in Germany.

A score of experienced administrators, drivers and secretaries had arrived with Terboven on 21 April 1940. Soon they were joined by others, and by the autumn of 1940 a total of 239 bureaucrats – the *Reichskommissariat* – were running Norway from the recently vacated offices of the Storting. Apart from the translators, all were German nationals. The Reichskommissariat also established regional branches in Trondheim, Bergen, Stavanger, Kristiansand, Harstad, Narvik, Tromsø, Hammerfest and Kirkenes.

Terboven structured a 'watchdog' German administration in four main sections that would give him full insight and control over every piece of legislation and policy initiated by his new cabinet of Norwegian ministers. The *Hauptabteilung Verwaltung* monitored the activities of the departments responsible for home affairs, the labour market, the judiciary and finances; the *Hauptabteilung Volkswirtschaft* scrutinised legislation concerning trade and business, farming, fisheries, price regulation, forestry, communications and social welfare; the *Hauptabteilung Volksaufklärung und Propaganda* followed legislation bearing on propaganda, the press, broadcasting, culture, schools and education; and the *Hauptabteilung Technik* new proposals relating to energy, roads, buildings and bridges. Norwegian law continued to be the law of the land except in cases involving the interests of the Wehrmacht, which were tried under German law. The Reichskommissar was, however, at liberty to create laws whenever he thought it necessary. These were known as *forordninger* (Resolutions) and their status was guaranteed by publication in both Norwegian and German in a bulletin, *Verordnungsblatt für die besetzten norwegischen Gebiete* (Resolutions for the Occupied Norwegian Territories).

Most resolutions and laws, however, were the work of the new National Unity departments and dealt with matters such as price regulation and rationing policies and restrictions. Even here, the last word remained always with the German 'advisers' of the four *Hauptabteilungen*. An official letter of 10 October 1940 to all government departments reminded recipients specifically that '*all* resolutions from departmental heads are to be submitted to the Reichskommissariat before publication. In each case *written approval* of the resolution must be sent to the department involved.'[17]

Behind these powers, and guaranteeing them, lay the formidable German Wehrmacht, comprising the *Heer* (army), the *Kriegsmarine* (navy) and the *Luftwaffe* (air force). Unlike the practice in the other German occupied territories, where a civil administration was formed behind the front, Norway retained its status as a Wehrmacht Operational Area for the duration of the war. In practice this meant that the armed forces' attention and potential field of activity remained directed outward, towards the larger theatres of war. Stability and security within occupied Norway were, instead, the responsibility of the SS. Originally formed in 1925 as the *Schutzstaffel*, Hitler's personal bodyguard, the cadre had been taken over in 1929 by Heinrich Himmler and developed into a nationwide police force with a wide range of extraordinary powers that included the right to imprison suspects for an indeterminate length of time without given reason and without interrogation. SS members were also empowered to search houses at will, to confiscate property, censor or ban newspapers, tap telephone wires and dissolve undesirable parties and organisations. The head of the organisation in Norway was Wilhelm Rediess, who was also supreme head of all German police in the country. Directly answerable to Terboven, he had his own staff, with sub-departments each with its own area of specialisation: for prisoners of war, including the thousands from Eastern Europe sent as slave labour to Norway; for recruitment to the SS; for the ideological education of the force's members; for the welfare of SS members and, in March 1941, for a *Lebensborn* programme set up to take care of Norwegian mothers with children by German fathers.

The *Sicherheitspolizei* (Sipo, the Security Police), of which Himmler was also supreme head, consisted of a political police force and a law-and-order force. It was active in Norway by the end of April 1940 and for most of the war was under the command of Heinrich Fehlis, a trained jurist who had become a member of the Nazi Party in 1933 and joined the Gestapo in 1935. Following the example of Reynard Heydrich, the Sipo head in Berlin, Fehlis divided the Norwegian branch of the organisation into sections with separate responsibilities for administration, security, law and order, and a foreign intelligence service. Section Four of the Sipo structure was the *Geheime Staatspolizei* (Secret State Police), better known as the Gestapo, responsible for the arrest of Norwegian patriots suspected of acts of resistance and their interrogation.

The methods used included what was euphemistically termed *skjerpet avhør* ('enhanced interrogation'), meaning torture, where ordinary interrogation failed to produce the desired result. From January 1942 to the end of the war the head of the Gestapo in Norway was Hellmuth Reinhard, another trained jurist.

Sipo made use of a number of prisons in Norway. One was Møllergata 19, formerly the main police station in central Oslo, looking down over the central square of Youngstorget. Another was the newly built prison at Grini, just beyond Røa in the west of Oslo. Originally intended as a prison for women, since the end of April 1940 it had been used as a prisoner-of-war camp for Norwegians who had taken part in the fighting that came to an end with the surrender of 10 June 1940. Some 700 soldiers detained there had been released once hostilities ended, in exchange for a promise not to take up arms again. But Grini remained in use for political prisoners and for Norwegians guilty of grave but not capital offences, such as the production and distribution of illegal newspapers. By the end of the war some 20,000 men and women had spent longer or shorter periods incarcerated behind Grini's barbed-wire fences.

Lord of all this apparatus of administrative, political and cultural dread was Josef Terboven. The Reichskommissar made his status clear in June 1940 when he requisitioned Haakon VII's country mansion at Skaugum, on the western outskirts of Oslo, as his own home.

With Quisling a formally absent but still dominant presence in its deliberations, the newly appointed cabinet of National Unity's *kommissariske statsråder* now set about the daunting task of imposing a national socialist revolution on a population that was politically more to the Left than any other democracy in Western Europe at the time. A brief series of measures introduced by Albert Hagelin at the Ministry of the Interior in the first days after 25 September abolished democracy at the local government level and replaced it with the Führer principle central to national socialist ideology. The elected offices of *lensmann* (sheriff) and *ordfører* (mayor) were turned into personal appointments made at the discretion of the minister to men of proven National Unity credentials. In a directive of 16 December 1940, Hagelin required his appointees actively to work for the future success of National Unity and the promotion of a national socialist ideology in Norway.

Sverre Riisnæs at the Department of Justice followed a similar path. On a number of occasions since the start of the occupation, the Supreme Court had displayed a reluctance to be manipulated by the new regime. Following the introduction of the one-party state on 25 September 1940, the court had bravely tried to insist on its constitutional power to continue to pronounce on the constitutional legitimacy or otherwise of the Resolutions issued by Terboven or his Norwegian ministers. Riisnæs' response was to lower the retirement age of Supreme Court members from seventy to sixty-five, a move that would force instant retirement on seven of the court's thirteen members. The political complexion of their replacements would then be entirely up to Riisnæs. Rather than wait for Riisnæs to carry out his threat, the entire court resigned from office on 21 December 1940 and with that the last vestige of legitimate judicial authority in Norway was gone. Shortly afterwards, as expected, Riisnæs appointed ten new members who were openly supportive of the new regime.

Among the first propaganda bureaucrats to arrive from Germany after 9 April was G.W. Müller, head of the German *Presseabteilung* and a protégé of Joseph Goebbels, the master of political propaganda in national socialist Germany. Müller headed a Norwegian branch of the *Presseabteilung* for the 'education' of the public, a significant aspect of which involved bringing the free press to heel. One obvious ideological target, the left-wing *Arbeiderbladet* (The Daily Worker), was permanently closed down in August 1940. Even simple expressions of opinion were forbidden. Disliking the tone of its report of the Belgian surrender in June of that year, Müller imposed a ten-day suspension on *Dagbladet*, a daily with a nationwide circulation. The editor of the Stavanger newspaper *1ste. Mai* was arrested and his newspaper permanently closed down following an article critical of Terboven's 25 September speech. Müller also instructed Norwegian newspaper editors to stop referring to Vidkun Quisling as National Unity's *fører*. Instead they were to describe him as its *Leder* (Leader). Müller brought a certain bleak humour to what he knew was the uphill task of promoting national socialist German culture to Norwegians. In a welcome speech he gave to a visiting German theatre group in the foyer of the National Theatre in Oslo on 2 January 1941, he assured the actors that the Norwegians were a cultured people, but warned them this tour would be unlike any other 'cultural exchange' they had ever experienced. They would be performing, he told them, for audiences that were 'ninety-eight per cent anglophile'. He encouraged them to think of themselves as 'spiritual artillery, as if you were in a bomber flying over London, or in the trenches'. Things would be even worse in Bergen, he added, 'where a hundred and fifty per cent of them are anglophile'.[18]

Perhaps not coincidentally, the informal 'demotion' of Quisling from *Fører* to *Leder* occurred shortly after the arrival in Oslo of Heinrich Himmler on 28 January 1941. With the first year of the occupation drawing to a close, the main purpose of his trip was to make a fact-finding assessment of the state of affairs in Norway and report back to Berlin. Another was to encourage a revival of the 'Germanic' spirit among Norwegians, and to this end on 30 January he presided over an oath-taking ceremony for the volunteers to *Regiment Nordland*, a Norwegian division of the Waffen-SS recently established by Quisling for those wishing to fight 'the English', as National Unity's promotional literature insistently described their opponents. *Regiment Nordland* turned out to be only the first in a series of attempts the Nazis made to persuade young Norwegians to join the war effort on the German side. Later units included *Den norske Legion* (the Norwegian Legion); the *Hirdvaktbataljonen av 1942* (the Hird Guard Battalion of 1942); the *Pansergrenader-regiment Norge* (the Norwegian Armoured Grenadiers); and the *Skijæger bataljonen* (the Ski Hunters Company). The various initiatives were never particularly successful, although enlistment increased notably following the German invasion of Russia in June 1941 and the resumption of the Winter War between Finland and the Soviet Union, which enabled National Unity's propagandists to sell enlistment to potential volunteers as a way of helping *broderfolket i Finland* ('our brothers in Finland') against the Russians. In all, some 5,000 young Norwegians were recruited to these units over the next four years. Most ended up fighting not for the Finns but for the Germans, and on the Eastern Front. Seven hundred so-called *Frontkjempere* (Front Fighters) lost their lives in what they perhaps never even thought of as the promotion of a national socialist revolution in Norway. As good Pan-Germanists, two of Terboven's *kommissariske statsråder*, Jonas Lie and Sverre Riisnæs, were among the first to enlist in *Regiment Nordland*. 'Let us not bring shame on our forefathers who in their day conquered England,' Himmler urged new recruits at the oath-taking ceremony, 'for the power of the Nordic race is not yet dead in Norwegian hearts'.

The rhetoric of racial and historical pride sounded the keynote of what some modern historians have described as Himmler's *rasesafari* ('racial safari'). In the course of what would turn out to be a three-week stay, the *Reichsführer-SS* indulged to the full his remarkable but hopelessly blinkered infatuation with Norway and its history. Before leaving on a trip that would take him as far north as the Lofoten Islands, he carried out a short programme of official functions in the Oslo area, first visiting the German war cemetery at Ekeberg, before crossing Kongsveien road to study the palaeolithic rock carvings in the grounds of the Sjømannsskolen (Seamen's College) on the other side. Later he was taken to the *folkemuseum* (Folk Museum) on the Bygdøy peninsula just outside Oslo. As the trip was to be used for propaganda purposes back home, a photographer travelling with the party duly photographed Himmler listening raptly as an elderly man named Ole Brenno performed for him on the *langeleik*, a droned zither that is, along with the *hardingfele* (hardanger fiddle), one of Norway's two great traditional musical instruments. Brenno came from a poor farming family in the village of Bagn in Sør-Aurdal in what was then the county of Hedmark/Oppland in the south-east of Norway. Over seventy years old at the time of the German invasion, he was paid to perform at the museum wearing a wadmal jacket of coarse wool with metal buttons and a peasant's skull cap as a living embodiment of the kind of person who would have inhabited one of the ancient timber houses in the outdoor museum, and a demonstration of how these former inhabitants would have entertained themselves in the days before the radio and the gramophone. The photographs were duly printed in the German newspapers as proof of how the invasion of Norway had been welcomed by the local population. Brenno was afterwards rebuked for having agreed to play for Hitler, to which he could only respond that the visitor had 'seemed so interested'.

While at Bygdøy, Himmler also visited the Viking Ship Museum that housed the Oseberg and Tune ships and was entertained by a programme of Norwegian folk music and readings from the Old Norse sagas. Finally, it was time to leave Oslo and head north. Jonas Lie, Josef Terboven and Wilhelm Rediess were among those who accompanied him on his pursuit of Norwegian history and culture. He was given a guided tour of the Maihaugen museum in Lillehammer and visited the medieval Tofte *gård* near Dombås in Gudbrandsdalen, an ancient residence of the kings of Norway mentioned in Snorri Sturluson's *Saga of Harald Hårfagre*, before reaching Trondheim, where he was shown around Nidarosdomen, the cathedral built above the grave of the Norwegian saint-king, Olav (995–1030).

This tourist attraction was particularly appropriate, for Himmler's 'racial safari' also had something of the character of a pilgrimage to it. His reasons for undertaking it were intimately related to the racial mysticism underpinning Nazi ideology in the 1920s and 1930s, and shed light on several otherwise puzzling aspects of the patience ideologically committed Nazis were willing to display towards Norwegians they encountered who were manifestly not sympathetic to the message of the coming 'new age'. In the first year of the occupation, many Norwegians appeared before the German military courts accused of acts hostile to the occupation. These might be radio transmissions to England reporting German ship movements, or the construction of military installations such as airports and barracks. They might be accused of organising refugee routes across the North Sea for Norwegians hoping to join the fighting from Britain. Yet of the several death sentences passed by the German military courts during the first year of the occupation only one was carried out, and the rest commuted to imprisonment. The reason for this leniency was that Nazi ideologists such as Himmler hoped that Norwegians would in time – and in spite of rather than because of Vidkun Quisling – come to see the true significance of racial brotherhood in the 'new order' towards which the Nazis were leading Europe. The belief derived from a radically focused version of an 'us and them' mentality in which 'we' were members of an ancient tribal brotherhood known variously as Aryans, Germans or Nordics, and a 'they' who were everybody else. At the time of Adolf Hitler's rise to political prominence in the 1920 and 1930s, this Germanic world saw itself as threatened with extinction by the combined influences of Jews, with the corrupting brilliance of their adaptability, their perceived restlessness and their cultivation of capitalism as an economic model, and communist revolutionary leaders, very often Jews themselves, who dreamed of a world in which people were bound together in natural union by the pursuit of social equality and the abolition of hereditary privilege rather than by national borders.

For the Nazis, those who had best preserved the ideal values associated with this tribal mysticism and continued to best represent them in the twentieth century were the inhabitants of northern Europe. They included the Dutch, the Danes and the Swedes; but of them all, the *Übergermaner* were the Norwegians. Their very geographical remoteness was supposed to have preserved their Aryan blood from dilution by immigration and interracial marriage. From his father Himmler had inherited a fondness for the saga literature of Norway and the Old Icelandic commonwealth and seems to have regarded the sagas as more or less historical accounts of the culture and deeds of the northern branch of the Aryan tribe during its last period of greatness. For him, the Vikings, with their risk-taking, their boldness and their sense of adventure, represented everything that was best about the tribe. Norway and the Norwegians were his great hope.

So while it might have looked like photogenic propaganda, Himmler's attitude of rapt attention, whether peering at the Ekeberg rock carvings or listening in trance-like stillness to Ola Brenno performing on the *langeleik*, was entirely genuine. His so-called Ahnenerbe Institute had been up and running in Germany since 1935. This pseudo-academic institute was dedicated to a study of the roots of Germanic tribal culture, and one of its articles of faith was that Norwegian folk music was the authentic ancient voice of the tribe. His absorption in the 'ancestral roots' of the Germanic tribe had even caused him to have a man sent from Norway to Germany to instruct members of the SS in how to brew *mjød* (mead), an alcoholic drink made from honey, yeast and water that was drunk by the Vikings. Throughout his tour of the country and its ancient monuments, Himmler conducted himself with the unpredictable self-confidence of the autodidact; Arne Fjellbu, the priest who was ordered to give him the guided tour of Nidarosdomen, recalled him pontificating on details of the cathedral's architecture. Elsewhere Himmler noted for further study by the scholars at his Ahnenerbe Institute the uncanny resemblance he had noticed between the Ancient Greek word *phyle* (meaning tribe or clan) and the Norwegian word *fylke* (meaning county).

Such enthusiasms were the building blocks of Himmler's dream of life in the future *Germania*, once the war was over and the Thousand-Year Reich established in Europe. Large colonies would be founded, one in Russia, another in Poland and a third in the Crimea and the lower regions of Ukraine.[19] Settlements of thirty or forty individual farms would be worked by ethnic Germans under the leadership of SS men and women of impeccable racial pedigree. Each township would have its central square or *tingplass*, just as described in the Old Norse sagas and histories. This bizarre idyll was the dream Himmler offered SS recruits as a reward for engaging in what he presented to them as the necessary cruelties and violence of their activities as SS members, including the murder on an industrial scale of unarmed men, women and children in the regions of Eastern Europe that would have to be cleared to make way for the establishment of these future settlements.

Throughout the three weeks of his visit to Norway, Himmler scarcely acknowledged the existence of National Unity's leader Vidkun Quisling and spent little more time in his company than the initial hour at the oath-taking ceremony for *Regiment Nordland*. The problem was Quisling's manifest lack of personal charisma. This absence remained an enigma to most of the prominent Nazis who met him, as did the continued support Quisling enjoyed from Adolf Hitler. Even strong-minded figures in the senior ranks of National Unity such as Jonas Lie behaved as though Quisling did, in fact, possess this mysterious quality. The illusion may have owed something to Quisling's work with Fridtjof Nansen in the years immediately following the Russian Revolution, when the two men led famine relief efforts in the Ukraine, an association which left Quisling's name permanently burnished with the reflected glow of Nansen's very obvious charisma following the death of Norway's greatest hero in 1930. As such it was a peculiarly Norwegian response that remained inexplicable and perhaps even incommunicable to those not born in the country.

For all Norwegians were supposed to be born leaders, and history demonstrated this to be the case. In his *Historia Normannorum*, from the early eleventh century, Dudo of St Quentin tells the story of an emissary sent by the French king, Charles the Simple, to negotiate a peace treaty with Viking pirates in Normandy who had taken control of the Seine. On asking to speak to their leader, Rollo, the emissary was informed that 'among us there is no leader, we are all equal, you will have to negotiate with us all'.[20] History as precedent was important to Nazi ideologists, and the story of Rollo might have helped them to explain to themselves the disappointing 'normality' of the average twentieth-century Norwegian they encountered. Norwegians *were* born leaders, one of the German arguments ran, but with no inferior tribes nearby to dominate they had been faced with the impossible task of dominating each other and in sheer despair succumbed to egalitarianism and a peaceable way of life. Himmler offered an analysis along these lines at a later stage of the war, when fielding complaints from his officers about a lack of discipline among Norwegian members of newly created volunteer units like the 5th SS Panzer-Division Wiking. It seems that these men filled their letters home with endless complaints about life in the unit. Himmler's response was to remind his officers that they were dealing with the aristocrats of the Germanic tribe, and that their training must take account of this. So instead of rebuking their Norwegian recruits, the officers found themselves attending a fourteen-day sensitivity course in the proper way to handle them.[21]

This attitude of tolerant patience was never extended to Vidkun Quisling. One who did experience it in person was the man who would presently become Quisling's nemesis, Eivind Berggrav, Bishop of Oslo and Primate of the Norwegian Church. Following the dissolution of the Administrative Council of which he had been a prominent member, and the resignation of the Supreme Court in December 1940, Berggrav's had become an increasingly active voice of protest against the new regime. Over the winter the unique status National Unity now enjoyed as the 'only way to freedom and independence' for Norway had led to a series of violent confrontations between students and uniformed members of Quisling's *hird*. On 27 November 1940 the president of the Trondheim Students Union had complained to the local *hird* leader that members of the organisation had put up posters in the union's private club rooms. The following day the president was visited and beaten up by fifteen members of the *hird*. The only response to a complaint to the Minister of Justice Sverre Riisnæs was that a national socialist was *always* entitled to react with violence when confronted with disrespect. *Hirdmannen*, a weekly supplement to National Unity's own newspaper *Fritt Folk* (Free People), repeated the doctrine following a similar incident at the Oslo *Handelsgymnasium*. After complaints that teachers had taken no action when National Unity pupils – who insisted on attending school in their *hird* uniforms – were subjected to the mockery and insults of *jøssing* pupils, senior *hird* members entered the school, beat up the director and several teachers and arrested a number of pupils. One pupil was abducted from his home at night, driven away in a car, stripped naked and whipped by *hird* thugs. Incidents such as these led to a large protest demonstration in central Oslo in December against National Unity and the behaviour of the *hird*, at which there was a further outbreak of violence. Jonas Lie at the Department of Policing ordered the Norwegian police not to intervene but instead 'actively to support the *hird*'.[22]

It was in response to these acts of state-condoned violence that a *hyrdebrev* ('pastoral letter') was sent to Ragnar Skancke at the Ministry of Church and Education in January 1941. Largely drafted by Eivind Berggrav, it was signed by all the Norwegian bishops and expressed the church's dismay at another Resolution from Jonas Lie's department, issued on 13 December 1940, decreeing that a priest's vow of confidentiality could by overruled by order of the state. The police were further empowered to imprison a priest without trial in pursuit of information that was regarded as important for state security.

Ragnar Skancke's response to the *hyrdebrev* failed to satisfy the bishops, and Berggrav arranged for his pastoral letter to be duplicated. Fifty thousand copies were illegally printed and posted to every priest in the country. All of them duly read it to their congregations on the morning of Sunday 9 February 1941. As a result, Berggrav found himself summoned to meet Himmler and Terboven at the Reichskommissar's home in Skaugum. Like many of his generation and social class the bishop was fluent in German and no interpreter was required at their afternoon meeting. It lasted three and a half hours, which was more time than Himmler spent with Quisling during the entire three weeks of his stay in Norway. In a memoir published in 1945, just months after the end of the war, Berggrav published a near-verbatim account of the conversation that provided, among other things, further demonstration of the extent of Himmler's tribal attachment to the Norwegians. Himmler's evident personal liking for Berggrav created a remarkable atmosphere of bonhomie at the meeting that Berggrav was able to sustain without ever losing his dignity. He and Himmler even shared a joke which left Terboven stony-faced. Berggrav thus became one of the very few people to have seen Norway's illegitimate but all-powerful Reichskommissar reduced to the role of spectator in what was an intense ideological discussion between bishop and Reichsführer-SS.

On just two occasions was the convivial mood threatened. At one point, Berggrav was asked to give his word that he would show any future pastoral letters to Terboven before distributing them. Berggrav agreed, but only if, in his opinion, the content could be defined as political. The obvious difficulty here was that the whole national socialist project was in direct opposition to every meaningful tenet of the Christian religion. Inevitably this led to a discussion on the subject of God, with Berggrav affirming that the word of God was sovereign in all matters, political or not, and that he and his fellow bishops had no choice but to obey: 'Our firm and unshakeable belief in God is our greatest joy.'

Apparently affronted by the forceful way in which Berggrav said this, Himmler offered the sharp rejoinder: 'Are you suggesting that *we* don't believe in God?' In his memoir of the encounter, Berggrav reports that Himmler seemed embarrassed by the vehemence of his own interjection. He glanced uncertainly in Terboven's direction before adding, as though he thought it redeemed all his uncertainties: 'Are you aware that Hitler believes in God?' Berggrav, sensing grave danger if the conversation turned to the subject of the Führer, offered a diplomatic reply: 'I understand what you are saying and I have no reason to question it.'

The second occasion was revealing in a different and more predictable way. They began to discuss the Church's objections to the violent activities of the *hird*. The Church's carefully worded complaint alleged that the police simply stood by and watched as *hird* members set about kicking and punching innocent bystanders, guilty of perhaps nothing more than a disparaging remark about Quisling, or of protest at the breaking of a shop window because the proprietor was Jewish. Uniformed *hird* members had carried out raids on schools and colleges and started brawls with pro-English students. No one was ever arrested, none brought to trial. It all signalled, said Berggrav, a general breakdown of law and order under the new regime:

> HIMMLER (friendly, but also sharply): I'm afraid, bishop, that you are seeing things from the pulpit and not from the point of view of life.

BERGGRAV: Not at all. I have detailed knowledge of these incidents.

TERBOVEN: You certainly do not. I, on the other hand, have all the relevant documents and I know exactly what happened and in what order.

HIMMLER (to me): You should examine the matter from this perspective as carefully as you have examined it from the other.

BERGGRAV (to Terboven): In that case, may I see these documents?

TERBOVEN: No. Because that would make you an *over-rikskommissar*.

BERGGRAV (addressing Himmler): Then how am I to 'examine the matter from this perspective' when I am not permitted to see the relevant documents?

HIMMLER: It is your responsibility to investigate matters before you pronounce upon them.

BERGGRAV: Well now hold on, I'm not a police officer conducting an investigation. But what I have written regarding this business still stands. For me, the point is that the police have taken no action. No action has been taken to ensure that justice is not only done but is seen to be done. It is *this* we cannot remain silent about. Just look at the schools!

HIMMLER (to Terboven): What is this about the schools?

TERBOVEN: Oh, there's a dreadful fuss going on at the moment. These schools should watch themselves. We don't need all the academics they produce. If the schools want to go on strike well then let them. We have an urgent need for barracks, so by all means, let me have the schools.

BERGGRAV: This is a very serious matter. It is intolerable that our children should be assaulted by the *hird* in this way.

TERBOVEN (angrily): It is the others who start the trouble. Why don't the bishops do something about that?

BERGGRAV: In our memorandum to the Minister for Education and Religious Affairs, which we have unfortunately been unable to distribute because it has been forbidden, we make it clear, in no

uncertain terms, that we condemn provocation and violence, no matter who is responsible. This business about the *hird* and the schools has to be stopped.
HIMMLER: Why is the church so afraid of a little brutality?[23]

This is the only time in the course of the meeting that Himmler's civilised mask slips. At times, in the face of his autodidact's enthusiasm for archaeology and ancient history, his unembarrassed fascination with the lost continent of Atlantis, his efforts to prove Buddha was of Aryan origin, the exaggerated earnestness of his absorption in Ole Brenno's *langeleik* playing or the naïve charm of getting Hugo Boss's company to design and produce the SS uniforms so that his recruits would look stylish, these eccentricities can come perilously close to making the Reichsführer-SS appear a normal if eccentric human being. The sudden interjection to Berggrav was a chilling reminder of what else that charm was capable of. Working behind the line of the advancing German armies in 1939, his SS *Einsatzgruppen* (task forces) had already killed tens of thousands of unarmed Poles and Jews. One of his officers, SS-*Obergruppenführer* Karl Wolff, described a mass execution near Minsk in 1941 at which Himmler himself was present, for the specific purpose of hardening himself to the sight of a 'little brutality'. A group of naked women and children were ordered to jump into an open grave and lie face down, Wolff writes. When a sufficient number had been shot to cover the bottom of the grave, a second group were ordered down to lie across the bodies and were then shot themselves. Himmler, writes Wolff, had never seen dead people before. In his curiosity he was leaning forward and over the triangular pit, peering down into it as the shooting was going on. At some point matter from the brain of one of the victims splashed up and splattered his face and his coat. He stumbled back, green and pale, retching and swaying as Wolff helped him away. The experience is believed to have been instrumental in Himmler's search for a means of conducting mass executions in a way that was less personally distressing to the executioners involved, and that in due course led to the innovation of the gas chamber.

Himmler's report to Berlin on the current state of affairs in Norway almost a year into the occupation has not survived. He would have seen for himself how unpopular Quisling was with the average Norwegian, and what a dangerous provocation his promotion to prime minister would be, and his assessment of the situation must have been sufficiently negative to persuade Hitler to postpone the plan agreed upon in September 1940 for Quisling to take over as leader of a Norwegian national socialist administration by the spring of 1941, and put it on hold until a more opportune moment.

For Nazi ideologists like Heinrich Himmler one of the most puzzling aspects of modern Norway must have been the country's fondness for the extreme socialism of the Soviet Union. This source of bafflement turned into sudden and present danger following the German invasion of the Soviet Union on 22 June 1941. Codenamed *Barbarossa* (after the twelfth-century crusading German emperor Frederick Barbarossa), it was a unilateral abrogation of the unlikely non-aggression pact that had existed between the two powers since August 1939 and was not due to expire until 1949. At a stroke this attack on the home of international and expansionist communism turned Norway's *Landsorganisasjon* (LO, the Norwegian Confederation of Trade Unions),* well organised, militant and fiercely loyal to Moscow, into a grave potential danger for the occupying force. It also played a part in delaying still further Quisling's hopes of being entrusted with leadership of an entirely Norwegian nationalist socialist government. Strikes, and in particular a general strike, could make the job of administering the country and keeping the wheels of production turning more

---

* At the time and until 1957 the confederation was known as *Arbeidernes Faglige Landsorganisasjon*.

difficult as well as more dangerous. Such a task was clearly beyond the capabilities of a man like Quisling and the Reichskommissar would have to deal with it himself. Terboven therefore devoted much of the summer and autumn of 1941 to neutralising any potential threat from the trade union movement. He did so using brutality on a scale not so far seen during the occupation.

The saga of Terboven's battle with the trade unions had started earlier in the year, on 3 April 1941, when the leaders of twenty-two organisations in the public sector addressed a letter to him protesting against the many undemocratic irregularities introduced by his National Unity *kommissariske statsråd* since 25 September, and in particular the creation on 15 February 1941 of a new body governing employment in the public sector. The letter complained that by making membership of National Unity rather than practical ability the deciding factor in filling job vacancies, the new organisation NSPOT (National Unity Office for Public Service Personnel) represented a blatant politicisation of the traditionally politically neutral public sector. A copy of the letter reached the lawful Norwegian authorities in London and was broadcast on the BBC's Norwegian service even before Terboven had received the original. Deeply offended, he ignored it.

Six weeks passed. Unease continued to grow over the constant demands for 'loyalty' to the new regime in public sectors like the schools and establishments of higher education across the country, including Oslo University, and on 17 May a second letter of protest on the same theme was addressed to the Reichskommissar. This time it was signed by the leaders of forty-three labour organisations. For the first time since the invasion, Norwegians were beginning to assess the weapons at their disposal to counter the hostile occupation. Inevitably, the possibility of using strike action arose. In a minor matter involving the politically motivated dismissal of a medical superintendent at Dikemark Hospital in Asker, just outside Oslo, the threat of strikes by doctors across Oslo had proved sufficient to have him reinstated. This success encouraged belief in the tactic as a response to the new regime. The letter of

17 May also reiterated the widespread outrage at the behaviour of members of Quisling's *hird* of which Berggrav had complained to Himmler earlier in the year:

> We see constantly proof that membership of National Unity has become a critical condition of employment and promotion, and that formal qualifications are accorded little weight. Pressure and threats on members to join the party or actively to promote it are experienced as deliberate attempts to force members to act against their own consciences and turn their backs on what they believe to be the right and proper course of conduct [...] In recent times our feelings of disquiet and irritation have brought us close to a state of bitterness.[24]

Again Terboven declined to respond. But then, on 18 June, four days before the German invasion of the Soviet Union, the signatories to the letter were summoned at short notice to attend at the Storting building, which now housed Terboven's Reichskommissariat administration. The Reichskommissar made his audience wait an hour before flaying them with a speech of undisguised hostility in which he ridiculed the value of communal protests such as theirs. All other things being equal, members of National Unity would *always* receive preferential treatment when it came to job appointments and promotions. He then called out the names of five union officials who had signed the letter on behalf of their organisations and told them he was giving them an opportunity to ponder their actions in the 'contemplative silence' of a prison cell. Gestapo officers then led the five men out. Henning Bøtker and Erling Steen, the two men believed to have drafted the letter, had already been arrested earlier in the day.

Terboven then gave way to the Minister of the Interior Albert Hagelin, who announced a series of measures that amounted to the most serious attempt so far to impose national socialism on Norwegian society: many of the organisations that had signed the letter would be dissolved, while others would be given new leadership that was politically compatible with national socialist ideals.

The response of the LO was to refuse to have anything to do with Hagelin's new NSPOT organisation. Instead it declared that it would negotiate trade union matters with the German authorities only. That the LO would prefer to deal with the German occupants rather than a National Unity minister was striking evidence of how deeply the party was loathed in the country. It constituted a severe blow to the party's prestige, and on 30 July the LO's leader Jens Tangen and the organisation's lawyer Viggo Hansteen were summoned to a meeting with Terboven at which the Reichskommissar insisted that pay rises, for example, could only be achieved through direct negotiation with NSPOT. Tangen objected that NSPOT failed to recognise the LO as a negotiating body. He and Hansteen continued to insist that the LO would discuss pay only with the Germans, and that the boycott of NSPOT would go on. They also demanded the release of the five shop stewards arrested at the meeting on 18 June.

Hansteen and Tangen may have been taken aback when Terboven agreed to both demands. And he kept his word: the five men were released the following day. But the victory was pyrrhic. On 2 August, above a story boasting that 35,000 Soviet troops had been captured after fierce fighting south and east of Smolensk, a proclamation signed by the Reichskommissar appeared on the front page of all national newspapers announcing the creation of a new instrument of state control, the Civilian State of Emergency (CSE). A preamble explained that the measure was being introduced owing to 'recent developments in the international situation'. The 'recent developments' were, of course, Barbarossa and the invasion of the Soviet Union. If and when a CSE were ever imposed it would give unprecedented powers to both the German and the Norwegian police, empowering them to do 'whatever may be necessary for the maintenance or restoration of public order and safety', even where this contravened Norwegian law. Its most sinister innovation was provision for trial before *standrett* (drumhead courts) 'for all actions that threaten public order and safety, economic stability and peaceful conditions at work'. Punishments available to the courts included the death sentence, which would be carried out immediately; life imprisonment with hard labour; forced labour for a period of not less than ten years; and the forfeit of all personal property.

Following the public announcement of its creation, Terboven waited just six weeks before announcing the first use of a CSE in Oslo and invoking these new powers. He did so as part of a plan to terrorise the trade union movement into complete and lasting submission. He had been stiffened in his resolve by a short visit paid to Norway by Reinhard Heydrich, Himmler's second-in-command of the SS and the newly appointed Acting Reich Protector of Bohemia and Moravia. Heydrich had been involved in planning the *Kristallnacht* assault on German and Austrian Jews in 1938 and would, in the course of the war, be a leading advocate of the 'final solution' policy which aimed to eliminate the Jewish race entirely. For a man whom Adolf Hitler once described as having an 'iron heart' nothing was out of bounds. There is no official record of what he and Terboven talked about during the three days of his stay in Oslo, but the dreadful power of the Civilian State of Emergency was discussed.[25] Heydrich flew back to Berlin on 6 September and four days later Terboven declared the first Civilian State of Emergency in Oslo.

From his negotiations earlier in the summer with the LO, Terboven already knew Viggo Hansteen. He was the organisation's legal adviser and the man generally recognised as being its real leader. Hansteen came from a privileged background. An only child, he grew up in an eight-roomed house in the West End of Oslo. His grandfather Christopher Hansteen was Professor of Astronomy and Applied Mathematics and Astronomy at 'Det kongelige Frederiks Universitet i Christiania', as the earliest incarnation of what is now Oslo University was known. One of Norway's most prominent early feminists, the painter Aasta Hansteen, was his great-aunt. Personable, always stylishly dressed, Hansteen was the public face of the LO. In the tense 1930s he functioned as a sort of personal guarantor for the decency and reliability of the organisation for many anxious middle- and upper-class Norwegians. In the aftermath of the violent events at Menstad he defended several of the strikers brought to trial, where his courtroom opponent was Sverre Riisnæs, the man later to become Terboven's and subsequently Quisling's Minister of Justice. Passionately convinced of the rightness of communism, he had nevertheless resigned from the party early in 1940 in protest at the Soviet invasion of Finland in 1939.

Hansteen was a prime example of the type of person the Nazi leadership feared most. Terboven referred to them as the 'spiritual inspirators' of opposition to the new regime. With the non-aggression pact between Soviet Russia and Nazi Germany abruptly a thing of the past he became convinced that the communists, led by Hansteen, were actively engaged in trying to take control of the LO. The fact that Hansteen was listed as a Jew in a series of anti-semitic publications called *Hvem er hvem in jødeverden* (Who's Who in the World of Jews), by the journalist Mikal Sylten, where he was described as 'Defending Counsel in the Court of Appeal for the Muscovites' for his role in the Menstad trials, served only to encourage Terboven in this belief. Sylten had published his listing of Norwegian Jews, actual and supposed, for the first time in 1925, and further editions appeared in 1932, 1938 and 1941. The only criterion for entry was the compiler's personal conviction that these were people of Jewish origin. His assumptions were frequently wrong, as they were in the case of Viggo Hansteen.

Another labour activist who had already come to the attention of the Nazi authorities was Rolf Wickstrøm. Twenty-eight at the time of the occupation, he came from the opposite end of the social spectrum from Viggo Hansteen. He grew up in a family of seven in a one-room flat in Tøyen in the East End of Oslo. On leaving school he was unable to find regular employment for several years. He obtained a qualification as an arc-welder and in 1935 began full-time work at the Skabo Jernbanevognfabrikk, a firm of coachbuilders.[26] By 1940 he was a shop-steward at the factory. International Workers' Day, 1 May, was an important date in the calendar of the union movement, and in protest at the new regime's insistence that it be treated as a normal workday Wickstrøm had been among the first to down tools and leave his place of work at midday. The owner of the plant blamed him for the walkout and gave his name to the Norwegian policeman who had arrived to make a report of the incident. As a result, Wickstrøm and sixteen other men were arrested and held at Møllergata 19 in central Oslo for the next three weeks before being released. To the factory owner, Birger Mørk, the detention might have seemed punishment enough. He could have had no idea what this apparently trivial episode would ultimately lead to.

By the summer of 1941 food shortages were starting to bite. Seasonal fruits were hard to come by, potatoes were scarce, and fish was too, even in the coastal villages. Most of the available food went to German troops on the Eastern Front, or to the barracks housing the 300,000 Wehrmacht solders now stationed in Norway. Milk was in short supply too. On 9 September, for the second morning in succession, milk rations for the morning break failed to arrive at factories in the Oslo area. By nine in the morning the first walkouts had occurred. By the middle of the day workforces were out at fifty-four larger and smaller industrial sites, including the Skabo coach-making factory where Wickström worked. By the end of the day 20,000 were out on strike. At his home in Risløkka in north Oslo, Wickstrøm was getting ready to leave for *Folkets Hus* (The People's House) in Youngstorget in central Oslo for a meeting about progress in wage negotiations between the LO and the Germans. As his young son Tore played out in the street a black car pulled up and three men wearing long coats emerged, strode up the garden path and entered his house. A few moments later they emerged with his father. All four got into the car and it then drove off.

By the end of the same day fifty-two other union activists had been arrested. A formal declaration of the Civilian State of Emergency under which the arrests had been made did not appear until the following morning's newspapers. The notice was prefaced with Terboven's explanatory statement:

> In recent days, communist and Marxist elements in the trade unions and especially their leaders have engaged in the criminal disturbance of peaceful conditions of work by preparing for a general strike. I therefore declare, within the police districts of Oslo and Akershus, effective from this morning 10 September 1941 at five o'clock and until further notice, a Civilian State of Emergency.

A curfew was imposed between 8 p.m. and 5 a.m. All transport except the railways closed down at seven. Cinemas, theatres, dances, public gatherings and the sale of alcohol were banned. All of this to create a framework of fear and unease among the general population and give the regime peace in which to pursue the real purpose of the declaration: the castration of the union movement. Viggo Hansteen had been arrested in the early hours of 10 September at his home at 33 Bernhard Herres vei in Smestad and taken to Gestapo headquarters in Victoria terrasse. In a simultaneous action the Gestapo raided the LO's offices and closed them. Over 120 union activists were arrested. Wickstrøm was taken first to the prison at Møllergata 19 and then transferred to Gestapo headquarters in Victoria terrasse where he was accused of having played a leading role in organising the walkout the preceding day.

In the afternoon Hansteen, Wickstrøm and three other LO leaders were taken to Kristinelundveien 20 to appear before a German *standrett*. Each man appeared separately. The proceedings were brief, all the briefer for the trials being without a defending counsel. Hansteen was charged with posing a threat to public law and order by his actions in forming a communist resistance group opposed to the occupier and seeking the collaboration of other groups likewise opposed to the occupier. He was accused of having organised the milk strike as a deliberate 'dress-rehearsal' for a full-scale general strike of Norwegian workers. No summary of the proceedings survives, but the evidence presented appears to have been entirely circumstantial, referring to his known communist sympathies, his sometime membership of the party, his frequent visits in the pre-war years to Moscow and his general status as the effective head and instigator of all the LO's disruptive and communist-inspired activities. He was found guilty and sentenced to death. Wickstrøm, who followed him into court, met a similar fate. The three other LO leaders tried that afternoon were luckier; two were sentenced to fifteen years with hard labour, one to ten years.

Hansteen and Wickstrøm were told they had the right to appeal for clemency and waited in the foyer at Kristinelundveien 20 to hear the result of their appeals to Terboven. Ivar Sæther, a fitter and turner who was another of the defendants, caught a brief glimpse of the two men as he was walked through the foyer for his appearance before the court at about 4 p.m. Wickstrøm was sitting in the sofa, Hansteen standing with his back to it.* Within the hour the appeals were rejected and the two were driven to the Oslo Østre Rifle Club's shooting-range at Stig, in Årvoll, where they were blindfolded and shot shortly after 5.30 in the afternoon. Their executions and the long prison sentences given to the three others were announced on the front page of *Aftenposten* on 11 September. By what must surely have been design the report was directly above a story headlined 'New Leadership for the LO' that announced the names of the LO's two new, regime approved leaders.

Hansteen's murder was a message to the socialist intelligentsia and Wickstrøm's a warning to the socialist shopfloor: this is what will happen to you if you listen to people like these. Here was the 'little brutality' of which Himmler had spoken to Bishop Berggrav. It

---

* Sæther was sentenced to ten years imprisonment with hard labour.

was devastating in precisely the way intended. On 13 September, from Berlin, Reinhard Heydrich wrote to von Ribbentrop, Hitler's Foreign Minister, explaining the need for the drastic new, non-military 'Civilian State of Emergency' that had been introduced in Norway. He referred to the LO as 'Norway's only really disciplined organisation' and as a dangerous focus of opposition to the occupation, both as a military threat and as a threat to productivity by strike action. Like Terboven, he viewed the 'milk strike' as a well-planned rehearsal for a general strike:

> With particular reference to the Norwegian trades' unions, our discussions led us to conclude that psychological and tactical considerations dictated that the first stage of response should involve an intensive programme of surveillance, but at the very first opportunity action of the most ruthless kind be taken, to make it finally clear to the Norwegians that measures announced by the Germans must be taken seriously. Hence the first employment of this new conception, the Civilian State of Emergency, as a way of eliminating the need to invoke an inappropriately *military* state of emergency to deal with what are political matters. The opportunity appeared with surprising speed following the attempted disruptions of recent days.[27]

Heydrich further informed von Ribbentrop that 'the radical measures taken so far have been most effective. [...] The measures introduced as part of the Civilian State of Emergency, in particular the *standrett*, have had impressively sobering results. The people now understand the seriousness of the situation [...] The death sentences have had a devastating effect. They have created an atmosphere of the most extreme reticence.'

Reticent the atmosphere certainly was. And by early December 1941, with German troops just a few kilometres outside Moscow and with the power of the 'Bolshevik' trade unions to disrupt the administration of the country effectively terrorised into submission, Quisling must have thought that now, at last, the time had come for him to take his appointed place as leader of the new Norway. And indeed it had. The great day was planned for 1 February 1942. Unfortunately for him, it was Reichskommissar Terboven who had done the planning.

4

Legislation for a National Socialist Revolution, 1942

The *Statsakt* (State Act) of 1 February 1942, in which Terboven formally accepted the resignations of the *kommissariske statsråd* who had served him since 25 September 1940 and their transfer to the government of the new leader of the civil administration in Norway, Minister-President Vidkun Quisling, was a huge moment in the little party's short history.* It was celebrated with pomp, flags, uniforms and trumpets at a ceremony at Akershus Fortress, a consummate piece of Nazi theatre, complete with a statement of legitimacy from the now Nazified Supreme Court. 'A day greater than 17 May 1814 and 7 June 1905,'[†] *Aftenposten* wrote in its account of the proceedings of 1 February, quoting Quisling's own description in the first of the twelve pages it devoted to the ceremony. Future generations of Norwegians would mention the name of Quisling in the same breath as those of Saint Olaf, Harald Hårfagre and Olaf Tryggvason.

Terboven spoke first. He devoted much of his speech to a

---

* In 1941, on the first anniversary of his 25 September speech, Terboven had given the *kommissariske statsråd* permission to style themselves 'Ministers'.
† The dates, respectively, of the drafting of the Norwegian Constitution and of Norway's independence from Sweden.

personal attack on the Bishop of Oslo, Eivind Berggrav. Terboven tried to destroy his credibility as a man of principle by quoting liberally from a 'secret' diary that had come into his possession. Writing shortly before the outbreak of war, Berggrav had openly suggested that he thought Germany more likely than Great Britain to respect Norway's neutrality. In what was clearly to him a devasting undermining of Berggrav's claim to know what had 'really' been going on in Germany since the 1930s, Terboven continued: 'He claims to know about national socialism – and the source of his information is a Jew!' The absurdity was left to speak for itself. Only towards the close of his speech did Terboven mention Quisling. He praised the new minister-president as an expert on Russian affairs, noting the keen insight this had given him into Soviet Russia's plans for world domination, and he reminded his audience that international communism was the brainchild of the Jews, themselves a people without a nation. He ended by praising Quisling's courage in the face of what he readily admitted was the herculean task of converting Norway's near-communist population into a nation of devout national socialists.

Quisling then spoke. He praised the occasion as demonstrating to the whole world:

> … that Germany, and our Germanic brothers, have an honourable, honest and friendly attitude towards the Norwegian people. This

proof of the honesty of Germany's intentions in Norway was in and of itself unnecessary for me personally, for I have known all along of the Führer's desire to allow Norway to win back its freedom and independence through our movement. It has never been part of Germany's plan to turn Norway or Scandinavia into a second Ireland, for Germany came here not as an enemy but as a friend, to protect Norway against an attack that was already under way from the English, and to protect its own just interests against the sinister breaches of neutrality perpetrated by the English. And yet this protective peace-keeping initiative was greeted with hostility by the then government of Norway, whose concern was not the interests of Norway but those of England and Moscow. That government of traitors long ago ceased to be a Norwegian government.

He reminisced about his own failures and disappointments as party leader, for which he blamed the blindness and perfidy of others, never himself, before analysing the magnitude of the task that lay before National Unity now that the party was finally in power:

Norway's future cannot be saved by a strong government alone. Norway's misfortune has not merely been the system. Norway's real misfortune has been the damage done to the soul of the Norwegian people. And when the *interior* was troubled in this way then more and more was the *exterior* affected. Materialistic individualism and liberalism, and the imported spirit of the Jews corrupted the heart of our people and prepared the ground for Bolshevism. English propaganda did the rest. All these life-lies have led to the breakdown of the old society. They operate still to poison the minds of men.

Looking ahead, he spoke of his plans to permanently replace the democratically elected Storting with a new *riksting* (National Assembly) composed of representatives from all fields of social and professional life, with delegates not elected but instead announcing their fitness as a result of 'the Führer principle of responsibility that must also, under all normal circumstances, remain the fundament of our state and society. National Unity and the national government will unite all Norwegians in national cooperation. Our government is not a party-political government. Still less is it a class-war government, as Nygaardsvold's was. We are a *national* government. A government for *all* people.'

He concluded his speech with an exhortation and a warning:

> And now we ask of all Norwegians – indeed, we have a right to *demand* it – that every loyal citizen helps this government in its efforts to fulfil its national duty, which is to secure and build a new Norway. Harald Hårfagre united a kingdom; we shall unite and lead a people. This is the obligation that has been placed upon the shoulders of our national government. So let the words of our great prophet-poet continue to inspire us:
> – Norway was a kingdom. It must become a people.
> That is the task that lies ahead now for the government of Norway.[28]

As he returned to his seat and waited for the applause to die down, Quisling was probably unaware that his attempt to requisition Henrik Ibsen for national socialism in Norway contained an unintentional irony, for in a letter to the Danish critic Georg Brandes several decades earlier the great dramatist had referred to the Jews as the 'aristocrats of the human race'. Pondering the mystery of their survival in the face of centuries of isolation and hostility, Ibsen hypothesised that it was because the Jews 'had no state to burden them down. Had they stayed in Palestine they would long ago have lost track of their identity, just like all other peoples. The state must go!' was Ibsen's conclusion. 'Now *there's* a revolution I would support.'[29]

That was hardly the kind of endorsement Quisling would like to have heard from the man who, long before his death in 1906, had become the conscience of modern Norway. But the minister-president must, in any event, have been painfully aware by now that the whole State Act pageant was a sham. In a letter of 26 January 1942 to Terboven, he had requested that the Reichskommissar include in his speech an announcement that the two of them would share power for a period of no longer than two months following the passing of the act, after which it would pass into Quisling's hands alone as leader of a fully independent – although still occupied – Norway. Terboven had ignored his request. Nor had there been any mention in his speech of Norway regaining its independence, and nothing about a peace treaty between Norway and Germany that would allow Norwegians to fight alongside Germans as their allies against the Bolsheviks and the British.

Quisling had visited Hitler in Berlin again early in December of 1941 and returned full of optimism from his trip. But as Josef Goebbels had noted in his diary entry for 24 January 1942, Quisling's imminent elevation to minister-president would change nothing in Norway: 'the structure of the Norwegian state and the position of the Reichskommissar will remain the same. Quisling will be incorporated into the state.'[30] Terboven himself, in a briefing to his staff on 29 January, gave them assurances that Minister-President Quisling would 'naturally, be completely under my command'.[31] Signalling the reality of all this, as soon as the applause following Quisling's speech had died down, the band struck up the German national anthem. This was followed by a rendition of the Horst Wessel song, the battle hymn of the NSDAP. Only then was it time for *Ja vi elsker*, the Norwegian national anthem. Nothing could have demonstrated more clearly to Quisling and his new ministry that the Reichskommissar remained as firmly in charge of proceedings as ever.

On 5 February Quisling led the first meeting of his new government, now with Terboven's three non-party experts in the ministries of Trade, Industry and Finance replaced by National

Unity members. Two new pieces of legislation that emerged from the first session announced the start of a sustained attempt to indoctrinate Norwegian children from the age of ten upwards into the national socialist way of thinking. The first was the *Lov om nasjonale ungdomstjeneste* (Law Concerning National Youth Service), modelled on legislation in Nazi Germany that had created the *Hitlerjugend* (Hitler Youth) and the *Bund Deutscher Mädel* (League of German Girls):

1. For the benefit of their nationalist upbringing, and to serve their people and fatherland, every Norwegian boy and girl shall serve in National Unity's Young People's Movement. The obligation begins on 1 January of the year in which the child turns ten and ends on 31 December of the year in which the child turns eighteen.
2. The Minister for Labour and Sport will in consultation with the Minister for Church Affairs and Education in due course provide further detail concerning the law and its application.
3. The Law comes into force on 1 March 1942.

The second law, the *Lov om Norges Lærersamband* (Law Concerning the Norwegian Teachers' Organisation), was an obvious corollary to the first and proposed to Nazify the teaching profession by dissolving all previously existing teachers' unions and replacing them with a single new, national socialist Teachers' Organisation. This was to be headed by Orvar Sæther, a teacher himself and national head of the *Rikshird*, the elite section of the *hird*. Membership was compulsory, as was membership of National Unity. Both pieces of legislation aimed at the application of the Führer principle on which the party had been formed in 1933 to cover the administration of the whole country. This was a manifestation of the elitist belief that power flows downwards, with decisions always being taken by the best and the most able men. Within any such hierarchy the leaders are appointed from above. Those appointed owe a duty of unquestioning obedience to the one doing the appointing. They are in turn responsible for the appointment of the leader immediately below them and compel the same absolute obedience as they owe the leader above them. To objections raised in the social democratic Norway of the immediate pre-war years that such a system amounted to dictatorship, National Unity's legal experts invoked Paragraph 30 of the Norwegian Constitution,[32] which states that the king listens to his advisers before taking his decisions *efter sit eget omdømme* ('following his own counsel'). And under the terms of the February State Act, Quisling had now assumed the constitutional powers of a Norwegian monarch.

Some of the ground for this had already been prepared by Dean Sigmund Feyling, Quisling's director general at the Ministry for Church Affairs and author of a textbook of religious instruction widely used in schools prior to the occupation. A new edition published in 1941 had contained Feyling's revised commentary on the Fourth Commandment ('Thou shalt honour thy father and thy mother') that gave a distinctly anti-democratic spin to orthodox Christian teaching on the duty of obedience:

> Most of all we owe obedience to the *fører* (leader) and to the government. To set oneself up against authority and the state is to defy the word of God. Punishment will follow.

At this stage of the occupation the Germans were not interested in alienating a 'silent majority' of Norwegians by the fanatical promotion of national socialist values. That could wait until after the victory. But Quisling felt he had something to prove to his Nazi masters, and the two new laws were a statement of intention addressed to the occupiers as well as to his fellow Norwegians. They united people against National Unity as nothing had done before. An immediate and sustained campaign of protest known as the *holdningskamp* (Conscience Struggle) got under way. Nationwide and non-violent, it united teachers, bishops and thousands of parents and schoolchildren in common cause against the new regime. In various ways it would occupy most of the country for most of the year.

The state church led the way with a dramatic response on the very day of the State Act ceremony itself. A parallel ceremony had been arranged to take place in Nidaros Cathedral in Trondheim. About a week before the ceremony – the details of which had been kept secret – the Bishop of Trondheim, Johan Støren, received a telegram from the Department of Church Affairs informing him that the service on 1 February would be a special one in celebration of the historic occasion. A visiting priest would lead it, Peder Blessing-Dahle. Blessing-Dahle was one of the few priests to join National Unity. Indeed he was a founding member of the party, having joined in 1933. Støren passed the information on to Arne Fjellbu, who had been due to lead the service that Sunday, noting that he didn't think there was much they could do about it.

LEGISLATION FOR A NATIONAL SOCIALIST REVOLUTION

Arne Fjellbu was of another mind. As early as the autumn of the first year of the occupation he had been active in organising a united church front to the one-party state introduced by Terboven. He had been one of a number of priests who ignored the injunction from the Terboven government for priests to omit from their regular Sunday services the prayer 'for the King and his House, Parliament, the King's Council and all our Authorities' as being no longer appropriate. He was appalled by Bishop Støren's shrugging reaction and visited the bishop to discuss the matter with him in person. At one point the bishop raised the question of whether or not the two of them should personally attend the service led by Blessing-Dahle. Fjellbu refused even to discuss the possibility. 'It's out of the question,' he said. 'No one at all must attend the service.'

Støren's wife was in the same room. 'Well,' she began, 'my husband...'

'I intend to protest as loudly as possible against this,' Fjellbu interjected. Fjellbu later wrote that the bishop's wife rewarded his interruption with an approving glance. Perhaps she wasn't too surprised; Fjellbu had already had several minor confrontations with the Nazi authorities. Shortly after the invasion, as the dean of the cathedral, he had received a visit from a high-ranking German Nazi. The visitor explained that his visit was a courtesy call. In what he later recalled as a frank exchange of views, Fjellbu informed him that national socialism and Christianity were as 'incompatible as fire and water'. National socialism, he said, demanded *everything* of the individual; in his world, only God could make such a demand. His statement puzzled the visitor, who suggested that it was just the priest in him speaking. Not so, was Fjellbu's rejoinder; it was the Christian. As early as the summer of 1940 he had composed on behalf of the Trondheim diocese a letter to members of the Storting urging them not to support plans to request the abdication of King Haakon VII. The result was four hours of interrogation at Gestapo headquarters in Trondheim. As Fjellbu remarked in an interview with an American radio journalist in 1945, this was the period of the Norwegian version of the 'phoney war' in which the invaders were still on their best behaviour, and Fjellbu was allowed to leave after his interrogation. But his spirit of outraged rejection was not to be denied. In the spring of 1941, a combined British and Norwegian commando raid on the Lofoten Islands known as Operation Claymore ended in a rare triumph for the Allies. Three hundred Norwegians joined the British for military training when the expedition returned home, with over 200 German prisoners of war. Incidents such as this ended German attempts to win over the population by means of propaganda, and among the reprisals Terboven ordered a number of houses to be razed to the ground in Svolvær, leaving the families homeless. Fjellbu organised a relief action for those affected. Terboven immediately forbade any such relief. Fjellbu lodged a protest but was ignored. Not long afterwards he protested against the persecution and intimidation of Trondheim's Jewish community, the second largest in Norway. For these combined infractions he was fined a thousand kroner.

As far as the Nazis were concerned Fjellbu was a major confrontation waiting to happen, and his determination to ruin the State Act celebrations in Trondheim on 1 February 1942 marked a point of no return in the Conscience Struggle from which it was impossible to turn back. At 11 on the morning of the ceremony, Blessing-Dahle began his sermon before a sea of Sun Crosses and swastikas to a congregation of *hird* and National Unity party members. He preached on the unparalleled threat to Christianity in Europe from the militant atheism of Soviet communism, basing his sermon on Matthew chapter 19, verses 27 to 30, where Peter asks Jesus what is to be his disciples' reward for abandoning everything to place themselves in his hands, and Jesus responds by prophesying a visionary future for them. Blessing-Dahle's spin on this was Norway's unprecedented need at such a moment in its history for a leader to take charge of all the lost sheep and lead them on to a similar glorious future. Such a man had appeared among them, he assured the congregation. His name was Vidkun Quisling.

The day before the ceremony, Fjellbu had inserted a notice in the Saturday edition of the local newspaper announcing that his service would not be held at the Cathedral at the usual time on Sunday morning but instead at 2 p.m. The notice was mysteriously absent from the evening edition of the paper and early on Sunday morning the police arrived at Fjellbu's house to detain him for the duration of Blessing-Dahle's service. Fjellbu, however, had already gone into hiding in an architect's office adjacent to the cathedral that gave access to a hidden staircase leading into the church. From there he had been able to watch the marching, flag-waving columns of members of the *hird* in all its many subdivisions and the party dignitaries as they arrived and entered the cathedral.

Blessing-Dahle's service passed without incident and when it was over the congregation, including a few non-party members such as Fjellbu's own son, present as observers, made their way out. Police and *hird* members who had been stationed at the doors to prevent possible disturbance left the scene. Not long afterwards, on a bitterly cold February morning, with the temperature at minus 35, a crowd of people loyal to the king and the London government began to congregate in the cathedral square to hear Fjellbu's postponed service. As the size of the crowd grew the police and the *hird* were ordered to return to their posts as local National Unity officials continued to work against the clock to track Fjellbu down and inform him that if he attempted to go ahead with it his proposed service would be regarded as an illegal act of hostility towards the regime and he would be arrested.

From the window of the architect's office Fjellbu could now look down on a scene of growing chaos outside the main western doors of the cathedral. He saw the police bar the main entrance and refuse to allow the crowd, now numbering several hundred, inside. People trying to force their way in were driven back by the baton-wielding police and *hird* guards. Bishop Støren arrived to complain about the violence. He urged the crowd to disperse. No one listened.

As 2 p.m. approached Fjellbu made his way from the architect's office to the cathedral using the secret staircase. He passed through the cathedral workshop and entered the church. Expecting to be placed under immediate arrest he walked not to the pulpit but straight to the altar, following the advice of his wife, who had urged him to force his enemies to arrest him in the holiest place in the cathedral. Many had managed to get inside before the police barricaded the doors. Even the organist had made it, and as the service got under way the Chief of Police approached Bishop Søren in the sacristy and informed him that the service was a 'political demonstration' and that he intended to stop it. Støren pointed out that it was already under way and there was no legal way he could do so since the law of the land stated that a church service once started could not be stopped. The chief took the point and ordered his men to stand down and let Fjellbu preach. They could arrest him afterwards.

In view of the violence he had witnessed from the office window looking down over the cathedral square, Fjellbu had decided to depart from his originally prepared sermon and instead speak of the blasphemous outrage of preventing people from attending a legal church service. At the last moment, however, he changed his mind again, reflecting that a sermon like that would leave him open to a charge of politicising his office. This had already become a favourite mantra of both German and Norwegian Nazis and to avoid the possibility he reverted to the subject of his original sermon.

The crowd outside had swelled to thousands. People remained calm in the bitter cold. Suddenly a lone voice struck up the first line of Martin Luther's hymn 'A mighty fortress is our God', and the extempore congregation of thousands joined in. It must have been audible inside the cathedral.

At the end of the service Fjellbu and his family left the cathedral, again using the secret staircase. Using one of the smaller entrances at the rear of the building they emerged unseen into the street and made their way home. A modest celebratory dinner that evening was interrupted by the arrival of a Norwegian State Police

(*Stapo*) officer to take a statement from Fjellbu. At the request of the Germans Fjellbu was also asked to provide a copy of his sermon. He was placed under house arrest and ordered to report twice daily to the local Stapo headquarters. As he later recalled, his daily visits to register his presence were recorded by a young girl who had once been one of his confirmands but who had, as he put it, 'taken the other path'.

On 18 February Quisling returned from a visit to Germany and at a government meeting the next day Fjellbu was dismissed from his post and expelled from the diocese of Nidaros.* Bishop Støren, whose instinct had so often been to go along to get along, resigned in support of him on 24 February 1942. So did the other bishops in the Norwegian Lutheran Church. As Easter approached the new government's crisis deepened with the appearance of *Kirkens Grunn* (The Foundation of the Church), a document co-written by Eivind Berggrav, which announced the theological impossibility of the Lutheran Church continuing as a state church under a national socialist regime, and explained why its servants had to resign. Illegally distributed to churches throughout the country, it was read to congregations from their pulpit by priests who made it their last official act before resigning office. The union of church and state that had existed in one form or another since the Reformation in 1537 and had become such a central part of the democratic functioning of the country had come to an end:

> Events in Norway after 25 September 1940, and especially after 1 February 1942, with all the repercussions and changes that have followed, compel us to make this statement regarding the Foundation of the Church. As long as these changed conditions

---

* Fjellbu was banished to Hvitsten. Following accusations of 'anti-state activities' he was further banished to Andøya. In the summer of 1944 he was ordered to Lillehammer, which had become National Unity's favoured location for holding troublesome priests. Tired of being told what to do, he instead escaped to Sweden with the help of Sami border guides.

endure and are sustained by further changes and interventions then the church and its servants must live and act according to their commitment to the word of God and to their faith, and take every consequence this may have...³³

Support for the protest was impressive. Of a total of 858 priests, 797 resigned on Easter Sunday, 5 April 1942. Berggrav, a moving spirit behind the resignations, had by this time become a figure of hate for the minister-president; for his role in the collapse of Quisling's 9 April coup and the formation of the Administrative Council that had so effectively sidelined Quisling for the first two years of the occupation; for the recent humiliation of ousting Quisling as a focus of Terboven's State Act speech; and now for the further humiliation of the mass resignations. In April 1942 he ordered the house arrest of the Bishop of Oslo, confining him to the family's cabin home in Borgen, in Asker, where Berggrav remained until almost the final moments of the liberation in 1945.

Minister-President Quisling now assumed the 'deposed' Haakon VII's function as head of the Norwegian church. Learning that his own home parish of Fyresdal in Telemark had become a hotbed of resistance to everything his new government stood for, he arrived in the village one day in August 1942 with a full complement of bodyguards, National Unity party officials and Stapo officers, interviewing village leaders and officials, confronting them with anti-regime statements they were alleged to have made and issuing threats about what would happen if they did not mend their ways. On 12 August it was the turn of the local priest, a man named Otto Irgens. Quisling visited him at the rectory, the place where he had spent the first four years of his own life as the son of the man who was then Fyresdal's parish priest, Jon Lauritz Quisling.

The meeting began civilly enough, until Quisling brought up the subject of a vote Irgens had arranged in the church to discuss Quisling's new 'Law Concerning National Youth Service' – why had he done that? Irgens' reply was that it was in the church's interest to keep people informed of what was going on in society.

Not at all, responded Quisling. The church had only one job, and that was to preach the word of God to parishioners and to make better people of them. On learning that Irgens was one of those who had resigned from office in protest against his new legislation, Quisling expressed outrage at the fact that the priest was still living in the rectory. He gave him and his wife fourteen days in which to leave not only their home but the county of Telemark, confiscated his assets and those of his wife, and informed him that anyone offering him financial assistance would receive the same treatment. On 28 September the couple left the village with nothing but the clothes they stood up in and a handful of personal belongings.

Quisling's problem as new head of the Norwegian church was that there was now hardly a Norwegian church to be head of. A few National Unity priests found themselves fast-tracked into bishoprics. A contemporary photograph shows the sheepishness they felt at this unworthy and sudden promotion. Shortly after

Irgens' departure from Fyresdal, a National Unity priest was appointed to the vacant living and took up residence in the rectory. Like most other National Unity priests, the new incumbent found himself preaching to congregations in single figures, while outside the church doors the legitimate priests of the parishes continued to preach and preside over social and religious rites such as marriage ceremonies, baptisms and funerals.* No longer able to draw wages as state employees, the priests became dependent on the charity of their parishioners and benefactors. In all, 127 priests were expelled from their parishes; 92 of them spent shorter or longer periods in jail.

The fourth of the six points in 'The Foundation of the Church' was a justification of the church's rejection of the Quisling government's plans to create a Norwegian equivalent to the Hitlerjugend in Germany:

> Every Christian father and mother has the duty and the right to raise their children in the Christian faith [...] The church would betray its obligations as an educator if it merely looked on while a worldly authority organises a moral and social education that takes no heed of the Christian view. No attempt should be made to compel parents and teachers to act against their conscience by putting their children in the hands of educators who propose to 'revolutionise their minds' and initiate them into a 'new vision of life' that is alien to the Christian faith.[34]

In backing this up the schoolteachers responded to the new plans to Nazify the educational system by following the lead shown by the bishops and priests. Among their leaders was Einar Høigård, a thirty-five-year-old teacher at Oslo Cathedral School,

---

* These had to be ratified afterwards by National Unity authorities to become legal.

where he was also the librarian. In 1935 Høigård had spent a year in Hamburg as a lecturer in Norwegian at the university and seen for himself the practical consequences of adopting national socialism as a political system. The prospect of its arrival in Norway filled him with dread as what had originally been principally a military occupation intended to guarantee the supply of iron ore from the mines of northern Sweden now evolved into a determined attempt by native Norwegian adherents of the system to impose national socialist values on the population. By the autumn of 1941 Høigård had already drafted a statement of principled response in anticipation of exactly the type of assault on the teaching profession made by the February 1942 legislation. It consisted of four cardinal points teachers were asked to consider in the event of any attempt to indoctrinate pupils and teachers:

1. Demands for membership or declarations of loyalty to National Unity to be rejected.
2. Any attempt to introduce National Unity propaganda into the classroom to be rejected.
3. Any order issued without competent authority to be rejected.
4. Any involvement with National Unity's Youth Movement to be rejected.

Following the February 1942 legislation the circumstances envisaged by Høigård had become reality and on 14 February, at a meeting of the Secret Educational Committee, it was decided to advise all teachers to sign a standard 'declaration of conscience' and post the letters to the headquarters of the Norwegian Teachers' Organisation:

> I find I am unable to contribute to the education of Norway's young people in the direction associated with National Unity's Young People's Movement as my conscience will not allow it. Membership of the union would oblige me to provide such an education, according to the union's national leader, and would

moreover oblige me to act in other ways at variance with the terms of my employment. I therefore have no option but to inform you that I cannot consider myself a member of the Norwegian Teachers' Organisation.

Letters from 12,000 of the country's 14,000 teachers duly arrived at the offices of the Teachers Organisation in Kristian Augusts gate 19, each one including the full name, address and place of employment of the signatories. Orvar Sæther summoned head teachers from schools in the Oslo region to discuss the impasse. There was no chance of a negotiated settlement and shortly afterwards the Ministry for Education and Religious Affairs delivered its ultimatum: anyone refusing to join the new union by 1 March would face dismissal.

The threat had no immediate effect, and in a face-saving move intended to give him more time to deal with the problem Ragnar Skancke abruptly ordered the closure of all schools on 26 February, on the pretext that there was a nationwide shortage of firewood. Alas for the face-saving side of the move, the weather at once turned mild and remained so for several weeks. Skancke may have hoped that the economic burden of life without a regular income would bring the teachers to order but, as was happening at the same time with the priests and bishops, collections were clandestinely organised and money raised to support them and their families.

Stirred by the response of the teachers, the parents of the children affected now came together and voiced their own protest against developments. This also took the form of a standard letter to the department that raised the same conscientious objection to the proposed Nazification of the schools and the curriculum as the teachers', their letter having the added impact of the objection to a national socialist education being raised on behalf of 'my child'. The parents' campaign was instigated and largely run by women. Using the tactic employed by the schoolteachers, parents all posted their letters on the same day and as far as possible at the same hour. This had a dual purpose: to overwhelm the bureaucratic resources of the department, and to preclude any possibility of the senders of the first letters to arrive being singled out for punishment. Between two and three hundred thousand identical letters duly arrived at the offices of the Ministry for Education and Religious Affairs.[35]

National Unity's response was to take the gloves off. On 26 March about 1,100 teachers from all parts of the country were arrested. In keeping with the occupiers' policy of staying well in the background in such matters as this, ordinary local Norwegian police officers made the actual arrests. Only male teachers were taken. The national socialist view of women was that they belonged in the kitchen and in the bed and could scarcely be held accountable for their actions when venturing outside these two arenas. Most of the teachers arrested in southern Norway were imprisoned in Grini and offered a chance to reconsider their refusal to join the new union: if they did so by 30 March they would be free to go home and resume their lives. When the deadline arrived, only three of the 294 had accepted the offer. The remainder were informed that they were to be transported to the far north of the country and put to work there as slave labour.

Once the teachers held at Grini had been joined by those from other camps the complete group was transported in cattle trucks to Fåberg station, and from there marched to a notoriously squalid concentration camp at Jørdstadmoen. Here, in two weeks of waiting while their transport to the north was arranged, they were subjected to humiliating punishment exercises, punctuated by punches and bayonet jabs from the adolescent thugs in charge of them. On 3 April – Good Friday – the teachers were summoned on parade and given one last chance to reconsider. Of the 786 now held at Jørdstadmoen, only eleven decided that enough was enough and were allowed to leave the camp.

On 8 April their long journey to the far north began – first by train to Trondheim and then aboard an old coastal steamer, the D/S *Skjerstad*. Four hundred and ninety-eight teachers were packed on board a ship designed to accommodate 150, with a Norwegian crew and fifty German guards. The Norwegian skipper initially refused to sail until sufficient lifejackets had been provided for the overcrowded vessel. On a visit to Berlin in May Terboven related this detail to Hitler. Mistakenly supposing the captain involved to have been German, Hitler despaired of the typically German decency the man had shown and suggested that what the teachers really deserved was to have the *Skjerstad* torpedoed by 'their beloved Englishmen' and sent to the bottom of the ocean. Along with the physical discomforts of the voyage the teachers had to live with the very real fear that the Allies would attack the ship.

Arriving in Kirkenes on 28 April, the teachers faced instead the strong possibility of being killed by one of the 328 Allied bombing raids which that small town on the Norway–Russia border was subjected to over the course of the war. In Kirkenes they were delivered into the relatively civilised care of the local Wehrmacht and put to work as navvies, longshoremen and stevedores alongside Russian and east European slave labourers.

Even as the *Skjerstad* was still at sea, however, Orvar Sæther had conceded defeat in the face of the teachers' overwhelming opposition. The whole standoff had been the result of a 'misunderstanding', he explained. The new union was a professional organisation only. Membership carried no obligation to promote a specific set of values or political views. The same press release included the promise that 'no honest teacher shall be required to do or say anything that is at odds with their own conscience'. Membership of the new Teachers' Organisation was automatic; there would be no dues to pay. The only obligation members faced was to teach pupils 'to believe in and aspire to all that is true and just'.[36] On these terms, female teachers and those males not placed under arrest were able to return to work on 9 May, members of a now meaningless union. Like the men of principle they were, however, the teachers who had been banished to Kirkenes proved such good and conscientious workers that the Germans were reluctant to let them go. Not until the onset of a bitterly cold November put their survival at risk were they finally released to return to their homes, families and jobs in the south.

Einar Høigård had been active organising fund-raising for the dependents of the exiled teachers. National Unity attempts to Nazify Oslo University had run concurrently with the attack on the school system. The rector, Didrik Arup Seip, had been dismissed, arrested and imprisoned and replaced in September 1941 by Adolf Hoel, an assistant professor in geography with a more sympathetic attitude towards National Unity. Høigård was among the leaders of a group opposed to any cooperation with Hoel, and the battle lines hardened when new criteria for entry into the medical faculty were introduced in the summer of 1942 to favour applicants who were members of National Unity. It was a smart and sinister move, at a time when members of the medical profession enjoyed an almost godlike status among the general public. Numbers admitted on the basis of party membership almost doubled the agreed intake for the next academic year. Høigård worked behind the scenes to persuade faculty heads in the medical and other departments to insist that merit alone could qualify applicants for places in their departments. They were urged to make sure that students who owed their matriculation to party membership would have problems arranging laboratory time and could not be certain they would be allowed to sit their final exams. The response of National Unity was to order the arrest of ten professors and sixty-three activists. Høigård's name was top of the list, but by the time of the raid on 15 October he had been tipped off and gone into hiding.

With his wife and children in a safe house in Vågå in Gudbrandsdal, some 250 kilometres north of Oslo, Høigård boarded the Halden train on 23 October intending to cross the border into Sweden. His flight was arranged by Rolf Nielsen, one of many serving Norwegian police officers who found this and similar acts of illegality the only way to deal with the unthinkable moral gymnastics imposed upon them in their daily work since the invasion of 9 April 1940. Nielsen, who helped over 1,400

Norwegian refugees over to Sweden, said after the war that he had not realised how significant a figure Høigård was at the time, or he would have taken greater care with the arrangements. As it was Høigård was arrested on board the train by a Norwegian-American border policeman named Holgeir John Stabell. He was held in Halden for two days before being transferred to Bredtveit Prison in Oslo and accused of illegal political activity as well as attempting to leave the country without permission, a new crime introduced by the Quisling regime that carried a possible, if rarely used, death sentence.

Høigård was held at Bredtveit for a month. Never a man to waste his time – during his months in hiding he had written a significant textbook, *Pedagogical Statistics* – he occupied his mind in a statistical experiment that involved tossing a small 'coin' made from cardboard and marked on each side with 'heads' and 'tails', in pursuit of practical proof that things always even out in the long run. He tossed his little carboard coin a total of 10,000 times and came remarkably close to a perfect demonstration of the theory, recording 5,007 tails and 4,993 heads.

His constant fear over the years of his active opposition to the attempt to bring the national socialist revolution to Norway's schools and its university was of being arrested and tortured. He once confided to Harald Schelderup, a professor of psychology who led the university's Action Committee, that he was deeply uneasy at the thought that he wouldn't be able to endure it and would reach a point at which he would begin naming names. From his prison cell he managed to send out a message to his associates: 'I know what I must do if it becomes necessary. My way is clear.' He may have been tortured by his Norwegian captors while in Bredtveit; after the war a woman imprisoned in the cell next to a university teacher recalled how she was once ordered to clean the floor of the scholar as he lay there on his bunk, too reduced following a session of 'focused interrogation' to do so himself. She didn't know his name, but the circumstantial evidence is strong that the teacher was Einar Høigård.

On 25 November, Høigård was transferred to Victoria terrasse in central Oslo to be handed over to the Gestapo. In an effort to forestall this he asked to be allowed to speak to a Norwegian Stapo officer named Gottfrid Skule, a man with a reputation for relative decency. He was given permission to do so, but in a curiously amateur moment the policeman who was to take him to Skule delivered him instead to the wrong place, an office up on the fifth floor. Unaware that the man at his door was a prisoner, the occupant told him Skule's office was down on the third floor. On his way back down the stairs Høigård stopped at a window on a landing. With an instinctive tidiness he then removed his glasses and hat and placed them on the windowsill before opening the window and jumping to his death.[37]

At his widow Elfrida's request, a pathologist at *Rikshospitalet* (the National Hospital) conducted a private autopsy on Høigård's body. Along with the fractured skull and numerous broken bones, he found evidence of burn marks on the fingertips that suggested he may have been tortured not long before his death. Høigård left a letter inside his sock, with instructions that it be read to his three children when they were old enough to understand his decision. A month after his death Elfrida gave birth to his fourth child. This last letter did not survive. Perhaps it was along the lines of something he wrote to one of his students while in hiding in the summer of that same year:

Conditions today have given rise in all of us to thoughts and qualities we wish had been ours before. I mean decency, and courage. Clear thinking and an understanding of the values that are ours. In short, the will and the ability to stand up against the Nazi ruination not only of our country but of our inner selves. It isn't enough to see that it's happening, and to comfort oneself with the thought that one has no part in it: one has to do something, risk something, sacrifice something to sustain what we build our lives upon.[38]

5

The Conscience Struggle, 1942

The Conscience Struggle of 1942 that was galvanised by Quisling's legislation was a mass movement of unsung heroes; it did not spawn icons of resistance who became legendary for their striking individual contributions. But of those it did produce none symbolises better the enigmatic power of the movement than Ingrid Bjerkås, and none gives us a better insight into why ordinary Norwegians were better able to counter the threat of national socialism than that hapless conscript she had observed from the kitchen window of her Bærum home as he straddled her back garden fence on the morning of 9 April 1940. Her record of protest went back to an afternoon some seven weeks following the invasion, when she disrupted a speech being given by Josef Terboven on 1 June in front of the royal palace, the Reichskommissar's first in public since arriving to take office in late April. In the weeks following her first terrifying sighting of those German soldiers invading Oslo, Bjerkås had experienced a religious awakening. It had been so intense that there were times when she, a woman of no previous religious conviction, feared for her own sanity. The religious awakening brought with it a compulsion to follow her instincts as a Christian with no care as

to where this might lead her. Wearing her *lotte* (reservist nurse) uniform beneath her coat, and with a biblical text in her handbag – 'I tell you, my friends, do not be afraid of those who kill the body and after that can do no more. But I will show you whom you should fear: Fear him who, after your body has been killed, has authority to throw you into hell. Yes, I tell you, fear him'[39] – she had taken the tram into central Oslo and made her way to the large open square in front of the royal palace. Somebody was already speaking when she got there. Not Terboven but, as she realised later, General Nikolaus von Falkenhorst, the architect of the Weserübung invasion plan. Finding a gap in the protective cordon of police and soldiers around the square, she had headed quickly towards the podium. Reaching inside her coat pocket, she pulled out the copy of a German Bible she had purchased on the journey in. She kept on walking until she was no more than five metres away from the podium. The man addressing the troops fell silent and stared at her. Holding the German Bible aloft in her hand and straining towards the microphone clipped to the front of the podium, she shouted out the words she had been rehearsing all the way in on her tram journey to the centre: 'No speeches by Germans! The king and the Nygaardsvold government are the only rightful rulers here!'[40]

Bjerkås was arrested and taken to Gestapo headquarters five minutes away in Victoria terrasse, where she was questioned by a Gestapo officer who struggled to maintain his anger in the face of his greater bewilderment. Eventually she was released on the promise that she would commit no further disturbances of the peace. She was escorted out of the building by a Norwegian policewoman, who told her that the men stationed at the palace had been equipped with water cannon in anticipation of crowd trouble – 'But as it turned out, fru Bjerkås, you were the only one.'

Her record of personal protest continued with a brief campaign of letter-writing to Quisling that caused considerable alarm in circles around the minister-president. She began it following a radio broadcast on 5 September 1941 in which Quisling had spoken of the 'decisive world struggle' that faced all Norwegians as they forged ahead into 'the new age', and laid the blame for all the ills that had befallen the country over the preceding eighteen months on the king and his government.

The following day Bjerkås addressed a letter to him:

Herr Quisling –

After hearing your speech on the radio yesterday I believe I have the right and duty to approach you in this way.

Herr Quisling, you have already done greater damage to our country than probably any single other man before you ever has. Yet still you don't think it is enough, still you persist.

If you were still able to say that you are quite certain Hitler will win the war then that would be an extenuating circumstance for your course of action. But you simply cannot say this. You simply believe it, assume it and hope for it, and based on this you persist in drawing more and more weak

Norwegians with you along the failed path you have yourself taken.

Herr Quisling, let me tell you: I know that Hitler and Nazi Germany will not win the war; that England cannot be humiliated, and that our own king, the crown prince's family and his family, government and our sailors and all the others will return to a free and liberated Norway. And knowing this as I do, I must ask: How dare you, Herr Quisling, entice and seduce Norwegians into being betrayers and traitors, criminals opposed to their own people, disgracing us in front of the whole world, and despised by their own?

No, if you really are a Norwegian, Mr. Quisling, and have at the heart of you the same feelings as every true Norwegian, then there is only one thing you can do:

Dissolve your party and admit to yourself and the world that the path you have chosen leads not upwards but downwards into wretchedness.

It takes courage to do that. But in your speech you used the phrase 'Christianity in practice', so you know that whoever does the right thing does not have to be afraid of anyone or anything, for he has God with him.

If you are a Norwegian, Herr Quisling, then do the right thing and do it soon.

I am an ordinary anonymous Norwegian citizen, but in the name of decency I sign myself –

Ingrid Bjerkås

In the purity of her anger she seems genuinely to have expected to see, if not the actual dissolution of National Unity, at least some sign that Quisling would moderate the intense hostility of his rhetoric towards people who did not share his views. So when a month had passed without seeing any sign of improvement, she resent the letter, registered delivery this time, and with a covering note urging Quisling to follow her advice:

Herr Quisling

It has been over a month since I sent the original of the attached letter. As I have not yet seen any result of it I must allow the possibility that you did not receive it and I have therefore made this typewritten duplicate which I send to you today by registered post.

At the same time I take this opportunity to tell you that it is not for fun, nor out of curiosity nor in response to some hysterical whim that I have decided to approach you in this way. It is because I regard it as necessary to invest everything in the effort to bring about the dissolution of N.S. so that the Norwegian people can stand together as one in these evil times.

That is why I turn in the first instance to you. Can you not see for yourself that you still have the chance to wash away so many of the shameful stains with which you have soiled the name of Norway, as well as your own name? Make the effort now. Show the world that Quislings at heart are true Norwegians and not, as they seem today, the slaves of Germans.

Ingrid Bjerkås

Quisling received this second delivery and on 21 October Bjerkås was summoned to Norwegian State Police headquarters in Kirkeveien and questioned about the letters. She denied any wrongdoing but agreed not to write any more. She would not, however, promise to abandon her campaign for the dissolution of Quisling's party. Her remarkable and passionate conviction puzzled Ragnvald Kranz, the Norwegian Stapo officer in charge of the case, and he shared his anxieties about her mental stability with his friend, Dr Hans Eng, Quisling's personal physician. Eng, a confident and arrogant man with an unshakeable belief in the correctness of his own understandings, offered his diagnosis to Kranz:

Herr politifullmektig Ragnvald Krantz. (sic)

Re fru Ingrid Bjerkås, b. 8.5.1901. Kringsjåveien 8 – Jar.

Before going into detail on the above case let me give a brief account of what I understand by Jøssingism.

Jøssingism denotes intellectual tendencies the aim of which is to break down or oppose the ideology of National Unity or of anyone working to implement the new direction in our society.

Jøssingism is a collective term for a variety of forms of anti-social behaviour. However, these different asocial types have a number of characteristic features and in some cases it can be difficult to distinguish the different types.

...

The subject in question, fru Ingrid Bjerkås, exhibits a number of delusional beliefs. She knows that Hitler will not win the war, but she has no logical basis for the belief. She sees it as her task to disband National Unity but has not the slightest knowledge of the party's programme. She makes threats against National Unity and against the Germans but has not 'decided' what means she will use. She tried to interrupt Terboven's speech in front of the palace. This is an action no human being (regardless of their political persuasion) would attempt in a normal state. The relevant documents indicate that she suffers from psychopathic jøssingismus (methodologically it might be termed jøssingismus anglemanicus paranoidformis i.e., a psychopothic anglophilia Jøssingisme with delusions of persecution).

My recommendation is that she be placed under guardianship or else be detained by the police and placed under psychiatric observation.

Heil og sæl

Hans Eng

Quisling had wanted a charge of *ærekrenkelse* (defamation of character) to be considered against Bjerkås on the basis of the letters, but with this 'diagnosis' she was instead released into the 'guardianship' of her husband Sigurd, who gave the police his assurance that he did not believe his wife capable of physical violence. But even as 'head of the household' he was unable to promise that she would not write any more letters to Quisling, though he gave his word that he would try to persuade her not to, and to impress upon her the likelihood of a prison sentence if she did.

As the hugely symbolic moment of the State Act approached, early in 1942 Eng recalled his 'diagnosis' of Bjerkås, and that passing reference to her attempt 'to interrupt Terboven's speech in front of the palace'. The thought of Ingrid Bjerkås somehow repeating the interruption and reducing the State Act ceremony to an undignified farce exercised him so much that on the day before it he raised his anxieties with the Minister of Justice, Sverre Riisnæs, as well as his Stapo friend, Ragnvald Kranz. He urged Kranz to have Bjerkås taken into custody until the whole thing was over. Kranz sent a man to her house, only to learn that Bjerkås was spending the nights at the local hospital where her daughter, Uni, lay seriously ill with peritonitis. On request she gave the authorities her written assurance that as long as her daughter remained in hospital she would refrain from doing anything that might trouble or embarrass the authorities. She also promised to inform the authorities once Uni's recovery released her from the promise.

Once the ceremony was over and her daughter recovered Bjerkås then called, unannounced, on Dr Eng at his home in Kirkeveien 90. Somehow she had learned of his *jøssingismus* diagnosis and now demanded to know by what right he had diagnosed her as mentally ill, without even subjecting her to a personal examination. It seems that she reduced this powerful and self-assured man to a stammering defence in which he was obliged to explain that behind his diagnosis lay the simple certainty that anyone who did what she had done – interrupt a Nazi German general in the middle of addressing his troops – would, by definition, have to be insane to do so.*

Her daughter's illness might have prevented Bjerkås from any possible disruption of the State Act ceremony but her personal crusade against Quisling and National Unity was still not over. The flaring up of the Conscience Struggle in the wake of the February 1942 legislation brought her once more onto a collision course with the Norwegian Führer. This time it led to a personal encounter. The local secondary school in Stabekk attended by her two children, Trond and Uni, had become a centre of opposition to Quisling's plans for a new Norwegian Teachers' Organisation. It made the school an ideal place at which to set an example that would hopefully bring the teachers into line and on 22 May 1942 Quisling himself, his Minister for Education and Religious Affairs Ragnar Skancke, and Jonas Lie from the Ministry of Policing made a surprise visit to the school. Thirty policemen accompanied them. The children were sent home as the three politicians in turn tried to cajole and bully the teachers into joining the new union. Two eventually complied; the remainder who didn't were arrested and imprisoned.

Ingrid Bjerkås was active in organising collections to support the families of imprisoned teachers. She took the arrest of the

---

* There may also be some truth in the explanation Eng offered at his trial in 1948, that he wrote it partly as a joke, and partly in the attempt to prevent Bjerkås from being sent to a prison camp in Germany.

teachers up personally with the new National Unity head of the school, who told her there was nothing he could do about it; the resolution of the dispute wasn't in his hands. Did that mean it was in Quisling's hands? Yes, it did. Which meant another session at the typewriter and a letter to Quisling demanding the release and reinstatement of the teachers.

Following the State Act, Quisling had moved his offices to the royal palace and was now administering the country from what had formerly been the royal family's living room. So when a telephone call summoned her to a meeting with Quisling to discuss her letter, it was to the palace she had to go. She was made to wait, and from the corridor at the foot of the staircase up to Quisling's office observed, through the open door of the guard-room, members of Quisling's *hird* as they sat smoking, with chairs tipped back and their feet up on the table.

The first thing she noticed on entering what had now become Quisling's office was that a hole had been crudely cut in the carpet to accommodate a microphone on a stand. Then Quisling was walking towards her. To her surprise he proffered his hand. She took it, determined to do whatever was necessary for there to be a useful outcome to the meeting.

The minister-president gestured for her to take a seat and she sat down. He sat down facing her on the other side of the desk. Skancke occupied the chair to her right and an officer in military uniform to whom she was not introduced was on her left. Quisling was studying a document on the desk in front of him. He was frowning. From where she sat she could see it was her letter. Presently he began to read aloud from it. When he reached the point at which she had written that the parents intended to keep their children away from school until the teachers were freed and reinstated, he stopped and looked up at her.

'Strike?' he said, looking up, his fingertip still held on the offending sentence. 'You are proposing that the children go on *strike*?'

She opened her mouth, intending to put the suggestion in context.

'Wait until I have finished speaking,' he shouted, glaring at her, his jowls quivering. The change in his demeanour was so sudden she felt herself tense. For the first time she was reminded of newsreel footage she had seen at the cinema of Adolf Hitler addressing a crowd and seemingly in the throes of some strange demagogic fit. She realised that the word 'strike' might have triggered the change as Quisling ranted for a long minute or two on the general immorality of *all* strike action, and expressed his despair of a generation of parents and teachers who would not only permit but encourage innocent children to adopt the tactics of the Bolsheviks.

When he had stopped, dropping the letter and thumping the desktop heavily with the side of his fist as though in punctuation, she let several seconds pass before replying, anxious not to repeat her earlier mistake. On the tram ride into town she had rehearsed a defence of her protest, but this outburst of sudden, false rage surprised her, and it occurred to her for the first time that Quisling might not be a rational man. She took a deep breath and then said only that, as parents, they should be glad they had teachers who acted according to their consciences. That having a conscience and acting on it didn't necessarily make them bad schoolteachers.

'Do you know what you are doing?' he said. This time she knew better than to respond. 'You are trying to break down everything that we in National Unity are working to build up. You are putting not only your own future but the future of your children in jeopardy. Do you suppose, when the Bolshevik hordes come, for the sake of argument, do you suppose the Bolsheviks will tolerate *conscience* among your teachers?'

He gave the word a heavy, ironic stress and she waited for him to continue. He pushed her letter to one side, looked directly at her then closed his eyes and shook his head wearily from side to side.

'Fru Bjerkås, I don't know what to do with you, I really don't. Skancke,' he said abruptly. 'This is your problem. You must decide on a suitable punishment.'

She turned to look at Skancke. He caught her look and held it.

'Well, one thing is clear: there will be no more schooling for your children in this country.'

He reached inside to his jacket pocket, took out a notebook and balanced it on his lap.

'What does your husband do?'

'He's an accountant,' she said.

'Then he won't be an accountant for much longer.'

He scribbled a note and put the notebook back in his jacket pocket. Quisling was staring at her. The puffy face, the hair parted on the wrong side. Suddenly she knew she had been right and that he was insane and that she had to get out of there as soon as possible. Trying to disguise the sense of urgency she felt, she stood up.

'I can see we aren't going to get anywhere as regards the matter I came to see you about, so I'll be on my way.'

There was no response from any of the three men in the room with her. With her heart in her mouth she bent to pick up her handbag, turned and walked towards the door. Her shoulder brushed against the microphone stand as she passed and it swayed away from her. When she came to the door she stopped. To her astonishment the uniformed officer who had sat in silence throughout the encounter now hurried past her and held the door open for her.

Sigurd was home when she got back, and she gave him a full account of the meeting with Quisling. The threats had opened a new dimension in her world of protest and as soon as she had finished she took the radio from its hiding place in the loft, broke it into pieces and buried it in the back garden.* In due course Trond and Uni's names duly appeared on a list that was circulated among the Oslo schools of pupils who were to be denied admittance to classes, but the threat against Sigurd's job never materialised, and

---

* The set was illegal. In the autumn of 1941 all radios had to be handed in to the authorities. Only members of National Unity were allowed to keep theirs.

while the teachers remained in jail the children's education was continued in private homes.

One might suppose that a tirade from the Norwegian Führer himself in the awe-inspiring setting of the royal palace would have been enough to dissuade Ingrid Bjerkås from any further protests, but a last return to the fray as a voice of individual protest proved her undoing. On 28 November 1943, following a fire at the university in central Oslo which Terboven believed had been deliberately started by students, the university was closed. Thirty teachers and several hundred students were arrested. Many others were able to avoid arrest by fleeing to the Oslo *marka*, the dense belt of pine forest that surrounds the city, where they lived rough for the duration of the war. All the female students arrested were released later the same day, but 700 male students were sent to Germany for a 'political re-education'. This turned out to consist largely of bewildered attempts on the part of their tutors to awaken a slumbering sense of tribal pride in being Aryans. Their 'racial heritage' meant the students were treated better than most other prisoners, but there were no converts to the Aryan cause.

Bjerkås' response to the fate of these students was another letter rebuking the authorities. This time she addressed it to Josef Terboven himself. The letter itself has not survived, but in her autobiography *Mitt kall* (My Calling), she writes that she was arrested for writing 'a letter to Terboven in which I held him responsible for all the sufferings, the killings and horrors which our country had suffered since his arrival'. Norwegian Stapo officers arrested her at her home just before Christmas 1943 and for two months the family had no news of her. Then, in February 1944, a letter arrived from the prison camp at Grini:

> My dear, dear Uni and Trond and Loll* and Mamma and Pappa,
> I hope you're all well. I worry so much about how you're getting on without me. And that I didn't have time to tidy up

---

* Her husband Sigurd.

the house before Christmas nor do the washing. But I hope you managed and that you're all doing well. Once I get out of here I'll work twice as hard and make up for all the things I'm neglecting now. My health is excellent, and in every way I feel fine. Thank you so much for the sleeping bag, it's so good to have that, I really mean it. And thank you for all the other things. I'm always thinking of you. Look after yourselves and please take extra good care of Uni and Trond. I don't worry because I know God is looking after you, as he is looking after me.[41]

With the help of an old school friend who had joined National Unity, Sigurd Bjerkås was able to have Ingrid transferred from Grini to the psychiatric wing of a hospital in Bærum for the final few months of her incarceration. Prison had left her in poor physical shape, but the regime and the healthy food at the hospital enabled her to recover well and she was released in time to spend Christmas of 1944 at home with her family.

By the end of 1942 it was clear that the shell of a national socialist state was in place in Norway but inside it was empty. There would be no Nazification of the schools and universities, no Nazification of the young, no Nazification of the church. The Conscience Struggle produced as few martyrs as it did memorable individuals, but martyrs there were. Einar Høigård's suicide was a martyr's death. So was the death of a priest named Arne Thu, whose insistence on including prayers for the king and elected government as part of his Sunday service after these became illegal led to his arrest in February 1942. A comfortably overweight man in his early fifties, Thu died at Grini on 27 July 1944 following a particularly gruelling session of punishment exercises the prison guards sometimes arranged to amuse themselves. These could involve the prisoners sprinting at the double until punctuated by a shouted *hinlegen* ('Down!'), a signal to lie flat on the ground and wriggle forward using the elbows, or squirm along on their backs, or bunny hopping, being driven in this fashion to the point of exhaustion. This particular punishment session had been ordered when a book written in English was discovered in Thu's hut. But in spite of such losses, and the sufferings endured by teachers and priests alike, the relative success of the campaign of 1942 marked a rare triumph at a time when the German cause appeared invincible on every front. For one small group of Norwegians, however, 1942 was a year of unthinkable tragedy.

6

The Norwegian Holocaust,
14 March 1942 – 26 November 1942

The national socialist campaign against Norway's Jewish population began in earnest days after the passage of the State Act on 1 February 1942, and occupied most of 1942, reaching its nadir in the winter of that year. But from the earliest days of the occupation the invaders had signalled that the demonising of the Jews was a priority of the dawning 'new age'. A mere four weeks after the invasion, on 10 May 1940, Jews – and Jews only – were ordered to hand in their radio sets to the authorities. Kaare Sørum's grotesque 'public information' poster, with its slogan 'Tenk Dig Om!' (Think About It!), of which 50,000 copies were printed, explained the reason. Receipts were issued and gave a spurious air of legitimacy to the move by suggesting the measure was only temporary. Newspapers were told to neither report nor comment on the confiscations.* Less than a week later, on 15 May 1940, *Det Mosaiske Trossamfund* (the Society of Jews in Norway) was asked to provide a list of all registered members of the Jewish community in Norway. In the autumn of the same year

---

* A second round of confiscations in the autumn of 1941 applied to all Norwegians except members of National Unity.

a similar request resulted in the registration of all Jewish-owned property in Norway. On 22 January 1942, a week before the State Act, a notice appeared in the national newspapers announcing, among the adverts for hairdressers, dentists and chiropodists, an 'Important Proclamation from the Police Department': identity cards belonging to all Jews were to be stamped with a 'J'. The idea to adopt what had been common practice in Germany since the mid-1930s came from Heinrich Fehlis of the German Sipo (Civilian Police) in Norway and met with no resistance from National Unity politicians. The notice also instructed Jews to provide a precise account of the family history and relationships that would define a person as Jewish and, as such, obliged them to obtain such a stamp before 1 March. Failure to attend the local police station (or, in the countryside, the sheriff's office) to obtain such a stamp would be punishable by a fine or a three-month jail sentence. As though they were being offered some kind of service, Jews were informed that the stamp would cost them nothing, it was free.

As ever, the occupiers had taken care to remain in the background and let National Unity front these potentially controversial initiatives.[42] Fehlis did not give the requirement the status of a governmental directive, which left Jonas Lie at the Ministry of Policing wondering how to respond to any Jew who failed to act on it. In a draft translation of the order the Norwegians had accordingly inserted a line saying that the directive was *etter tyske ordre* ('on German orders'), and another that it came 'at the request' of the *Befehlshaber der Sicherheitspolizei und des SD* ('Commander of the Security Police and the SD"). Fehlis expressed himself content with the general wording of the document but insisted that references to the role of the Germans in the announcement be removed before publication. Fifteen hundred and thirty-six Jews duly had their ID cards stamped with a dark pink capital 'J' two centimetres high. They filled out, in triplicate, an 'Enquiry Form for Jews' giving their names, place and date of birth, family relationships, and providing information on their economic status, the nature of their employment and any criminal record. The figure of 1,536 who complied with the directive was several hundred less than Norway's actual population of Jews, and provided bleakly ironic confirmation of a comment made by Martin Luther, one of the delegates at a conference on the fate of the European Jews being held at the same time in Wannsee, a suburb of Berlin, to the effect that occupied Scandinavia had such a small number of Jews one could not properly speak of Norway and Denmark as having any kind of 'Jewish problem' at all.[43] It made no difference. As Norway's Reichskommissar once put it, there was 'no Jewish problem to be solved, only a solution'.

Many of those who did not turn up to have their ID cards stamped had realised they were already on an escalator to hell and arranged to be smuggled across the border into Sweden or over the North Sea to England. Those who did not leave were so daunted at the thought of the upheaval involved that they somehow persuaded themselves it wasn't necessary and that registration was as far as the process would go. But, as with the doggedly pursued campaign to revolutionise the schools and the teaching profession, Quisling and National Unity seemed determined to show their Nazi sponsors and protectors that the introduction of the 'new era' in its every aspect could safely be left in their hands. The greater the speed and efficiency with which the party could

---

* The *Sicherheitsdienst* (SD) was the intelligence agency of the SS.

do so, the more likely it was that Hitler would recall Terboven and formally declare a military alliance with an independent Norway under native Nazi leadership. Perhaps fired by Terboven's evident contempt for him, Quisling had somehow persuaded himself that such a scenario was still possible. It wasn't; on 22 January 1942 Hitler declared Norway a *Schicksalzone*, a region of critical importance to the successful outcome of his war. So great was his fear of an Allied invasion in the north, with his troops caught between a British expeditionary force landing somewhere in central Norway and Soviet troops crossing the border at Kirkenes, that he now ruled out any further significant change to the administration of the country until the war was over and the victory won.

Undaunted, Quisling and his ministers went ahead with the next step in the national socialist revolution. This was the reinstatement, on 14 March 1942, of the second paragraph of the constitution of 1814 that prohibited Jews from entering Norway. This always contentious restriction had been removed from the constitution in 1851 following years of campaigning by the poet Henrik Wergeland. Quisling's 'expert' on Jewish affairs, Fru Halldis Neegaard Østbye, a founding member of National Unity and a prominent feminist as well as an antisemite, had long been urging the restoration of this paragraph, and Sverre Riisnæs at the Ministry of Justice duly obliged. At a party gathering on 21 February 1942 at Klingenberg cinema in central Oslo she told a full house that the 'Jewish problem is the key to the world's problem'.[44] With a surreal disregard for the facts she put the number of Jews in Norway at between eight and ten thousand.*

Riisnæs presented the reform as a straightforward act of constitutional fundamentalism, announcing it in a major policy speech at Lier, a town some 40 kilometres outside Oslo, on 13 March. In his speech he condemned the 'weak liberalism' of the previous century that had permitted the 'disfigurement' of the constitution in 1851 and praised the courage of the constitutional

---

* As noted above, the actual figure was under 2,000.

fathers of 1814 for their determined adherence to the 'Nordic understanding of life'. The reinstatement was all the more urgent, he said, since 'the threat posed to our tribe from Judaism' was so much greater in 1942 than it had been in 1814.

At a stroke, the paragraph made the mere presence of Jews in Norway a criminal offence. In doing so it marked a crucial step in the direction of the Norwegian holocaust. What was still required was some proof of the perfidy and treachery of the Jews that would give the final stage of the holocaust a moral and legal logic of its own, and in the autumn of 1942 a combination of violent events provided just such an opportunity. On 6 September, in a gun battle at Majavatn, on the eastern shores of Lake Majavatnet on the border between Nord-Trøndelag and Nordland, Norwegian resistance fighters killed three German SS men. Shortly afterwards, on 21 September, a group of British and Norwegian commandos sabotaged a power station at Glomfjord in Meløy in Nordland and halted production of aluminium at the Haugvik factory that was used to make aircraft for the Luftwaffe.

Sharing Hitler's fear that all this activity was the prelude to a British invasion in the north, Terboven declared a Civilian State of Emergency in west-central Norway on 6 October 1942. About 2,000 men, including German Sipo officers, Gestapo, SS men, Wehrmacht conscripts and Norwegian State Police officers drafted in from Oslo, took part in the operation. Over the next six days nearly 13,000 people had their credentials checked. Some 1,500 houses and farms were searched. Ninety-one arrests were made for infringements ranging from illegal ownership of a radio set to being in possession of a large sum of money and unable to account for it. On 7 October ten *sonofre* ('scapegoat victims') were executed.* Twenty-four men from Majavatn were condemned to death before a *standrett* and shot on 8 and 9 October.

In a speech not long after the State of Emergency ended on 12 October, Henrik Rogstad, National Unity party leader in the

---

* For further detail on the background to these executions, see p. 178.

South Trøndelag region where the action was concentrated, revisited a theme that was becoming a familiar one to Norwegians: the recent spate of acts of violence was blamed on 'Norwegian emigrants', which was National Unity code for the British-trained Norwegian commandos who carried them out; but, according to Rogstad, the ultimate responsibility lay with the Jews. It was Jews who had financed and commissioned the violence, Jews who, with their usual cunning, had contrived to obscure their involvement by getting others to carry it out for them. In the newspaper list of the names of the ten *sonofre* executed in reprisal for the recent attacks only one, a Trondheim businessman named Hirsch Komissar, was further identified by the addition of the word *Jøde* ('Jew') in brackets after his name.

In this atmosphere of heightened hostility all that was required was a 'Sarajevo incident' that would provide an excuse to set in motion the final stage of the campaign, and it presented itself on the night of 22 October 1942. Karsten Løvestad, a twenty-six-year-old fireman from Trøgstad in Østfold who also worked as a border guide for refugees, was travelling with a group of eight Jewish refugees on a train bound for Halden, a border town 12 kilometres east of the crossing to Sweden at Svinesund. The journey had been arranged in haste and the conductor on the train had not been informed of their presence, as was the usual procedure if the guard was a known *jøssing* sympathiser prepared to warn groups about police checks on the train.

As the train trundled along between Skjeberg and Døle stations, two *Grepos* (border policemen), Arne Hvam and his partner, began checking the passengers' IDs. Hvam was a committed Nazi and among the first graduates of the *hird*'s very own Viking Hird Training Centre. Wearing civilian clothes, the two men attracted little attention as they moved through the train. Hvam slid open the door to the compartment where Løvestad was sitting with two Jewish men, Willy Schermann and Herman Feldmann. Løvestad was travelling with a forged passport under the name of 'Harald Jensen', but both the young Jews had only their legal ID cards stamped with the large red 'J'. Hvam told them to follow him out into the corridor and ordered his young *Grepo* partner to tell the guard to alert the Halden police when the train stopped at the next station. Realising things had gone badly wrong, Løvestad followed the border police into the corridor, pulled out a gun and shot and killed Hvam.

As the train slowed to cross the Besseberg bridge the three men jumped out and ran off into the night. The remainder of the group, unaware of what had happened, continued on their journey and got off the train at Halden. The plan was to cross over into Sweden and safety by boat, but there was no guide to meet them. Instead they found themselves arrested and taken to Halden jail.

Meanwhile the alarm had been raised, with roads blocked and houses and farms in the area searched in the hunt for the three fugitives. Police with dogs joined the search. Both the Jewish refugees had sustained injuries in the jump. Feldman had a broken arm. He was found after asking a farmer for help in repairing his torn clothing so that he would not attract undue attention on his way over to Sweden. Schermann was found in a potato cellar on a farm not far from where the three had jumped from the train. Weak and bloodied, he had tried to cut his wrists with a shard of glass. Karsten Løvestad managed to evade capture for five days before being arrested and sent to Grini to await trial.

It was Løvestad who had done the shooting, but the headline in National Unity's own newspaper *Fritt Folk* the following day preferred to make its own assumption: 'Another shameful deed: Norwegian policeman gunned down by Jews.' And from this point onwards there could be no way back. On 24 October the Quisling government passed emergency legislation allowing the arrest of anyone suspected of 'promoting activities directed against the people or the state'. On the morning of 25 October the Stapo head Karl Marthinsen wired every police station and sheriff's office in the country with orders to detain all male Jews over the age of fifteen. The arrests began that same day, using information gathered from the 'J' stamp registrations of 20 January earlier in the year. A law of 26 October ruled that all property and assets belonging to arrested Jews could legally be confiscated and would become the property of National Unity. An exception was made for jewellery, watches and items of precious metals which were handed over to the occupying authorities.

In Oslo and Asker 126 police officers organised in sixty-two patrols under the command of a Stapo officer began the operation. Each Stapo man was issued with a list of names of the ten Jews it was his professional duty to arrest. In carrying out the arrests the police were to present those arrested with a copy of the document that legalised the arrest. Bearing the signatures of Vidkun Quisling, Sverre Riisnæs and Rolf Fuglesang, it informed them that their property, assets and money and that of their families were now state property. Any attempt to evade the law of 26 October by transferring money or assets to someone outside the family of non-Jewish heritage would incur the severest punishment. Wives, mothers or the oldest surviving members of the family were not arrested but ordered to report daily to the police.

Their turn came a month later. On 25 November Jewish women, children, the elderly and the sick were arrested and transported in a fleet of 100 taxis directly to the Vippetangen docks to join the husbands, fathers, brothers and friends gathered there after their overnight transport from the prison camp at Berg, near Tønsberg. The SS *Donau*, a German transport ship, was docked at Pir 1, waiting for them to board.

True to their tactic of making their most controversial actions appear to be solely the work of the National Unity government, the Germans had left the actual arrests and transportation to Pir 1 to the Norwegian police. But it was Hellmuth Reinhardt, head of the Gestapo in Norway, who had been responsible for commissioning the *Donau*, and once the Jews boarded they came under the control of German SS guards. The ship sailed at 2.55 p.m. with 582 Jews on board, bound for Stettin in Poland. From there the journey continued by rail to Auschwitz. Later that same day the

Monte Rosa left for the same destination with another twenty-six. Jews who were transported from different parts of the country to Oslo but arrived too late for these sailings were deported on the *Gotenland* on 25 February 1943.

The number transported on the *Donau*, the *Monte Rosa* and the *Gotenland* was marginally less than half of all the Jews living in Norway at the time. They comprised citizens of the country as well as those who had arrived in Norway as refugees and been trapped following the German invasion of April 1940. Most of those who escaped the Norwegian holocaust of 1942 did so through the agency of an informal rescue operation that came to be known as 'Carl Fredriksens Transport', the name itself a hidden loyalist allusion to King Haakon VII, whose baptismal name before becoming king of Norway was Carl, and who was the son of Frederik VIII of Denmark. Alf Pettersen, the man who led the operation, was a former policeman who had been dismissed from the force for refusing to take a pledge of loyalty to Quisling. His new job as transport manager in charge of a fleet of lorries gave him an intimate knowledge of the routes from Oslo to the Swedish border and a legitimate reason for having lorries with covered cargo beds travelling the border roads at all hours of the day and night. Very often the transport for the final leg of the journey, made on foot to the border itself, would be the responsibility of a volunteer *grenselos* or border guide. Thus far in the occupation their work had largely been confined to taking young, fit and usually male resistance fighters operatives wanted by the Germans over into Sweden. Now suddenly they found themselves responsible for the safe transport of entire families, including the old, the sick, children and infants too young to understand the need for silence. One trip emptied a hospital ward of its patients and included a man who had just been operated on and had to be carried lying flat on his back. Another was insane. Efficiency was hampered by the fact that people often tried to take with them as much as their wretched circumstances would allow. Many carried suitcases. A guide carrying an elderly woman across a river in the Østfold border regions slipped on a stone. 'My stamps!' she cried as her precious album slipped from beneath her grasp and disappeared beneath the cold water.[45] Hard and cruel decisions had to be made on the spur of the moment. On one occasion a group of Jewish refugees already on board a lorry were told they had to leave because a group of resistance men had to leave as a matter of urgency. The brutal logic of the situation was that while Jews were hunted simply for being Jews, an arrested resistance member would likely be subjected to torture and as a result do untold damage to the organisation and put the lives of numerous others at risk.

'Carl Fredriksens Transport' existed for six weeks. During that time, working five nights a week and using two covered lorries carrying an average of forty refugees on each trip, the drivers and their shotgun-carrying mates saved the lives of hundreds of Norwegian Jews who had managed to evade arrest on those two fateful nights in the autumn of 1942. In mid-January 1943 the group was betrayed by an informer posing as a refugee.

The drivers and their mates were arrested, tortured and executed. Others, including Pettersen himself and his heavily pregnant wife, escaped to Sweden.

A second group involved in the rescue of Norwegian Jews was a *Sivorg** circle in which women played a particularly prominent part. Among these was Sigrid Helliesen Lund, who was forty-eight years old when the war came to Norway. She lived in a villa on Tuengen allé, in the Vindern district of Oslo, with her husband and two sons, Bernt and Erik. Among Lund's closest associates and helpers in the rescue operation was a thirty-seven-year-old Englishwoman from Cambridge named Myrtle Wright.

Their friendship began in spring 1940 when Wright, a practising Quaker who worked full-time for the Society of Friends in England, arrived in Norway on her way to Copenhagen, where she was due to have talks with the Danish Society of Friends. Arriving in Oslo on 6 April she was detained by stormy weather. She was still stranded three days later when the Germans invaded. Over the next few days she made several fruitless attempts to leave the country legally, and in the course of her dealings with the German bureaucracy her passport was taken and severe restrictions placed on her travel. Other than that, she was left to her own devices. In the patronising chivalry of the national socialist world no woman, not even an Englishwoman, was considered a potential danger to the revolution.

So for the next four years Wright found herself living in occupied Norway with a suitcase she had packed for a two-week stay in Denmark. She and Lund met through a mutual friend who was a Quaker. Learning of Wright's plight, the Lunds invited her to move into the family home in Vindern, an offer which she gratefully accepted. Apart from a young son, Erik, born with Down's syndrome, the whole Lund family – Diderich the husband and Bernt, their

---

* The name of a civil resistance organisation (see p. 134).

sixteen-year-old son – was active in the resistance in various ways. Inevitably, as she began to pick up the language, Wright was drawn into these activities, principally as a sort of assistant and conversation partner to Sigrid Helliesen Lund in the many ways in which this extraordinary and tireless woman helped others.

On the night of 25 October 1942 an anonymous caller had telephoned the house and delivered a simple but enigmatic message: *Det blir et stort selskap i kveld. Men det er bare de store pakkene vi skal ha* ('There's a big arrangement on tonight. But we're only taking the big packages'). Sigrid and Myrtle then tried to puzzle out what the message meant. *Selskap* was a code that warned of trouble; but what could 'big packages' mean? Finally, and almost simultaneously, the two women had it: the caller was a *jøssing* police officer and he was informing them that the arrest of the Jews was imminent, but that only Jewish men – the 'big packages' – were to be taken. Phone calls could be monitored, hence the need for code. Wright's diary for the years 1942–4* takes up the story. It gives a remarkable street-level view of the tensions and concerns of everyday life in a *jøssing* household during this period; the difficulties and tensions, dangers and joys that were the companions of everyday life for those who chose to get involved in the struggle. The following passages relate to the two main waves of arrest but also contain passing references to the protest actions involving teachers and parents in which Lund and Wright were involved, as well as Lund's visit to her son Bernt, arrested and imprisoned in Grini† in 1942 for the distribution

---

* *Norwegian Diary 1940–1945* by Myrtle Wright was published in 1974 by the Friends Peace and International Relations Committee. The manuscript of this little-used source is in the Hjemmefront Museum (Resistance Museum) in Akershus Fortress, Oslo. Wright kept the diary beneath the floor of the hencoop at Tuengen allé until January 1944. Lund's sister, a librarian, then hid it in the Tibetan literature section of the National Library, with the patriotic call number H7.

† Bernt Lund was later transferred to the camp at Sachsenhausen. He survived the war.

of illegal newspapers. (Passages in italics are Wright's own later editorial insertions and usually explain the use of coded words in casethe diary fell into the wrong hands.)

Sunday 25 October

Sigrid went to visit two small girls (*Czech Jewish children*), one of whom has a birthday.

She hears rumours that American citizens have been taken into internment in Grini. They can have parcels, visits, books. Said to be reprisal for an action of the American government.

News on radio of offensive in Africa on a big scale, especially in the air.* This must be the awaited offensive. Churchill, according to Norwegian papers, is in Gibraltar.

Quiet morning; played some English hymn tunes, especially Whittier's 'Words are less than deeds' – 'the shadow of thy Cross is better than the sun' – 'the wrong of man to man on thee inflicts a deeper wrong'. These words came all too true in the evening when rumour reached us that Jews were to be arrested early tomorrow morning – this has been current for some days.

But we had many guests – all the Müllers, Gulim, Marie and George stayed the night.

(*This, for obvious reasons, is the only reference to the night of the arrest of all male Jews. The news was brought to the door by a strange man. Sigrid Lund was out until the early hours of the morning warning all she knew. Several were brought to spend the night. I stayed at home and received them.*)

Monday 26 October

All too true – telephone message that there had been a 'big party' last night. Went down with Sigrid to Odd Nansen's office, then to Ruth Rønneberg and Bertha Erichsen's.

(*All male Jews who could be found had been arrested and*

---

* BBC news listened to on an illegal set.

taken to Berg prison, Tønsberg. *The visits referred to were all in connection with the hiding of Jews in families.*)

Tuesday 27 October

Sigrid was down at Nansenhjelp office all day – many of the wives of the arrested Jews came for advice.

I went on a shopping tour – 'cotton wool' is made of paper, sugar is not only saccharine but a substitute for that! Darning wool is goodness knows what kind of cellular product, toothbrushes have ceased to exist. Hoarded a little toilet paper.

Sigrid very tired when she came home – an exhausting day.

Wednesday 28 October

At last I have been to Grini! Sigrid and I took a taxi out with two parcels of clothes for Bernti; drove to the outer gate and walked up to the Guards' House. The buildings lie well hidden in woods, long, newly built red brick with both Swastika and S.S. flag flying. New barracks of good quality material built in front with stone pillars and verandah. Tall, square watchtowers in various places. Otherwise not much to suggest a prison. The guards were in a private looking house by the gate inside a second fence. A young boy in prison uniform was sweeping the steps. The guard opened the door and took the parcels inside. 'Only clothes', said Sigrid. 'No tobacco?' asked the guard rather officially. Sigrid innocently replied, 'Oh, but that isn't allowed, is it?' and it sounded quite genuine, and the guards melted and both of them were very willing to converse. Sigrid asked if they knew Bernti 'with red hair'. 'Ach, ja, er ist immer fröhlich' (Oh, yes, he is always cheerful), they replied, and they would give greetings from his mother. As we went out we passed the young boy; Sigrid looked straight ahead but said 'Hils Bernti' (greet Bernti) and I saw that he nodded. It was sunny and beautiful as we walked through the woods and then over the open farm land to Roa station. We called at a farm where Bernti had worked, and Sigrid went to a home for

14 small Jewish children from Vienna. Will they start sending children from here, as they have done from France?

Friday 30 October
Now things are really pleasant! Death penalty for having secret papers in the house and not reporting them to the police; also for helping people over into Sweden, if you want a more difficult way of ending your life!

Since Monday's arrests and the news of the treatment of those arrested the sense of indignation and the wrongness of the whole thing has grown. Most people are filled with a sense of helplessness, but it was suggested that, if the feelings of the Norwegian people are expressed loudly enough, it might prevent the same fate coming to the women and children.

Engineer Viig had had a visit from a Jew and had not given him a bed and was very repentant. He was a man Diderich knew and neither of them liked.

Got an evening alone – read, except for the endless ringing of the phone.

Saturday 21 November
I found this quotation from von Hügel: –*

'No baseness or cruelty so deep or so tragic shall enter our human world but that loyal love shall be able in due time to oppose to just that deed of treason its fitting deed of atonement. You say first, "This deed was made possible by that treason", and secondly, "The world as transformed by this creative deed is better than it would have been had all else remained the same, but had that deed of treason not been done at all".'

Here is the root of the matter in this Jewish question; the cruelty and baseness of the deed can only be matched by some act of loyal and understanding love, the risk taken, the price

---

* Friedrich von Hügel (1852–1925) was an Austrian-British philosopher and religious thinker.

paid must be great indeed before it can be too high to atone for so great a crime against human personality.

In the latter part of the quotation is also a useful thought in connection with the problem of the fine and noble things that have been brought out by the war and its horrors. Do we need such terrible happenings in order to bring out so much that is good? Must we say that the courage and devotion and energy and 'greatness' of personality which we see is due to the war? The quotation gives the reply – the world is transformed by these deeds and is better for them, but would have been even better if the 'treason' had never been done at all.

The 400 prisoners from the North are today back at Grini; those who are teachers have gone home. It was dysentery and not bad weather which has kept them ship-bound. Odd Nansen looks well, says his sister-in-law.* She also says her friend has had so many guests – seven at a time (*Jews in hiding*).

But from Grini Jews and some other Norwegians have been sent to Germany – said also to be a punishment for a recent escape from Grini. These Jews were under German control at Grini, while the main body of Jews arrested recently are at Tønsberg under N.S. guard.

Monday 23 November

My birthday – woken according to tradition by the strains of the gramophone and as a rousing finale 'The International'!

One of the few fine days we have had – some frost but also sunshine. Sigrid and I, with the dog, Tasso, took the tram up to Frognerseter and went for a four-hour walk in Nordmarka. At Tyrvannstua the ski-run was not yet snow-covered, but the lake frozen and boys were skating. We got coffee substitute, without sugar but with milk, at the hut on the way up. We spoke of the future of Nansenhjelp; what it could do in face of

---

* Fridtjof Nansen's son, arrested and imprisoned at Grini early in 1942 and transferred to Sachsenhausen in 1943.

the need for humanitarian relief after the war. I cannot think of help which has a narrower basis than human need, and indeed, it is this lesson of the significance of individuals which those with whom we now struggle need to know. We may have many things to say to members of different nations, but our response to need must be unqualified. Indeed it may be their need which opens the way to reach those whose policies we now condemn. For me all work in the future must have the same underlying aim, as in the past, the bringing of the right spirit among men – most completely and shortly described as the Christ-like spirit.

On 25 November the Lund household received a second cryptic warning. The doorbell rang at Tuengen allé 9. Sigrid opened the door to a stranger: 'There's another big arrangement tonight. We're taking the small packages this time,'* he said, then turned and walked back into the street. Having cracked the code on the earlier occasion Helliesen Lund knew that most of the night ahead would be spent out ringing on doorbells and trying to warn as many Jewish families as possible to make ready to leave instantly, as well as telephoning round to organise safe houses for those who heeded the warning. Wright would remain at the house in Vindern to receive those sent by Sigrid to wait while safe houses were found for them.

Helliesen Lund's first call was to the wife and three children of the rabbi of Oslo, Isak Julius Samuel, at Meltzers gate 3. Rabbi Samuel himself had been arrested as early as September and taken to Grini to await transportation. She was able to take the two older children to safe homes without incident, but was almost caught as she was moving the third child, three-year-old Amos, who was to be taken to a different safe house, on Colbjørnsons gate. To keep people off the streets and forestall such attempts to subvert the operation the Germans had adopted the tactic of sounding air-raid sirens at frequent intervals throughout the night.

---

* These details were not included in the diary for security reasons.

As Sigrid was walking down Meltzers gate with Amos and passing the Swedish embassy, a jeep cruised by with a revolving searchlight mounted on the roof. As the beam swept towards her, she dropped to the pavement, pulled her coat over little Amos and covered her head with her elbows. She could almost feel the light as it brushed over her. Then the jeep was gone and she stood up and they continued the journey to safety.* Realising that another prime target for the arrests would be children living in the Jewish Children's Home in Holbergs gate 21 in central Oslo, she then made her way there. Some of the children she had personally brought to the apparent safety of Norway three years earlier, as part of a group of thirty-seven, in the fatal lull between the German invasions of Czechoslovakia in March 1939 and of Norway almost exactly a year later. Most had been housed with foster parents outside Oslo but fourteen remained at the home. On arrival she found Dr Nic Waal already there.† Waal had had the same thought and driven to Holbergs gate. Between them the two women and the children's 'foster-mother,' Nina Hasvold, managed to spirit the children to safety just hours before the

---
* Henriette Samuel and her three children all escaped to Sweden. Isak Samuel was killed at Auschwitz on 16 December 1942.
† Caroline Schweigaard Nicolaysen 'Nic' Waal had been a supporter and close associate of Wilhelm Reich during Reich's five years in Norway as a refugee from Nazi Germany in the 1930s.

operation to collect the 'small packages' got under way. Waal made three trips, with the children hiding under rugs and cushions on the back seat of the car. With the air-raid sirens still wailing at frequent intervals she was stopped in her first trip by soldiers at a checkpoint on Hegdehaugsveien. She bluffed her way past them, angrily pointing to the sticker on her windscreen that showed she was a doctor out on business and fully entitled to be on the streets. In *Alltid underveis* (Always on the Move), her memoir of the times, Helliesen Lund writes that most of those who agreed to hide Jewish families in their homes, always at huge personal risk, were 'older women living alone'. Pressure on the 'export business', as the transports into Sweden were known, was intense at the time and those in hiding had to wait weeks and often months before their turn came. There was the added burden of extra mouths to feed in already hard times, and of doing so without arousing the suspicions of an unsympathetic neighbour who could be moved to report them to the authorities. Helliesen Lund notes that the tendency to give priority to resistance fugitives over Jewish refugees was often criticised after the war but, as she forlornly confirmed, '*Vi var jo på den tiden ikke klar over hva jødene gikk til når de var tatt. Det het så pent "internering"*' ('Of course, we didn't know at the time what happened to the Jews once they were arrested. 'Internment' was the euphemism used by the authorities').[46]

Neither Helliesen Lund nor 'Fredriksens Transport' were able to save Nathan Fein. A Lithuanian born in 1887, Fein had come to Norway in 1907 and established himself in the rag trade. In time he had done well enough to buy a flat for himself and his wife Rachel, coincidentally in the same block as Quisling's doctor, Hans Eng, at Kirkeveien 90, in Majorstua.

On 2 September 1942, several weeks before the Halden train incident, Fein was arrested on a trumped-up charge of involvement in producing an illegal newspaper and sent to Grini. On 20 November 1942 he was deported on the *Monte Rosa*, along with twenty others, mostly elderly Jews.⁴⁷ Rachel went into hiding and escaped to Sweden in December 1942. Nathan and the others were disembarked at Aarhus in Denmark then transported by rail to Berlin, and from there to Auschwitz. Fifty-five years old at the time, Fein somehow survived the initial crude process of 'selection' on arrival that would otherwise have sent him straight to the gas chambers along with the women and children as being too old for work.

At Auschwitz Fein met a twenty-one-year-old Norwegian Jew named Kai Feinberg who had lived not 200 metres from him at Jonas Reins gate 9, on the other side of Kirkeveien, with his parents Elias and Clara, his sister Rachel and a ten-year-old Austrian refugee named Johan Reiss. On the day before the arrests of Jewish men in October 1942 Kai had been warned and gone into hiding. The police who arrived to arrest him left a message that they would be back the following day and if he wasn't there then they would take Rachel as a hostage when they left.

The following day Kai reported, as instructed, to the Stapo headquarters on Kirkeveien, opposite the main entrance to Vigelands Park. There he was placed under arrest and sent to Bredtveit prison, and shortly afterwards transferred to the Berg camp. His father was left at liberty and given the task of arranging support for the Jewish women and children now that these families had lost their breadwinners as well as all their earthly possessions. With the second wave of arrests on 25 November, Elias' function became redundant and the entire Feinberg family was on board the *Donau* when it sailed from Pier 1 at 2.55 p.m. the following afternoon.

The family were allowed to stay together on the *Donau*, but immediately separated on arrival at Auschwitz. Kai's mother, his sister and Austrian foster brother Johan were loaded onto a lorry and driven straight to the gas chamber within twenty minutes of arriving at Birkenau. Kai could see his sister standing on the back of one of the trucks. She was wearing her red woollen hat and she took it off and waved goodbye to him as the truck drove off.[48] He recalled later the almost surreal nature of the thought that struck him at the time, that at least the Nazis weren't making the women and children, the sick and the old, walk to the camp, at least they had the decency to drive them there. It showed they must have some heart. Kai and his father were then marched to Auschwitz-Birkenau.

Within weeks Elias Feinberg died, from grief, despair and pneumonia. Kai was put to work as slave labour at the Buna Manowitz plant run by the chemicals giant I. G. Farben. At unpredictable intervals there would be roll calls for the purposes of 'selection' at which the prisoners had to assemble naked outside the barracks for health inspection by a doctor. Anyone deemed incapable of further useful work would be called out from these musters and sent to the gas chamber. Feinberg recalled that even a man in good health might be sent there should the doctor dislike the way he looked at him.

Despite his health frequently breaking down with the inhuman living conditions and starvation rations in the camp, Kai survived these roll calls. Of the progress of the war in the larger world outside he and his fellow prisoners knew nothing and cared less. Their only hope was that the Allies might bomb the camp and bring the whole nightmare to an end. But once news of the Soviet victory at Stalingrad filtered through, prisoners and guards alike realised it announced a turning point in the war. As the end approached Kai could look from his barracks window and see German and Russian tanks firing at each other less than a kilometre away. Then, on 27 January 1945, a solitary Russian soldier suddenly appeared, driving through the camp gates on a horse and cart.

Auschwitz-Birkenau was liberated, its staff arrested and imprisoned. In a gesture much appreciated by the former inmates the Russians obliged their German prisoners to remove their caps whenever they passed a Jew.

Norway remained an occupied country and Kai stayed on at the camp until April before starting his long journey home. He spent several weeks in Bucharest, where he was given a Norwegian passport at the Swedish legation and was temporarily employed in weeding out people falsely claiming to have been at Auschwitz in order to qualify for financial aid. From Bucharest he travelled on to Bari in Italy, where the British arrested and held him for a few days while they checked his passport, finding it suspiciously new and in suspiciously good order. From Bari he travelled on, passing through Switzerland and Germany before finally arriving back in Norway on 27 October, almost three years to the day since his departure.

On arrival he reported to the Freemasons Lodge in Kongens gate in Oslo, at the back of the Storting, which the Norwegian authorities were using as a registration office, before going on to spend the night with an uncle and aunt at Løvenskiolds gate 3 B. In the morning he made his way up Kirkeveien, past Vigelands Park, up through the junction at Majorstua and on for a couple of hundred metres past the junction with Suhms gate at Marienlyst. He crossed Kirkeveien and turned into Jonas Reins gate. Standing outside the family home at Number 9, looking up through the windows at the curtains and ornaments on the windowsills, he could see that people were living there.

He rang the bell. As he waited, he turned and peered across Kirkeveien towards the junction with Suhms gate. Shielding his eyes from the morning sun he tried to work out from the windows which flat would have been Nathan's. He knew Nathan was dead, that he'd been shot at Dachau in April 1945 during a forced march to evacuate Auschwitz as part of Himmler's attempt to hide all traces of what the camp had been used for. In his memoir *Fange nr 79108 vender tilbake* (Prisoner Number 79108 Returns

Home), Feinberg describes the last time he saw him. Nathan had come to visit him in his barracks before leaving on the march. He had not wanted to go. Kai had tried to persuade him he didn't have to. But Nathan wouldn't believe him. He was convinced he would be shot if he refused or tried to hide.

Feinberg heard the door open. He was tired. He didn't feel up to making a scene with the people who had taken over his home, hardly even cared who they were. He turned to see saw a young couple, strangers, peering out at him through the half-open door.

'My name is Kai Feinberg,' he said. 'I live here.'

PART 3

VIOLENCE AND CULTURE

7

'Osvald', 'Yellow Cheese' and the Violent Resistance, 1941-4

In an unofficial contribution to National Unity's celebrations of the State Act, bombs left in two suitcases in the waiting rooms of Oslo's main railway stations, Østbanen and Vestbanen, exploded on the night of 2 February 1942. No lives were lost but both buildings suffered extensive structural damage. It was the first act of sabotage in the Oslo region since the invasion, and it had been over eighteen months in coming. Beyond the two months of initial fighting that led to the surrender in June 1940, a violent reaction to the invasion had proved difficult for the Norwegians. In the brief span of its history as a small and independent modern nation it had had no previous experience of war. The policy of neutrality, which had served Norway so well during the First World War, failed in the Second. In the face of the German invasion of April 1940, and the Riksråd negotiations that followed in the summer of that year, the country's beleaguered parliamentarians had shown themselves willing to go to almost any lengths to meet German demands, including the abolition of both democracy and the monarchy. The paradoxes involved in the person and career of a naval officer named Olaf Kullmann present a telling example of the country's deep-seated reluctance to engage in physical violence. Born in 1892 at Stord, in Vestlandet, Kullmann's father had been a priest, a parental background he shared with Vidkun Quisling. Also like Quisling, Kullmann had graduated from his military training – in his case at the Norwegian Naval Academy – with the best marks of any candidate in the academy's history. There the similarity between the two men ends.

Kullmann was a socialist and had been a defence policy adviser to the Labour Party in 1932 and an influential voice in the party's proposal to replace Norway's armed forces with a partially armed 'civilian guard' that lay behind the savage cuts made to the defence budget in 1933. Kullmann claimed that the Soviet Union was a guarantor for peace in the world, and at an Anti-War Congress in Amsterdam in the summer of 1932 he supported a motion proposing that military men in every country 'oppose war openly and by deed'. Quisling was Minister of Defence in Hundseid's short-lived *Bondepartiet* government at the time of Kullmann's return from Amsterdam. Dismayed by his conduct, he at once initiated a series of court actions against Kullmann that resulted in his suspension from the rank of captain and his being relieved of his duties as commander of the torpedo batteries at Oscarsborg.*

After the German invasion Kullmann travelled the country, mostly by bicycle, lecturing and preaching the pacifist cause. On 23 June 1941, he was arrested and imprisoned in Grini. In due course he was offered freedom in exchange for a promise to cease his pacifist activities. He declined. In the spring of 1942 he was transferred to Sachsenhausen concentration camp in Oranienburg in Germany, where he died three months later, from the combined effects of tuberculosis and hard physical labour. His fellow prisoners were humbled and impressed by the way he would share his meagre portion of rations with those whom he felt needed it more than he did.

---

* It was guns and torpedoes from the Oscarsborg fortress that sank the *Blücher* seven years later, on the night of 9 April 1940. The invasion and the nature of the subsequent occupation might have followed a very different path had a pacifist Kullmann still been in command of the island's guns.

The extreme example of Kullmann's life and fate convey the difficulties most Norwegians would have encountered when faced with the harsh realities of the Nazi occupation of their country, and the need, under certain circumstances, to take another human life. In a diary entry of 28 April 1943, relating to an incident in central Oslo on 31 March 1943 in which two informers, Finn Roald Andersen and Charles Anderson, had been found murdered in a flat in Løvenskiolds gate 17, Myrtle Wright tried to articulate the difficulty:

> Shortly before Easter two Norwegians were found murdered in a flat in Løvenskioldsgate. The police were seen carrying out two corpses; the story soon got round town and I heard it from many sources, so the details are not in doubt. A *hirdman* was found a flat by one of the German Gestapo, presumably Fehmer,* whose spy the man was. It was no doubt a confiscated flat and none of the neighbours likely to want to have anything to do with him. It was noticed, however, that a smell came from the flat and, on being broken into, two bodies were found, one with a knife still in the breast. This is the fate of those who betray their countrymen; it raises very difficult questions of morality. Such men, who spy on others and deliberately give information to the Germans or Norwegian Nazis, are responsible for the imprisonment and death of others. There seems no possible way to render them harmless except to take their lives. No authority will arrest them, for they are the servants of those who have political power. To kidnap them and hold them in secret is impossible and would risk the lives of everyone concerned. To ship such a man over the frontier presents also an insoluble problem. Whatever principles one may have and still maintain, the problem of 'the informer' is a terrible one under the conditions we have here.[49]

In the absence of any recognised legal authority in the country

---

* Fehmer was head of German counter-espionage in Norway.

following the flight of the king and government on 7 June 1940 and the resignation of members of the Supreme Court in December in the same year, two influential organisations arose to coordinate resistance to the demands of the Reichskommissariat and, in due course, of the Quisling government.

One, known as *Sivorg*, an abbreviation of *Sivil Organisasjonen* (Civil Organisation), was responsible for the organisation of many of the mass protests involved in the Conscience Campaign of 1942 against the attempted Nazification of the schools, the teaching profession and the church. The circle around Sigrid Helliesen Lund and Myrtle Wright worked under the umbrella of *Sivorg*. Their main fields of activity involved the transport of refugees; all types of communication and information; and financial and moral support to the dependents of Norwegians executed or imprisoned by the authorities. Helliesen Lund writes in her memoirs of how uncomfortable it was to walk through Frogner Park on one such errand with 25,000 kroner in notes wedged inside her shoes as insoles; and of how, the day after Viggo Hansteen had been executed, she was told to visit his widow Kirsten with a bunch of flowers from the London government.

Leadership of *Sivorg* was shared between two groups. *Kretsen* (the Circle/Group) was a self-appointed group of leading private citizens that liaised with the government in London, advising and making demands of it in regard to its policies, its responses and its recommendations to those still living in occupied Norway. *Koordinasjonskomiteen* (KK, the Coordinating Committee) was made up of representatives of the professions – doctors, lawyers, teachers, barristers, priests – and focused on countering National Unity's initiatives aimed at the abolition of democracy in everyday life, including the implementation of the Führer principle. Its activities often took the form of *paroles*, which were statements of principled response to these initiatives, spread by word of mouth and via the illegal press and having something close to the force of law among *jøssing* Norwegians. Einar Høigård's widely disseminated and widely observed 'cardinal principles of response' to the attempted Nazification of the educational system in the year of the Conscience Struggle were a prime example of the power of such *paroles*. Both Kretsen and KK were strictly non-violent organisations.

The second group that arose in the vacuum of authority left by the flight of the king and government was known as Milorg, an abbreviation of *militære motstandsorganisasjonen* (Military Resistance Organisation). It came into being in the spring and summer of 1941, and as its name implies, it was dedicated to the use of force in its attempts to frustrate the occupying power and its political ideology. It sought and on 11 November 1941 obtained formal recognition from the government in London as its military arm in Norway. In principle this gave it democratic legitimacy for a range of intended activities as a military unit that would potentially include sabotage, 'liquidations' and assassinations. But two experiences in particular that year led to an extreme reluctance on the part of the 'official' leadership to resort to violence. One was the 'trial' and execution of the trade unionists Viggo Hansteen and Rolf Wickstrøm in September 1941 for the simple act of being associated with a strike action. The other arose following an incident earlier in the year, on 26 April 1941, when an informer led a group of twelve Gestapo men to a house in Telavåg, on the west coast island of Sotra. The village had become a centre for North Sea refugee traffic and for the landing and picking up of agents. Two Norwegian resistance men were resting at the house prior to travelling onwards to carry out their assignments. In the ensuing gunfight two Germans and one Norwegian were killed. A search of the village uncovered a large cache of weapons, ammunition and radio equipment recently arrived from England. In reprisal the Germans burned every house in the village, scuppered every boat and confiscated all livestock. Eighteen young men who had no connection either with the village or the incident were summarily shot in Trandum Forest. All male villagers between the ages of sixteen and sixty were deported to Sachsenhausen concentration camp, where half of them died. The women and children were interned at Framnes concentration camp in Norheimsund in Hardanger where they remained for the next two years. In the wake of the action, other resistance groups in Stavanger, Oslo, Sunnfjord and Bergen were broken up. In the face of this kind of response the government's attitude, as communicated to Milorg operatives in Norway, was one of what Reinhard Heydrich would probably have described as 'extreme reticence'. This reticence lasted well into 1942, when Milorg leadership issued an order to its operatives not to shoot at Germans, 'not even in self-defence'.[50] And in a speech broadcast from London in September 1942 Prime Minister Nygaardsvold expressed the hope that 'people desist from individual actions that serve no sensible purpose but only bring more terror from the quislings and the Germans'.

In the face of this understandable reluctance to risk civilian lives, from what quarter was any violent response to the violence of the occupation likely to come? Cue the appearance of two groups who fell outside principled objections to the use of force: one, the dedicated, working-class communist; the other, the career criminal.

Asbjørn Sunde was the man responsible for the explosions at the two railway stations early in February 1942 that took some of the sparkle off Quisling's State Act celebrations. Sunde was born in the northern Trøndelag, in central Norway, in 1909, to a mother who died of tuberculosis when he was eleven years old. He was raised by his father, a cobbler and fisherman, as one of seven children. He went to sea after leaving school. Inheriting his father's radical and active socialism, he joined the Norwegian Communist Party (NKP) and in January 1937 travelled to Spain to join the International Brigade in the Spanish Civil War to fight against fascism. There he picked up the skills of guerrilla warfare, including sabotage and 'silent killing'. When the brigade was disbanded in July 1938 he returned home and shortly afterwards took over as leader of the Norwegian branch of the Wollweber Organisation, or to give it its official title, the 'Organisation for the Defence of the Soviet Union and against Fascism'. Formed by the German Communist Ernst Wollweber, the organisation specialised in the sabotage of shipping that served Nazi and fascist regimes across Europe, including weapons to Franco's Spain. Given that most of its operatives were seamen and dockworkers it was a natural choice of action. Equally naturally, for security reasons, none of the group were listed as members of the Communist Party.

By 1940 Wollweber's organisation was destroyed in countries occupied by Nazi Germany and survived only in Norway. Norway's communists remained loyal to Moscow and the non-aggression pact between the Soviet Union and Germany for the first fifteen months of the occupation of Norway, comforting themselves uneasily with the view that the war was an imperialist power struggle in which workers should have no part. Following the German invasion of the USSR on 22 June 1941, couriers from the Soviet legation in Stockholm arrived in Norway with orders for Norwegian communists to begin sabotage activities. The leaders of the NKP, banned since August 1940, had gone underground and were neither ready nor willing to comply. Sunde, however, who was still at the head of the Wollweber Organisation (which contained several veterans of the civil war in Spain), needed no second bidding. Within a month the group had carried out its first sabotage action, blowing up the railway lines at Nyland station in Groruddalen, an eastern suburb of Oslo. It was the prelude to a campaign that lasted until the disbanding of the group in the autumn of 1944. Known as the Osvald Group from one of the many aliases Sunde used, it numbered only thirteen at the start of the campaign but well over 260 by the time it was over. It was respected and feared above all other opponents by the Gestapo and the Norwegian Stapo. The intense efforts on their part to bring down the Osvald Group and kill its leader meant that the losses the group suffered – as many as thirty-five dead – were proportionately high.

Osvald and his group had no compunction about killing informers. The year 1941 had seen a dramatic increase in the activities of such individuals. Some of the earliest responses to the invasion on the part of loyal Norwegians involved attempts to establish radio communications with the British in order to pass on information about the location of barracks, troop movements, coastal sea traffic, the construction of airfields, bridges and roads and other logistical enterprises. These earliest resistance efforts were destroyed with dismaying ease because the groups involved did so with a naivety that left them wide open to infiltration.* In the weeks following the invasion, networks in Bergen and Arendal, both of them dangerously large and unwieldy, were betrayed to the Gestapo. As this was in the 'honeymoon' period of the occupation, of the seventy-five arrested in Arendal just five were sentenced to death, with only one sentence being carried out.

In Haugesund, on Norway's south-west coast, an informer betrayed one of these communications groups. Eighteen were arrested, and ten sentenced to death. Five men from Ålesund were arrested and executed when the refugee route they operated over the North Sea was betrayed. By this time the most notorious of all informers, the Trondheim-based Henry Rinnan, had a large network up and running with a chilling efficiency. Among his most successful agents was Marino Nilssen, who was responsible

---

* In his post-war history of intelligence activity in Norway during the occupation, the resistance operative Ragnar Ulstein called the first of the three volumes *The Time of the Amateur*.

THE VIOLENT RESISTANCE

in October 1941 for bringing down an independent organisation formed in Bergen by Kristian Stein that was engaged in weapons training, smuggling refugees to England, producing and distributing illegal newspapers, and intelligence photographing and reporting. By the time Nilssen infiltrated and betrayed Stein's group it consisted of over 1,500 people. More than 200 were arrested in a Gestapo *razzia* on 2 October. Nine, including Stein, were executed – some beheaded – and a further forty-six died in a German concentration camp. In Farsund and Kristiansand in the south-west of Norway a single informer, a twenty-four-year-old journalist named Thorleif Øymoen, was responsible for the arrest in the winter of 1943/44 of 113 men. Some were shot without trial, others endured weeks of torture in the town's notorious *Arkivet* at the hands of sadistic and drunken Norwegian and German policemen before being released.

Among the few who got out in time were Arne and Ruth Moy, two of the three passengers in a car with an Oslo border guide named Knut Mathiesen that was stopped close to the Swedish border on 20 April 1944. Ruth Moy's brother, Mardon Fiveland, was a regional courier for Milorg. Inadvertently betrayed to Thorleif Øymoen by his brother-in-law Arne, Fiveland was arrested and for ten days, from 9 to 19 February 1943, subjected to incessant torture. He was admitted to Kristiansand Hospital, from where he made a dramatic escape on 24 August and succeeded in crossing over into Sweden. With his cover blown, Thorleif Øymoen was given a new name by his Gestapo minder Lipicki and continued his devastating operations, now as a stool pigeon among the prisoners at Asylet. He gained the trust of a cell-mate, Guttorm Koteng, a high-ranking police officer from Arendal being held on suspicion of resistance activities, and reported him to Lipicki. Koteng was duly tortured, and seventy-one more men were arrested in Aust-Agder. In this way whole resistance communities, ranging from those who simply listened to illegal broadcasts from London to those who sent reports the other way describing activity on and around the strategically important military air base at Lista, could be destroyed by the malice of a single informer willing to engage in *spill i den negative sektor* ('activity in the negative sector').

Once the line of communication to Moscow broke down Sunde and his group were left to their own devices. Sunde generally chose his own targets and discussed his choices with no one. He also worked on an *ad hoc* basis with Milorg. The killing of the two informers in the flat in Løvenskiolds gate at the end of March 1943 that led Myrtle Wright to meditate on the terrible need for such responses was the work of his group, in an operation commissioned and financed by Milorg. These sub-contracted operations frequently involved targeted killings which Milorg's own operatives were either unable or unwilling to carry out.

On 21 August 1942, following a failed attempt to assassinate Dr Hans Eng in his apartment at Kirkeveien 90 earlier in the evening, Sunde and a small group carried out an attack on the headquarters of the Norwegian State Police (Stapo) in Henrik Ibsen's gate 7. Under the auspices of Karl A. Marthinsen, this political police force – a Norwegian version of the German Gestapo/Sipo – had been operational for just over a year and had already established a reputation for ruthlessness in its pursuit of all opposition to the new regime. The goal of the raid was the theft of Stapo's own archives and records, and to kill and injure as many as possible of a group of four officers who used the office and who were notorious for their use of torture in interrogating prisoners. At half past two on the morning of 21 August 1942, writes Sunde in his autobiographical account of the group's activities, *Menn i mørket* (Men in Darkness), he and his men set off down Møllergata:

> ... Oskar, '13', Trond, Dagfinn and me. The night was dark, with a hard drizzle whipped on a bitterly cold wind. We didn't speak, there was nothing more to say. A couple walked by arm in arm along Youngs gate. Otherwise there was no one. We stopped outside No. 7. The windows were completely blacked out, only the slight sliver of light here and there. The Germans were working. For

a few seconds we stood without saying anything. Our guns were loaded, safety catches off. I motioned for the guys to follow me and we entered the building. There was the far-off buzzing rattle of typewriters. Slowly and silently we crept up the stairs and reached the sixth floor without being detected. I pushed the key into the lock of no. 11 and turned. We crept in, leaving the door ajar. For a few seconds we held our breath and listened. There was no sound except that far-off clatter of the Germans' typewriters. Trond and Oskar started removing papers from the filing cabinets and desk drawers, '13' stood guard outside the door and Dagfinn and I started to prepare the explosives. All worked with shaded torches. We already knew that the power from the telephone network was not strong enough to activate a detonator, so the cable that led to the telephone apparatus had to be opened and a wire cut. We then had to connect two ordinary torch batteries and two detonators. We used a control lamp all the time we were working, didn't want to run any risk of blowing ourselves up. Dagfinn held the torch and I worked non-stop.

Sunde's account continues:

It was a horrible job, lying on my back and fiddling with those wires. Pretty soon I was drenched in sweat. We took one last check. Then, very carefully, we packed the detonators in two and a half kilos of dynamite and pushed the whole thing in under a cupboard. It was a perfect fit. We looked at each other and grinned. Maybe we'd get caught. Maybe have to shoot our way out. But nothing could stop it now, the Nazis would be flying through the air in the morning. We looked out into the corridor. The lookout was still there, we could see his silhouette through the frosted glass. One by one, we sneaked out into the hallway and down the stairs. The far-off rattle of typewriters sounded like machine-gun fire. From all sides we could hear the hum of voices speaking in German. '13' and I took off our shoes, tied the laces together and hung them around our necks. We didn't have rubber soles and it was best not to make too much noise. Once down on the fourth floor we put our shoes back on. We managed to lock the door behind us without anyone hearing it. It felt good to get out into the cool, misty rain. I opened my mouth and felt the cold moisture touch far down in my throat. Outside the Deichman library we jumped into the car that was waiting for us, laughing and gabbling like idiots as the car sped off. Oskar, '13' and Trond were dropped off where they lived. Dagfinn and I drove up to Sinsen. I had borrowed a room from a friend who was on holiday. Dagfinn had moved in with Oskar and Gerd. We had a smoke and a drink and talked about what was going to happen. We had to make sure that a call was made to room no. 11 just as Tofteberg, Dønnum, Vogt and Torhus entered the office in the morning. One of our contacts in the building was to appear in a window facing Møllergata and signal by wiping his nose with a white handkerchief. One of us would be standing on the street below, another outside the public library. Another three were posted to keep the telephone booth outside the old Aker police station open for us. As soon as they saw the handkerchief, one of us was to call the State Police and ask to be put through to room 11. As soon as the receiver was picked up the charge would go off. And anyone who happened to be in the room at the time would have a pretty rough time of it. The heavy desk and the other fittings in the room would make sure of that.[51]

This part went according to plan: at half past eight in the morning Arne Tofteberg arrived for work. He saw at once that the filing cabinets had been emptied, he picked up the telephone and the explosion went off. By midday Tofteberg had died from his injuries. But this turned out to be meagre comfort for Sunde. By an unlucky coincidence three members of the sabotage group, Alf Kristiansen ('Dagfinn'), Håkon Eriksen ('Tretten/'13'), and Sigurd Hansen ('Oskar') were arrested the following day by the German Sipo in a long-planned action that had nothing to do with Tofteberg's death. The three saboteurs were tortured, tried, sentenced to death and shot in the forest at Trandum on 7 September.

Rigmor Hansen, Sigurd's wife, who worked as a courier for the group, was also arrested. She died in Grini on 29 October while being tortured.

Phone traffic in and out of Gestapo headquarters at Victoria terrasse was monitored by Milorg's P-Group, and very shortly after the arrests and torture of the saboteurs Sunde learned that the Germans now knew his real identity. He spent the next night sleeping rough in Stensparken and woke in the morning to find 'Wanted' posters with his picture on already pasted up on walls, shop windows and lamp-posts across Oslo. Fifty thousand kroner was being offered for information leading to his arrest. Through safe contacts he accepted the offer of surgery at *Rikshospitalet* in the form of paraffin injections, one below each eye and one above the bridge of his nose. When, four days later, he rejoined his comrades in Nesbyen in Hallingdal, with his shaven head, bruised cheekbones and bandaged hand – he had had a tattoo removed while in hospital – the only thing they recognised about him was his voice.

The relative success of the Conscience Struggle of 1942 did not mean the end of National Unity's attempts to impose a national socialist revolution on Norwegians, principally by the indoctrination of the young through the school system, and through organised leisure time activities arranged by the party. In the early days of the occupation, National Unity had introduced a scheme known as *Arbeidstjeneste* (AT, Work Service). The purpose was to combat unemployment and foster good health and a feeling of community among the young. At first the *Arbeidstjeneste* was voluntary and its tasks politically harmless projects that largely involved work on the land. In due course this was extended to clearing up damage from Allied bombing raids or acts of sabotage. From the spring of 1941 it had become compulsory for men, and over the following two years Work Service assumed some distinctly military characteristics: National Unity's *heil og sæl* greeting was introduced, conscripts were questioned about their attitudes towards *den nye tid* ('the new age') and were expected to parade to work with shouldered farm implements. Despite these developments, leaders of the resistance movement remained unwilling to issue *paroles* ordering male Norwegians to refuse to be conscripted to the service. This official ambivalence lasted until the early part of 1943. On 22 February Reichskommissar Josef Terboven and Minister-President Vidkun Quisling sent a joint telegram to Adolf Hitler:

Führer!

The announcement of total war as a unanimous response of the German people to the heroic struggle of its sons in Stalingrad and as an expression that it is prepared to meet any eventuality was a signal that is heard and understood also in Norway. At a crowded mass meeting where thousands of others failed to gain access, and where we both spoke, the minister-president, to the rapturous acclaim of the gathering, announced the concentration and total dedication of this entire country's manpower in the struggle of the Germanic peoples and all of Europe against Bolshevism. All for Victory – from this day onwards that is the resolution that overshadows all else, here too in a Norway led by the national government. Together and in unbreakable comradely cooperation we shall translate this slogan into action.

Heil dem Führer!
Terboven – Reichskommissar
Quisling – Minister-President
Oslo 22/2/1943

Very shortly afterwards the Quisling government did indeed start translating the slogan into action. At the beginning of April, 300 young Norwegian Work Service conscripts were sent north to Svelvik to be employed by the Speer Organisation. They were ordered to sign a German military contract that bound them for the duration of the war, issued with German uniforms and drilled by German officers in German. An oath of loyalty to Hitler was demanded. Rumours quickly spread that their eventual destination was the Eastern Front, and on 13 April resistance leaders issued a *parole* that appeared in several illegal newspapers and forbade anyone conscripted to the service from complying with German orders.

A week later, at 10.30 p.m. on 20 April, a lorry containing Asbjørn Sunde and five others cruised down Universitetsgata from St Olavs plass and turned right into Pilestredet. Sunde's younger brother was one of the five. As the lorry passed number 31 and the offices of the Work Service Administration, Sunde hammered twice on the roof of the cab as a signal for the driver to stop. The street was still swarming with people. 'Get out of here!' Sunde yelled at them. Moments later he threw his first Molotov cocktail through the office windows. As he was preparing to throw the second the driver, not waiting for the agreed second set of double-taps on the cab roof, put his foot down. The lorry lurched forward, and Sunde was blown off the flatbed. 'I landed on my stomach,' he writes, 'and the bottle I had up my right sleeve shattered against the cobblestones and it was as though I was hurtling through a sea of fire and brimstone, spinning at high speed towards the seabed. Sparks were flying everywhere, I struggled to make my way up and out of that inferno. Dark figures dancing wildly around me, throwing things.' He forced himself up onto one knee and saw his brother Haakon and another man, Arvid Falkenberg, whom they called 'the Architect', in the act of hurling more flaming cocktails through the office windows. There was another explosive roar and a tongue of fire licked across him. Through the chaos he heard a German voice – *Da ist der eine! Halt ihn fest!* ('There's one of them! Grab him!'). He felt a body pinion him to the ground, and a jacket being pressed over his face. With a huge effort he managed to raise his left shoulder enough to work his pistol free and fired two shots through the body holding him down. He felt the weight pressing down on him as the life drained out of the dead soldier and struggled to his feet. He saw German soldiers running up the street towards him. He fired and the man closest to him went down. Now he found himself alone in the street and was able to see for the first time the swirling inferno of the Work Service offices behind him. As the Germans re-emerged from shelter to resume their pursuit of him, a sudden gust of wind blew a wall of smoke between them and he was able to run around the corner unseen. He came to an open doorway and joined several other people standing sheltering off the pavement. Noticing he was injured someone took him upstairs and into an apartment. In a surreal moment, as they walked in, he saw a young woman standing by a long table ironing a shirt. People crowded round, asking had he just been passing by at the exact moment the bombs went off? Yes, he said. Bloody saboteurs. What's the point? Now the Germans will take more hostages, that'll be the only result. To his relief this irritated salvo was greeted with silence and he knew he was among sympathisers and could relax.

The operation had been a success. Pilestredet 31 was left a burned-out shell and records containing personal details of thousands of young men and women to be conscripted for Work Service destroyed. A second action against another Work Service office – led by Milorg's Jens Christian Hauge and due to have taken place at the same time – had been altogether less successful. The driver employed to drive them to Heimdalsgata had got cold feet and failed to turn up. They were unable to find a replacement at short notice and the operation had to be abandoned. Given that this was one of the first times Milorg had openly attempted an action of the kind Sunde and his group had been carrying out for over two years, Sunde was understandably caustic about Milorg's failure. He'd been calling his own action group *den sorte hånd* (the Black Hand) and in mild dismissal of the failure of Hauge's group he dubbed them *den bleke hånd* (the Pale Hand).

But, as always, the success of the Black Hand came at a price. Sunde's brother Haakon was arrested by the Germans after a gun battle a few days later and executed in Trandum forest early in 1944. Johan Petter Bruun, with Sunde the only other survivor of the earlier attack on the Stapo headquarters in Henrik Ibsens gate the previous year, was arrested as part of the same action and also shot in Trandum forest. Reidar Holtman, a Milorg member temporarily affiliated to the Osvald Group, was killed in the initial encounter. Of the five men who attacked the Work Service offices at Pilestredet 31 on 20 April 1943 only one, a second Milorg affiliate named Arvid Falkenberg, survived unharmed. Sunde himself was badly burned and remained out of action for several months. While convalescing, he could console himself for the savage losses his little group had sustained with the thought that they had, in this small but bloodily effective way, contributed to making Adolf Hitler's fifty-fourth birthday somewhat less of a day of celebration for the occupying Germans.

And Milorg would quickly redeem the early failure of *den bleke hånd* with several similar actions that rendered Quisling's idea of providing Hitler with cohorts of willing young Norwegians for use as cannon fodder in his total war against Bolshevism a bureaucratic impossibility. The bank robbery carried out by the Osvald Group at the Modum Sparebank on the night of 17 April 1944 was the fourth and last of the group's 'signature' operations and another part of the small complex of events and coincidences that led to 20 April and what became known as 'catastrophe night' for the resistance movement. Money was a constant problem for Sunde's organisation. Weapons, transport, explosives, living expenses, all had to be paid for. For most of its active period the group's main source of funding had been the NKP, under the leadership of Peder Furubotn. The ties between Sunde and Furubotn had been good, and several of Sunde's best men had been on semi-permanent loan to Furubotn as his bodyguard. But they had grown tired of 'watching over a bigshot politician' and began talking about wanting to return to active service with Sunde. Furubotn chose to see this as a power struggle. In what was essentially a communist variant of the Führer principle, his response was to announce that he was taking personal charge of all future communist sabotage operations. In view of this the NKP cut its funding to the Osvald Group, with the last known payment being made at the beginning of February 1944.

Sunde was not impressed: 'As regards Furubotn,' he wrote later, 'he was no saboteur. He was mostly talk. Wrote long articles which he sent to England, but he wasn't the man to carry out active resistance work.'

The bottom line was that by the spring of 1944 Sunde's group had run out of money and with no prospect of being able to remedy this state of affairs by non-violent means they turned to robbing banks. A raid on 15 March on the Aker Sparebank in Holtet, a suburb of Oslo near Nordstrand, served as a sort of practice run. Three of the group were involved. One kept a lookout on the street door, one kept an eye on the bank staff – having held them up at gunpoint – and the third emptied the safe and the tills. Afterwards they split up, one boarding a passing tram and the others hailing taxis. When they counted the money at Sunde's safe house that evening the haul amounted to 12,000 kroner.*

The proceeds pale compared to those from the Modum Sparebank which the group raided the following month. As was often the case in such operations, those involved wore stolen Stapo uniforms and used a Chevrolet pickup truck painted to look like a police vehicle. An added sophistication was the rusting wood gas generator mounted at the back on the left-hand side, to disguise the fact that the truck was running on petrol. Four heavily armed members of the Osvald Group set out for Modum. A second truck containing five men left the safe farmhouse at Einastranda at the same time as the Chevrolet and headed in the direction of Ringerike, where their task was to blow up the iron bridge at Geithus as a diversionary manoeuvre. Sunde was not a member of either group on this occasion.

It was late at night when the Chevrolet arrived at the bank in Vikersund. The gang rang the doorbell of an employee whom they knew lived in an apartment above the bank and demanded

---

* Just over 18,000 pounds sterling.

to be admitted to the bank vaults to follow up a tipoff about an illegal printing press they had reason to believe was in operation there. On this occasion the group had a singular advantage in that one of their number was an Austrian Luftwaffe deserter, a twenty-three-year-old named Günter Scheskat, whom they had dressed in the uniform of a Wehrmacht soldier and who now used his German voice to full and terrifying effect to compel compliance from the keyholder. To keep matters simple the group maintained the fiction that they were German and Norwegian Nazis looking for an illegal printing press until they were inside the vault. Only then did the leader, Harry Sønsterød, reveal that they were loyal Norwegians who needed the money to finance their resistance operations, and to sustain the widows and families of Norwegians imprisoned or executed in the service of their country.

With the money safely bagged the plan was to lock the keyholder and his wife in the vault. The keyholder protested that there was no ventilation in the vault and they would suffocate to death. The group argued briefly among themselves about what to do. Sønsterød decided to trust his hostages and offered to lock them in one of the basement cellars on condition that they did not attempt to escape for two hours. On the drive back to Einastranda they sang communist battle hymns. The Chevrolet made it safely back to base, where Sunde heard the explosion as the bridge at Geithus went up. They then began the long business of counting the proceeds of the raid.

It was a stupendous haul, 157.371 kroner and 66 øre, in contemporary terms a little over 3.2 million kroner. The following week Sunde sent the bank manager a receipt for the exact amount taken. Somewhat improbably, Harry Sønsterød later claimed not to have been aware that Sunde's group was a communist-inspired organisation. 'Sunde never talked about communism when I was with him,' he told a journalist after the war. 'He said we were fighting against fascism.' But in the same interview he made a joke about the size of the haul – 'You know, those farmers made a lot of money during the war' – that hinted at a class-based rationalisation of the operation.

Asbjørn Sunde was a man born to thrive in the chaotic context of war. His commitment to the cause of resistance was total and his authority unquestioned. 'He was a very good leader,' Sønsterød recalled after the war. 'Hard as nails to deal with, but mild and comradely, and with a good sense of humour.' Sunde's unwavering dedication to the cause was what provided the group with the moral justification certain of them sometimes felt the need of. As a young man brought up in a Christian home Sønsterød was particularly uneasy when Sunde asked them to turn bank robbers – by the time this particular phase of their activities was over, six banks had been robbed. 'No, it wasn't easy,' he said. 'But war is war. You have to do things that go against the grain. You know that it's morally wrong. But on the other hand, you've got all the rest of it that matters. We were fighting with all the means at our disposal; and even before we started out we were told we wouldn't make it.'

Only once did Sunde's moral compass come close to failing the group. On 1 May, less than two weeks after he had played a central role in the raid on the Modum Sparebank, the group's 'Austrian deserter' Günter Scheskat was sent out hunting with another member of the group, Norman Iversen. Scheskat was nominally the group's cook and perhaps had a professional interest in what Iversen might shoot. It turned out to be him. Though Scheskat had been with the group for several months and taken part in several actions, Sunde had never trusted him enough to allow him to carry a weapon. When the killing was discussed within the group later that day only two of them voiced doubts about the propriety of Sunde's decision to liquidate a man whom he had become convinced was a spy. One was a Ukrainian known as 'Nils' who had joined the group after escaping from a prison camp outside Bergen, who gruffly urged the leader to 'remember democracy'. The other was Harry Sønsterød, who piously expressed the hope that Sunde had had 'real proof' against the Austrian before taking his decision. No very convincing evidence of the accusation was ever offered, and Scheskat appeared under his real name on a contemporary German list of deserters that emerged later. The subdued nature of these objections probably reflects the sheer difficulty of attempting to query the actions of a man as pathologically untrusting as Sunde. He had, after all, lived for years on the edge of a consuming paranoia, fuelled by the ever-present fear of betrayal, capture, torture and the painful death that was the certain fate of the whole group as 'Bolsheviks', should they ever be betrayed.

The killing of Scheskat came just a month before Sunde's long-interrupted lines of communication with Moscow were restored. A courier arrived with a coded message ordering him to disband the group and send its active members across into Sweden. Here they would join the thousands of other young Norwegians already training to police the German surrender in Norway, which, by the middle of 1944, seemed inevitable. Religiously committed to Communist Party discipline, Sunde finally disbanded the Osvald Group in December 1944, after a lingering farewell to active service that included several more attacks on Work Service offices in Drammen and Tønsberg and on railway lines and timber yards. Milorg operatives who had been instructed by London to blow up munitions factories, railway lines and bridges – and in general make it as difficult as possible for any of the German troops stationed in Norway to join the fighting in France – were enthusiastic participants in these operations.

In its three years of active service the group had carried out over a hundred actions, making it by far the most active sabotage group during the five years of the Nazi occupation of Norway.[52]

Johannes Andersen, nicknamed *Gulosten* or 'Yellow Cheese', was born in 1898 and from an early age had proved resistant to authority of any kind. At fourteen he was sent to Bastøy Approved School as being beyond parental control. Two years later he went to sea. Having lost his job during the Depression, when prohibition was introduced to Norway he became a smug-  gler and started a career as a full-time criminal. He was arrested and imprisoned numerous times during the 1920s and 1930s. A combination of Jimmy Cagney gangster looks and two daring escapes from custody – on one occasion he jumped overboard from a ship returning him from Germany to Norway following an extradition request, and on another leapt through the window of a Drammen courthouse as he was waiting to be sentenced – had made 'Gulosten' a household name. His nickname derived from his days at the Bastøy Approved School and the food parcels he received from home that invariably contained yellow cheese. Following the German invasion of April 1940 his notoriety led to a remarkable and psychologically complex stand-off with the new regime. He had at once identified the Nazis as his enemies, perhaps not so much from a love of democracy as from an instinctive detestation of the premium national socialism put on discipline and submission to authority, and when a BBC broadcast to Norway claimed that the arch-criminal Johannes Andersen was a member of Quisling's *hird*, Gulosten went to surprising lengths to deny the rumour. The episode developed into a variant of Groucho Marx's observation that he wouldn't want to be a member of any club that would have someone like him as a member. The rumour had probably been started and communicated to London by *jøssing* Norwegians as a way of denigrating the *hird* and providing proof that its members were typically violent and uneducated criminals – a common and largely accurate observation. The ideological defenders of the *hird* were clearly as anxious as Gulosten to make a public denial of his membership. On 22 February 1941 he was given column space in *Fritt Folk* for a carefully worded refutation:

> Sir –
> Might I ask for your help in the correction and mortification of a certain untruth concerning me which I gather is now spread about town and has even been broadcast over the radio from London? It is claimed that I am a member of the *Hird*, that I have been seen about town wearing the uniform of the *Hird*, and that I have even risen through the ranks of the *Hird* to a position of leadership. I am not a member of the *Hird*. I have never applied for membership of the *Hird*. I am not even a member of National Unity. One untruth more or less at a time such as this hardly matters, but since people claim that there are already so many 'criminals' in the *Hird* then I think you will agree that they can manage well enough without adding my name to the list.
> Sincerely Johannes Andersen (Gulosten)

The disavowal was greeted with relief and pleasure by the editor of *Hirdmannen*, as anxious for the truth to come out as Andersen, though for different reasons:

> The notorious safe-breaker Johannes Andersen ('Gulosten') thus confirms that neither he nor anyone like him has any connection with National Unity or the *hird*. In this he shows a better understanding than the English fabricators of these lies. He understands that our movement, with its exalted and idealistic goals, is no place for criminals of any sort.

For reasons that remain obscure but may have been connected to his own claim to have pasted up loyalist posters bearing King Haakon's picture in the streets of Oslo, and which certainly involved the theft of a large quantity of tobacco from a warehouse in Welhavens gate, Andersen was arrested by the Gestapo on 3 March, tried and given a twelve-month jail sentence. While serving his time he became friendly with another inmate, a policeman named Øyvind Ask, whose small resistance group had set up a radio transmitter in Sandefjord but had been betrayed. Ask and two others were sentenced to death by a German military court and transferred to Akershus Fortress. The Akershus prison chaplain, Dagfinn Hauge, ministered to the condemned men in the days before sentence was carried out. Like Andersen, he was moved by Ask's warmth, sensitivity and decency.

Andersen served part of his sentence in Germany. While there he learned of the executions, and that the informer who had sealed the men's fate was a certain Raymond Colberg. On his return to Norway he got wind that the police intended to re-arrest him for a number of ordinary crimes, including the organised and large-scale theft of bicycles. He abandoned his flat in Kristian Augusts gate, where he had been working as a caretaker, and went into hiding at the Cheval Animal Hospital in Holmen's gate in central Oslo. Andersen had brought back from Germany messages from Norwegian prisoners to friends and dependants back home in Oslo, and it was while delivering one of these that he met Annæus Schjødt and his wife, Hedevig. Hedevig was already a member of a resistance group known as 2A that specialised in refugee transports and intelligence work. Her husband was a High Court lawyer. The Schjødts were not immediately aware that their new friend was the notorious criminal Gulosten, but what they heard about his recent experience in Germany convinced them that he was a loyal Norwegian looking for the chance to do something for his country. On learning that he was a wanted man living in hiding they offered to help him cross into Sweden. Andersen's response was to accept, but on condition that he first perform some useful and valuable act for the resistance. Albert Wiesener, part of Øyvind Ask's defence counsel, recalled a private conversation with his client during a break in the trial: 'Had I known the price of what I was doing,' he said, 'I could have done something bigger, more useful and more fateful.' Perhaps some such thought was in Andersen's mind when he went on to suggest the name of Raymond Colberg as a target for what turned out to be the first semi-official 'liquidation' of an informer by the Norwegian resistance movement.

Colberg was, like Gulosten, a career criminal. The difference between them was that for Colberg, informing was just another crime, just another way to make money. It was also less trouble than working the black market that had emerged in response to the increasing scarcity of numerous everyday commodities such as coffee, stockings, soap, meat and tobacco. The idea of killing him was discussed at the next meeting of 2A, and informal approval of his suggestion was conveyed to Andersen. Fearful of reprisal killings by the German authorities, the group stressed that Colberg must disappear without a trace.

As a fellow criminal and dedicated immoralist, Colberg had little reason to suspect anything when he agreed to meet Andersen around midnight on the night of 31 March 1942 behind the National Theatre in the centre of Oslo. He believed he was going to be offered several sacks of coffee on the black market and willingly accompanied Andersen on the five-minute walk to the Cheval Animal Hospital. Arne Stølen and Johannes Larsen, who both worked at the hospital, met them there. The four then made their way up the ramps connecting the floors until they reached the door to the stables on the fourth floor. At this point Andersen took the gun he had been given by Hedevig Schjødt from his pocket and pointed it at Colberg.

'You've sent enough people to their deaths,' he said. 'You won't be sending any more.'

Colberg must have turned, for Andersen's first shot went through his right eye. He fell to the floor. As he lay there Andersen shot him a second time. The three men then stripped Colberg of his ID papers and his wallet, carried the body down into the hospital's back yard and hid it inside a bin where the corpses of unclaimed stray dogs were piled. Andersen then went to see

Hedevig Schjødt to tell her Colberg was dead, and to return the pistol to her. She arranged for a lorry and a driver to come to the hospital in the early morning and the corpse, now swathed and tied inside a mattress sack, was loaded onto the flatbed by Andersen, Larsen and the driver. They drove it to the Bispebrua bridge behind the Central Railway Station and parked beside a hole in the fence. First checking to make sure they were unobserved they then rolled Colberg's body over the side of the bridge and into the Akerselva river.

Ten weeks later it was fished out of the water further down the river by an employee at Nylands mekaniske verksted. Long before that the Schjødts and Johannes Andersen had crossed the border into Sweden. From there Andersen was transported to England by plane, a benefit of his new-found celebrity as resistance hero. Another – more unexpected – benefit was an invitation to meet and dine with the king of Norway. Haakon took a liking to Gulosten and would remain his friend and financial supporter during what was an eventful and always morally dubious career in post-war Norway.

In Britain, Andersen linked up with Norwegian Independent Company 1, the Norwegian commando unit based in the United Kingdom and trained by the British Special Operations Executive (SOE), an organisation established in 1940 to carry out espionage, sabotage and reconnaissance activities in territories occupied by the German forces, and to train and liaise with local resistance groups. Norwegian Independent Company was known informally as *Kompani Linge*.* After a brief period of training in October 1942 Andersen and three other Norwegians were parachuted back into Norway on a mission known as Operation Bittern. Its goal was devastatingly simple: to liquidate as many prominent Norwegian Nazis as possible on a list of names that ran into double figures.

---

* So named to commemorate Martin Linge, a Norwegian actor and patriot killed in the joint British–Norwegian commando raid on Måløy in late December 1941.

Andersen's liquidation of Raymond Colberg had broken down Norwegian resistance to the kind of violent action their British associates in the SOE had been urging on them for some time: namely assassination as a means of curbing the activities of informers who had been able to operate with impunity in the two years since the occupation began.

The list of planned liquidations was ambitious and included government ministers as well as informers. Jonas Lie was one name on it. In fact, it proved too ambitious for the Milorg operatives who were given the task of liaising with the members of Operation Bittern. Fearing reprisals on the scale of the response to Heydrich's assassination in Prague earlier in the year – which resulted in the razing of two villages, the shooting of all males above the age of fourteen and the deportation of the women and children to concentration camps – the local Milorg authorities vetoed the entire project. Instead, the Bittern group concentrated on the second part of their assignment, the training of willing young patriots in the arts of sabotage, safe-cracking, silent killing and other aspects of clandestine warfare.

Andersen rapidly became bored with this and, on 6 November, on the pretext of needing dental treatment, he travelled into Oslo to see a dentist. Milorg, less than thrilled at being ordered to cooperate with a man they knew only as a hardened criminal and violent amoralist, sent someone to chaperone him and make sure he did nothing but visit the dentist and return. Andersen gave his chaperone the slip and disappeared for the next forty-eight hours. When he returned to base at Holmen in Asker he was so drunk he couldn't find his way home, knocked at the door of a family he had got to know while staying in the area and spent the night there. When questioned he claimed that all he could remember was that he had visited his wife Ruth.

Aware that the whole Bittern operation might be compromised, the other members of his group now offered him a face-saving manoeuvre that involved his travelling to Sweden carrying important messages for Milorg contacts in Stockholm. Even there he remained resolutely himself, continuing to indulge in his use of cocaine as both a recreational and professional necessity, boasting casually to complete strangers of his clandestine activities with the resistance, once with five Jewish refugees with whom he shared a compartment on the train journey to Kjesäter. From this point onwards he was removed from any theatre of war that depended on discretion, silence and stealth for its success and transferred to service on the MTB (Motor Torpedo Boats), where he served out the rest of the war at sea and appears to have done so with credit. Andersen's unorthodox and amoral personality was the catalyst that forced many ordinary Norwegians to accept the need to kill those whose activities as informers were responsible for the imprisonment, torture and execution of literally hundreds of loyal Norwegians, both as a discouragement to others and as a preventative measure.

Milorg's real value to the Allied cause belongs to a later chapter of the war, from the Normandy landings of June 1944 onwards, when its campaign of sabotage of railway lines and bridges did much to prevent soldiers from the vast Wehrmacht presence in Norway being transported to mainland Europe to join the main German force defending Germany's borders from the approaching Allied forces. It was nevertheless active during these early and middle years, and among the most celebrated actions of the war, in Europe as well as in Norway, was the attack Milorg operatives carried out on Norsk Hydro's heavy water plant at Vemork, near Rjukan in Telemark.* The action, codenamed Grouse, involved a group of Norwegian commandos who were dropped on Hardangervidda in late 1942 with the task of marking a landing

---

* In 1965 the raid was the subject of a Hollywood film, *The Heroes of Telemark*, starring Kirk Douglas and Richard Harris. Norwegian State Television (NRK) dramatised the episode in 2015 in a six-part series as *Kampen om tungtvannet* (The Heavy Water Affair).

site for the nighttime arrival in November of two British planes. Each had a glider in tow transporting commandos of the British Royal Engineers whose job it was to attack and destroy the plant. The Norwegian commandos, handpicked for their local knowledge, would then guide them to safety

Heavy cloud cover on the night of the landing meant that the towing planes never spotted the markers laid out for them by the Norwegians on the ground. In the ensuing panic one of the tow-ropes broke and the glider crash-landed south of the Lysefjord, and the second plane developed technical problems that forced it to cut its glider loose. Both lead planes crashed. All of those in the towing plane were killed, but nine British commandos in the glider that landed south of the fjord survived. Five of them were later executed in Trandum Forest, the four others in Stavanger following extensive torture. The fourteen who survived the crash landing in Egersund were all executed the following day. The failed operation cost forty-one British lives.

The four Norwegian members of Grouse remained on Hardangervidda over the winter. Early in 1943, under the new team name 'Swallow', they began to prepare for the arrival of a second group of commandos, with whom they would join forces to launch a fresh attack on the plant at Vemork – Operation Gunnerside. The six commandos dropped by parachute on the night of 16 February were Norwegians, all members of *Kompani Linge* who had been specially trained for the operation at Brickendonbury, not far from Hertford. In view of the fate of their British predecessors, all had been issued with suicide tablets. The night of the attack itself, 27 February, proved remarkable for its lack of incident. The nine saboteurs approached the site along the unguarded and little-used railway line that ran between Rjukan and Vemork, then cut through the perimeter fence. Lookouts posted to deal with any sentries patrolling saw no one. At some point they encountered the Norwegian caretaker, a man named Johansen, who raised no objection to the plan. The saboteurs then gained entry to the plant itself and laid their charges on the heavy water electrolysis chambers, using a short, thirty-second fuse to eliminate any possibility of its being severed. Just as the fuses were about to be lit, Johansen discovered he had misplaced his spectacles. A hurried search of the laboratory ensued, the glasses were found, and the fuses duly lit. The saboteurs then made their retreat.

Claus Helberg, on lookout duty for the Swallow team, heard a dull thud and the shatter of broken glass. The thud was enough to rouse a German sentry who came wandering out from his post, torch in hand. He directed the beam here and there. The building remained quite undamaged and seeing nothing suspicious the sentry presently returned to the comfort of his post. Five of the saboteurs subsequently made their getaway across Hardangervidda on skis, into Sweden and from there to Britain. One travelled down the Numedal valley through Eggedal and Krøderen. Helberg skied alone to Geilo and then boarded a train to Oslo. In the extensive German enquiry into the attack it later transpired that the guards on watch that night had not even known where the switch to turn on the plant's floodlights was located.

The blast destroyed the equipment that carried out the process of electrolysis, but within three months the plant was operational again. A fleet of 161 American aircraft then carpet-bombed the Vemork plant on 16 November 1943 without doing significant damage to the vital centres of production but killing twenty-one Norwegian civilians. Production was again halted, but again the pause was only temporary.

At this point the Germans decided to dismantle the equipment and resume the operation in Germany. Learning of the plan, Milorg sabotaged the ferry carrying the heavy water across Lake Tinnsjø on 19 February 1944, blowing it up halfway across and sending it, along with its cargo of jars of heavy water, to the bottom. Eighteen lives were lost in the explosion, fourteen Norwegian passengers and four German soldiers. The action had a significant, morale-boosting effect, although it emerged later that German scientists were not dangerously close to being able to produce a hydrogen bomb from the heavy water. Hitler had greater faith in the destructive power of the V2 supersonic guided missile. Well over a thousand of these landed on London in the months following the rocket's first deployment in September 1944.

In a tidying-up operation, Claus Helberg returned three weeks later to the remote cabin at Skrykken on Hardangervidda where Grouse had spent the winter while they waited for Gunnerside to recover weapons and explosives that had been left there. The military repercussions from the raid were still ongoing and large numbers of German troops were still combing the terrain looking for what they assumed to be a group of British saboteurs. At the cabin, Helberg was surprised by a German ski patrol and a dramatic chase ensued. He managed to outdistance his pursuers all save for one persistent man. Helberg despaired of ever shaking him off, but then he realised that in the course of the pursuit the soldier must have emptied his gun. He stopped in his tracks, turned round and began shooting, at which point his pursuer finally abandoned the chase.

Helberg continued his journey. As darkness fell, he had the misfortune to ski over a hidden drop and break his arm. In due course he reached the shelter of a store whose owner he knew. He knocked on the door and was surprised when a German soldier opened it. With great presence of mind he improvised a story that while guiding a German patrol in the region he had fallen and broken his arm and been told to make his way to Rauland for treatment from a German military doctor. His bluff worked, he was invited inside and spent the night sleeping on the floor alongside the very people who had been sent to track and capture him. In the morning he was examined and treated by the doctor and told to make his way to the hospital at Skien to have his arm properly seen to.

He was then given a lift with the German convoy to the hotel at Dalen, where he was to spend the night. His intention was to take the boat down the Telemark canal to Skien the following morning. Later in the evening the Reichskommissar himself, Josef Terboven, arrived. When one of the hotel's female guests insulted him in some way, Terboven ordered the arrest of every single guest. They were to be transported to the camp at Grini by bus in the morning.

Helberg spent the night in his hotel room under armed guard, and in the morning boarded the bus with the other guests, now prisoners. He found himself sitting next to the young woman who had offended Terboven. Evidently he enjoyed her company too much for the liking of the German guard at the front of the bus, who at some point ordered Helberg to swap places with him. After a drive of nine hours, as the bus began the narrow, twisting climb up from Drammen to Liertoppen, he knew he had no choice but to try to escape. He could not risk being interrogated and tortured once it emerged that his story was false. As the bus crawled over the brow of the hill he wrenched the door open, leapt out and began running. He ran blindly through the garden of a roadside house just as its occupant was emerging from his outside toilet. The German motorcyclist riding shotgun behind the bus threw a grenade at Helberg. It bounced off his back and didn't explode until several seconds later. In the confusion the motorcyclist arrested the bewildered houseowner while Helberg disappeared into the shelter of a nearby wood and made his getaway. With the help of a *jøssing* doctor he was admitted to a hospital in Drammen under a false name and spent three weeks there until he was well enough to leave and go into hiding in Oslo and await plans for his flight to Britain.

In Oslo he came in contact with the circle around Sigrid Helliesen Lund and Myrtle Wright, who knew him as 'Arne'. He remained in hiding at the home of family friends for the next three weeks, successfully concealing his presence even from his own brother, who was occupying a room near the front door of the same apartment. Milorg were unable to verify his identity and feared he might be a 'plant'. In the end he lost patience and asked Helliesen Lund to use her own contacts to get him onto one of the ordinary refugee transports to Sweden. Through Lund, Helberg became friendly with her English friend, Myrtle Wright, and while waiting for his transport he and Wright often went walking together in the streets around Tuengen allé. He promised he would visit her mother in Cambridge if he made it safely over to England. As luck would have it her address in Cambridge at 171 Huntingdon Road was easily remembered using Haakon 7's monogram, with a 7 superimposed between the parallel bars of an H, by this time the most widely used symbol of resistance among patriotic Norwegians.* Claus Helberg did indeed visit her once he arrived in England. It happened to be Mrs Wright's birthday and he joined her for a celebratory meal. At one point, following Norwegian custom, he rose to stand behind his chair and deliver a short speech in honour of the eighty-year-old Quaker.

Helberg remained in England until October 1944, when he returned to Norway to take part in Operation Sunshine. With victory by this time looking a likely if still distant prospect, Operation Sunshine was a joint British and Norwegian operation aimed at protecting essential Norwegian installations and industry from possible destruction by the retreating German forces. The operation lasted until the end of the war and cost the lives of several members of the group.

---

* See the illustration on p. 32.

8

Revolution as Reaction: Culture Under Quisling, 1940–5

Dispiriting as it was for the regime, the success of the Conscience Struggle in the schools and universities was not enough to persuade the Quisling government that its attempted revolution of the mind was doomed to failure. In 1936, at the last parliamentary election held before the occupation, National Unity had taken just 1.8 per cent of the vote, insufficient to give it even one mandate in the Storting. As of 9 April 1940 the party had some 2,700 officially registered members. Over the next six months a further 3,000 joined. A second and larger wave of enrolments occurred following Terboven's decision of 25 September 1940 to outlaw all political parties except National Unity, and by the end of the first year the party had more than 25,000 registered members. Recruitment continued to rise and reached its height in the winter of 1943, when it had over 43,000 members. A further encouragement may have been the relative success of the Lebensborn institutions in occupied Norway. The Lebensborn project, launched by Heinrich Himmler in Germany in 1935, aimed to preserve the presumed Aryan 'purity' and genetic heritage of the Germanic race. Lebensborn maternity homes in Norway were modelled on those in Germany and took care of

Norwegian mothers who were carrying the children of German soldiers. At least part of their purpose was to prevent the mothers involved from having abortions. The programme opened in the spring of 1941 and in due course numbered nine centres, with facilities for some 600 infants, at different geographical locations across the country. All were staffed by Germans. Over the five years of the occupation somewhere between ten and twelve thousand Norwegian-German children were born in these homes. As they did with the steadily increasing number of people joining the party, National Unity leaders preferred to interpret this evidence of widespread fraternisation as further proof that, despite the setbacks suffered during the Conscience Struggle, the goal of a national socialist Norway still lay within reach, if only the war would last long enough, if only Germany could win it.

So the long-term project of shaping Norwegian culture for a coming 'new age' continued apace. It had started within the first few weeks of the occupation. Norwegian Wikipedia tells us that Norway's first Minister of Culture was a man named Lars Roar Langslet, who held the post in Kåre Willoch's conservative government between 1981 and 1986.[53] In fact, the portfolio was introduced to Norway by the German Reichskommissar and the first holder of the office was Gulbrand Lunde, one of the acting ministers appointed following Terboven's speech of 25 September 1940. Dubious as the culture he promoted was, Gulbrand Lund was nevertheless a real Minister of Culture in one recognisable respect in that his task was to promote the values and ideals of a particular political philosophy through the medium of the arts. The creation of the post in Norway was as a direct result of Josef Goebbels' insight into the crucial role culture plays in moulding minds, whether through the awesome pageantry of the Nazi Party's Nuremberg rallies of the 1930s, or in the private darkness of a seat at the local cinema. Goebbels sent one of his most trusted associates, Wilhelm Müller-Scheld, to Norway shortly after the invasion with the specific task of re-shaping Norwegian cultural life in the direction of national socialist ideals.

The day after Terboven's speech the offices of the Tiden publishing house were raided and closed. Tiden had a long tradition as a left-wing publisher and among the books on its list was Karl Marx's *Das Kapital* (Capital: A Critique of Political Economy). The company's entire stock, some 400,000 volumes, was seized and destroyed, the justification given being that the paper was needed for recycling in order to produce books promoting the more useful ideas of the 'new era'. The head of Tiden, Kolbjørn Fjell, was arrested and interrogated at Gestapo headquarters in Victoria terrasse and then sent to Grini prison, and Tiden acquired a new board consisting of National Unity members and sympathisers. All the company's most important writers, however, had already taken their work elsewhere, and for the duration of the occupation Tiden existed in name only.

Few Norwegian writers supported the occupation, and those that opposed it could scarcely expect to be allowed to express their views openly in books. Their union, the Norwegian Society of Authors, was not Nazified but it kept a low profile throughout the war. It had been started in 1893 by Erik Lie, a minor writer himself, son of the celebrated novelist Jonas Lie and father of Quisling's Minister for Policing, Jonas Lie. Like the better-known Knut Hamsun, Erik Lie was a Germanophile and one of the small number of Norwegians who supported the German cause during both World Wars. His funeral in May 1943 was one of the more bleakly surreal moments of the occupation, bringing together at the crematorium three of the Norwegian Society of Authors' most prominent members, the chairman Alex Brinchmann, the journalist and playwright Georg Brochmann, and the novelist Johan Bojer, author of the international best-seller *The Last of the Vikings*, with Jonas Lie, Sverre Riisnæs and Fredrik Prytz, all of whom were members of the National Unity government. Brinchmann's wreath from the Society was laid next to Vidkun Quisling's tribute. It was a difficult but honourable tribute from the society to the man responsible for its formation.

Vern om norsk bokheim (Protection of Norwegian Literature) was the name given to a list of banned books that was distributed in October 1940 to bookshops and public libraries with orders to remove them from the shelves. A little more hands-on than the 'trigger warnings' of our age, the idea was in many ways similar, to shield readers from degenerate and depressing literary truths, as well as to prevent the spread of pernicious social ideas, books either critical of German national socialism or which actively promoted communist ideology. It was one of the earliest shots fired in National Unity's battle to impose a national socialist worldview on Norwegians.

On 17 February 1941 Gulbrand Lunde and his advisers issued a second censorship list consisting of further books from Tiden's catalogue, as well as books published by the Norwegian Labour Party's own press, and other smaller socialist publishing houses. Authors published by Gyldendal and Aschehoug, Norway's two largest and most economically stable publishing houses at the time, accounted for only 10 per cent of the names on the list of 350 titles. On 25 July 1941 a third list appeared with a varied selection of both Norwegian and foreign authors, but in the main this consisted of new titles from authors who had already been banned. These lists offered curiosities and enigmas. Norway's Nobel laureate Knut Hamsun, who made no secret of his hatred of communism and his Anglophobia, was not, of course, on the list, but it seems that on his own initiative the librarian at Ørsta in Sunnmøre removed Hamsun's books from the shelves anyway, presumably on the grounds that by the standards of the time they were considered 'dirty'. This attempt to discourage *griseliteratur* ('dirty books') seems to have been unique to the Norwegian version of the national socialist cultural revolution. Louis-Ferdinand Céline's first and greatest novel *Journey to the End of the Night* made the official list, probably on the same grounds of immorality, though had the compilers known of his antisemitic polemic *Bagatelles pour un massacre* (Trifles for a Massacre) lthey might have been inclined to give the benefit of the doubt to his masterpiece.

Bertolt Brecht was among those proscribed in the 'Protection of Norwegian Literature' lists, as were Ernest Hemingway, the renegade fascist Curzio Malaparte, Robert Musil and Erich Maria Remarque, author of *All Quiet on the Western Front*. Four of Sinclair Lewis's books were listed, including *It Can't Happen Here*, his 1935 satire on the rise to power of an American Adolf Hitler that the Storting's President C.J. Hambro had translated into Norwegian in 1935. Upton Sinclair was also on the list, as was the anthroposophic visionary Rudolf Steiner.

As a loyal supporter of Quisling and one of the earliest members of the party, Lunde might have seemed a good choice to the German authorities, but there was always a division in National Unity between the Pan-Germanists and those like Lunde and Quisling himself for whom the cause of Norwegian nationalism within the framework of a new Germania was the greater goal. Lunde's death by drowning in October 1942 was believed by some to be a German-inspired assassination to get rid of someone not as 'on message' as he ought to have been. On the evening of Sunday 25 October he and his wife Marie were asleep in the back seat of the car as they waited for the Romsdalsfjord ferry to take them across from Våge to Eidsbygda. As the ferry was preparing to leave, the driver pulled forward a few metres from the quay onto the connecting ramp then stopped and got out of the car. Intending to reverse closer to the quay, the captain somehow caused the ferry to move forward, the ramp slipped clear of the ferry and the car plunged into the icy waters of the fjord. A third passenger in the car managed to swim clear, but Lunde and his wife drowned. Rolf Fuglesang, a National Unity member closer to the Pan-Germanist wing of the party than the fiercely nationalist Lunde, was appointed to replace him, a move that gave rise to suspicions in some quarters that Lunde's accidental death was in fact a political assassination.

Fuglesang would also issue lists of banned books, but they were shorter – in some cases they contained just a few book titles – and were unsystematically distributed. Some lists merely noted the names of authors whose entire oeuvre was forbidden. As late as August 1944 new lists of forbidden books were still being issued by the department, but by then the missionary zeal of the 1941 actions had run out of steam. All but the most deluded accepted the failure of the hoped-for national socialist revolution in Norway and the prohibitions were pursued with decidedly muted enthusiasm. Books were never actually burned in Norway, but the whole exercise remains as a depressing example of what can happen when fanatical idealists find themselves in charge of the cultural life of a nation.

One of Lunde's more memorable initiatives during his short tenure as Minister for Culture was to set up *Kunst og ukunst* ('Art and Non-Art'), an exhibition of paintings held between April and May 1942 and curated by Søren Onsager, his appointee as the new director of the National Gallery. 'Art and Non-Art' was directly inspired by the exhibitions of *Entartete Kunst* ('degenerate art') in 1937 in Munich and elsewhere in Germany. Onsager himself was a capable painter in the academic style.

The visitor to 'Art and Non-Art' was guided through a succession of rooms showing mostly Norwegian art. The first displayed the great landscapes of early-nineteenth-century masters such as J.C. Dahl, August Cappelen, Hans Gude and Adolf Tiedemann, moving forward and into the early twentieth century with Harriet Backer, Kitty Kielland, Eilif Peterssen and Fritz Thaulow, and arriving at what was referred to as 'the Room of the Masters': Nikolai Astrup, Halfdan Egedius, Hans Heyerdal, Christian Krogh, Gerhard Munthe, Harald Sohlberg, Erik Werenskiold. Onsager also loyally displayed four of Edvard Munch's paintings among the masterpieces, including *Spring* and *White Night*. *Scream* and other examples of Munch's more strikingly Expressionist work, eighty-two of which had been removed from German galleries in 1937 as examples of *entartete Kunst*, were quietly ignored. All of this was preparatory to what was called 'the Chambers of Horrors', a room featuring art that was either abstract, expressionist, or politically wrong-headed, like Willi Middelfart's 1932 *The Police Attack*, which Onsager damned as simple communist propaganda. There was lots more of it down in the basement, he told journalists. Paintings by what he called the *real* painters on show were not secured to their frames, and in the event of an air raid, three men had been specially trained in how to roll these up and spirit them away to safety. The degenerate paintings, on the other hand, would just have to take their chances in their frames.

Here and there small notices on the wall beside the exhibits gave further information; next to one of Kai Fjell's paintings in the Chamber of Horrors was a curatorial note informing visitors that this was from Kai Fjell's 'early and confused' period, before he had seen the light. Looked at now, the choices seem curious. Given Onsager's explanation of the criteria involved – that the bad art was degenerate, depressing, the figures deformed – the inclusion of the two Edvard Munch paintings (*Spring*, according to the critic of the now National Unity-run *Aftenposten*, 'completely dominated' the Masters room) is surprising, for Munch failed to make the cut at every exhibition of *entartete* art mounted in the same spirit in German galleries, where *Scream* no doubt was at the centre of any 'demoralising' Chamber of Horrors.

Munch was not a political artist and kept his distance from party politics all his life. Knut Hamsun's son Tore had direct personal experience of this when he visited the old man in 1943, the year of Munch's great self-portrait *Mellom klokken og sengen* (Between the Clock and the Bed). Tore's mission was to try to get Munch's support in a protest against an attempt by National Unity to impose the Führer principle on the Artists' Union. Tore Hamsun was a painter and National Unity member himself, and his role as emissary underscores the enigmas and contradictions that could be involved in being a Norwegian Nazi during the occupation. Tore Hamsun began by asking Munch straight out if he was prepared to support the existing, democratic format of the organisation. Munch, being old and neither a good listener nor a good union man, interrupted and with a dismissive wave of the hand explained that he didn't want to get involved in anything to do with the Germans and National Unity. Tore Hamsun explained that he was asking him to do the opposite and keep the Germans away from the organisation. Munch was still not interested. The Germans, he muttered, would do whatever they wanted anyway.

Before dismissing the *Kunst og ukunst* exhibition as pure Nazi propaganda it is worth recalling that Norway had been independent from Sweden for a mere thirty-five years in 1940 and similar attitudes decrying foreign influence on the country's artists in the name of patriotism could have been heard at any point over the decades since 1905. But the *Aftenposten* journalist who covered the opening was only playing devil's advocate when he put it to Onsager that it might be a little unfair to pillory fellow artists in such a public way. Not at all, replied Onsager, because they weren't actually artists at all, they were just confidence tricksters who had worked out how to exploit the public's ignorance of art. Onsager's rage against the fads and fashions of modern art might have been amusing and even sympathetic to a traditionalist had there not been, in among the hostility to Picasso, Braque and all foreign influences on Norwegian artists generally, a reference to what he called *jødekunsten* ('Jewish art'). Onsager didn't bother to define this term and, indeed, in the year of the Norwegian holocaust, there would have been no need to define it, since there were no longer any Jews left in Norway to produce *jødekunsten*.

After the German surrender Onsager was arrested and charged with treason, but died in prison in 1946 of a long-standing illness before his trial came up. Unsurprisingly, he had purchased very little art for the National Gallery during his tenure of office, and the little he had bought was quietly returned to the artists concerned after the war.

Probably the most prominent martyr in the struggle to protect the integrity of Norwegian culture during these years was a Trondheim theatre manager and actor named Henry Gleditsch.

The son of a Scottish mother and Norwegian father, Gleditsch had started the Trøndelag theatre in 1937 and by 1940 it was already an established part of the city's cultural life. As luck would have it, on the night of 9 April 1940 Gleditsch was in Oslo and staying at the Continental Hotel, where Vidkun Quisling also spent the night before the invasion. Gleditsch immediately headed back up to Trondheim to begin work on the theatre's response. By the end of October his colleague at the National Theatre in Oslo, Axel Otto Normann, had been informed by National Unity's police chief in Oslo that 'nowhere in the text of a performance shall there be insults directed towards the German authorities, their representative or their interests, or towards National Unity, its members or its ideology. Individual performances must not contain new material or new ways of performing lines etc, for example, pregnant "pauses", certain gestures with the hand etc that may be offensive to the above-mentioned bodies, persons or interests and ideas.' Each major theatre received a similar set of instructions, and a censor was appointed to each individually. As a sort of guide to what was acceptable, in December the *Reichsministerium für Volksaufklärung und Propaganda* in Germany sent over a list of twenty-eight plays which it recommended as particularly suitable for Norwegian audiences.

As part of the same cultural overture, theatre directors were invited to send a group of Norwegian actors, one or two from each theatre, on a study trip to Germany to experience German theatre for themselves. Gleditsch was from the start opposed to any contact between the two worlds that could be exploited for propaganda purposes and replied that the Trøndelag company was so small he was unable to spare even a single actor to join the group. He followed this up with a campaign of bureaucratic filibustering that turned the invitation into a nightmare for those issuing it, requesting that the invitations be formal and individual, quibbling incessantly about the date and exact hour of the departure, and in general making such a nuisance of himself that in the end the trip was cancelled.

The abortive study strip had originally been planned as a prelude to the visit of a company of actors from the Hamburger Staatliche Schauspielhaus. When they arrived in Norway in January 1941, Gleditsch furloughed his entire company and, to eliminate any possibility of fraternisation, told them to stay away from the theatre for the duration of the German actors' visit.

He then persuaded the city's dentists to buy up all the tickets for the performance by the German visitors, asking them to ensure that none were used on the night. Our sources cannot explain exactly why dentists were so well suited to this task, but the tactic was a great success. As the minutes ticked by and curtain up approached, the manager of the German company expressed consternation at the fact that there was no audience. Gleditsch assured him that everything was fine, the show was a sell-out, not a vacant seat left. In desperation the visitor suggested requisitioning off-duty German soldiers to fill the empty seats. Gleditsch told him that, alas, it was simply not possible to give away seats for which others had already bought tickets.

The curtain duly went up and the first act was played out to a largely empty theatre. By the opening of the second act, German soldiers had been ordered in to fill the seats for what remained of the performance. The Trøndelag's stage manager, Birger Straume, had been requisitioned to man the spotlights and see to the raising and lowering of the curtain and the correct timing of sound effects, functions which he carried out with such enthusiastic incompetence that partway through the evening he was ordered to stand down and let a German technician take over for the remainder of the performance. In a final small but symbolically significant gesture, Gleditsch 'forgot' to arrange for flowers to be presented to the visitors at the close of the performance.

The German troop left Trondheim on the last day of January and on the very next evening Gleditsch presented the première of a *Norsk aften* ('Norwegian Evening') of patriotic songs – including the national anthem *Ja vi elsker* – and poetry, the intention being, according to the programme, to present the audience with 'an evening uniting that which was with that which is to come', with no need to specify that the woeful present was no part of the celebration.

Tightening its grip on the country's theatres, National Unity arrested and imprisoned the board of the National Theatre in Oslo in the summer of 1941 and appointed party members to run it. New regulations introduced by Gulbrand Lunde made it mandatory for every theatre to seek a licence, and withheld state support from those that attempted to run without one. Henry Gleditsch's Trøndelag theatre in Trondheim was at that time the only one functioning without a licence and was facing closure on Lunde's personal orders. Gleditsch therefore had no option but to begin the application process, doing so with practised pedantry. He refused to apply without first seeing a contract that stipulated the conditions governing the issue of such a licence. When one materialised, he objected in particular to a paragraph stating that the director was responsible for ensuring that 'no plays by Jews, emigrants or dramatists at war with Germany are staged'.[54] Gleditsch's suggested amendment was that it was 'the responsibility of the theatre to ensure that plays not approved by the *Teaterdirektoratet* are not to be staged'. It was rejected. It seems that the demand came from the Germans and was unconditional.

Naturally, none of the twenty-eight plays on the German list of recommendations were ever performed in Trondheim. Instead Gleditsch used the subtle metaphoric power of the drama to accentuate his *jøssing* credentials for delighted Norwegian audiences. *Brand*, Henrik Ibsen's play about a priest whom most Norwegians of the time admired as quintessentially Norwegian and admirable in his obstinacy to compromise, was chosen by Gleditsch to reopen the theatre in the autumn of 1940.[55] Hans Wiers-Jenssen's *Anne Pedersdotter*, from 1908, was revived just two weeks after the bleak pomp of the State Act ceremony in Oslo and Vidkun Quisling's elevation to minister-president. The plot of Wiers-Jensen's play was based on a real-life episode of witch hysteria in seventeenth-century Bergen which resulted in Anne Pedersdotter being burned at the stake. Wiers-Jenssen's play predates by some decades Arthur Miller's *The Crucible*, which dramatised a similar case of mass hysteria in Salem, Massachusetts, in 1692 to expose Senator Joseph McCarthy's persecution of suspected communists in the USA in the early 1950s. The winter season of 1942 opened with Ibsen's *The Wild Duck*, directed by Gleditsch, who also cast himself as Dr Relling. His desire to play a character so implacably opposed to fanaticism of any sort was hardly without significance.

As things turned out he never did get to play the part. He had the ill luck to cross his own real-life Gregers Werle in the person of Trondheim's young National Unity leader Henrik Rogstad, and an encounter that began almost as farce ended up a tragedy that cost Gleditsch his life. A National Unity gathering had been arranged to take place in Trondheim between 14 and 17 November 1941 and the usual order went out from the local authorities for flags to be hoisted on all public buildings for the duration of the gathering. The local newspaper *Dagsposten*, now under National Unity control as were all newspapers, explained the reason: 'Norway's saviour and leader Vidkun Quisling arrives in Trondheim on Friday. Show him the honour he deserves. Fly your flag high during the four days in which he is the guest of our city. Whoever does not do so is not a true Norwegian.' The day before Quisling was due to arrive the mayor of the city, in anticipation of trouble from Gleditsch, sent him a personal letter reminding him of his moral obligation, as a recipient of state support at the Trøndelag Theatre, to fly the national flag outside his theatre. But Gleditsch was alert to any attempt by the Quisling regime to identify itself with mainstream patriotism, and when the party gathering opened on the 14th the flagpoles outside the Trøndelag building were conspicuously bare. Acting on his own initiative, Rogstad telephoned Gleditsch and told him to hoist the flags. Gleditsch explained that the flagpoles standing outside the theatre technically belonged to the Theatre Café, which was part of the theatre complex but administratively independent of it. Not being in receipt of state support it was under no obligation to hoist a flag when asked to do so. Suspecting that the matter might not end there, Gleditsch then ordered his carpenters to remove the flagpoles and had them sent to the workshop for 'necessary repairs'. So when Rogstad again telephoned to insist that flags be flown Gleditsch could reply in all honesty that this was simply impossible, since he no longer had any flagpoles.

It was an apparently trivial victory over a particularly driven young Norwegian Nazi. There was a replay a couple of months afterwards, on the occasion of the State Act. The Theatre Directorate sent Gleditsch a telegram reminding him that flags were to be flown on all public buildings on 1, 2 and 3 February in celebration of National Unity's great day. Gleditsch put a slightly different spin on his response this time: the theatre couldn't fly any flags because the theatre didn't have any flags. Again, no flags flew on the appointed days, and Gleditsch had once again emerged triumphant from an encounter with the National Unity authorities. But these were dangerous triumphs.

By this time the authorities were communicating with Gleditsch through the office of the *Teaterdirektoratet*. Not having a flag was a legitimate excuse for not flying one, and early in July 1942 he received a letter from the head of the *Teaterdirektoratet*, Finn Halvorsen, offering to provide as many flags as he needed; how many *did* he need? Despite a reminder that the matter was urgent Gleditsch did not deign to reply until late August, his letter of response his trademark mixture of insolence lightly disguised as bureaucratic pedantry. Aware that the patience of his opponents might be wearing thin by this time, he concluded by saying that *of course* the theatre would like to have a flag, and that he would do his best to find a suitable place outside the theatre to put a flagpole from which to fly his new flag, once he had it.

In all its bureaucratic absurdity this long-running battle of the flags was what led to Gleditsch's death. Probably inspired directly by his experiences with Gleditsch and the way in which the director had turned his theatre into what was viewed in local National Unity circles as a *jøssingreir* ('den of traitors'), early in 1942 Henrik Rogstad had issued a secret order to National Unity officials in the region to begin compiling lists of names of the most prominent *jøssinger* in their areas, and to grade them 'according to the degree of danger posed and the degree of hostility shown'. Most of those he approached had little enthusiasm for the project and quietly ignored the order. But Rogstad was serious about the national socialist revolution. He drew up his own list, and Henry Gleditsch's was probably the first name on it as a voice whose influence on loyal Norwegians he, along with the Reichskommissar and Vidkun Quisling, feared even more than the bombs and firearms of the Osvald Group and the saboteurs of Milorg. In the absence of a native aristocracy – abolished by law in Norway in 1827 – intellectual voices of conscience such as Gleditsch's had become a cultural elite capable of strongly influencing public opinion on matters of national importance for what remained a very small society.

The Nazis referred to such people as the opposition's *åndelige opphavsmenn* ('spiritual inspirators') and, as Bishop Berggrav, Viggo Hansteen and Einar Høigård had been in their time, so now did Gleditsch become a focus of their attention. As part of the second Civilian State of Emergency declared in the Trøndelag region on 6 October 1942 following the Majavatn raid,* Gleditsch became one of ten prominent local individuals arrested as 'scapegoat victims'. He was picked up at his theatre, where he had been making last-minute preparations for the opening night of *The Wild Duck*, and marched through the streets to Gestapo headquarters at the Misjonshotell (Mission Hotel) and locked in a room. At 8 p.m. he had the eerie and terrifying experience of hearing the announcement of his own execution and that of the nine others over loudspeakers that boomed the news out across Trondheim's deserted city centre as though these had already taken place. At 10 p.m. he was taken from the hotel and driven with the others the 70 kilometres to Falstad concentration camp where two more men from the list were picked up. They were then driven the short distance to a densely wooded place, the van stopped, the back door was opened and the German officer in charge of the execution detail, Oskar Hans, told them to get out. He informed them they had been found guilty of supporting criminal sabotage activities and the sentence of death would be carried out immediately. Gleditsch, who spoke German, translated for the others. They were then taken, two by two, blindfolded and with hands tied behind their back, to stand at the edge of a large open grave into which they fell when shot by the ten members of the firing squad.[56]

For obvious reasons, the première of *The Wild Duck* was postponed until the state of emergency was over. And when it did open two weeks later the audience rose to their feet at the curtain and simply stood for long moments in a silent tribute to Gleditsch's memory before going home. Two years after Gleditsch's death, an actor named Knut Riise Jacobsen was arrested after he was found to have been operating a radio transmitter in the catwalk above the stage, disguising it as part of the theatre's own electrical

---

* See p. 109.

network. It is sobering to reflect that a man who neglected to buy flowers for a visiting troop of German actors, who ran out of flags and flagpoles, and who put on plays about obstinate men of God in remote Norwegian valleys and seventeenth-century witch hunts in Bergen was considered such an obstacle to the success of the national socialist revolution in Norway that it cost him his life; while another, who transmitted sensitive military information from the same venue to the Allies, was merely sent to the prison camp at Grini and spent the rest of the war there.

In the earliest period of the occupation, with people too depressed to even want to be entertained, attendances at the cinema sank. After radios were confiscated, however, it was only natural that Norwegians in search of escape should turn to film. Films from Britain and the United States were banned in the first year of the occupation, but in addition to the obligatory German films audiences could see films from Denmark and Sweden, France and Hungary. Attendances rose dramatically, from 11 million tickets sold in 1940 to 26 million in 1945. The Germans initially tried to persuade Norwegians that as a minor member of the brotherhood of Germanic peoples they had no right to a film industry of their own, but the appointment of the Nationalist Gulbrand Lunde as Minister of Culture and General Education changed the situation and the film industry was left to develop alone, provided it did so along lines acceptable to the German authorities. The result was the establishment of *Statens Filmdirektoratet* (the State Film Department). It was left largely to finance itself, which it did by raising tax on tickets – categorised as a luxury tax – from a pre-war level of 10 per cent to 30 and later 40 per cent of the gross income from ticket sales for foreign films, and from 5 per cent to 25 per cent on Norwegian-made films. This brought in a huge amount of money, but as few Norwegian film directors were interested in making films that promoted national socialism as a way of life the money was left unused and in due course earmarked for the creation of a studio village. Originally planned for the northern outskirts of Oslo where the student village of Kringsjå now stands, this came to nothing, and by the end of the war the State Film Department had amassed a sum of money from the tax on ticket sales equivalent in value to 18 million pounds sterling today. This vast sum of money was retained after the war for the creation of a new body, still state-run but to very different ends, an arrangement which survives to this day as the Norwegian Film Institute.

National Unity's hopes for a film industry that would change the way people thought and felt and so play its part in the proposed national socialist revolution of the country soon had to be abandoned as Norwegians voted with their backsides for farces, smutty comedies, romantic melodramas and other diversions from the awfulness of everyday life. The most popular Norwegian film during the occupation years was *Vigdis*, a romantic comedy directed by Helge Lunde. It had its première in Oslo on 2 August 1943. Vigdis is the daughter of a schoolteacher and a choirmaster. A happy, fun-loving girl, her pious parents worry she'll get herself a bad name in the village. She's secretly in love with the local doctor, Falck, who has no idea who she is and is anyway engaged to be married to someone else. After a dance in the village hall Vigdis hides in the back seat of his car and on the drive home he finds her there. One thing leads to another and they end up kissing. Various other characters appear to confuse the situation and then, nine months later, Vigdis gives birth to a child. She refuses to say who the father is. Finally, the magistrate presiding over a paternity hearing learns that his old friend Dr Falck is the father. The film ends with Vigdis and Falck setting up home together. *Vigdis* is not unlike a Norwegian version of the George Formby films that were popular with wartime audiences in the United Kingdom, but with a morality that would have seemed out of place in a Formby film. With its small-town setting, its doctors and lawyers, its bedroom secrets and sometimes inscrutable morality, *Vigdis* evokes rather the world of the later plays of Henrik Ibsen.

Vigdis was based on a 1931 novel entitled *Vigdis and the Fathers of Her Child* by the pseudonymous 'Franz Ferdinand'. The author's real name was Albert Wiesener, a lawyer and early member of National Unity who was expelled from the party in 1937 for his opposition to Quisling's leadership. Wiesener was frequently ordered to defend Norwegians brought before German military courts on charges of espionage and crimes of violence against the occupying forces. In spite of his political sympathies, he was known to be a decent man who put the law above his own political inclinations. Norwegian audiences that queued to see *Vigdis* in record numbers in 1943 would have known they would have to sit through a propaganda newsreel film before the escapist fun could begin. In the early days of the occupation it was possible simply to turn up late in order to miss it, until National Unity authorities got wise to the ploy and ordered the doors to be closed after the advertised start of the evening's programme. Audiences responded by indulging in sustained fits of coughing throughout the newsreel screening, fusillades of artificial flatulence, catcalls and so on during reports featuring the doings of Nazi politicians, *hird* members and German soldiers. It might have seemed innocent enough, but Norwegian Nazis knew that few things are more devastating to power than being laughed at and audience members were frequently reported for such behaviour and sometimes arrested and fined. Many of these cases landed on the desk of a Norwegian policeman named Gunnar Waaler in his role as legal adviser to National Unity's public prosecutor.

PART 4

GUNNAR WAALER'S WAR

9

Waaler's Work

From the start it was obvious to the invaders that the task of administering occupied Norway would be greatly simplified if they were able to reach a *modus vivendi* with the native police force. That made it a matter of urgency to set about a process of Nazifying the Norwegian police. Success would enable them in due course to leave in their hands many of the most controversial and distasteful measures involved in subjugating the population, including, when the time came, arresting Norwegian Jews and arranging for their expulsion. Following Terboven's speech of 25 September 1940 and the appointment of National Unity as the party of government, this process of Nazification was pursued with a rare dedication that saw 30 per cent of ordinary Norwegian policemen join the party, a far higher percentage than any other comparable professional group. However, though party membership was recommended and urged, it was not compulsory. For many who joined after 25 September, membership was no more than a bureaucratic detail. They neither paid their subscriptions nor attended party meetings.

One of the earliest administrative changes following the establishment of the one-party state had been to split the Department of Justice into separate departments of Justice and Policing. The new ministers in charge, respectively Sverre Riisnæs and Jonas Lie, had together set about the ideological and structural reform of the Norwegian police force. New uniforms had been introduced. A new branch of the police force, the *Statspoliti* (*Stapo*), was introduced in the summer of 1941, on the model of the German *Geheime Staatspolizei* (Gestapo). Membership of National Unity was compulsory in this ideologically bound force. Its brief was to identify and deal with 'political crimes'. In the context of the occupation that meant any expression of opposition, verbally or by deed, to the progress of the national socialist revolution. It was Gunnar Waaler's posting to the legal department serving this new branch of the force in the summer of 1941 that started him on his career as a 'spiritual saboteur' of the 'new age' and in due course turned him into one of Milorg's most valuable double-agents.

Waaler was a thirty-six-year-old career policeman, the son of a parish priest and his wife from Lillestrøm, some 30 kilometres north of Oslo.[57] Following military and legal training he moved in 1936 to Bergen where he worked as a *politifullmektig* (police prosecutor), meaning that it was his job to study the facts of a case and decide whether to recommend it for prosecution or dismiss it. He lived alone with his dog, Varja. On the night of the invasion he had been out with a friend from his student days, Gerhard Mathiesen, and a local businessman named Ludvig Gåsland. They finished the evening at Waaler's flat in the Kalmarhuset on Jon Smørs gate. At some point the sound of gunfire was heard from out in the fjord. Waaler and one of his guests went out onto the balcony to see what was going on. The caretaker of the flats, a man named Fredrik Helle, observed them from his window. In a sworn statement made on 30 June 1946 as part of the judicial reckoning after the liberation, Helle described what he then saw. Both men were visibly drunk. Waaler was waving and gesticulating with a sabre which Helle had earlier seen hanging on the wall of his apartment. The air-raid sirens sounded and Waaler's companion at once made his way down to the air-raid shelter. Waaler remained where he was. As the air-raid warden Helle then had to go down into the shelter himself, where he saw Waaler's friend, 'sitting with the women', as he pointedly remarked. A half hour later, after the all-clear had sounded, he saw the two again on Waaler's terrace and could hear Waaler mocking his companion for his timidity. Helle went on to describe another incident in Bergen, from the winter of 1941. Some children had been throwing snowballs at passersby from a nearby bridge. Waaler suddenly appeared behind them brandishing 'a large dog-whip', which he often carried when out walking with Varja. He was wearing his police uniform and was 'beside himself with rage'. He began to whip the children. Helle stood in his doorway and watched as passersby remonstrated with Waaler. 'No one throws snowballs at me!' was Waaler's unrepentant response. In a final observation Helle told the police officer interviewing him that he had once noticed Waaler had a dagger hanging on the wall next to the sabre. 'It had some kind of inscription on it,' he remembered, 'Something like *Blut und Ehre*.' Summing things up, he recalled that Waaler seemed to him 'very pro-German. I considered him a Nazi though I didn't know whether or not he was a member of National Unity. Waaler was a brutal and unsympathetic person who could often be extremely crude in his manner. That's how most people thought of him.'

Truth may well be the first casualty of war, but it can as frequently be the last. These were the bitter and vengeful accusations made after the liberation by a man facing prosecution as a member of National Unity and concerned to do all he could to blacken Waaler's name and make his claim to have been a loyalist from the start of the invasion as difficult to prove as possible. Arrested and interviewed, former colleagues in the Norwegian State Police recalled his 'jubilation' at the German invasion; his mockery of the Norwegians who resisted it; his approval of the return of the death penalty under the Germans. With particularly damning attention to detail, one colleague recalled Waaler's conduct on a trip to Berlin in September 1940 to study German police methods. The hand-picked group of officers all spoke the language. None were Nazis, but this was part of the German 'charm offensive' that characterised the earliest period of the occupation, when the Nazi belief in racial brotherhood persuaded them that Norwegians could, potentially, be persuaded to join Germania voluntarily, and before they had become aware of the extent and ferocity of Norwegian opposition to national socialism. The group had been informed that at some point they would meet and dine with Reinhard Heydrich, operational head of the German SS and Heinrich Himmler's second-in-command, and that they might be invited to join the SS as honorary members.

Himmler had taken charge of this organisation in the late 1920s and by 1933 had turned it from an elite personal bodyguard for Adolf Hitler into an armed force of over 52,000 men, indoctrinated with the values associated with warrior cults like the Japanese samurai and the Knights of Bushido. Between them Himmler and Heydrich had managed to invest the SS with a dark glamour that exerted a fascination for any young man with an authoritarian cast of mind, and this youthful group of Norwegian officers were no different from any others in this respect.

Prior to the dinner with Heydrich there was much discussion among some of the group of Norwegians about entry criteria into the SS. Little was known of these, and some wild claims were made. Rampant virility and an indifference to disgust were believed to be among the desired qualities, and Waaler's former colleagues were keen to stress their former colleague's fervent desire to be found acceptable. One evening the group were taken to the Berlin Institute of Pathology to be shown the day's harvest of suicides and unidentified dead in the mortuary. An officer named Nils Dagestad later claimed that, while most of them recoiled in disgust from the sight and smell of these unfortunates, Waaler had mocked them for their weak stomachs. He made a point of touching the corpses and pressed his nose as close to the flesh as possible the better to demonstrate his indifference to the smell.

The same informant noted that Waaler was the last to leave the mortuary. In a sworn statement after the war Dagestad originally used a word – which he modified on signature – implying that Waaler was so keen to prove his fitness to join the SS that he had taken the opportunity to molest one of the corpses. In a similar but less dramatic vein, Waaler's colleagues reported that he had made a fool of himself at a Berlin nightclub, buying a huge bunch of flowers for the club's torch singer in hopes of bedding her later and then having the gall to ask fellow officers to pay for the flowers with a whip-round.

In the immediate aftermath of the liberation, Waaler had to confront and refute these and other accusations made against him by men for whom his betrayal of friendship was, in their eyes, a greater crime than their own in having supported the occupiers. He set about the task with judicial thoroughness. It had not been him waving the sabre on the balcony on the night of 9 April. That was his friend Mathiesen, who had been using it as a pointer as they tried to ascertain the nationality of the approaching warships. He had not touched alcohol that evening. In Helle's account the caretaker had confused two knives. The incisions on the one hanging next to the sabre were not German but Chinese pictograms, the meaning of which, Waaler noted, he had never troubled to find out. The knife with *Blut und Ehre* and the swastika was one he used in his office as a letter opener. He described it as 'a quite ordinary Hitlerjugend knife'. A friend had brought it back as a present after a trip to Germany in the summer of 1933. It was a cheap souvenir bought for a couple of marks from a street-trader. 'On 9 April 1940 I carefully packed that knife away and it has never seen the light of day since.' As for the accusation that he – Waaler – was generally regarded as a brutal, crude and unsympathetic person, 'well', he wrote, 'that may be so. But all the time I was in Bergen I never saw any sign of it from Helle. You might suppose he would have been a little reserved when in the company of a common Nazi who was so brutal, crude and unsympathetic. Under the difficult circumstances it's understandable that he tried to avoid being openly rude – but did he really have to go to the opposite extreme and come rushing up to me with a big smile on his face every time he saw me and then detain me with his inane babble for the next thirty minutes?' As for the accusation of necrophilia in the Berlin mortuary, Waaler responded that he had 'quietly followed the tour like everyone else. Everyone was in everyone else's sight at all times, and if anyone had behaved in an unusual or inappropriate way then all present would have noticed. I spent the entire time in the company of Officer Eek from Aker, Officer Aamodt and Superintendent Hauge.' The 'nightclub' was a quite ordinary Berlin restaurant and the 'torch singer' a Hungarian woman whose job it was briefly to provide male guests with female company, sitting at their table for a half hour before moving on. In conventionally courteous response, he concluded, he had bought her a couple of flowers.

Oddly, there were no revelations about Waaler's pathological desire to join the SS on the evening of the actual dinner with the head of Hitler's *Schutzstaffel*. A select group of four were invited to dine with Heydrich, and it was Heydrich himself who raised the subject of SS membership for foreign nationals. This led to a discussion among the Norwegians about the degree to which such a thing would be appropriate, given the circumstances. One guest wondered how a German would have been regarded who had been admitted to a comparable French organisation during the French occupation of the Rhineland; as a traitor, surely? Heydrich protested vigorously, saying that the only intention behind any invitation made to foreigners lay in the honour; there was no question of active military involvement. Any foreigners admitted to the cult-like organisation would be free to leave whenever they liked, unlike German initiates who were bound to it for life, along with their families.

The guests were asked for a response. Egil Olbjørn expressed his appreciation of the offer but declined to accept it. Erik Muhle rejected it on the grounds of the circumstances – the occupation. Olbjørn then gestured towards Waaler: what did he think of Heydrich's offer? Waaler had so far not spoken at all. 'If one is sympathetic towards national socialism,' he began. 'And one believes that a closer co-operation between Norway and Germany would be of mutual benefit, then one should accept the offer. Otherwise not.' It was an exemplary judicial response, hard to respond to and clinically free of anything resembling a personal opinion. In the occupation years that followed, and after his arrest by the Gestapo, when none of his resistance contacts expected ever to see him again, it was this talent for answering without actually answering at all that enabled Waaler to escape with his life.

Gunnar Waaler was culturally pro-German and a fluent speaker of the language, but his sense of outrage at the imposition of the occupation never wavered. He had spent the first two months of the occupation trying to join the fighting as a *vernepliktig* (conscripted reservist). He attempted to join a Norwegian unit still fighting at Voss, but even before he left Bergen the force there had surrendered. At the end of April he made his way north by sea to join the fighting at Åndalsnes and Dombås, but on reaching Eivindvik in Sogn he learned that the troops at Åndalsnes had withdrawn, leaving him with no option but to return to Bergen.

In the middle of May he sailed once more from Bergen, bound for Oslo. His plan was to cross into Sweden, travel north and cross the border back into northern Norway, where heavy fighting was still taking place. He made his way via Rødenes in Østfold and through the forest into Sweden, but his party were stopped and sent back into Norway by a Swedish border patrol. They crossed again the following night at a point further north. From here he made his way to Stockholm, where he reported for duty at the Norwegian legation. A Major Just put him in command of a troop of sixty men, with orders to lead them north to Rovaniemi, the capital of Lapland, in northern Finland and cross into Norway at Kirkenes. Before he could do this Norway had surrendered, and Waaler and his men were stopped by the Finns at Torneå and sent back to Sweden. Back in Stockholm, Waaler and a French-speaking Danish officer then approached the French embassy to offer their services. Plans were made to send them via Moscow and Odessa to join Maxine Weygand's French 'oriental army' in Syria, but this time it was the French capitulation that put a stop to Waaler's efforts to join the fighting. In desperation the two men then approached the British Embassy. There was briefly talk of sending them to Canada, but nothing came of this either. They had no money left to finance any further attempts to join the fighting and when the Swedes arranged for a special refugee train for stranded Norwegians who wanted to go home, Waaler accepted the situation, boarded the train and made his way back to Bergen, where he resumed his work as a police prosecutor.

By the autumn of 1940, with the occupation a fact of life and the prospect of a British counter-invasion remote, Waaler had drifted into the widespread ambivalence that characterised the response of most of those in positions of authority. Many looked to the situation in Denmark, where the king and government, denied the option of flight by the swiftness of the German invasion, were taking a credible stand against attempts to impose national socialist values on the country by the Germans. The Germans for their part were content with the strategic gain that made them masters of the Baltic and deferred any attempt to impose a national socialist revolution on the Danes until a later date. The native Danish Nazi Party enjoyed as little electoral support as National Unity did in Norway, but crucially, the party had not produced a Quisling of its own.

By the time Waaler returned from the study trip to Berlin in September 1940, National Unity was the only legal political party left in Norway. Not long after Terboven's speech of 25 September 1940 a conference of senior police officers was held in Oslo at which both Jonas Lie and Sverre Riisnæs were present. Lie gave a keynote speech on the role of the police in the new era of national socialist Norway. Officially the position remained that party membership was a matter for the individual conscience, recommended but not compulsory. During session breaks Lie was seen in intense conversation with the Bergen police chief, a man named August Pedersen. On his return to Bergen Pedersen called a meeting of his senior officers and told them that every officer in the Oslo and Trondheim forces had already joined National Unity. The announcement had its intended effect; the Bergen force enrolled *en masse*.

Like the majority of the forces' more experienced officers, Waaler's principal concern in joining remained the protection of the Norwegian public at a difficult time. A refusal to join National Unity would see their functions taken over by Germans or, even worse, by members of the Quisling's *hird*, whose reputation for physical violence, established during National Unity's election campaigns in the 1930s and confirmed during the campaigns of the Conscience Struggle, had worsened with the arrival of their spiritual mentors. Waaler recalled after the war that at the time enrolment seemed no more than a bureaucratic triviality. But August Pedersen's lie would have serious repercussions once the Nygaardsvold government in London declared National Unity an illegal organisation in December 1944 and criminalised membership, with retroactive effect.

In the spring of 1941 Waaler was transferred to Oslo to serve as a police prosecutor in the *utrykningspolitiet* (Active Response Group). A month later this would change its name to become the *Statspolitiet* (the Norwegian State Police), always abbreviated as Stapo, and commence operations as a political branch of the police dedicated to the prevention of crimes 'against the new order'. Waaler was ordered to serve as case adviser to the new public prosecutor, Jørgen Nordvik. All crimes defined by the new regime as being political and directed against the Nazi state landed on Waaler's desk. It was a poisoned chalice of a job. True to the Führer principle at the heart of the attempted revolution that was now under way, Waaler's functions were limited to advising Nordvik on whether or not to proceed in the 'political' cases that landed on his desk. The final decision was Nordvik's.

From his first days in Nordvik's office the experience shocked and disheartened Waaler. For many non-adherents, national socialism still seemed essentially an ideology in passionate opposition to revolutionary international communism. In Norway the ideology had not as yet been tainted by an increasingly savage and exclusive insistence on the 'national' element in the Nazis' alternative version of socialism. The scales fell from Waaler's eyes as one so-called 'political' case after another landed on his desk:

> In the course of my work on political cases in the summer of 1941 I got an insight into the inner workings of National Unity to which I had previously not been privy. Among the party leaders crime and corruption were rife. No party member was to be punished. Members of the *hird* carried out the most savage attacks on innocent people – and the cases were dismissed. *Jøssinger* were persecuted, held in prison and punished for things that were not contrary to Norwegian law. From that time onwards my attitude towards National Unity, its leaders and its whole nature became one of complete opposition. It was not simply that I should be compelled to deal with these cases; I was now on public display as Special Police Prosecutor for all of Oslo.

As his own notes and comments from the period of his secondment as Special Police Prosecutor to the attorney general show, Waaler now commenced a game of great subtlety that involved a spiritual sabotage of the national socialist revolution. In a world of deception, illusions, lies, dishonesties and doublethink, in which a colleague's true colours were impossible to gauge, he played to perfection the role of the highly principled 'good' Nazi. In a party in which conscience counted for little he played the part of the conscience of national socialism. Waaler's notes of the hundreds of cases that crossed his desk during his three years at the Public Prosecutor's Office provide a remarkable record of the banal awfulness of life in occupied Norway during those years. The petty corruptions. The score-settling and tale-telling. The curtailments of the basic rights to freedom of speech and thought. They also show how persistently he tried to sabotage any attempt by National Unity members to define the party as essentially a self-help and self-protection organisation by claiming that virtually any case in which a party member was the subject of a complaint or accusation be handled as a 'political case' and therefore not subject to the due processes of law. With an unwavering and even tedious uprightness he denies over and over again to his superior Nordvik that these cases have any 'political' dimension at all. That his arguments were frequently ignored by the public prosecutor was hardly his fault:

5) – Case – IV – 6
Serious assault on a Jew. – People watching. A *hirdman* suddenly walks over and punches a bystander in the face and knocks him over.
W:* Sent with relevant documents Police Dept. in compliance with Justice Dept. circular of 21/1 41 $ 3. i.f.
According to paragraph $228 anyone who acts violently towards another is to be punished, unless the assailant can show he acted in response to a preceding assault or other provocation. A presumption or suspicion that such provocation must have existed is not sufficient grounds for impunity.
In this particular case there is no supplementary evidence whatever of such a provocation beyond the assailant's own claim. That any such provocation came specifically from the victim not even the accused is able to maintain, (cf the accused's own explanation: '... but if the complainant himself was responsible for any of these (shouted insults) I am unable to say with certainty.'
As in this case there can be no question of impunity on the ground of provocation, and as there appear to be no other legal grounds for impunity, I find that Arne Riedeger must appear before the People's Court to face a charge under Strfl. $228

---

* W. is Waaler himself.

Not accepted. – The charge against *hirdman* Riedeger was dropped by the Public Prosecutor.

11) Case VII – 1
   Charles Stravseth, *hirdman*.
   Sadistic treatment of interned schoolteachers in Ørlandet.
   Even Stapo suggest charges be made.
   W. (in the absence of the Public Prosecutor) confers with Ålvik Pedersen of the People's Court. – What follows is a report of the meeting dated 25/7 42:
   On Thursday 23/7 I had a meeting with Judge Ålvik Pedersen of the People's Court to discuss this case and read the most important extracts to him. – My own view of this matter – I then said to him – is that this type of person should be punished with extreme severity, the findings made public, and the one involved permanently expelled from the party. It is undeniable that a large number of the worst kinds of people, including those who have been in and out of jail many times, have joined the party and then allowed their criminal propensities free rein as being under the protection of the party. A man like this does more damage to National Unity than a hundred propaganda broadcasts from London. The National Unity must ruthlessly weed out and expel these types, or the party will be destroyed from within.
   Instead – I went on – Nordvik has consistently followed a line that under any and all circumstances, *the law will hold a protective hand over National Unity members, regardless of the nature of their crime.* This case is by no means an isolated incident. During the year in which I have been working in the Public Prosecutor's Office there has been a long series of cases in which National Unity members have been guilty of the worst crimes imaginable, without a single charge being raised against any of them. Not a single one of these cases has ever led to an appearance before the People's Court. They are guilty of the most violent physical attacks and assaults, the

most outrageous manipulation of the rationing system, yet nothing is ever done about them. The idea surely is that the party should work towards achieving the goals it has set for itself, not simply be a group of people dedicated to protecting their own and each other's interest at any price. It's bad enough when people see National Unity members and *hirdmen* behaving in this way, and it makes it ten times worse when people see the constituted authority holding a protecting hand over them and accepting such criminal activity. If one makes an example of this particular man in this particular case and makes it clear that such behaviour is simply intolerable to National Unity, then this would do more to make the party respected than a hundred propaganda lectures.

The reason I've come here to talk to you about this – I continued – is because I intend to request that the court issue a custody warrant in this case and hand down a term of imprisonment in a subsequent trial – so I need to know beforehand whether I can count on such a request being met. If – as happened in a recent case – a man with both a permanent address and a full-time job can be held in custody for five weeks for nothing more serious than having torn the *solkors* logo out of his tram ticket, then surely a man like this can be held in custody too.

The judge responded that as it was now some time since the alleged incidents had taken place (in April this year, the case only now having reached this stage), the man had a permanent address and was, after all, a policeman (in charge of the kennels), then there was little danger of his doing it again, or of trying to influence witnesses…

To this I responded that in a large number of cases involving people from the other side who had committed some crime, often of the most trivial nature, and all other circumstances being equal, the People's Court had not had any hesitation in ordering detention in custody, often for long periods (cf the man with the tram ticket). I am aware of all these other circumstances you mention, but in my view we should be making it very clear that behaviour like this will simply not be tolerated.

My reason for wanting to talk to you about this is not essentially because of this one single case but because I believe that firm action in this particular case can be used to signal a *widespread* change of attitude in such cases involving party members.

The judge replied that he would take a closer look at the matter and get back to me.

The next day I received the documents in return with a note attached:

'I see no reason to issue an arrest warrant in this case. Å P'

(This note written and signed in Ålvik Pedersen's own hand) – Note is in doc. coll. VII – 1

W: raises the case verbally with Nordvik.

Public Prosecutor drops the case, citing 85 II

Case XXX – 14

Cramer Norbye – syphilitic *hirdman* and Kruse Bruu, *hirdman* – in full uniform visit a 76-year-old woman on Bygdø and by threats get her to bequeath her house to a girlfriend of one of the *hirdmen*. They search her shop for tobacco, demand permission to pick her redcurrant bushes, etc etc.

Oslo Criminal Pol. Send the case to statsadv* in Oslo and suggest an arraignment at Aker District Court.

The statsadvokat (Jak. Andersen) refers the case to the Public Prosecutor's Office 'in case you find there to be a political dimension to this case...'

W: Case returned to statsadv. Oslo.

I see no reason to regard this case as having any political dimension. Beyond the fact that the two culprits are both National Unity members it has no other possible political

---

* *Statsadvokat*, public prosecutor

aspect. The case is therefore to be treated as a matter for ordinary criminal law and the state prosecutors themselves to decide whether or not to formally charge these two.

28 October 1942 GW

Public Prosecutor refers the case to the National Unity General secretariat.

It remains there for several months.

Two reminders sent in 1942 – a third in 1943.

Additionally twice sent a secretary from the Public Prosecutor's Office to the General Secretariat requesting the documents in the case be returned – in vain.

Documents finally released in February.

W. repeats his earlier suggestion of 28/10 42.

Public Prosecutor accepts.

Case tried in May 1943 in Aker Kriminalrett:

Six months' jail for each *hirdman*.

21) Case V – 23

Man removed the *solkors* emblem from his tram ticket.

Held in custody 26/6 – Judge Dale of the People's Court extends custody order to 30/7 42. – Stapo propose the case be put before the People's Court on the basis of the ordinance governing respect for the flag.

In the Public Prosecutor's absence W. issues a fine of NOK 150 – subs. 21 days jail already served in custody. W. orders the man's immediate release.

33) Case IX – 1

Bureau head Feyling has information regarding secret address of the Church Free Leadership organisation and orders Stapo to raid the Arguskontoret.

Feyling sends a copy of the order to the Public Prosecutor's Office.

W. informed Hallesbye. – Church Free Leadership archives moved, nothing found when Stapo make the raid.

Oct/Nov. 1942

6) Case X – 3

A man arrested for saying Quisling ought to be tied up and eaten by rats.

Insufficient evidence and the police chief in Lillehammer suggests the case be dismissed.

W: Case returned to the Chief of Police in Lillehammer advising the case be dismissed as suggested.

9/2 43 GW

Accepted by PP.

39) Case XV – 3

Woman at the cinema as the minister-president appears on the screen: 'Look at the fat pig!'

Stapo/Police Chief Rød suggests arraignment before the People's Court for contravention of the law of 12/3 42 $2 prohibiting 'the public expression of provocative utterances concerning persons of authority and intended to undermine public trust in the leadership of the state, in such a way that...'

W:

'Returned to Stapo. – As described the situation is hardly covered by the legislation mentioned, as it seems to me that 'public trust in the leadership of the state' is hardly undermined or perturbed by the alleged words of fru Lina Skaug at the Eldorado Cinema on Tuesday 16 February 1943 at 19.00.

The case may be resolved by the imposition of a fine of NOK 50 – subs. 9 d.f. under para. $ 350

2/6 43 GW

A particularly fateful case that came before Waaler was that of Karsten Løvestad, the border guide who shot and killed a Nazi policeman aboard the Halden train on the night of 22 October 1942

while taking a group of Jewish refugees to the Swedish border.*
Løvestad had been awaiting trial at Grini since his arrest. Waaler
tried to argue against the prosecution's demand for the death
penalty for Løvestad:

> 38) Case IX – 33
> Copy of W's note dated 21/1/43 (in document collection IX – 33):
> '... I then asked the PP if it really was so absolutely necessary to have this Løvestad sentenced to death. – I urged him to consider the fact that carrying out a death sentence would be a terrible mistake, that any death sentence handed down by National Unity authorities would cause a sensation and provide our opponents with invaluable propaganda. –
> To which he (Nordvik) remarked only that a death sentence was necessary on generally preventative grounds. He referred to the numerous attacks on and killings of Norwegian policemen (*Stapo* men).
> In response I said that the numerous death sentences already carried out by the Germans had not had any preventative effect, and that a death sentence handed down by a Norwegian court was unlikely to be any more effective in that regard. I repeated the argument that the negative propaganda effect of a death sentence was of much greater significance. – I also suggested to him that when he, as Public Prosecutor, recommended that the People's Court hand down a death sentence this would exonerate him from any blame from the likes of Riisnæs and others, since the matter would then be entirely in the hands of the People's Court (A majority of the People's Court had already announced that they would not hand down death sentences).
> I also drew his attention to the fact that handing the case over to the Germans was the same as ensuring that Løvestad

---

* See p. 210.

would be given a death sentence. The Public Prosecutor's response was that he was aware of this.

At this point the telephone in Nordvik's office started ringing and our conversation ended. And there was really little more to be said on the matter.

21/1 43 GW

Though a National Unity creation, the People's Court had proved surprisingly resilient in the face of attempts to turn it into an instrument of party policy and remained faithful to the concept of impartiality before the law. In discussions with the court's foreman Waaler had obtained assurances that it would not, under any circumstances, hand down a death sentence. However, Sverre Riisnæs at the Ministry of Justice had foreseen this eventuality and handed the case over to be tried by the Germans. To Riisnæs other members of the National Unity government, anxious to prove themselves capable of imposing a hardline national socialist revolution on Norway without German assistance, the case presented a strong argument for the creation of a special Norwegian court that had the power to pass death sentences on its own without the embarrassing need for German help. An ideal opportunity for the creation of just such a court would arise in the late summer of 1943.

10

The Execution of Inspector Gunnar Eilifsen, August 1943

For Reichskommissar Josef Terboven, the inability and even unwillingness of the People's Court to hand down a death sentence was further evidence of the squeamish nature of Norwegian national socialism. A showdown between the hardcore Nazism of the occupiers and the softer understandings of Quisling's National Unity was inevitable. Precipitated perhaps by the Løvestad impasse and its resolution, in the late summer of 1943 a situation arose almost out of nothing to force the issue.

The final defeat of the German Sixth Army at Stalingrad in February 1943 was seen by both sides as a turning point in the war. Hitler became convinced that the Allies were planning an imminent invasion in the north of Norway, a possibility that made the imposition of domestic stability in the country more of a priority than ever. Sabotage activities were on the increase. Resistance to the 'call-up' to Work Service was widespread. Respect for the Quisling government was dwindling still further and Terboven was becoming increasingly concerned about its ability to control the population. In 1942, the year of the Conscience Struggle, at a time when Germany was otherwise triumphant on all fronts,

National Unity had failed in all its various attempts to enforce loyalty to Quisling and inculcate party values in the schools, universities, churches and sports clubs. By early 1943, with the beginnings of a crisis becoming visible, Quisling stepped up his attempts to impress Hitler with the number of ideologically inspired young men and women he would be able to provide for his leader. On 22 February his government passed a law ordering all men between the ages of eighteen and fifty-five and women between twenty-one and forty to report for Work Service.[58] The justification was that there was a pressing need for a national programme to ensure supplies of food from the farms, but on the basis of inside information from, among others, Gunnar Waaler, the resistance movement issued another of its *paroles* urging conscripts to ignore the order. A second *parole* followed in June urging loyal police officers to refuse to arrest anyone who failed to respond when conscripted for Work Service. This *parole* led directly to the return of the death penalty to Norwegian law after an absence of almost forty years.

Gunnar Eilifsen was a forty-six-year-old career policeman. Like Waaler, he had joined National Unity while serving in Bergen in late 1940 as part of the mass enrolment. Four months later he changed his mind and resigned, to the annoyance of his friend and colleague Jonas Lie, who took the resignation personally. When he remonstrated with Eilifsen, Eilifsen insisted it was a matter of conscience and nothing else. He quoted from the gospel of Mark – 'For what shall it profit a man if he shall gain the whole world and lose his own soul?' – to which Lie replied: 'Then you can go to hell.'

Lie then proceeded to demote his friend, and by the spring of 1943 Eilifsen was at a suburban station in Oslo dealing with ordinary criminal offences. On 9 August he was contacted by Bernard Askvig, Chief of Police in Oslo, with a request for five of his men to be seconded to the State Police for a particular job. The request was not unusual, the nature of the assignment not specified, and Eilifsen routinely agreed to it. Shortly afterwards one of the five returned to the station and complained that they had been ordered to arrest three young women who had failed to attend for Work Service. All five had refused on the grounds that this was not an appropriate task for ordinary police officers.

They asked Eilifsen to support them in their protest and he did. He telephoned Askvig, described what had happened, and explained that he was supporting his men as a matter of conscience. He would certainly have known of an earlier case of subordination that involved two officers who had refused to sign documents legalising the confiscation of food. Jonas Lie had sentenced both to several months' imprisonment at Bredtveit and there was no reason to suppose the response would be any different now. Askvig again ordered Eilifsen to obey and he refused a second time. Askvig then informed Jonas Lie's right-hand man Egil Olbjørn of the situation and Olbjørn ordered Eilifsen's arrest. Jonas Lie tried to remonstrate with him. 'You make things very difficult and uncomfortable for me by refusing to obey this order.' Eilifsen remained unrepentant and the matter went back to Askvig. He tried once again to get Eilifsen to change his mind, and heard once again from Eilifsen that he could not, it was a matter of conscience.

Askvig may well have been surprised to hear that such a thing still existed among his officers. He reported the matter to Terboven. On Friday 13 August Sverre Riisnæs was summoned to a meeting with Terboven. Wilhelm Rediess, head of the German police in Norway, was present, as were Quisling and Jonas Lie. Terboven opened with some general remarks on the progress of the war, Germany's problems on the Eastern Front, Mussolini's fall and the loss of Italy to the Allies. He raised the ever more vivid spectre of a British invasion of northern Norway before broaching the subject of Eilifsen's insubordination and the appropriate response. That a senior police officer should refuse to obey an order from a superior *on the grounds of conscience* – what possible future could there be for such a society in the new Germania? Such a man should be tried, sentenced to death and executed. A

Norwegian court should be responsible for the whole procedure. It should be over and done with inside forty-eight hours. If not, then the Germans would take over the case and see to it that matters were brought to the proper conclusion. And if it should come to that, he added, the Norwegians should know that the relationship between the Norwegian and the German police forces would need to be radically redefined.

Riisnæs made the point that there was no provision in Norwegian law for the death penalty for a police officer who refused to obey an order. Terboven's response was that in that case the minister-president must simply create one. So, with the help of Terboven's own legal adviser, Riisnæs at once set about drafting such a provision and later that same day was able to present for Quisling's approval the draft of a 'Temporary Law concerning Means for the Maintenance of Law and Order during Wartime'. Offered as a supplement to the military penal code of 22 May 1902, this new paragraph decreed that in time of war the police must be considered part of the country's military and therefore be subject to military law. The following day, 14 August, Quisling signed the new law and the *Særdomstol* (Police Special Court) came into existence. Its verdicts could not be appealed. The only recourse the court allowed was an appeal for clemency to the minister-president. Most of those involved in the process comforted themselves with the existence of this option, and that it would be used. In the face of Terboven's ultimatum they had no real choice. Albert Wiesener was appointed Eilifsen's defence counsel for a trial before the new court that was to take place less than twenty-four hours later. Naturally he requested an adjournment. Naturally the request was refused.

Jonas Lie appointed three judges to try the case; Egil Olbjørn, Karl A. Marthinsen, who was head of Stapo, and, as jury foreman, the High Court judge Egil Reichborn-Kjennerud. On the evening before the trial – a Saturday – two of them, Olbjørn and Reichborn-Kjennerud, dined at Oslo's Grand Hotel with their host, Sverre

Riisnæs. Marthinsen was unable to attend. In the course of the meal Riisnæs outlined the situation to the judges, informed them of Terboven's insistence on the death penalty, and that their way out of it would be the appeal for clemency to Minister-President Quisling. Both guests protested that they must be free to reach whatever verdict the evidence suggested. Riisnæs, who perhaps knew that none of it mattered anyway, agreed.

In circumstances of the utmost secrecy the trial got under way the following morning at 11.00 a.m. in Oslo Tinghus, in Apotekergate. The enormity of what was taking place was not lost on any of those present as a handcuffed Eilifsen entered the building accompanied by armed Stapo officers. The group stopped inside the main entrance. Eilifsen smoked a cigarette. He looked calm. It was hardly possible he was aware of the pressured discussions and legislation of the last forty-eight hours.

Reichborn-Kjennerud opened by announcing that it was strictly forbidden to make any report of or reference to the proceedings that were about to take place. Eilifsen then took the stand and in response to Wiesener's questions spoke of the numerous occasions on which he had carried out orders from National Unity authorities and his own superiors, isolating this as the single instance in which he had felt obliged to disobey and again citing conscience as his grounds: it seemed to him wrong to send young Norwegian women to work in a factory making ammunition for German guns. That wasn't what Work Service was supposed to be about. Several character witnesses then took the stand, all giving him exemplary references as a good man and an outstanding officer. At this point a verdict of guilty seemed so inconceivable that the defendant smiled and nodded to colleagues seated in the spectators' benches, although not, one supposes, to either Jonas Lie or Sverre Riisnæs. Both were in attendance and cast a symbolic pall over the gathering in their black SS Norge uniforms. At a brief adjournment both spoke to Reichborn-Kjennerud, urging him to move proceedings along and get the thing over with.

When the trial resumed Albert Wiesener delivered what was generally regarded as an outstanding and even irrefutable defence of his client, urging on the judges the unconstitutional nature of the legislation under which Inspector Eilifsen was being tried for an unlawful act committed five days before the act was even defined as unlawful.

By 7 p.m. the trial was over, Eilifsen was back in his cell, and the judges had begun their deliberations. At their own trials after the liberation it emerged that between then and 11 p.m. these three men between them consumed two bottles of cognac and a bottle of aquavit. As judges they were in an impossible and even humiliating position, central characters in a farce that had to end in tragedy. Their need for alcohol in such quantities is not hard to fathom.

Or at least not hard to fathom for two of them. Reichborn-Kjennerud and Olbjørn were firmly opposed to handing down a death sentence. Reichborn-Kjennerud, the only one of the three with a legal training, was of the opinion that a jail sentence of four years would be appropriate. Olbjørn doubled that to eight. None of their arguments carried much weight with Karl Marthinsen, perhaps the only one whose practical understanding of national socialism in action the Germans themselves would have recognised without difficulty. Whether the legislation was retroactive or not meant nothing to him. In August 1942 he had outlined for Stapo members some operational guidelines in the 'new time':

A. It is better that one innocent person be imprisoned than one guilty person escape.
B. The processes of law, procedural and police instructions should not be followed slavishly. They can be adapted and should never be a hindrance to efficient service. I draw your attention to the changed situation of the individual in a national socialist state *contra* a democratic state.
C. At a revolutionary time such as we are now experiencing in our country it will often be the case that appropriate laws do

not exist to cover certain crimes and misdemeanours. In other cases the laws we have are outdated and old-fashioned and inhibit an appropriate reaction. Here the Stapo officer must not allow himself to be confused or hampered. We do not *need* law in order to act against the enemies of our society. Our mission – always to ensure the security of the state – gives us not only the right but also the obligation to intervene when we see the necessity of doing so, regardless of whether the individual paragraphs of the law allow it or not.[59]

Among Waaler's notes to his Milorg contacts he included a colleague's characterisation of Marthinsen: 'he is the devil incarnate. Very smart. Intelligent. Forgets nothing. Ambitious. Ruthless. The type who can get tears in his eyes when someone sings *Når fjordene blåner* [When the Soft Blue Falls over the Fjords] and the next moment turn round and give the order to have someone shot.' Such a man was hardly likely to concern himself with the fact that a piece of legislation might be retroactive, and his response to his fellow judges' suggestion was consistent with his understanding of 'the new time' they had all entered. 'You don't understand anything,' he told them. 'He's going to be shot, whatever you say.'

Nevertheless, when the three men left the premises late that evening to inform Lie and Riisnæs of their verdict, the two others were still holding out for a prison sentence. In a witness statement after the war the caretaker who locked up after them later remembered that all three had seemed 'unsteady on their feet', though Reichborn-Kjennerud remained clear-headed enough to get him to go back and check the room where they had been sitting to make sure they hadn't left any cigarettes burning.

Lie and Riisnæs were furious when they heard of the failure to pass a death sentence. Even though it was a formality they still insisted that it be done; Quisling would then use his powers to commute the sentence to one of imprisonment. So the judges were immediately reconvened to resume their deliberations. A fourth bottle of spirits was opened and Eilifsen's fate discussed for a further three hours. Finally Marthinsen's patience ran out and in the early hours of the morning he stood up and threatened to leave the room to report the impasse to the Gestapo. Reichborn-Kjennerud remained unmoved by the threat, but Olbjørn capitulated, giving the court the necessary two-thirds majority it needed to pass the death sentence.

As soon as he received the news Riisnæs drove out to Bygdøy to inform Quisling at Gimle. Quisling, perhaps unaware of the extent to which his prerogative had been used to persuade the dissident Olbjørn, voiced his doubts about whether Terboven would agree to commute the sentence. He suggested Riisnæs himself make the awkward call to the Reichskommissar. Terboven's response summed up in a few humiliating words the plight of the whole wretched Quisling administration throughout the three years of its illusory status as the government of Norway: 'Do you suppose, minister, that you can bargain with me in a matter such as this?'

Riisnæs replaced the receiver and relayed Terboven's answer to Quisling. Quisling duly rejected the plea for clemency. Eilifsen was taken from his cell and driven south from Oslo along Enebakkveien in the early hours of 16 August, a Monday morning. He was blindfolded, tied to a tree and shot by a firing squad of seven men. Two had to be drafted in as replacements for boys who were too drunk to shoot straight. Hans Eng was there in his capacity as Stapo's own doctor at what would turn out to be the first of nineteen death sentences carried out following appearances before the Police Special Court. He carried with him a little pistol with which he administered the *coup de grace*.

The whole episode was used to carry out a long-planned joint operation involving Germans and Norwegian Nazis that had the same general intention of redressing a perceived lack of rigour among the police at a time of intense military unease. On the morning of Eilifsen's execution several hundred policemen in the major population centres of the country were either arrested at their homes or, as in Oslo, ordered to report to the main police barracks in Majorstuen at six in the morning. Almost 500 men were assembled in the main courtyard inside the Majorstuen barracks and the exits were then blocked and guarded by armed German SD and Norwegian Stapo officers. Senior policemen were lined up in the centre of the courtyard, in front of a small table. Rediess then briefly addressed them in German, to impress upon them the importance of obeying orders and remaining at one's post. Jonas Lie then replaced him at the table to repeat the warning in Norwegian. He informed them that a senior police officer had earlier that morning been executed for insubordination. In order to prevent any recurrence of this particular officer's crime – he avoided mentioning Eilifsen by name – Lie went on to say that an oath of loyalty had been prepared which he wanted every one of them to sign. In doing so they would undertake to cooperate with the German authorities and obey without question any order given. He then invited the officers to come forward and sign the document.

Only two men stepped forward, and for the first time Lie realised that he might have a problem. He ordered the reluctant officers into the building and then called for the rank and file to step forward and sign. Many of the 470 did so without hesitation; but many followed the examples of their superiors and declined. These too were ordered inside.

Presently the first group of officers re-emerged, came forward to the table and signed Lie's document. The rumour was that they had been given the option of doing so or facing a firing squad. The threat appeared to have been successful. Over the next few minutes most of the reluctant officers and men now declared their willingness to sign. Having done so they were allowed to leave and return to work. That left only a small group of between thirty and forty men. Bernard Askvig pleaded with them to sign, but could give them no firm assurances as to what would happen to them if they still refused. Two were deputed to approach Lie and put the same question to Lie: 'You will be court-martialled and shot early tomorrow morning,' he replied without hesitation.

Was he bluffing? It was impossible to tell. But the uncertainty proved too much for some, who duly stepped forward and added their names. Only sixteen were now left who still refused to sign the oath. They were arrested and transported to Victoria terrasse. There, to their surprise, they encountered a number of officers from other parts of the country who had already been arrested as part of what was called *Aktion Polarkreis*, a nationwide attempt to weed out 'unreliable' members of the police force.

Neither the Oslo sixteen nor any of the others were shot. Instead the whole group, numbering almost 300 men, was sent to the Stutthof prison camp in Germany, where they remained for the duration of the war. There, like the Norwegian students before them, they were subjected to futile attempts to turn them into Nazis. Lie's attempt to 'stop the rot' failed dismally. Recruitment to the police had always been slow. Following Eilifsen's trial and execution and *Aktion Polarkreis* it dried up altogether. Demoralisation became endemic. Senior officers like Askvig and Olbjørn abandoned themselves to alcohol. All of these developments were communicated in Gunnar Waaler's secret despatches to his Milorg contacts.

The Police Special Court handed down several more death sentences. Two were young deaf-mutes found guilty of raping a woman in the chaotic hours following the huge munitions explosion at the Filipstad docks on 19 December 1943. They were executed on 26 February 1944, their deaths marking the only occasion on which the government in London did not voice any kind of protest. The one priest able to communicate using sign language was refused permission to attend the execution, and on the 17-kilometre drive out to the forest where they were to be shot the car carrying the boys made a brief stop at his home in Nordstrand so that he could administer the last rites to them, an obligation that almost beggars the imagination. Another was a thirty-four-year-old factory worker from Notodden named Olaf Moen. Moen's case underlines how desperate National Unity authorities now were to persuade the Germans that the party had enough authority to make a contribution to the German military through a reformed and militarised Work Service. Moen's crime was to have threatened three local youths with repercussions should they obey a summons to report for Work Service, telling them that he would personally make sure they faced prosecution after the war if they did so.

Before being executed Moen had been tortured by his Stapo interrogators, who whipped and beat him. Splinters were forced beneath his fingernails and set on fire with a cigarette lighter. The technique of the *skjerpet avhør* ('focused interrogation'), as it was known, was something Stapo officers learned from their German comrades in the Gestapo; but refinements such as this reflect a personal darkness that was often intensified by alcohol abuse. Another Stapo officer in the course of another 'focused interrogation' bound his suspect to a chair, personally shaved his head, suspended a punctured saucepan of water above his head and left him to the torment of the drips for several hours.

It is a relief to turn from the depravity within the ranks of the Norwegian State Police to the activities of Gunnar Waaler. On five separate occasions he had conducted a total of eighteen refugees across the border to the safety of neutral Sweden. One crossing was made on 8 May, only two days after he was present in an official capacity at the execution of a young man named Knut Mathiesen who had shot and killed a Nazi policeman while guiding a group of refugees to the Swedish border. Waaler continued to sabotage – on a daily basis – the Nazified court system's attempts to brand everything as a political crime. But his most important contribution to the work of the resistance was the transcribing and photographing of the sensitive documents to which his position gave him relatively easy access, and his delivery to his Milorg contact Major Langeland of written reports containing information passed to him in the course of carefully orchestrated conversations he had over the months and years with his Stapo colleagues – none of whom, it seems, ever suspected him.

This branch of his activity had started in the late summer of 1941. Ordered much against his will to the post of legal adviser to the public prosecutor, his thoughts had turned once again to the possibility of crossing into Sweden and from there making his way to Scotland to join the Norwegians being trained in sabotage and other military activities by the British. He abandoned this plan when he met Ludvig Engeseth, head of the Municipal Archives in Oslo. Waaler had known Engeseth before the war and he was someone Waaler looked up to and admired. In the course of their conversation following their chance reunion he had become sufficiently convinced of Engeseth's national loyalties to confide in him. He spoke of his distress over the 'political' work he had been forced into and of his plans to cross the North Sea.

Engeseth was already active in the resistance and as soon as he realised the importance of Waaler's position he urged him to abandon these plans. There were enough eager young patriots in England already, he told him; one man more or less wouldn't make much difference. If Waaler really wanted to serve his country the best thing he could do was remain where he was, retain his membership of National Unity, and begin to work clandestinely against the Nazis along lines he was prepared to suggest.

Waaler remained sceptical, for the understandable reason that it would mean continuing in a role he found extremely distasteful. His personal pride, not to mention the social distress such a course of action would involve, militated against it. Engeseth persisted. He urged on him the potential value of the work he would be able to do for the resistance if he could just bring himself to endure the distaste of most of those he liked, and the camaraderie and friendship of many he didn't. In the end, Engeseth's insistence on the uniquely valuable nature of the information he would be able to provide prevailed, and Waaler returned to his desk, content in the knowledge that he was now finally engaged in meaningful resistance work.

11

Waaler's Arrest, 1944

The demoralisation of the police that began with Gunnar Eilifsen's execution and the deportation to a German concentration camp of hundreds of Norwegian police officers entered a new phase with the killing of Inspector Gunnar Lindvig, shot dead on the steps of his flat in Langaards gate on the morning of 24 May 1944. His two unknown assailants arrived and departed on bicycles. Lindvig was regarded by resistance leaders as one of their most dangerous opponents, a man whose fanaticism increased as the war progressed and who possessed a dangerous knowledge of the organisation's activities. His devotion to the cause was so puritanical he once boasted to a colleague that he would not hesitate to arrest his own father and brother if he believed them to have broken the law. Lindvig had been in charge of the secretive execution of the border guide Knut Mathiesen and Waaler had named him in the report he delivered to Milorg, who duly forwarded it to the Norwegian authorities in London. Shortly before Lindvig's killing the BBC's Norwegian service had carried a mysteriously detailed account of Mathiesen's trial and execution. It was a slipup of sorts, and there was little doubt in Waaler's mind that he was himself responsible for Lindvig's killing so soon after Mathiesen's execution.

Waaler's activities had by this time attracted the attention of the head of Milorg himself, Jens Christian Hauge. Hauge, Waaler and Major Langeland began discussing ways to make even greater use of Waaler's evidently extraordinary plausible personality, his acting skills, his intelligence and daring. At the end of May 1944 Hauge and Langeland asked him to put his membership of National Unity in order, and he did. They told him he must continue to present himself as a driven Nazi. The only point on which he dug his heels in was when they told him he must take the oath of loyalty to Vidkun Quisling demanded of all recruits to the State Police. When he protested Hauge told him it was an order. Lindvig's killing marked open season on Stapo officers and as Hauge was well aware, the risks Waaler now ran included the ironic possibility that some rogue loyalist over whom the organisation had no control, unaware of his true status, might try to kill him.

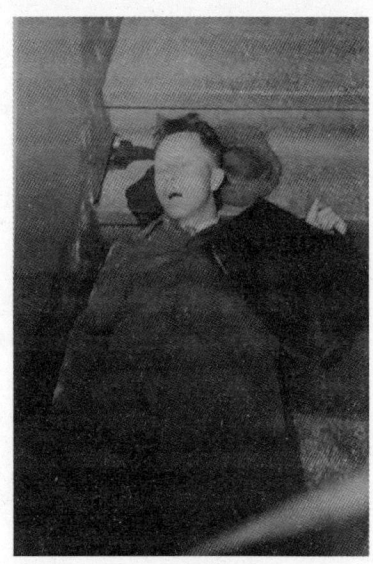

On the morning of Monday 14 August 1944, Waaler arrived for work as usual at Stapo headquarters in Kronprinsens gate. At about 11 a.m. a colleague in the office next to his, Erling Søvik, asked him to step inside for a moment. Waaler did so. Søvik had two colleagues with him. Inspector Sverre Thorhus and Inspector Rolf Skjønhaug had both been involved in the trials and executions of Norwegians sentenced to death by the Special Court. Waaler knew that Søvik liked and respected him. It was Søvik who had arranged for him to attend the trial of Knut Mathiesen and the execution afterwards. Søvik had personally signed the pass that allowed him to travel unrestricted in the border area. But Waaler sensed at once the tension in the air.

Søvik closed the door behind him and turned round: 'Are you armed?' he asked.

Waaler knew instantly that he had been betrayed.

'No,' he said.

'Search him.' Søvik gestured to Skjønhaug, who stepped forward and carried out a perfunctory slapping of his pockets before stepping back with a nod to Søvik.

Søvik turned his back on the room and walked slowly towards the window. He folded his arms. He dipped his head to one side for a few moments, as though following something going on in the street below.

'Tell me, Waaler,' he said, still without turning around. 'Do you know a man named Arnfinn Sunde? He was a Front Fighter with the 5th SS Division Wiking.'

He turned around and gestured briefly in the direction of his own eye: 'Has a glass eye from a grenade splinter.'

Waaler paused before replying. 'The name is familiar. I believe I may have met him, yes. What's all this about?'

With his gaze fixed just above Waaler's head he said in a strained monotone, 'There have been some serious accusations against you.'

Waaler frowned, then gave a puzzled smile: 'Accusations in regard to what?'

'You'll be told in due course. In the meantime, consider yourself under arrest. Take him to his office,' he continued to Thorhus. 'Put a man in there with him. Make sure he's armed.'

Waaler spent the next two hours sitting in his own office under the watchful eye of a guard who sat on the corner of his desk, one dangling leg swinging in a constant small arc, ostentatiously loading and unloading bullets into the chamber of his gun while staring fixedly at Waaler. At about 1 p.m. the door opened. Waaler was ordered to his feet and escorted back into Søvik's office. The three who had been in attendance before were there, this time joined by Karl Marthinsen.

Marthinsen fixed him with his intense, dark eyes and said, in a not unfriendly way:

'This is a very strange story, Waaler.'

Waaler parted his hands slightly but said nothing. Søvik then opened the door to his waiting room and beckoned to someone in there. Moments later, Arnfinn Sunde entered the office.

Waaler studied him quickly for signs of torture, bruising, blood. He looked into his eyes but was disconcerted as always by the dull immobility of that glassy blue stone.

Skjønhaug addressed him in a falsely sweet voice: 'Now tell us, Sunde, exactly what you told me on Saturday.'

Waaler listened in mounting horror as Sunde gave a version of his recruitment to Waaler's group. It was adapted to serve his own cause. He described how he had been threatened by Waaler and forced to enrol in Stapo for the specific purpose of breaking into offices and photographing documents. There were more threats when he was reassigned to the border police. Waaler had said that if he didn't arrange to have the archives at Mysen photographed then he would…

Sunde fell silent.

'What do you mean when you say he threatened you?' Marthinsen interrupted.

'He frightened me.'

'What exactly did he say?'

'It was more that…' So far Sunde had avoided looking at Waaler. Now he raised his head and looked straight at him.

'He's capable of anything. He'll do anything. I was afraid he'd kill me if I didn't do as he said.'

'I see.' Marthinsen smiled enigmatically. He shook his head several times before turning to Waaler: 'Well, what do you have to say to all this?'

How does an innocent man behave? Waaler wondered whether to respond to Marthinsen's smile. Or laugh out loud and shake his head in disbelieving wonder. He decided to do neither. Best to retain his military bearing and allow just a hint of outrage to trouble his reply as he opened his mouth and embarked on the story he had feverishly been honing ever since Sunde entered the room and identified himself as the source of the accusations against him.

'I can see what's going on here,' he announced, glaring at Sunde. 'I met this man a couple of times about a year ago. It was at Wessmann's house, I was there to discuss the shooting on the Halden train with Wessmann. At some point he has become involved in illegal activity. Now he's been caught and he's looking for a way out. He's trying to use a casual encounter with me to try to blacken my name and destroy my reputation. I very much hope that no one here is taken in by his lies.'

The touch of anger wasn't hard to simulate. He *was* angry. Aware that Arnfinn Sunde was a heavy drinker, Milorg had still encouraged him to recruit the man. He realised that Sunde had already told his interrogators far more than they could possibly have hoped or expected he would know. In his description of the photographing of the archive at Mysen, he had given them the name of the photographer Waaler worked with, Wolff. In the course of his explanation the circumstances of Sunde's arrest had become apparent. A few days previously, while travelling near the Swedish border in a car carrying two refugees, he had been stopped by a border patrol. They'd let him drive on, but at a drinking party in the station mess-room in Hemnes a day or two later the subject had come up again. It was Sunde's day off but he'd come in anyway for the company, having already put away a half bottle of aquavit on his own.

On one level Waaler's anger lay in the contempt he felt for Sunde, who had been an insufficiently good story-teller to *lie* his way out of the questions his colleagues put to him concerning the incident. Instead of inventing some story, or joking the whole thing away, like some clown from an American gangster film he'd suddenly jumped up from his chair, run outside the border post, pulled the pin on a hand grenade and tossed it back in through the open window, where it rolled under a colleague's chair and blew off one of its legs. No one was injured. Sunde had then dived into the waters of nearby Bråtenvannet and started swimming until, drunk as he was and hindered by his clothes – he still had his shoes on – he had had to make his way back to dry land where, of course, he been arrested. He had then been driven to Oslo and interrogated by Skjønhaug, to whom he told the whole of his almost true story without, as far as Waaler could see, any need of a 'focused interrogation'.

Waaler, such an expertly unreliable narrator himself, could see only one benefit to him of the story as it now stood: it compelled Sunde to present himself as a pathetic and frightened clown. He knew instinctively that a man like Marthinsen would find Sunde contemptible, no matter whose side he was on. He was therefore gratified but only slightly relieved to hear Marthinsen say that he was inclined to believe Waaler was telling the truth and had difficulty accepting that a man of Waaler's moral character could be capable of duplicity on the level suggested by Sunde. Marthinsen then asked Sunde if he had some reason to be angry with Waaler, or held some grudge against him? Because these were very serious accusations indeed. Telling lies in such circumstances would be dangerous and damaging for all concerned. It was important to stick to the truth. Tell only the truth.

Marthinsen turned to Søvik: 'Where is this photographer, Wolff?'

Søvik replied that they'd been to his house and learned that he was away on holiday at his cabin in the mountains. He was expected back in Oslo the next day.

Marthinsen nodded. 'Then we'll see where things stand once we've talked to him. Is it still raining?' he asked vaguely, looking out the window, not expecting an answer, not getting one.

'So: tomorrow.' Marthinsen turned back towards the room and raised his arm in a distracted salute. The others responded, Waaler with his customary vigour. Marthinsen left.

1 (left). The sinking of the German heavy cruiser *Blücher* off Drøbak in the Oslofjord in the early hours of 9 April 1940.

2. (below). German troops marching past the university in central Oslo, with the royal palace in the background. Oslo fell in less than a day.

(above). Josef Terboven (left) became Hitler's Reichskommissar in Norway and remained there for the duration of the war. Wilhelm Rediess (right) was supreme head of the SS and the German police forces in Norway, including the Gestapo.

3 (above). Following the flight of the king and government, Vidkun Quisling announced himself as Norway's new prime minister. The abortive coup lasted just six days.

5 (*left*). Reinhard Heydrich (centre) visits the German war cemetery at Ekeberg in September 1941. He and Terboven discussed the imposition of a Civilian State of Emergency to eliminate the threat of a general strike.

6 (*far left*). The communist Viggo Hansteen, effectively the head of Norway's trades union movement, was tried and executed during the Civilian State of Emergency declared in September 1941

7 (*left*). Rolf Wickström, a shop-steward executed in September 1941 as part of the Nazi campaign to break the unions. He led a walkout in protest against a milk shortage.

8 (*left*). Terboven leaves the Akershus Fortress following Quisling's appointment as Norway's 'Minister-President' on 1 February 1941. As always, Quisling walks a pace behind Hitler's *Reichskommissar*.

9 (right). Quisling's so-called Second Government of 1942 of National Unity party members. Quisling and his deputy, Albert Hagelin, are on the left of the front row, Sverre Riisnæs and Jonas Lie behind them.

10 (above). Antisemitic graffiti on an Oslo shop window claiming that Jews were responsible for the German invasion of 9 April 1940. The Norwegian Holocaust was completed – with devastating efficiency – by the winter of 1942.

11 (above). Quisling inspecting a line of 'Front Fighters', Norwegians who had volunteered to fight the Russians on the Eastern Front.

12 (left). Jonas Lie with Heinrich Himmler. Himmler had a low opinion of Quisling and would have preferred to see the charismatic Lie leading Norway's Nazi party.

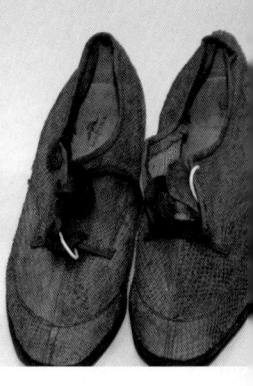

13 (*above*). The shortage of raw materials led to an explosion of creativity. Shoes made of paper and fish skin looked stylish but had a very short lifespan.

14 (*above left*). Tobacco was grown and refined in Norway following the sudden disappearance of British and American cigarettes from the market.

15 (*left*). Petrol rationing led to the use of generators mounted on the roof or rear of taxis and private cars. The engine ran on gas produced by wood burning inside the generator 'stoves'.

16 (*left*). The Sami people fell outside the rigid classification of Nazi racial theories and were even admired by some for their 'natural' way of life. German soldiers stationed in the north posed with them for photograph to be sent home.

17 (*above*). Gunnar Eilifsen, a police officer tried and executed for insubordination when he refused to arrest three Norwegian women who failed to turn up when conscripted for Work Service by Quisling's government.

18 (*above*). Karl Marthinsen, the powerful and much-feared head of the Norwegian State Police (Stapo). He was a member of the Norwegian *Særdomstol* (Special Court) that sentenced Gunnar Eilifsen to death.

19 (*left*). Forty-four passengers on the number 15 tram were killed in central Oslo when an Allied bombing raid on Gestapo headquarters on 31 December 1944 missed its target. Altogether 115 people died in the raid.

20 (*left*). The German ammunition ship *Selma* exploded on 19 December 1943 and destroyed large parts of central Oslo, rendering thousands homeless.

21 (*right*). Following the German scorched-earth policy in the northern county of Finnmark, in the winter of 1944, thousands of Norwegians fled their homes to live rough in the mountains.

22 (*left*). Kirkenes on the border with Soviet Russia was bombed 328 times during the occupation. The steps in the foreground are all that remain of Petterson's baker's shop.

23 (*left*). A community of Norwegians lived for two months in the tunnels of the Sydvaranger mining company at Bjørnevatn before the liberation of the north by Soviet troops in the winter of 1944–5.

24 (*left*). Quisling under arrest and awaiting trial at Akershus Fortress. He had hoped to retire to the quiet anonymity of life as a country priest following the end of the war.

25 (*below*). The German commander at Akershus formally surrenders control of the fortress to a Milorg operative, Sub-Lt. Terje Rollem.

26 (right). Quisling's Justice Minister, Sverre Riisnæs, had to be carried into court to face trial in June 1947. A verdict of guilty and a death sentence were inevitable, but the trial was abandoned on the grounds of Riisnæs' insanity. He was confined to Reitgjerdet mental hospital, where he remained until his release in 1960. Many continue to believe that his 'insanity' was a performance.

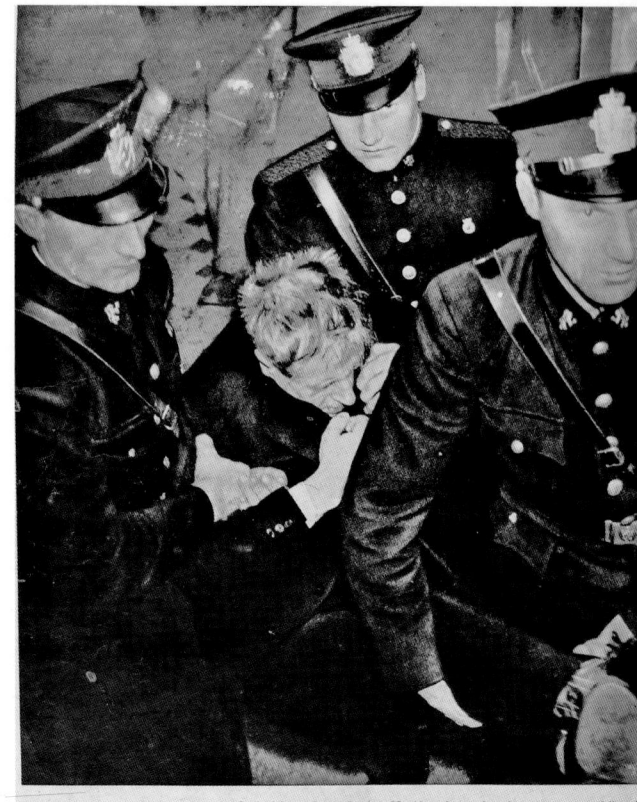

Riisnæs gjør entre i retten

27 (above). In a publicly broadcast sermon on NRK Radio following the liberation, the Larvik priest Kristian Ljostveit warned people of the dangers of being 'smitten' by the Nazi spirit in their pursuit of revenge.

28 (left). Eivind Berggrav, Bishop of Oslo and primate of the Church of Norway. A leader of the Conscience Struggle of 1942, he spent the last three years of the war under house-arrest. Following the liberation, he supported the criminalisation of Nazi party membership but was opposed to the death penalty.

Waaler was then escorted back to his office and as before placed under the armed guard.

At about 5 p.m. Søvik returned. His manner was changed. He seemed almost apologetic. Waaler realised that he, like Marthinsen, was so convinced of his own psychological acuity that he was finding it impossible to believe Waaler capable of deception on the level suggested. He sent the armed guard out of the room, took his place at the corner of the desk, even swung his jackbooted leg in the same way the guard had. But his tone was friendly. Once Wolff was back from his holiday and they had spoken to him he was sure this would all be cleared up and Waaler could get back to work. Until then, unfortunately, Waaler would have to remain in custody. Not in prison, not like some criminal, but at his own apartment on Bygdøy allé. In the meantime, Søvik suggested they all head down to Gamle Christiania in Stortorvet and get something to eat.

Waaler, Søvik and two rank-and-file Stapo men entered the dimly lit bar. They took a table beneath one of the several poorly executed paintings of scenes from Nordic mythology that decorated the walls of the restaurant. Waaler was invited to sit with his back to the room, opposite Søvik. The Stapo men sat one at each end of the small table. He'd seen them before but didn't know their names. Both wore civilian clothing, as was common for rank-and-file Stapo men. The atmosphere was a little uneasy. Conversation didn't come easily. In his many long silences Waaler kept his eyes fixed on the painting in front of him. It was oppressive but he didn't know where else to look. The thick, crude lines of the landscape seemed to sink down and envelop his head and shoulders. The conversation between the three others was largely work-oriented. He tried to listen, tried to follow, now and then tried to contribute, but it was impossible. At one point he picked up enough of a joke to be able to join in the laughter at the punch line. It was a *jøssing* joke Søvik told about how the Germans had decided to divide up Knut Hamsun's books: they were going to give themselves *Markens grøde* (The Growth of the Soil) and the

Norwegians would have to make do with *Sult* (Hunger). Waaler had heard it before, at one of his masked meetings with Jens Christian Hauge. In the version Hauge had told, the Allies were going to get Hamsun's *Victoria*.

Unthinkingly he found himself about to mention this to the group at the table and just managed to stop himself in time. This frightened him. He began to wonder how long he would be able to control his mind and his mouth. His thoughts raced and span at unearthly speed. He found himself hoping Wolff would die in a car crash on his way back from his mountain cabin. He knew Thorhus and Skjønhaug had searched his office in Kronprinsens gate and his apartment in Bygdøy allé without finding anything. There remained only his old office at the Public Prosecutor's Office. They would go through that in the morning. What would Wolff say when they interrogated him on Monday? Suddenly he recalled – saw it with photographic clarity – that he had a roll of film in Grubbegata, at his old office. What was on it? It was undeveloped. What was on it? They would have it developed. What was on it? He felt as though he was going to choke on his roast beef sandwich and reached for his glass of water to wash the blockage down. The film roll shouldn't have been there. He was always so careful to make sure nothing incriminating was ever left in any of his places of work or at home. Just this one time he'd left the roll of film there. He'd taken it when he went to see Østre, one of his couriers, the caretaker at the School of Applied Art on Ullevålsveien, for delivery to a contact, Herman Løvenskiold. After he'd been knocking for a couple of minutes a passerby stopped and told him Østre was dead. What happened to him? The informant didn't know. He thought it was a natural death. Waaler had almost stopped believing such things still occurred. He'd taken the film in its little metal drum back to the office, intending to find a courier to get it out to Løvenskiold himself at his Nesodden home on the Monday.

At the thought of Løvenskiold his blood ran cold. Suppose they tortured him, and he gave up Løvenskiold? He knew Løvenskiold kept copies of all the documents he'd photographed and transcribed for Milorg over the years. They were buried in a trunk somewhere on his estate on Nesodden.

Now he saw in his mind's eye one of the negatives, dim and ghostly brown: himself and the three Milorg men from Tønsberg he'd taken over the border before Easter. He cursed himself for allowing the picture to be taken and knew there was no way his Stapo colleagues could be allowed to see it. Somehow he had to get rid of it before Thorhus and Skjønhaug searched his office. As they were leaving Gamle Christiania he asked Søvik, as casually as he could, if they might just call in at his office around the corner in Grubbegata before taking the tram up Bygdøy allé – he'd borrowed a book from Skjønhaug, he explained, Jonas Lie's book about the trip to Mexico with Trotsky in 1936 as the Norwegian government's official representative after Trotsky had lost his refugee status in Norway. The best thing about it was that it was true. He *had* borrowed Lie's book *I Fred og Ufred* from Skjønhaug several months ago and failed to return it. He knew it was in one of his desk drawers. If he was lucky it would be in the same drawer as the roll of undeveloped film.

It was a fine August Sunday evening, warm and still too early for stars as the four men headed up Grensen. A minute or two later they turned into Grubbegata. Five minutes later they entered the Supreme Court Building. The place was almost deserted. Two men on guard duty recognised them and saluted. Waaler felt a thickness in his throat as they entered the lift and it clanked its way up to the third floor. In his office Waaler made a show of having forgotten where the Trotsky book was, scanning the spines of the books in the bookcase behind his desk, opening and shutting the drawers of the grey filing cabinet next to it. He cursed theatrically and turned his attention to the drawers in his desk. In the middle of the three drawers on the right-hand side he found them both, the roll of film and the book. With a little shout of triumph he held the book up in his right hand, at the same time slipping the roll of film into his left trouser pocket.

'What was that you just put in your pocket?' Søvik asked, his hand already held out to receive it.

'This?' Waaler opened his hand and stared at the film roll as if he'd never seen it before and had no idea how it had got into his hand. 'These are just some holiday snaps from the cabin. I'm having them developed tomorrow.'

'I'll take it, thank you.'

Søvik's hand was still open, extended over the desktop. Waaler raised his hand. The film was tightly wound around its spool. As he moved to hand it across to Søvik he used his thumb nail to flick up the small retaining tab of film from its slit and the spool scattered open across the leather inlay of the desktop with a flutter.

'Now that was very careless,' said Søvik, staring at Waaler as he slowly lowered his hand. 'Very careless indeed.' The door to the corridor had been left open. Now Søvik motioned with his head to one of the Stapo men who stepped back and closed it, then stationed himself in front of it, legs apart and hands crossed in front of him, a gun in one of them.

Waaler made a last attempt to rescue the situation. He gave a deep sigh and parted his hands in embarrassment. 'They're very private,' he said. 'There's a woman in them. She works here. I promised her.'

Søvik flicked at the curled negative with his fingertips. 'Well, now we'll never know what's on them, will we?'

As they stepped from the lift cage on the ground floor Waaler knew there would be no more talk of spending the night in Bygdøy allé. A black Citroen was waiting outside. With a Stapo man on each side of him, he sat in the back and was driven the short distance to Akershus Fortress.

Waaler was not interrogated until the early hours of Thursday. A handwritten notice on his door read: *Dieser Mann darf nicht an den Freistunden teilnehmen* ('This man is not permitted to take part in the free periods'). The light in his cell was left burning all night, not that it made any difference; he hardly slept. On Thursday he was woken at about 1 a.m. and walked briskly across the harbourfront to Kronprinsens gate. He was taken up to the fourth floor and pushed into a small room where three Stapo men were waiting. He recognised them: Georg Rosenlund, whom he knew had been part of the firing squad that shot Gunnar Eilifsen; a man in his late thirties, Carl Upwall, who had been in the squad that shot the factory worker Olaf Moen; and an officer named Johan Tjørn, whom Waaler knew by reputation to be a notorious sadist. All good Nazis.

Tjørn took the lead at once. From the start he conducted himself in a manner so extreme as to be almost a parody of the German style of interrogation, circling around the seated Waaler, pacing back and forth in front of him, all the while shouting and gesticulating like a man in the grip of uncontrollable rage. Waaler was not the man to be cowed by such an approach and at once began to reprise the role he had worked so hard at and played so well for so long, as the wounded conscience of what national socialism was *really* all about. He immediately informed his interrogators that, as an accused prisoner, he was under no obligation to explain himself: 'Our party's own programme states quite clearly that the proper procedures of the law and of common justice are to be observed at all times. The *fører* himself repeated the point in his most recent speech – he reminded us that National Unity's programme is not just a litany of empty phrases, it is something that must be followed in detail. Down to the very last letter.'

'You can reel off all the legal mumbo-jumbo you like, Waaler, none of it is going to help you here,' Tjørn bellowed. 'No one even knows you're here. What happens between these four walls tonight stays here. None of us will ever say a word about it. And you won't either. Because one thing is for certain and that is that you are a dead man. Very soon, in a few day's time, you'll be appearing in front of a Special Court. You'll be tried, convicted and sentenced to death. You'll be shot the same day. The only chance of that not happening is if you die first. There's something called "shot while trying to escape". In your case I can assure you, that is a very likely outcome.'

He paused for breath and turned to Upwall: 'Do you know what Riisnæs calls this man? He calls him *Norway's biggest spy*. I was there when the minister said it: *Norway's biggest spy!*'

He bent close to Waaler's face and sprayed him with spittle, smirking as Waaler jerked his head back in disgust. He straightened up.

'So,' he continued in a clipped, calm voice. 'Where are the films?'

Waaler didn't answer.

Tjørn cleared his throat and cupped both hands around Waaler's ear:

'*Where – are – the – films?*'

Still Waaler didn't answer.

Tjørn made a signal with his finger to Upwall and left the room. Only now did Waaler notice the gramophone player standing on a small wooden table in a corner of the room. He watched as Upwall moved towards it, flicked the switch and with ludicrous delicacy placed the needle of the pickup arm on the outer groove of the record spinning on the turntable. For a second or two there was the crackling and popping of shellac and then with the suddenness of an avalanche music exploded into the room. As he recognised the opening bars of Wagner's *Ride of the Valkyries*, he saw Upwall wince and subdue a reflex action to turn the volume down. Waaler knew Tjørn must have got this bizarre idea from a Gestapo torture session he had attended. Waaler knew that the most notorious Stapo torturers – with Section Leader Einar Dønnum the worst of them – sometimes followed cases that got handed on to the Gestapo and attended sessions of 'focused interrogation' conducted by the masters of the art. He had been in Søvik's office once when Dønnum returned unexpectedly from one such session in Victoria terrasse around the corner from Kronprinsens gate, explaining that what he had seen there was *for jævlig* ('just too fucking awful') to endure. For something to have been 'too fucking awful' for the former Sunday School teacher it must have been awful indeed.

Tjørn returned carrying an assortment of items under his arm. A brown rubber truncheon. A short-handled whip with several strands of thin, knotted wire. Two metal leg clamps. A tartan blanket which he dropped onto the floor and straightened with his foot before putting the implements of torture on the table next to the gramophone.

Tjørn turned round. 'Ten thousand documents,' he shouted above the music. 'Fifty-six thick folders.' Like somebody opening a concertina he stretched one hand open high above the other to indicate how tall the pile was. 'So you see how much we know.'

And with the mention of those absurdly precise figures Waaler knew that Wolff the photographer had been arrested and had talked. And not just about how he and Sunde – on Waaler's instructions – had photographed the *Grepo* archives at Mysen, where Sunde was stationed, which was all Sunde knew of Wolff's involvement and the only thing he had accused Waaler of involving him in. Wolff had been his photographer from the start. He had told them everything he knew. It was useless to deny anything anymore.

The music stopped.

Waaler knew that his only chance now lay in dropping his pose of arrogant outrage. He apologised. He slumped. He told the same story he had told Søvik and Skjønhaug. Yes, he'd photographed and transcribed documents. He was a disappointed idealist, gathering evidence for a national socialist day of reckoning that would come when the war was over and won, when all the corruptions that defiled their ideology would at last be confronted and removed. This time around, however, he made an important editorial amendment: he said he was gathering all this material for the Germans. It was a childish ploy and made him feel like a boy being bullied at school who threatens his tormentors with a big brother.

But, temporarily at least, it worked. In a profession which encouraged scepticism and suspicion in men, the extreme pressures of occupation had turned this habit of mind inwards.

A paranoid mentality was rife in the Stapo. Officers kept watch on each other. They didn't trust each other. They suspected each other. Waaler knew that Egil Olbjørn, head of the regular police force in Oslo and a close friend of Jonas Lie, kept a dossier on his colleagues. He knew this because Waaler had been his 'inside man' at the attorney general's office, feeding him documentary evidence of corruption within the Stapo. It gave Waaler an extraordinary insider's leverage in the situation he now found himself in and he used it to equate his own activities as a document collector with Olbjørn's. Very few Stapo officers were clean in this respect. He 'gave' them Olbjørn. Tjørn took off his handcuffs and offered him coffee and cigarettes. He made a phone call to Karl Marthinsen. Marthinsen had Olbjørn arrested. His offices were searched. Nothing was found. Olbjørn was released. The interrogations continued.

From the Stapo point of view, the most devastating of Waaler's betrayals was what thrilled his Milorg contacts the most: that he had been able to obtain for them copies of the General Staff's monthly reports on Stapo's activities and plans, a document so secret only Quisling, Jonas Lie, Olbjørn and the departmental head who wrote them had access to them. A copy was found in Waaler's desk. Over and over again, during ten days of interrogation in which kindness alternated with threats, his interrogators tried to discover his source. Some nights he was offered a choice of chicken or meatballs, coffee or red wine from Marthinsen's own private cellar, looted, as Waaler knew, from houses left deserted by Norwegian refugees and appropriated for members of the organisation. At other times the implements of torture would be displayed again and the tone of the interrogation become threatening, frightening, violent. And regardless of whether he told them anything or not, at no time was he left in any doubt about the fate that awaited him: trial before the Police Special Court, a guilty verdict, a drive out along Enebakkveien, blindfolded, tied to a tree and shot. All within a matter of days.

Early in the afternoon of 24 August – in daylight for once

– Waaler was driven in handcuffs from Akershus Fortress to Søvik's office in Kronprinsens gate and placed in a wooden chair. A few minutes later Jonas Lie arrived, ushered in by his adjutant, medals clinking on his black uniform. Lie stayed only for five minutes but made it clear they knew Waaler was still hiding information from them and they intended to get it. Their patience was at an end. It was time to tell them everything. The adjutant stepped forward, opened the door, and Lie departed. Almost immediately the telephone on Søvik's desk rang. He picked it up and listened. He turned his head to stare directly at Waaler, nodding, grunting quietly. He replaced the receiver and stood up.

'That was General Major Marthinsen,' he said. 'Tonight your interrogation will be "focused". You have no chance, Waaler. None at all. I'm going home now.'

'Tonight?'

'Yes, tonight.' He looked at his wristwatch. 'You'll be driven back to Akershus shortly, but you'll be brought back here this evening. That's when it will happen. That should give you something to think about.'

Søvik unhooked his trench coat from the wooden stand by the door, adjusted his homburg, opened the door and walked out. A Stapo constable in uniform entered, closed and locked the door, pressed his back against it and stared rigidly at the wall in front of him.

Waaler knew and could identify by face and by name the head of the entire Milorg central command, despite the fact that their encounters over the previous months had always been masked. Two years previously he had sat for a whole afternoon in a court room when the People's Court was in session and observed Jens Christian Hauge's face. Since then he had met Hauge many times, always masked but always knowing who was behind the mask. He had let Hauge use his flat on Bygdøy allé for his meeting with Waaler's Stapo colleague Captain Ola Fritzner to discuss a plan, never realised, to abduct Siegfrid Fehmer, head of German counter-espionage in Norway, and fly him to England. He knew who the head of the Oslo branch of Milorg, D13, was – Major Oliver Langeland. He knew enough for the Nazis to inflict catastrophic damage to the organisation if they should ever get it out of him, damage from which it would take a long time to recover. He went over in his mind the other things that would come out in the course of a session of 'focused interrogation': the names of loyal sheriffs in the region and the whereabouts of their secret stocks of weapons; the most used and successful refugee routes across into Sweden; his own enormous collection of documents in the possession of Herman Løvenskiold and hidden somewhere on Løvenskiold's estate; and exactly how he had come by those copies of Stapo's monthly reports to Minister-President Quisling that Tjørn had found in his desk.

He realised he had no choice and that at some point later in the day he would have to kill himself. The deprivations, slaps and occasional kicks he had been subjected to so far would be as nothing compared to what was in store for him now. He knew what people like Tjørn and Dønnum were capable of. The brutal violence of long and sustained beatings. Leg irons clamped to the knees and screwed tight. Wrists and ankles bound together and the prisoner left in an excruciating bowed posture on the floor in front of an electric fire that shrivelled the skin and burned away the hair and the eyebrows. Sinister and sadistic variations on these: burning oil poured into the rectum and preventing the processes of digestion and excretion. Sadists like Dønnum and Tjørn were quite capable of losing sight of the actual goal of an interrogation and simply indulging their appetite for extreme cruelty. The prospect was unendurable.

Presently the guard on the door was relieved by another, and the disturbance was enough to jolt Waaler from the terrible churnings of his imagination. He found some relief in a story a contact at the *Rikskriminallaboratoriet* (State Forensic Laboratory) had told him, about a recent case involving an engineer working at Akers *mekanisk verksted* who was found in the shallow waters of Gaustadbekken stream in the northern Oslo suburb of Blindern with his wrists cut. The man had been interrogated by Stapo officers the previous day and in a notebook found on the body he had written that he was taking his own life because of the things he had told them.

He'd died. But it had taken two hours. Waaler didn't have that kind of time. He'd have to try somehow to jump from the car on the way back to Akershus. If that didn't kill him he'd have to make sure he was shot while trying to escape. Or find some way to do it in his cell. Hang himself. Slit his wrists. Time passed. No car came. People came and went. Heads popped round the door. No one seemed to know what was going on. After he'd been sitting there for about two hours the guard was relieved by Upwall. Not long afterwards the door opened again. Tjørn came in. He stepped aside and held the door open for a small dark man wearing a civilian suit.

The small man stopped in front of Waaler and bowed slightly.

'Captain Waaler, I presume,' he said. 'Please will you accompany me around the corner to Victoria terrasse.' He spoke Norwegian, with enough of an accent for Waaler to identify him as German.

His joints stiff from having been seated so long, Waaler stood up a little unsteadily and followed the man in the suit. As he passed through the door Tjørn reached out and touched his shoulder. He had an odd smile on his face.

'That's Detective Superintendent Weiner,' he said. 'Reinhard's second-in-command. Gestapo. They invented the focused interrogation.'

Waaler had never heard him speak so quietly before.

12

Waaler Meets Albert Weiner

The Gestapo officer who now took over the case, Albert Weiner, had arrived in Norway in February 1944. He was the ninth in a family of eighteen, born in Neustadt an der Waldnaab in southern Germany. His father was a shopkeeper who went bankrupt in the 1920s, so young Albert had to abandon the theological studies he had recently embarked on in favour of something more practical. He joined the police. He joined the NSDAP in 1935 and was posted to serve in the Nuremberg police, where he was briefly in charge of monitoring the activities of religious groups in the region, no doubt as a result of his interest in religious and philosophical matters. It turned out to be bureaucratic rather than intellectually stimulating and after just a few months he succeeded in getting transferred to the *Abwehr*, the military intelligence service, where he learned the techniques of espionage and counter-espionage, and how to recruit and use agents. In 1937 he joined the Gestapo, and by the outbreak of the war was a member of the SS and regional head of SD, the Nazi Party's own security service. His main task was to monitor the private lives of certain leading Nazis, among them the unstable and volatile antisemite Julius Streicher. The work provided the stimulation his previous posting had not, introducing him to the unpredictable and morally chaotic world ushered in by national socialism. He proved so adept at the task that he remained in Nuremberg until being sent to Norway in early 1944. He was thirty years old at the time, married, with three children.

Shortly after arriving Weiner orchestrated a counter-resistance operation under the deeply cynical codename *Blumenpflücken* (Flower-picking). This took the form of a brief but deadly campaign of assassinations that ran from the summer of 1944 to early 1945 and cost eleven Norwegians their lives. All the victims were known *jøssing* and either active in or at least sympathetic to the resistance. Most were prominent members of society, doctors, lawyers or businessmen. As such the campaign marked an extension of Josef Terboven's earlier attempts to terrorise people tempted to follow the examples of men like Henry Gleditsch or Viggo Hansteen and those others executed during the two States of Civilian Emergency for being 'spiritual inspirators' of the resistance.

The existence of the *Blumenpflücken* campaign was a secret known only to Terboven; the supreme commander of the German police in Norway Wilhelm Rediess; and to the Gestapo boss Hellmuth Reinhard, with whom Weiner now shared a villa in Tennisveien 7 in the Oslo suburb of Slemdal. The aim of the campaign was the same as that of any terrorist campaign: to spread fear and confusion and to encourage the idea that anyone at all might be a victim, and for no apparent reason. To cause further confusion, care was taken to make the killings look like liquidations carried out by the undisciplined and chaotic Norwegian resistance movement itself.

Weiner himself was responsible for several of the eleven killings, including the one that opened the campaign. This was the murder on 12 June of Einar Hærland, a thirty-four-year-old police officer in charge of Civil Air Defence in Oslo. In circumstances that echoed the killing of Gunnar Lindvig three weeks earlier, to which this was a direct response, Hærland was shot dead in the stairwell of the flat at Sporveisgata 29 where he lived with his wife and two children. On 20 July Weiner tricked a resistance worker named Sigrid Hammerø into thinking she would be meeting her husband in Oslo, and that the pair of them would then be helped over into Sweden. She was arrested at Vestbanen railway station as she stepped off the train and taken straight to Victoria terrasse.

That same evening she was driven out to a quarry close to the prison at Grini with two other women. All three were blindfolded and their hands tied behind their backs. At Grini they were ordered out of the car. Realising what was about to happen, Sigrid Hammerø began to run. Albert Weiner shot her in the back. Oskar Hans, in charge of the *Sonderkommando* (execution squads) in occupied Norway, was busy preparing the execution site nearby when he heard the shot and rebuked Weiner furiously for his undisciplined improvisation. Shortly afterwards the two other women were shot in the approved fashion and buried in the large grave prepared for them, along with Sigrid Hammerø. One was Gulosten's wife Ruth Andersen, whose involvement in the killing of Raymond Colberg had finally been established by the Gestapo. The two men from the Cheval Animal Hospital who had helped Gulosten dispose of the informer's body were also executed and buried in the same grave. There were six corpses altogether in the grave, the sixth and last being a prisoner of whom nothing seems to be known beyond the fact that he was insane. For the Nazis that was a good enough reason to kill anyone. Albert Weiner was in the midst of directing and participating in this campaign of murders at the time he took over Gunnar Waaler's case.

At the same time as he was coordinating the *Blumenpflücken* campaign, Weiner, with Reinhard, became involved in another curious but less sinister Gestapo enterprise. As defeat became ever more likely Reinhard began looking at new ways of trying to win the hearts and minds of Norway's brightest and bravest, the task that National Unity had made its chief priority while in government but which had been thwarted by the Conscience Struggle. Instead of the imprisonment, torture and execution of individuals who were frequently intelligent and principled young men and women in a way that created an implacable hostility towards national socialism and everything it stood for, Reinhard, abetted by Weiner, now tried to show to a select group of young men being held at Grini, mainly for offences related to the illegal press, that national socialism had another side to it. That it had its own repertoire of tolerances, its own culture, that it was capable of a humane spontaneity, that beneath the swastikas Nazis were normal, approachable human beings.

The young men who became part of this campaign were held separate from the other, older prisoners in the so-called *Jugendabteilung* (Youth Section), a section of the prison housing young Norwegians who were considered likely candidates for successful indoctrination in national socialism. They were given German lessons and lectures on Nazi racial theories. Without prior warning, Reinhard began visiting the *Jugendabteilung*. He behaved in a friendly and approachable manner, engaged the boys in discussion on all sorts of subjects, then departed as unexpectedly as he had come. On 8 April 1944, the day after Good Friday, he arrived wearing his SS uniform, symbol of absolute power in the land. Three of the prisoners, Tor Bjerkedal, Rolf Grüner-Hegge and Knut Kleve, were summoned before him. He peered at them through his thick spectacles: 'I have an Easter present for you,' he told them. 'The three of you are to be released. But there is a condition: I want you to come to my house and dine with me next Sunday. You don't need to decide at once. I'll give you time to discuss the proposal.' In a memoir of the relationship written much later in life, Kleve recalled that it occurred to them all that the man might possibly be homosexual. But the three young men attended Reinhard's dinner party anyway, Kleve with Haakon VII's self-sacrificing motto sounding through his head, *Alt for Norge* ('Give All for Norway').[60]

In the event no such sacrifice was required and after two years in captivity Kleve and his companions presently found themselves free men. The first dinner invitation was followed by others, sometimes with all three men as guests, at other times individually. At each visit the boys would bring a list with the names of three Grini prisoners and each time the prisoners listed would be released. The gardens of the house in Tennisveien were patrolled constantly by armed guards and barking dogs. Every time he went there, Kleve recalled, he couldn't help thinking how like a Mafia boss Reinhard was. At those dinner parties his table groaned beneath the weight of dishes the average Norwegian household could only dream of during those days. Delicious meals accompanied by fine wines, all of it brought to the table on a silver tray by a white-jacketed waiter with a black Luger tucked inside his belt. Cigars and American or English cigarettes to go with the liqueurs afterwards. Beautiful young women wandered about through the rooms.

In his memoir Kleve describes Weiner and Reinhard as an unusual pair, Reinhard handsome, blonde and very Germanic, Weiner small and balding and, in Kleve's own phrase, of 'uncertain ethnicity'. Reinhard affected to find everything Weiner said ridiculous. Kleve recalled discussing with Weiner whether sex before marriage was a sin or not, and Reinhard's open contempt for the whole subject. The Gestapo chief was interested in art and would proudly show off a large painting by the Norwegian master J.C. Dahl that hung on the dining room wall of the villa in Tennisveien, oblivious to the fact that, like the villa itself, it was all actually the property of a shipping magnate and resistance man named Odd Berg who had fled to Sweden with his family in 1941. Reinhard would play recordings of music by Beethoven to which he would listen in a kind of distracted ecstasy. They discussed Kierkegaard's philosophy. The boys learned, among other things, of the true extent of the German contempt for Vidkun Quisling as Norway's Führer, and for National Unity as a Nazi Party: 'Quisling's just an old fool,' Reinhard commented on one occasion. 'As soon as we've got things properly organised he'll be out.' In the relaxed, drink-fuelled atmosphere around the table the Gestapo boss even confessed to 'hating' Terboven. Occasionally the little group would go for walks in the forest surrounding Oslo. Or play drunken tennis in the garden of the villa. On one occasion Albert

Weiner began groaning excerpts from an opera he claimed he had composed. It was, he told them, a celebration of the beauty of life.

On 25 August 1944 Gunnar Waaler was delivered into the hands of this singular man. In the weeks following the liberation, Waaler wrote his own version of what subsequently took place between the two men in an attempt to explain the complexities of his behaviour as a Stapo double-agent. In it he offers striking confirmation of something Knut Kleve recalled about those evenings at Tennisveien, where he found Weiner 'one of the most unusual and, I suppose I would have to say, *sinister* characters I have ever met. Sometimes, in conversation, I felt as though he were *a completely decent and normal human being* who inhabited more or less the same moral universe as me, at the same time as I knew – or as I now know – that he was capable of killing in cold blood, and had done so at least three times as part of the *Blumenpflücken* campaign of the summer of 1944.'[61] Waaler's long account often expresses a similar moral bewilderment. He recalls Weiner's first words to him: '*Sie haben gespielt – und Sie haben verloren*'* ('You played a game, and you've lost'). The next were: '*Danken Sie ihrem Gott dess wir Hand Sie genommen haben*' ('You can thank God you're in our hands now'). If Quisling had got hold of him, Weiner added, he would have torn him into little pieces.

Waaler's account of the relationship continues:

> The Germans had received a brief message from the Stapo about my case, but written in such a way that they knew there was more to it than met the eye. '*Dann habe ich gedacht: Dies ist keine Sache für die N.S.*' ('I thought at once: this matter is too important to be left to National Unity'). Weiner said he understood and respected my actions. He made it clear to me that, to a far greater extent than I had thought, the Germans despised National Unity. I should have come to them (the Germans) with my documents. If I had done so a year ago

---

* All German quotations are from Waaler's own account.

they would have informed the Führer in Berlin and that could well have meant the end of National Unity. As matters now stood they had to make do with what they had. But once the war was over and won there would be a showdown with National Unity. They'd be out, every one of them. Then the Germans would try working with decent Norwegians. He explained to me that my case was his personal *Vernehmung* ('interrogation'). He looked at it in a very different way from the State Police. But he had to have the matter in its entirety presented to him, with nothing held back. He made an elegant gesture in the direction of the pile of reports he had received from the State Police: '*Sie sind vernommen worden. Ich habe es gelesen. Dann habe ich gedacht: Der Mann hat gelogen*' ('You have been questioned. I have been through these interrogations. And I thought: this man was lying'). I must put myself entirely in his hands. He, in return, would give me his word of honour as a National Socialist officer that I should emerge from it all as lightly as possible, and my connections would not be arrested. *Ohne Strafe können Sie nicht davonkommen. Das verstehen Sie ja selbst* ('You won't escape punishment entirely. You must realise that yourself'). But I wouldn't end up in a concentration camp in Germany. *Da bekommen Sie es verhältnismässig gut* ('This will work out reasonably well for you'). But: *Jede Zeile wird nachgeprüft. Eine einzige bewusste Unwahrheit bringt Sie ins Grab* ('Everything will be checked. A single deliberate falsehood will see you in your grave'). And then I would be treated in the usual way and the case handed over to the *Polizeigericht* for adjudication. *Ein jedes Gericht wird Sie vom Leben verurteilen* ('And any such court would sentence you to death').

I thought about all this. I could almost believe that in this cunning way the Germans hoped to get me to betray myself and my connections and tell them everything I knew, and then, because of my confession, get rid of the lot of us. Weiner read my mind. He cynically remarked that it did indeed sometimes happen that they did things that way. But not this time. He was

WAALER MEETS ALBERT WEINER

ein glühender Nationalsozialist ('an ardent national socialist') but he also had *ein gutes Hertz* ('a good heart'). He would arrange everything in the best possible way for me. I could count on it. My situation was, of course, already very clear. It couldn't get any worse. By accepting his proposal I had a lot to gain and nothing to lose.

Waaler admitted to Weiner that he had had contact with the Milorg leaders 'Hamre' and 'Anker', but that he knew only their cover names and had only ever seen them wearing masks. He had no way of getting in touch with them or identifying them. He downplayed his importance, telling Weiner that those he had contact with were mostly insignificant National Unity members who could hardly be of serious interest to the Gestapo. Weiner appeared unconvinced and the following day had him driven out to Herman Løvenskiold's home in Nesodden in search of the reports he had passed on to Løvenskiold. Løvenskiold had already fled. Handcuffed, Waaler was led into the house. Fru Løvenskiold sat alone and crying. Weiner announced that they would be staying overnight, in case Løvenskiold returned. Fru Løvenskiold was allowed to go to bed and Weiner, another Gestapo man and Waaler spent the night in the living room. Waaler was still handcuffed. At one point Weiner casually wandered over to the window and stood there with his hands behind his back, staring out into the night. He had left his gun on the table in front of Waaler, but Waaler, realising it was a trap, made no move for it. In the morning Weiner courteously asked Fru Løvenskiold if she could provide them with breakfast, assuring her she would be paid for the food and given coupons. As Waaler recalled it, the atmosphere around the breakfast table was, to put it mildly, strained. Having been told by Waaler that the documents had been buried in the garden in a chest of some kind, Weiner then ordered the German soldiers accompanying them to start looking for it. In due course they came across signs of a freshly dug hole which they then re-opened. The hole turned out to be empty, and Waaler realised, to his enormous relief, that Løvenskiold had been able to remove the chest and its contents before fleeing. Afterwards they drove back to Oslo. As it was obvious Løvenskiold wouldn't be returning his wife was taken hostage and sent to Grini. She was imprisoned there for the remainder of the occupation.

Waaler was then taken to the National Archives to locate the documents he had admitted he knew to be hidden there. He was told to go into the reading room and ask for Løvenskiold. As expected, the acting head archivist in the reading room confirmed that Løvenskiold had not been in for several days. Weiner then entered and ordered the acting head archivist to summon his entire staff to the reading room. When the archivist politely asked to see his credentials, Weiner waved a revolver in his face and said '*Die erste Legitimation*' ('This is my first credential') before producing his ID card and announcing it as his second ('*und die zweite*'). The staff were duly summoned. Waaler was told to tell them that he had given Løvenskiold a number of documents for storage in the National Archives, and that it would be very much to his advantage if these documents could be recovered; if anyone knew where they were then they should say so. Naturally, no one did. The staff were dismissed, the National Archives closed and sealed, and Waaler once more driven back to his cell in Møllergate.

For the next few days, he was regularly picked up each morning and driven to Victoria terrasse. Weiner gave him an office and a typewriter and instructed him to make a start on the 'confession' he had promised to give him. Waaler sat there and wrote. Mostly he stuck to the truth. In order to convey the impression that he was giving them the complete and unvarnished truth, he made sure he included descriptions of certain relatively serious matters the Germans could otherwise not have found out about. He wrote openly about his refugee trips to Sweden, and never heard a word of reproach on that account. His description of his plans to abduct the German head of counter-espionage Fehmer and have him sent to England prompted not a single rebuke from Weiner. Waaler's tactic was to make the Germans believe that he had

WAALER MEETS ALBERT WEINER

agreed to tell *everything*, exactly as it was, and leave nothing out. 'It meant,' he wrote, 'writing at length and in detail about matters of no particular significance at all, the better to conceal from them those things which they must not learn at any cost.' These included the fact that although he did not himself know the real name of 'Hamre', the district head of Milorg in Oslo, he knew the names of two people who did, and that one of them was currently held in a prison camp. And because he wrote so openly about so many unimportant things it meant they also believed him when he said he knew nothing of significance about the people from the resistance with whom he was in contact. An added pressure as he sat at the typewriter in Victoria terrasse was the knowledge that the search for the missing documents at the now closed National Archives would be carried out only after his testimony had been completed. This meant he had no way of knowing exactly what the Germans would be able to check once they had resumed their search. 'Had I known for sure that they would not find these documents,' he wrote, 'I would have been able to omit a lot more.'

One day when he was in Weiner's office the secretary came in and told Weiner that 'Colonel' Søvik wanted to speak to him. Weiner hesitated, wrinkled his nose a bit, but told her to show him in. Waaler was sent into an adjacent room, but one of the connecting double doors was left ajar. Although he was unable to pick up the whole conversation, he nevertheless heard enough to know that Søvik wanted to know how the case against Waaler was going. It seems his former Stapo colleagues felt it was dragging on too long. Not long afterwards he heard a third voice, which he recognised as belonging to Karl A. Marthinsen, enter the conversation, urging Weiner to have Waaler eliminated as soon as possible since he represented an extremely serious threat to them all. To his surprise he heard Weiner repeatedly answering them back and defending him. At one point he clearly heard him say '*Schlecht ist der Mensch doch nicht*' ('But this is not a bad person').

When Waaler's 'confession' was finished the Germans told him that the document, despite its scope, was of little use to them. What they were looking for was 'connections upwards', but Waaler could not provide them. He pretended to be despondent at his 'failure'. He suggested they set him free for a few days to see what he could do. 'Anker', he was certain, would get in touch with him. But Weiner's trust in him had reached its limits and Waaler remained a prisoner, spending several weeks in solitary confinement in Møllergata. Then, at the beginning of November, he was driven back to the National Archives by the Gestapo to take part in another search for the missing documents. The head archivist and two of his assistants had also been brought in, and Waaler was instructed to tell them, over and over again, how important it was that the documents were found. He had to speak convincingly, aware that if by a single word or expression he revealed his fear of their actually being found, it would convey to the Gestapo that he was hiding something. Weiner further ratcheted up Waaler's anxiety by informing the archivists that, if the documents were not found, it was obvious what Waaler's fate would be.

The search then got under way, leaving Waaler both terrified that the staff would take Weiner's threat seriously and so uncover the documents, and terrified that they wouldn't. He had time to recall that among the more damning of the copied reports they were supposed to be searching for was one describing the trial and execution of the border guide Knut Mathiesen on 6 May earlier that year, and naming Gunnar Lindvig as the officer in charge of the execution, which had led to Lindvig's killing some three weeks later, on 24 May,* and another in which he had recommended the liquidation of Stapo officer Sverre Thorhus, advising his Milorg contact that this would give him a good chance of succeeding Thorhus as head of Stapo's espionage department. Waaler remembered with chilling clarity the exact wording of that second report – *he fully deserves the same fate as Lindvig, and as soon as possible*. He already knew via the prison grapevine in Møllergata that this report too had been acted on: at 8.57 a.m. on the morning of 3 November

---

* See p. 215.

Sverre Thorhus had been killed by unknown gunmen outside his home in Ruseløkkveien 61.⁶² If those reports should turn up now then not even a senior Gestapo officer like Albert Weiner would be able to save him from the wrath of his Stapo colleagues.

The archivist and his assistants searched the building from basement to attic. They opened every package and envelope. They found nothing. The Germans then took over and searched for another week, but all they found were copies of a couple of illegal newspapers in a broom cupboard. 'The Germans,' wrote Waaler, 'who had no sense of proportion, made a huge fuss about this, arrested the national archivist and sent him to Grini for several months.'

Back in his cell Waaler was visited by Weiner, who told him his case was now closed. As promised, he would not be sent to a concentration camp in Germany. And, as Weiner had also promised, none of the names he had felt obliged to mention in his 'confession' had been arrested. Not even the farmers he had named who had helped him with his refugee transports were approached. Before saying goodbye to him, Weiner informed him that if it later transpired that he had kept quiet about something, then his case would be reopened. Clearly aware of which way the wind was now blowing, Weiner also urged Waaler not to do as so many others did once they were free and 'tell tall tales of the torture and ill-treatment I had experienced in order to make myself interesting and get a martyr's crown. Even if the war ended in Germany's defeat, I should remember that I had been treated decently by him in my hour of need.'

On 15 November a guard entered his cell. *Fertig machen – alles mitnehmen* ('Get ready – take your stuff with you'). Securely handcuffed, he was driven with several others in a prison lorry to the camp at Grini and checked into Barrack Number 1. Soon after his arrival a message was smuggled in from 'Anker' asking for an account of what had happened to him and what he had told Weiner. A few days later he received a message thanking him for the information. He also learned from a recent arrival of a plan to smuggle a bottle containing diphtheria bacilli into the prison. Once Waaler displayed symptoms of being infected with this highly contagious disease, he would, it was assumed, be transferred to Ullevål Hospital, where an attempt would be made to free him. As luck would have it, however, the Germans had recently started treating all sick inmates in the camp hospital itself, and the idea had to be abandoned.

Before long, Waaler was joined at the camp by some familiar faces. Wolff the photographer was one; *Grepo* man Arnfinn Sunde, whom he blamed for his arrest, was another.

> He grinned at first, trying to pretend that nothing had happened. He reeled off a long speech intended to show himself in an advantageous light. Among other things, he said he imagined the State Police were already aware of the connection between him and me and only wanted him to confirm what they already knew. When I said his explanation was manifestly untrue and then asked him some questions he couldn't answer he turned rude and hostile. I didn't want to argue with the man so I broke off all connection with him. Later, whenever I passed him in the camp, he would stare rudely straight at my face without saying anything.

Waaler survived the war and was released from Grini following the liberation on 7 May 1945 and given a railway ticket home to Bergen. The pressures under which he had been living daily for most of the preceding three years were great. Firstly as a Stapo officer, hated and despised by all good *jøssing* as a Nazi and as such always the potential target of a loyalist assassin, and secondly as a double-agent for Milorg running the daily risk of exposure, imprisonment, torture and execution. A telegram from around the time of his release seems to suggest that in the end the pressures did finally get to him. Dated 15 May, and sent by the sheriff of Lista, in Farsund county in Agder, it reads:

> Inspector Gunnar Waaler subject of a missing persons report on the radio today was released from Grini on 10/5. He was very

nervous and believed he was being followed. Always wore a scarf around his neck pulled up to cover his mouth. In addition sunglasses. Always alone.

Gunnar Waaler is not a household name in Norway and is mentioned in only a few of the general histories of the occupation. A small pantheon of names that includes Gunnar Sønsteby, Claus Helberg and Max Manus was established shortly after the liberation, and in the shorthand of Norwegian war history these three have become synonymous with the heroism of the Milorg resistance organisation. They were members of *Oslogjengen* ('the Oslo Detachment'),* a sabotage group under the leadership of Sønsteby. It comprised ten men from different sections of the SOE and was particularly active in the Oslo area in the spring and summer of 1944. Their efforts were crucial to the further demoralisation of the national socialists and the ultimate failure of the attempted revolution. The acclaim for these brave and resourceful men, and for the two who lost their lives in action – Edvard Tallaksen (known as 'Tallak') and Gregers Gram – is fully deserved. But although Gunnar Waaler's contribution was less dramatic than theirs it was arguably more significant. One of the main functions of counterintelligence is to prevent the spectacular, to prevent drama and catastrophe. It is successful when things *don't* happen. The persistent drip of information from Waaler warning of impending raids, changes in manning policies, new thinking in campaigns against the resistance and in the tactics and even the uniforms of the state and the border police was of inestimable value in preventing things happening. 'His contribution in the extremely dangerous counterintelligence and double-agent role he played has quite simply been without parallel,' Major Langeland wrote after the liberation. 'In risking his life every day for a period of years what

---

* Not an exact correspondence. The term was coined by Lieutenant Colonel J.S. Wilson of the SOE's Norwegian section, and the Norwegian 'translation' was based on it.

he gave to the Norwegian resistance movement and to his fellow countrymen was beyond priceless. He microfilmed thousands of documents containing damning proof of the most heinous Nazi crimes. He obtained copies of the State Police's monthly reports to Quisling containing information that proved to be of incalculable value to the Norwegian security service. His timely warning to Professor Hallesby in 1942 prevented the church resistance group's archives from falling into the hands of the State Police and the inevitable destruction of the group.'

Waaler was not a natural social democrat. But unlike Vidkun Quisling and the members of National Unity he was able to live with the fact, and not oppose a way of doing things that he knew most of his fellow countrymen were in favour of. In what may or may not have been part of his complex survival strategy during interrogation he once told Weiner that he had always been fond of Germany and Germans. He understood German Nazism, he told him, but had come to realise it was essentially a *konjunkturfenomen* ('a product of the times') and not right for Norway. He may even have shared some of the simpler values of what made a man a good tribal German. In his post-war life as a district attorney in Tromsø in 1962 he once dismissed a case brought by a journalist against a ship's pilot for assault on the grounds that the journalist 'deserved what he got' for something he had written about the pilot in his paper.[63] As Himmler told Eivind Berggrav when the bishop had complained of *hird* brawling in Norwegian streets and schools, sorting things out with one's fists was 'the Germanic way'. 'I know some of the things on Weiner's record are bad,' Waaler wrote after the war. 'But my memory of him is coloured by the honest sympathy he had for me which is the only reason I am alive today. Weiner kept his promises to me. He made no use of the information I gave him. That a *Kriminalrat* in the German Gestapo, at great personal risk, should have kept this whole business to himself and held a protecting hand not only over me but over my connections is, I would think, unique.'

PART 5

LIBERATION AND AFTERMATH

13

The Beginning of the End

The addled decency and sense of honour that Weiner brought to his dealings with Gunnar Waaler in the autumn and early winter of 1944 may well have been influenced by the wider progress of the war. Nazi Germany's fortunes had turned irreversibly by early 1944. On 11 January 1944 an army of 800,000 Russian soldiers broke the German lines around Leningrad and ended a siege of the city that had been going on for 880 days. The German divisions that survived the onslaught had to fall back to the Panther-Wotan line, along the River Dneiper. The Finns, who had been fighting the Continuation War with the Soviet Union since the end of the Winter War in March 1940, and saw no prospect of success, began negotiating for a separate peace with the Soviets in March 1944. The talks dragged on, and the Continuation War continued, the territorial disputes involved still unresolved. On 6 June 1944 the Allied forces landed on the beaches of Normandy and began their rapid advance through France towards the German borders. It was obvious to any but the most blinkered observer that sooner rather than later the war would end in defeat for Germany. The only question was when and how.

On 21 June a Russian army of over 2 million men mounted a sustained assault on the German forces on the Eastern Front, Operation Bagration, on the same day as the Russians broke the Finnish line between Lake Ladoga and Lake Onega. Early in September the Finns accepted the Russian terms for peace, the most prominent of these being a demand that all German soldiers leave Finnish territory by 15 September. The demand turned out to have disastrous consequences for Norwegians living in the far north of the country, in the counties of Finnmark and Nord-Troms. On 4 October Hitler gave orders that the soldiers of the 20th Mountain Lapland Army (the 'Lapland Army') – all 204,000 of them – were to withdraw from their positions in Finland, cross the border, march across Norway and establish a line by the Lyngenfjord. From there they would continue to Mo i Rana, in Nordland. Trains would then transport them to southern Norway, from there they would be shipped to Denmark to be deployed in the defence of Germany's threatened borders. On 18 October the first Soviet troops entered Norway. Following a week of fierce fighting, Kirkenes – or what was left of it after 328 Allied bombing raids – was liberated. The Soviets advanced a further 150 kilometres into Norwegian territory before stopping at the River Tana on 8 November.

Hitler's response to fears that the Soviet army would continue to pursue his retreating soldiers into Norway was to order a scorched-earth policy in Finnmark and Nord-Troms that would make a barren wilderness of the two counties and leave the Russians with nothing to eat and nowhere to shelter. This required the immediate evacuation of the region. Vidkun Quisling was informed of the decision and, while not insensitive to the suffering it involved, he was convinced of its necessity, fearing that to leave the area inhabited raised the possibility of the Allies in the north inviting the legitimate government to return to Norway under their protection, a development that would spell the end for himself and his government and its spurious claims to legitimacy. He appointed his Minister for Policing Jonas Lie as Regional Overseer for Finnmark and Nord-Troms and sent the Minister for Social Affairs, Johan Andreas Lippestad, up north with Lie as his deputy to organise the evacuation of the region's 60,000 inhabitants.[64]

The plane carrying Lie and Lippestad landed at Høybuktmoen near Kirkenes on 11 October and the ministers at once set about the difficult and unpleasant task of persuading the population of the necessity of evacuation. So just as it had done in carrying through the Norwegian holocaust, the occupying power had again succeeded in getting collaborating Norwegians to do the dirtiest work. It pulled the strings, but the only visible effect was the dancing of Norwegian puppets.

The simultaneous evacuations of vast numbers of Norwegian civilians and German military personnel put an intolerable burden on the rudimentary infrastructure of the region. Inevitably it was the needs of the German army under their commander General Lothar Rendulic that took precedence. Hoping to keep the civilian evacuation at a manageable and steady trickle that would leave room for his troops, lorries, prisoners, wagons and horses, Rendulic initially permitted only a 'word-of-mouth' campaign to spread the news of the evacuation; but when after a week there was no sign of movement at all he gave Lie permission to have posters printed describing the need for evacuation and details of how it would be handled. Lie and his small group of National Unity associates then spent the next few weeks on a whistle-stop tour of towns, settlements and workplaces urging on his listeners the need to flee the area as soon as possible. He spoke of his own experiences in Bolshevik Russia and of what life under Russian occupation would be like if they didn't flee: 'I've had personal experience of communist Russia and I know what it would mean for a proud and noble people like the Norwegians. Murder. Plunder. Terror. Uncertainty. Rape. Godlessness. Moral destitution. Events in the war could mean you'll be facing this winter without a home. Think of your children. Think of their future. As strongly as I can I urge each and every one of you to take this opportunity to get out while there is still time. Seize this chance now. Very soon it will be too late and you will be left with nothing but regrets and the burden of responsibility. This is the awful truth.'

To Lie's disbelieving frustration few heeded his warnings. Norwegians living in the sparsely populated north had developed a *modus vivendi* with the occupying troops that gave the occupation a quite different character from that in the more populous cities and towns of mid-Norway and the south and east. Soldiers were billeted in private households. A small rent was often paid. Germans and Norwegians bathed together in the sauna. Many young Norwegian children were already fluent speakers of German. For, as Lie often heard in response to his fright-mongering, the experience of those in the north was that the average German soldier behaved in a disciplined and proper fashion. They treated the local people with respect, and people could see no reason why Russians would behave any differently.[65] The fact that the region was so sparsely populated, combined with the sheer geographical extent of Norway – if tipped on its axis it would extend as far south as Rome – had created significantly different experiences of the occupation for the north and the south. Milorg had no organisation in Finnmark. No illegal newspapers were produced north of Tromsø and the confiscation of radio sets in the early days of the war had been almost completely successful. Among other things this meant that the moral and practical guidelines known as *paroles* that resistance leaders and the authorities in London broadcast in response to specific events and initiatives from Quisling and the occupying powers rarely penetrated as far as the north.

On a brief visit to the north on 26 October the Reichskommissar saw for himself that the policy of suggesting to people that they leave their homes and farms so that these could be burned to the ground and the livestock killed was simply not going to work. Back in Oslo he urgently advised Hitler to make the process compulsory. Two days later Hitler issued the appropriate decree:

Owing to the reluctance of the inhabitants of northern Norway to evacuate voluntarily, the Führer has taken the Reichskommissar's advice and ordered that the entire Norwegian population living east of the Lyngenfjord be evacuated, by force, for their own safety. All houses are to be burned to the ground or otherwise destroyed. The German Supreme Commander in North Finland is responsible for the ruthless enactment of this order. Only in this way can the Russians, with their powerful forces, be prevented from taking advantage of the settlements and of a local population familiar with the region to pursue our troops and potentially reach the Lyngenfjord line as early as this winter. Sympathy for those involved is an inappropriate reaction.[66]

The final comment – added at Terboven's recommendation – indicates that even Adolf Hitler, in his dedicated pursuit of amorality as a weapon of war, must have had some sense of the enormity of what he was ordering. Over the next few weeks, as the main body of Wehrmacht soldiers made their way west across Finnmark and Nord-Troms, heading for the Lyngenfjord, 'burner-groups' brought up the rear, moving from house to house and settlement to settlement and leaving nothing standing in their wake. Bottles of petrol were hung from the rafters and light fittings in every house and farm building and the windows broken to improve the through-draught before the bottles were broken and the homes set on fire.

As people often do when confronted with an impossible imperative, some persuaded themselves that the order to evacuate did not apply to them. They found themselves woken in the early hours of the morning by soldiers and given thirty minutes in which to leave. In the belief that their houses would be left standing and waiting for their return still others gave their homes a thorough clean before locking the doors and heading for the designated local assembly points. No food must be left for the advancing Russians. That meant that all livestock was slaughtered save for horses, which were requisitioned for the needs of the huge army of retreating Wehrmacht soldiers. The moral horror of what they were about led to isolated incidents of drunken depravity among the burners. Sheep were doused with petrol and set on fire as living flares. As one farmer looked on soldiers emptied their machine guns into his cattle and he had to watch as the distraught animals ran into the cold waters of the nearby lake, their intestines floating around their bellowing heads. War at its most degraded and degrading.

Many of those made homeless preferred to take their chances in the wilderness rather than in the south and fled to the mountains. Soldiers were sent in pursuit of them with orders to bring them back for transport away from the region. A public proclamation warned inhabitants of the town of Lebesby that anyone fleeing to the mountains with the intention of remaining there until the Russians arrived would be arrested and shot as a spy. The final line of the announcement abandoned any attempt at logic and simply stated that anyone trying to remain hidden in any other way, or offering any resistance to the evacuation at all, would be shot.

Despite these threats thousands of those who fled managed to evade capture and eke out a harsh existence in tents and in *gammer*, shelters made of peat and earth laid across a wooden frame. Over 3,000 of the inhabitants of Kirkenes took refuge in the tunnels and mineshafts of the Sydvaranger company at Bjørnevatn. The mine had long been in use as an air-raid shelter and was already partially equipped for such an emergency, though it was never meant to accommodate such a large number. A small flock of goats and five or six cows provided the mine-dwellers with milk. Ten children first saw the light of day in that dim and shadowy world. The little community survived in the tunnels for over two months, emerging with the arrival of their Russian liberators.[67]

Jonas Lie, meanwhile, was still trying to carry out orders to move over 60,000 people out of the region. Given the logistical difficulties he faced the fact that some 40,000 were evacuated must have felt like some measure of success. Every conceivable means of transport had been requisitioned by the Wehrmacht for its own needs: buses, cars, lorries, vans, motorbikes, bicycles. For the devastatingly logical reason that these would no longer be needed, since fires were to be started and not extinguished, they even commandeered all the fire engines in the region. Petrol for civilian use was no longer available. All of this to transport the 170,000 German soldiers on the first leg of their journey back to Germany along the narrow ribbon of Riksvei 50, the Arctic Highway, a road that was never meant to deal with anything remotely approaching that volume of traffic. Eyewitnesses reported seeing a column of Russian prisoners of war being beaten and whipped along a road many of them had perhaps helped to build as Nazi slaves – stumbling along in rags, hollow-eyed with starvation, their feet swathed in filthy rotting fabric, their skin a sickly yellow. Like a procession of old men, someone said. It seems that not even the 40,000 horses and 13,000 lorries were enough to transport the army's weapons and equipment, for bringing up the rear of the 12-kilometre-long column of prisoners were four teams of human scarecrows, each sixteen-man team hitched to a four-wheeled wagon as they dragged it along the narrow road to Lyngen.

The campaign of burning and destruction would continue into February of the new year, but by the end of November 1944 Jonas Lie felt he had done as much as he could and made ready to return to Oslo. Eleven thousand homes had been destroyed. Four thousand barns and stables, 230 industrial sites, 420 business premises, 306 fishing communities, 53 hotels and boarding houses, 106 schools, 60 community halls, 21 hospitals and clinics, 140 assembly halls and 27 churches had been reduced to ashes. Roads, bridges, quays, boats, telephone poles, wells and lighthouses were all gone. The entire infrastructure of the region was devastated.

And it might all have been in vain. Having advanced 150 kilometres into Norwegian territory, the Russians did indeed stop at the Tana River. In a speech in Moscow announcing the liberation of Kirkenes on October 25 the Russian Foreign Minister Vyacheslav Molotov formally invited Norwegian troops and the legitimate Norwegian government to return and begin the process of reclaiming their country. An agreement reached in May of 1944 in which the Norwegian government had invited Russia to occupy the north of the country as a temporary sovereign power, with a similar offer being made to the British in the south, was adhered to by both parties. Elsewhere in Europe the Russians colonised the territories they had entered as a result of the war; Norway proved the exception. By 20 November the legitimate London government's Minister of Justice Terje Wold was in Kirkenes, arriving at about the same time as a symbolic force of 233 Norwegian soldiers from their base in Scotland. Arne Fjellbu, driven from his post as Dean of Trondheim Cathedral three years earlier for his protests against the State Act, returned from his refugee's exile in Sweden as the new bishop of a liberated Finnmark on 15 December. 'Morning service began at eleven o'clock,' he later recalled. 'The modest little church at Polmak was full of Lapps in their beautiful brightly coloured costumes. When all the seats were taken people sat on the floor. Even that wasn't sufficient. People sat on the steps of the pulpit. Even the ring of the altar was occupied.' Uncompromising as ever, Fjellbu then led them in a service that lasted over four hours.[68]

Jonas Lie, meanwhile, passed through Trondheim on the first leg of his journey back to Oslo. With the help of Henrik Rogstad, National Unity's senior party official in the region, he established a reception centre for the displaced refugees before booking seats on the night train to Oslo. Upon arriving at the railway station, Lie and his party were dismayed to find that the train comprised third-class carriages only. As a celebrity who had seen his fame soured to hatred almost overnight in 1940, he was deeply uncomfortable at the prospect of so many hours unprotected in the company of what he could safely assume would be a hostile crowd of fellow passengers. He suggested to the Station Master that one of the second-class carriages he had seen parked in a siding at the station be coupled to the train for himself and his party. The Station Master refused. A vehement argument ensued between this obstinate man and Lie that ended in inevitable victory for National Unity. A second-class carriage was hitched to the train and Lie and his associates were able to journey south in the privacy of their own accommodation. They did so in considerably more style and comfort than the thousands of northern evacuees who were stowed on board the *Adolf Binder* and the *Karl Arp* in freezing cargo holds on the first leg of their journey south from the embarkation point at Tana down to Narvik. These vessels had only minimal supplies of food and water and dysentery and diphtheria were rife. The voyage took a week and by the time the *Karl Arp* docked in Narvik, 95 per cent of those on board were too frail to disembark without assistance. For their own protection, the fire brigade personnel who helped them ashore had to wear gas masks.

As Lie's concern about his travel arrangements shows, he was well aware that, after Vidkun Quisling, he was probably the most hated Norwegian in the country. But Karl A. Marthinsen, by this time head of the state police, the criminal police and the border police as well as leader of the *hird*, ran him a close second. Lie was a government minister but it was debateable who wielded the greater authority of the two, who the resistance movement feared most, and who was considered the more urgent candidate for liquidation. The choice fell on Marthinsen and his was the name at the top of a list of seven potential targets for Milorg that was drawn up by the government in London in November. Responsibility for arranging his assassination was given to codename Number 24, Gunnar Sønsteby.[69]

Following the retirement of the communist-inspired Osvald Group, Sønsteby and his associates in the Oslo Gang took over as the most active saboteurs in the final stages of the war. In a bid to prevent the Germans from moving the large number of Wehrmacht troops still stationed in Norway to join the fighting in mainland Europe, they concentrated on disrupting the lines of rapid mass transportation, blowing up railway lines, bridges and roads. Sønsteby later explained that the absence of Vidkun Quisling's name from the listed targets resulted from a perception that the minister-president's habitual incompetence in dealing with the Germans was regarded as a distinct benefit by the resistance movement and not something they were interested in disrupting. There was also a feeling that Quisling was not bound to violence to quite the same extent as either Marthinsen or Jonas Lie. The resistance tapped Marthinsen's phone and had sporadic access to his mail and knew enough to suspect that his response to the prospect of defeat would be to fight to the death. He possessed the charisma Quisling lacked and there was a well-grounded fear that when the moment of surrender arrived he would summon it to urge those under his command to arm themselves and die fighting in a civil war that could cost thousands of Norwegian lives. Several weeks earlier he had lost his twenty-year-old-son Kjell Andreas, an SS-Untersturmführer in the Waffen-SS, when the plane carrying the boy home from Berlin crashed into a mountain, killing all fifteen on board. The loss might have knocked some of the fight out of Marthinsen, but one of his mantras was that *tapet er en del av krigens mening* (loss is part of the meaning of war). So he remained firmly in Milorg's sights, even though its leadership knew his death would mean the reprisal killings of a large number of innocent Norwegians.

By the beginning of 1945 Marthinsen was living in Blindernveien 74, in a large and stylish house named Villa Bellevue. The villa stood next to the Gaustadbekken, a stream whose tumbling waters – which effectively formed a protective moat around the back of the property – were undoubtedly one of the reasons Marthinsen requisitioned it for his own use in the first place. A few minutes after nine on the morning of 8 February his driver picked him up in his 1939 Graham to drive him to work. Marthinsen sat in the front passenger seat and the car set off down the hill. Slowing to cross the metro lines at the bottom, it began the ascent towards the students' hall of residence at the top. The petrol engine had been converted to run on gas and the weight of the generator further reduced the car's power. As it crawled over the crest of the hill where the road flattens out it was sprayed by gunfire from the Milorg operatives hidden behind a woodpile on the side of the road. Marthinsen and his driver were both hit, Marthinsen fatally. The car slewed to a halt and the driver managed to get out and run for the shelter of a nearby house. Before the eyes of shocked children making their way along the road to school, a gunman then approached and shot Marthinsen in the head through the car window.

The reprisals were immediate. Twenty-nine imprisoned Norwegians were placed before drumhead courts that same evening and within forty-eight hours all had been executed. Two of those taken were among the fifteen with whom Gunnar Waaler shared Room Number 9 in Barrack Number 1 at Grini. Four of those executed were not even prisoners but simply prominent citizens picked up and killed in revenge. A grieving Sverre Riisnæs insisted on joining one of the firing squads at Akershus Fortress for the executions as a way of expressing his anger at the loss of his friend Marthinsen. Drunk on wine, cognac and five or six Benzedrine tablets, he took his place alongside eight uniformed policemen as the blindfolded victims were brought out in groups of two and

three, a spotlight trained on them, and the order given to fire. He claimed later to have been so drunk he was unsure whether he'd hit any of them at all.[70] As Gunnar Waaler learned after the war, his own name was next on the list of those to be shot in the event of any further reprisal executions.

The number of those killed in reprisal was in excess of anything the resistance had anticipated. But it still fell short of the seventy-five Terboven had initially suggested, with both Jonas Lie and Sverre Riisnæs having to work hard to persuade Heinrich Fehlis, in charge of the Nazi response, of the futility of reprisal killings on such a scale. As the extravagant violence of Terboven's response to Marthinsen's killing might indicate, both sides in the conflict knew by this time that the end of the war and inevitable German defeat were only a matter of weeks away. In January the Russians had mounted a major offensive against the German army from the east, isolating East Prussia and Schleswig and entering Czechoslovakia and Hungary and, in due course, Austria, while Allied forces crossed the German border in the west as larger German towns such as Dresden and Hamburg were subjected to intense aerial bombardment. By 23 April Soviet troops had entered Berlin, and two days later linked up with American troops at the town of Torgau, in north-west Saxony. On 30 April Adolf Hitler, having first ordered his doctor to poison Blondi, his Alsatian dog, shot himself in his bunker deep beneath the Reich Chancellery building in Berlin.

The news did not appear in the Norwegian newspapers until Wednesday 2 May, with *Aftenposten* reporting that the Führer had died a hero's death, falling in the battle against communism.* Already with an eye on the coming day of reckoning for the National Unity administration and ministers, the Oslo Gang

---

* It was in the erroneous belief that Hitler had died in battle that Norway's Nobel Prize-winning novelist Knut Hamsun wrote his infamous necrology for the same newspaper on 7 May, in which he hailed Hitler as 'a warrior for mankind, and a prophet of the gospel of justice for all nations'.

under Gunnar Sønsteby raided the ministries of Policing and Justice in Akersgate in central Oslo on the evening of the same day, encountering no resistance as they removed vast quantities of archival material from the offices of both ministries, including a safe that weighed 700 kilograms. On Thursday 3 May the German Sipo released 1,200 Norwegian prisoners, all men over 55 years of age and all women over 50. On 5 May Quisling spoke for the last time on the radio as Norway's 'Minister-President', assuring listeners that the priority for him and his government was the avoidance of civil war. To the last he remained convinced of the rightness of his course of action, from the day of the invasion on 9 April 1940 onwards: 'The national Norwegian government is the country's legal government,' he said. 'And until it is relieved of its duties by another legal government it must therefore be obeyed.'[71] On 7 May, at Allied headquarters in the French city of Reims, General Alfred Jodl agreed to an unconditional German capitulation, with a ceasefire to take effect at midnight on 8 May. The news was broadcast on Norwegian radio in its German language transmission at 3.50 p.m. in the afternoon, and in Norwegian at 5.30. At 6.45 a.m. the following morning Quisling and six of his ministers arrived by car at the police station at Møllergata 19 to hand themselves over to the authorities.

On 7 May Terboven had offered Quisling the opportunity to flee the country using his private plane, a Heinkel 111, but the offer had been rejected. The Reichskommissar's own response to the last days of the war was that of a man who hated to lose, whether in battle or in the games of ping-pong he used to play with his secretary at Skaugum. On Adolf Hitler's fifty-sixth birthday on 20 April 1945 he had sent a congratulatory greeting to his Führer: 'Every one of us, no matter what uniform we wear, are prepared to offer our lives for the preservation of *Festung Norwegen* until Germany is victorious and the honour, freedom and future of our people is assured.' When the news of Hitler's suicide reached him ten days later he had wept. But his pitiless faith in the Führer survived unshaken, as he shortly afterwards confirmed in the only way possible.

On 3 May Terboven had been summoned to attend a meeting at Flensburg, in Schleswig-Holstein, with the man nominated by Hitler as his successor, Admiral Karl Dönitz. Among others present at the meeting were General Franz Böhme, head of the German armed forces in Norway. Terboven expressed his view that the fight must go on, there were still over 300,000 military and naval personnel stationed in Norway, a vast military resource. But as he soon realised, Dönitz's only use for the troops was to barter with the Allies for the time he needed – he estimated eight days – to get his troops out of Czechoslovakia and back into the west.

Back in Oslo, Terboven returned to his country residence at Skaugum. His secretary Gerda Hettich later reported overhearing him involved in a fierce argument in his office with Heinrich Fehlis.[72] She was unable to hear what the two were arguing about. When he emerged, somewhat to her surprise he invited her to join him in a game of table tennis in the basement. Depressed and frightened by the doom-laden atmosphere in the house, she then made her way into Oslo.

Next day, on 7 May, she turned up for work as usual. Following telephoned instructions from Rediess she spent most of the morning in Terboven's office, systematically burning all of his archived material and documents. Finally, using a hammer, she smashed the two small busts the former Reichskommissar kept on his desk, one of Adolf Hitler, the other of his ten-year-old daughter, Inge.[73] In the afternoon she was one of a small group sitting and drinking cognac in Rediess' nearby office. Among those present was Leon Degrelle, leader of the Belgian Nazi Party, who had recently arrived from Denmark. Presently they were joined by Oberfeldwebel Dühringen, Terboven's pilot. He informed them that Terboven had told him he had no use for the Heinkel 111 earlier declined by Quisling, and Dühringen could do as he pleased with it. The pilot had worked out that the plane had just enough fuel to reach Spain and offered seats to anyone who wanted to join him. Only Degrelle accepted, and the plane took off later in the day bound for Franco's Spain, with Peron's Argentina the ultimate destination.

Back at Skaugum, later that same evening, Rediess gave orders to the head of Terboven's personal bodyguard, Friedrich Barthel, that he was to move five drums of explosives into the bunker on the estate. He then smoked a cigarette and retired to his room. He failed to answer a number of phone calls made to him during the night. At 10 a.m. on 8 May, following Terboven's instructions, Barthel tried Rediess' door. It was locked. He carried a ladder from the garden shed, leant it against the outside wall and climbed over onto the balcony. The balcony door was unlocked and Barthel walked through the room, unlocked the interior door and admitted Terboven. Both wordlessly studied the body slumped on the sofa. Terboven leaned forward. He picked up the small pistol from Rediess' lifeless right hand and slipped it into his pocket. He turned to Barthel:

'He was too early,' he said. 'Lock this door and don't let anyone in. When it's dusk, carry him out to the bunker.'

Terboven spent the early afternoon saying goodbye to his bodyguards, drivers and domestic staff. At about a quarter to three, accompanied by Barthel, he walked through the garden to inspect the bunker where Rediess' body was to be brought later in the evening. As they walked Terboven asked about the five canisters of explosives: would that be enough? Barthel replied that five would be too many, one would suffice. Terboven insisted that no trace of his body must survive the explosion and Barthel reassured him that one drum would be sufficient to ensure the atomisation of the body.

Inside the bunker they spent a few minutes discussing exactly where this single drum of explosives should be placed. They then returned to the house. Terboven settled in a chair and picked up the book he was in the middle of reading, a crime novel by an English writer. For a few moments he seemed engrossed in it. Suddenly he looked up:

'Have all the women gone?'

'Not yet,' said Barthel.

'They must all be gone by seven,' said Terboven.

Barthel nodded. Terboven lowered his head and returned to his novel.

By 7 p.m. the only staff member remaining in the house was the butler, a man named Reimer. Barthel had moved the single drum of explosive out to the bunker and prepared the fuse. At Terboven's request it was five metres long. Barthel had protested that it would take over eight minutes to burn, but Terboven was adamant. He wanted five metres.

Shortly after 7 p.m. Reimer emerged from the kitchen carrying a tray with a plate of sandwiches, a bottle of beer, a pot of coffee and a miniature liqueur. He placed the tray on the coffee table in front of Terboven. Terboven laid the book face-down on the arm of the chair before looking up at Reimer and nodding his thanks. He ate the supper. Taking the liqueur and the book with him, he then retired to his study.

At 10.30 p.m. Barthel, helped by Rediess' adjutant Helmut Saur and a second member of Terboven's bodyguard, carried Rediess' body out to the bunker. Halfway along the path back to the main house a thought occurred to Barthel and he stopped. Though it had never been explicitly stated, he understood that Terboven himself intended to be in the bunker with Rediess' body when the explosion occurred. Concerned for the comfort of the former Reichskommissar during the eight minutes and twenty seconds he would be sitting on the drum before this occurred, he made his way back across the lawn to the garden shed, leaving the others to take Rediess into the bunker.

Inside the shed, and with difficulty, he searched in the dark for a suitable plank. He found one and carried it back across the grass and into the bunker. He made his way through the corridors to where the drum of explosives had been positioned and placed it across the top, pedantically adjusting it until satisfied that the small overlap was evenly distributed on each side.

He then returned to the house. He went to the ground-floor bathroom and washed his hands in the washbasin. He did so slowly. He towelled his hands thoroughly. Satisfied that they were dry, he left the bathroom and made his way down the carpeted corridor. He stopped outside Terboven's study and knocked on the door. Terboven called to him to come in. When Barthel entered he looked up quizzically from his book.

Barthel cleared his throat. He announced that everything was now ready. Terboven closed the novel and placed it on the floor next to his chair. He stood up. Barthel held the door open for him and followed him out of the room, followed him into the kitchen. Reimer the butler was standing in front of an open cupboard, looking up at some crockery. Terboven stopped in front of the back door. Reimer crossed the room and opened it for him and Terboven stepped outside. He looked up at the sky. It was a cloudy night. The temperature was mild. Terboven took a deep breath. 'If you happen to run across them when you get back to Germany,' he said, 'please remember me to my family.'

'I will do that,' Reimer assured him.

Reimer and Barthel then stood watching and listening as Terboven crunched down the gravel path, jackboots glinting briefly in a shaft of light from the kitchen window before the darkness swallowed him. Barthel looked at his watch 11.10 p.m. Reimer and Barthel turned and stepped back into the house, closing the door behind them. At 11.30, thirty minutes before the unconditional surrender order became operative, the bunker exploded. The windows in houses for miles around shook for a long second, and then stopped.*

*

---

* Terboven's death made him one of the eleven Nazi Gauleiters who committed suicide in 1945. Two more died fighting, one was shot by the SS, twenty-seven were imprisoned and eleven died under 'mysterious circumstances'. Seven were tried, condemned to death and executed. Two appear to have escaped.

All that survived the explosion at Skaugum were an Iron Cross and the twisted steel frames of a pair of spectacles. It was important to establish beyond all doubt that these were relics of Norway's late Reichskommissar Josef Terboven and, as luck would have it, the only part of the body left intact was a charred elbow bone which, on closer examination, showed signs of a break corresponding to an injury Terboven was known to have suffered in a plane crash seven years earlier. A mere twelve years after it had started, the Nazi dream of a Thousand-Year Reich in Europe seemed to have come to an end with the German surrender at midnight on 8 May; while the last vestiges of National Socialist Norway had apparently disappeared half an hour previously, with the detonation of 50 kilograms of dynamite at Skaugum. However, a bizarre endgame was still to be played out – over the course of three further days – at Skallum Manor, a farm on the western outskirts of Oslo.

14

Skallum

Two members of Quisling's government had defied Vidkun Quisling's orders to surrender without further violence following the German capitulation: Jonas Lie, the Minister of Policing, and Sverre Riisnæs, the Minister of Justice, made no secret of the fact that they intended to fight on to the death. In this they were joined by Henrik Rogstad, the former National Unity regional leader in the Trondheim area, whose personal feud with the theatre manager Henry Gleditsch had led to Gleditsch's death before a firing squad in October 1942. Within the disintegrating authority structure of the National Unity administration Rogstad was now head of the Stapo following the assassination of Karl A. Marthinsen in February, in spite of the fact that he had no previous experience of police work. Still only twenty-nine, considerably younger than either Lie or Riisnæs, Rogstad was now also national leader of the *hird*.

On the evening before the German capitulation was due to come into force these three had made their way to Skallum Manor, the smallest of Stabekk's four estate farms. Since March 1945 the farm had been the headquarters of a group of Norwegian Nazi commandos and was already heavily fortified and equipped as a small military base. Barbed wire surrounded the perimeter, the main driveway was protected by a barrier and a floodlight was hidden among nearby trees. A bunker with another floodlight had been built beside the driveway, and a second bunker closer to the house. There were large numbers of machine guns inside the main farmhouse, handguns and hand grenades, and plentiful supplies of ammunition for these. Inside the main bunker was a Sten gun, also well provided with ammunition. For men who dreamed of dying in a blaze of glory it must have seemed the perfect setting, and Lie can only have hoped that the group of sixty now assembled at the house with him, comprising members of the Ski Hunters Company and students enrolled at the police academy who had been hastily summoned to present themselves at Skallum, shared the thought with him. He had already taken a last farewell of his wife and two children, and his mother. He had given them suicide pills, obtained for him by Quisling's own doctor, Hans Eng, with instructions that they were to be used only in the event of a full-scale Russian occupation of Norway, with all the horrors Lie was certain would follow, including rape. When the German capitulation came into force at one minute past midnight on the morning of 9 May he announced to those remaining at the farm with him that the war was now over. Those who wished to leave were free to do so. All sixty of his audience, aware as Lie must have been that none of them faced the certain death penalty as certainly as their three leaders, did indeed slip away in the night, and no doubt to his great disappointment Lie awoke next morning to find himself alone, with only Sverre Riisnæs and Henrik Rogstad for company.[74]

Aware that something was afoot at Skallum, Milorg leaders had ordered section D13.313 (District 13 Oslo and Akershus, Division 3, area 1, group 3) of the organisation to surround Skallum. Under the command of Jens Wulfsberg the group had occupied Stabekk *Ungdomshuset*, a youth centre on Skogveien on Gamle Ringeriksvei not far from the main gateway to the Skallum estate.[75] Following the surrender and detention of the Quisling cabinet at Møllergata 19 in the early hours of Wednesday 9 May there were fears that the activity at Skallum might be a prelude to an assault on the city centre prison and an attempt to liberate the Norwegian *fører* and his colleagues. But by the morning of Wednesday 9 May Wulfsberg realised the situation was no longer urgent.

For several reasons, however, it remained precarious. Having stopped and questioned some of those leaving the house in the early hours of the morning Wulfsberg and his comrades were aware of how well-stocked it was with weapons and ammunition. They had also learned of the existence of 250 kilograms of plastic explosives stored in the basement of the west wing of the house. If the three desperadoes really did intend to go out fighting and made use of these resources then a great many lives might be lost. For the time being at least, Wulfsberg and his associates decided that a direct assault on the farmhouse was out of the question. They must wait and see how the situation developed.

Now, as he looked through his binoculars, Wulfsberg saw three men standing outside the main bunker, some 60 metres from the farmhouse. Jonas Lie, known for his personal vanity and love of uniform, was the one wearing full SS uniform and a steel helmet. The younger, dark-haired man in the long, belted police overcoat next to him was Henrik Rogstad. The third, wearing a similar uniform to Lie's, was Sverre Riisnæs. Lie and Rogstad were watching Riisnæs as he squatted over a drum of what looked like cable, turning it this way and that as though looking for the free end. Rogstad stooped beside him to offer his assistance.

On impulse Wulfsberg decided to telephone the farm and walked the short distance to a nearby private house with a telephone wire visible. It was some 200 metres from Skallum and afforded a clear view of the whole area between the bunker and the farmhouse. He knocked on the door and, when the owner answered, identified himself and requested to be allowed to use the telephone. It stood on a table facing a large bay window in the front room and he was able to watch as he heard the phone ringing at the other end and one of the three made his way over to the farmhouse, mounted the three wooden steps and disappeared inside. Moments later the ringing stopped as the phone was picked up.

'This is the head of the Milorg group surrounding Skallum,' he said into the silence. 'Who is this?'

'Riisnæs.'

More silence.

'Here is our ultimatum,' Wulfsberg continued. 'All three of you are to leave the house carrying a white flag. You are to be unarmed. Make your way on foot down the main drive and surrender to us. You have my word that no harm will come to you. You will be handed over to the legal authorities and you will in due course stand trial before a Norwegian court of law.'

He heard Riisnæs clear his throat: 'Jonas Lie is in command here at Skallum. I must first confer with him.'

Wulfsberg rested the receiver against his chin and watched through the window as Riisnæs reappeared, made his way at a trot across the grass to the bunker and passed the message on to Lie. They conversed. It was impossible at that distance to gauge the tenor of their conversation. A blue budgerigar in a cage on a stand on the other side of the window bay momentarily distracted him, furiously lunging at its own image in a small, round mirror wedged between two of the bars. He looked back at the farm just as Riisnæs was disappearing through the open front door.

'The minister proposes that your negotiators meet him at the bunker,' Riisnæs said, slightly out of breath.

'That is out of the question. Tell Jonas Lie that if he meets us at the main gate I guarantee his safe passage back to the farmhouse afterwards.'

As Wulfsberg watched Lie began making his unhurried way towards the open door. Moments later he was on the line himself.

'This is the Minister for Policing here. Surrender is completely out of the question. Completely. It's all over for us. We know that. We know you are in full control of the situation. But we are still in control of our own lives and of how we might choose to end them. So there's really nothing more to be said.'

His speech was slow and slightly slurred, but he spoke the last sentence with such finality that Wulfsberg, fearing he was about to hang up, offered a counter-suggestion: what if they met halfway between the bunker and the main gate? Both parties to be unarmed?

'Agreed,' said Lie after a moment's hesitation. 'I'd like to bring Rogstad as my adjutant.'

'Agreed,' Wulfsberg responded. 'I'll be accompanied by my adjutant too. The time now is', he shot back his cuff and checked his wristwatch, 'thirteen forty. We'll meet at two o'clock.'

Wulfsberg hung up as soon as he'd said this, deliberately depriving Lie of the satisfaction of ending the conversation. He then left the room, almost knocking over the houseowner as he opened the door to the hall.

'Are they going to surrender?'

'We'll have to wait and see,' said Wulfsberg. Then, greatly surprising himself, as he opened the front door he paused. 'Your budgerigar is lonely,' he said. 'You should either get it a companion or set it free.'

'He wouldn't last five minutes in the wild,' the owner responded in an aggrieved tone, suspecting he was being criticised.

'Even so.' Wulfsberg shrugged, thanked him for the use of his telephone and then made his way back to the command post.

Before beginning the long walk up the tree-lined driveway to the main house, Wulfsberg ordered two Bren guns and several snipers to cover the arranged meeting point; if Lie and Rogstad did anything unexpected at all he and Sandberg, his adjutant, would throw themselves to the ground and the snipers were to open fire. At exactly 1400 hours the two men set off, walking side by side down the driveway between the tall silver birches. As agreed, neither one of them was armed. The weather was mild, almost thirteen degrees, with the slight threat of rain from the low cloud cover.

Within a minute of passing between the gateposts they saw Lie and Rogstad emerging from the bunker that had been the scene of so much activity since the siege began and start to cross the grass in the direction of the driveway. As their paths intersected they stopped at a point that left some 10 metres between them. The two offered the straight-arm Nazi salute; the Milorg officers responded with conventional military salutes to the forehead. Jonas Lie was wearing his metal helmet, Rogstad a peaked cap. Wulfsberg noted Lie's puffy face and perceptible nervousness. His hand was shaking as he drew on his cigarette, then held it poised a few centimetres from his lips.

Discussions on a way of resolving the standoff began at once, and it was immediately clear to the Milorg delegation that their opponents had no clear idea of what their demands might be. Lie and Rogstad seemed most concerned to convey that under no circumstances would they surrender unconditionally, as Quisling had done, and his loyal ministers with him. Wulfsberg knew that Quisling had ordered both Lie and Riisnæs to join him and the other members of his illegal government at his home on Bygdøy, that the minister-president and his ministers had then driven into Oslo in two cars and surrendered to the police. Lie had already been formally dismissed from his post by Quisling, and it occurred to Wulfsberg that this refusal to obey the minister-president's orders was such a clear breach of the Führer principle that it was probably the first time he had done so since the war began.

But by now Lie's personality, which had chafed so long on the 'receiving end' of a principle that lay at the heart of the national socialist revolution, had reasserted itself. All that mattered to him now were his dignity and his honour, and under no circumstances was he prepared to allow himself to be locked up in a Møllergate cell and treated like a common criminal and be subject to the humiliation – as had Quisling – of having his belt and his shoelaces removed. Both sides knew that the resistance wanted to take the three Nazis alive. Both sides knew that, at some point in the not-too-distant future, they would be tried, found guilty and executed. What exercised them, in consequence, was the *manner* of their deaths. As was only natural, in the course of the conversation Terboven's death was alluded to. Wulfsberg, playing on what he knew to be the ex-minister's passionate concern for his own honour, argued that suicide was a coward's way out. It was soon evident that Lie was not persuaded, nor was Rogstad. Despite being younger by sixteen years, Rogstad appeared calmer than his leader. When he spoke he did so slowly, and with exaggerated clarity, as though he were tired of the very act of using words. Wulfsberg's impression was that he had already accepted his fate.

He was far from sure that Lie had done so, and Lie's persistent description of the ideal way to bring the situation to a conclusion from his point of view seemed further proof that he was in some profound way out of touch with it. He said he wanted to die fighting. Over and over again he invoked the concept of his 'honour' as he outlined his favourite scenario and tried to get Wulfsberg to agree to it: the twenty-five members of D13.331 laying siege to the farmhouse must attack and kill them. In the event of such an attack he, Riisnæs and Rogstad would undertake not to fire back directly at the attackers but instead aim over their heads, or off to the side. He appeared to mean this sincerely, and Wulfsberg was struck by what the scenario revealed about Lie, the way it suggested he had no concern for anyone's honour but his own, and seemed oblivious to the fact the Wulfsberg's own men would find such an arrangement incompatible with their own sense of honour. Perhaps sensing Wulfsberg's incredulity he concluded by sabotaging the offer, adding in an off-hand way that, of course, he couldn't guarantee that in the heat of his last moments he might not fire directly at his attackers.

When at last Lie and Rogstad were persuaded that Wulfsberg and D13.313 had no intention for the time being anyway of taking Skallum by force, Rogstad offered them what they had been waiting for; a proposal with conditions for their surrender. He delivered the terms in a mechanical fashion, as though he had committed them to memory in exact form:

> Lie, Riisnæs and Rogstad are to be treated as prisoners of war and interned in an officers' camp, possibly for life, with the guarantee that they will never be brought before a Norwegian court, neither military nor civilian. They will, however, allow themselves to be interrogated by the Norwegian authorities. Front Fighters innocent of any criminal activity are to be held in a prison camp with a guarantee that they will never be brought before a Norwegian court.

Wulfberg knew at once it was unlikely the authorities would accept these conditions, but in the interests of keeping the negotiations open he did not offer his personal opinion. He promised to convey the demands to his superiors. He then asked a question that suggested the offer would indeed be given serious consideration:

'Jonas Lie may well qualify for treatment as a prisoner of war. But can the same be said of Rogstad and Riisnæs?'

This was clearly something they had discussed at Skallum prior to the meeting. Lie responded without hesitation:

'Riisnæs has served for a time as a volunteer on the Eastern Front, and since the shooting of Marthinsen Rogstad has been head of the State Police. Both should on those grounds fulfil the requirements.'

Though he very much doubted the logic of Lie's answer Wulfsberg nevertheless continued to treat the demand seriously:

'What about the status of Front Fighters who have committed crimes following their return from the fighting?'

Lie stared at him from his red and swollen face. He had smoked at least three cigarettes during the meeting so far, discarding each one half-smoked and almost in the same gesture taking a fresh cigarette from the packet in the pocket of his uniform jacket, interrupting the conversation to concentrate on the exquisite ritual of fitting the new one into the end of his black cigarette holder, flicking open his lighter and bending his large, square face towards the fluttering flame behind the protective shield of his left palm.

Before answering he now lit a fourth, opened his mouth to speak and was overtaken by a violent coughing fit. He removed the cigarette holder from his mouth until the fit had subsided.

'What crimes?' he finally said in a hoarse whisper.

'Bank robberies. Looting.'

Lie was still struggling for breath and Rogstad answered: 'Anyone suspected of criminal activity can of course be tried as a common criminal. Our only concern is for the decent young man whose sole aim was to serve his country by fighting to protect it from the Bolshevik revolutionaries.'

Wulfsberg next raised the question of the large amount of explosives known to be stored at the house. Lie insisted they had no intention of detonating it. None of them were munitions experts, but they were well aware of the destructive potential of the depot.

'Only as a last resort,' said Lie. 'And in that case we will, of course, give you advance warning.'

'I sincerely hope you do not detonate it,' said Wulfsberg. 'Enough Norwegian blood has been spilt already. We should all be doing everything in our power to prevent any further bloodshed.'

Lie and Rogstad both muttered their assent to this. But to Wulfsberg and his adjutant Sandberg it was now clear that the three Nazis increasingly regarded the threat of the huge explosion as the strongest card still in their hands.

'So the London government is in power again,' said Lie, abruptly changing the subject. 'Are they back in Norway yet?'

'Not as far as I know.'

Lie took the holder from his mouth and removed the half-smoked cigarette. He flicked it away into the grass verge alongside the driveway and recommenced the ritual of pocket, packet, cigarette, filter, mouth, flame, smoke.

'It won't make any difference,' he said. 'Norway will simply be occupied by another great power. In this case Russia. The Bolsheviks.'

'That seems unlikely now,' countered Wulfsberg. 'A military commission from England and the United States has already arrived in Norway. It will guarantee law and order in Denmark and Norway for a period of weeks only and will be responsible for the disarmament and removal of the German armies.'

Lie gave him a look of incredulity: 'Really? The Russians have agreed to withdraw from Finnmark?'

'In all probability Norway will be entirely free of foreign troops by the end of the year.'

Lie tried to laugh but was distracted by another coughing fit.

'Well you may be blue-eyed, but that doesn't make you Germanic,' he said eventually. 'Anyway, I hope for all of your sakes that you are right.'

The racial reference and Lie's confident cynicism provoked Wulfsberg. In spite of his determination to remain professionally courteous he was beginning to find it hard, at this late stage of the negotiations, to maintain the level of politeness necessary to keep the conversation going. Pressing forward from the back of his mind were details of what he knew of Lie's personal involvement in the murders of good Norwegians. Deaths Lie thought of as legitimate executions. His responsibility for the establishment of the Police Special Court that had condemned at least five Norwegians to death. From details passed to D13 by Gunnar Waaler in the State Prosecutor's Office he knew that Jonas Lie had personally attended many of them. He knew of Lie's role in the execution of Olaf Moen, not to speak of his part in the fate of his former friend, Inspector Gunnar Eilifsen. Abruptly tiring of the falsely civilised tone of the encounter, Wulfsberg went on the attack:

'Finnmark, yes,' he said. 'Tell me, what on earth did you think you were doing when you ordered the evacuation and burning of the entire region and made thousands of people permanently homeless?'

'It wasn't me who ordered it. It was Adolf Hitler.'

'Hitler yes, but you supported it, you promoted it, you travelled the region pleading with people to leave their homes, have their livestock killed with no compensation, turning the whole region into a barren wilderness. And for what, exactly?'

He had tried to make the question sound rhetorical, aware of how far and how quickly he had strayed from his tactical decision to keep clear of politics, keep the discussion focused on the matter in hand: how to bring the siege to a peaceful end.

Lie, as Wulfsberg had feared he would, allowed himself to be provoked.

'I can assure you,' he said coldly, 'that had we not done so the Bolshevik armies would have been well south of Trondheim by now, 'liberating' as they went. And you would never have been able to get that large neighbour of ours out again, once you had left your "comrades" with food and shelter along the way. I had the doubtful pleasure of accompanying Leon Trotsky on his trip to Mexico as the government's official representative when he was expelled from Norway in 1937. I shall never forget him saying to me, on one particular occasion when he had completely lost his temper with the Norwegians, '*Om noen år vil De selv være en landflyktig mann*' ('In just a few years you yourself will be a refugee'). Now, what sort of threat do you think that was to make?'

Everything had to be shouted. Spontaneous speech was impossible under the circumstances. Wulfsberg was about to respond but suddenly felt dizzied by the chasm of misunderstanding Lie's words had opened up in the few metres that separated them. Lost for words, he turned to his adjutant for help.

Sandberg took his cue perfectly and within seconds had brought the conversation back into focus. Did they have enough to eat? Did they need any medical supplies? Jonas Lie volunteered that he was much plagued by a tropical condition he referred to as *volynisk feber*, a malarial condition he had contracted in the trenches on the Eastern Front – 'But we all know how this will end, one way or another, so a doctor hardly matters.' Then, returning to the matter at hand, he asked for names and telephone numbers. Rogstad took a pencil and notebook from his pocket and noted the answers from the Milorg men.

'Then we have your word of honour that there will be no

attack before we have received a response to our terms?' said Lie as Rogstad slipped the notebook back into the pocket of his greatcoat.

'You have my word of honour.'

Lie nodded. The meeting was at an end. The two Milorg men were getting ready to leave when Rogstad spoke up.

'We will be spending tonight in Bunker No. 2; is there a way you can let us know when you have a response to our proposals?'

This was one of the questions Wulfsberg had anticipated and he had his answer ready. The Stabekk chemist was only a couple of hundred metres away and in direct line of sight with the bunker. If a response came during the night they would send three long flashes from the chemist's shop. Five minutes later, Wulfsberg would telephone the farmhouse with the news. Rogstad had a supplementary request: if their offer was rejected, he requested an interval of twenty minutes before the ceasefire was broken. Wulfsberg agreed and again they began to walk back up the drive in the direction of the main gates. Again Rogstad detained them. With a peculiar intensity in his voice he made a special request: in the event of a full-scale attack, could Wulfsberg give them his word that regular army troops would be used? Wulfsberg, realising that Rogstad, and presumably Lie also, were still hoping to die fighting, replied that this would be a matter for his superiors to decide. Either that or, he thought with a chill, the twenty minutes were to arrange for the detonation of the plastic explosives.

'You will hear from us once your terms have been considered by my superiors,' Wulfsberg said with finality. He and Sandberg stood to attention and saluted. Lie and Rogstad stood to attention. Both gave the Nazi salute, but only Rogstad accompanied it with a loud expression of loyalty to Adolf Hitler, his dead Führer.

Journalists from countries all over the world had made their way, via Stockholm, to Skallum to report at first hand on what was already being described as the last bastion of Nazi resistance in Europe. Wulfsberg and D13 were unfamiliar with this level of media attention and had little idea how to handle the journalists' demands nor any hint of how versatile and inventive journalists in search of a story could be. On the day after the encounter between the two sides in the standoff on the driveway of the Skallum estate, Thursday 10 May, it transpired that a Danish journalist named Nielsen working for the Reuters news agency had managed to get an interview with Jonas Lie over the telephone. Wulfsberg had previously ordered that the direct line to Skallum be closed following a phone call he had received from Lie earlier in the morning. Lie said he had heard on the radio that his wife Evje and his children had been arrested. He claimed to have information from another source that the resistance movement was now arresting not just National Unity members and sympathisers but their children too. Wulfsberg's sharp response was that the days of random arrests were now over. Only people actually suspected of committing offences were being arrested. Lie had then requested that any news of his wife's fate and well-being be passed on to him. Wulfsberg agreed to this. Following the call he then contacted the exchange at Stabekk and told the operator to close the Skallum line for outgoing calls and pass incoming calls only from himself.

This attempt to increase the psychological pressure on the three Nazis backfired when a senior police officer, Lars L'Abée Lund, telephoned from Oslo and ordered the line opened so that he could speak to Lie personally and try to persuade him to surrender. When their conversation ended the line was inadvertently left open and the Reuters man was able to get through and talk to Lie. In writing up the interview for publication he addressed Quisling's former Minister for Policing in the third person:

'Lie is presumably aware that he is being held responsible for all the death sentences passed in Norway during the occupation?'

'Please don't misunderstand me,' Lie replied. 'In the few hours

I have left I feel no need to worry about my reputation. However, in point of fact, all of those executed were given a fair trial before an impartial court, exactly as the law prescribes.'

'Did Lie have the option to commute those death sentences to a prison sentence, as the new laws allowed for?'

'No. Absolutely not. That decision rested entirely with Quisling.'

'The incidents of torture that have become notorious, did these take place with your knowledge?'

'No they did not. I have never tortured anyone. Remember that there were two separate and independent factions in the country at the time, the Norwegian and the German.'

'Is Lie implying that only the Germans engaged in torturing prisoners?'

'Exactly.'

'In that case, allow me to inform you that at Grini Prison Camp yesterday I spoke to several Norwegian patriots who have been rendered lifelong cripples following torture by Norwegian quislings.'

'Really. I find that hard to believe. This must be the case of a single unfortunate individual.'

'How would Lie describe the relationship between himself and Quisling?' he tried.

'Good, in the main. The minister-president always followed my recommendations.'

'The minister-president always followed your recommendations: is that what you're saying?'

'Yes.'

'Then in that case could not Lie have commuted the death sentences through a simple act of recommendation to Quisling?'

Nielsen listened to the slow, heavy wheezing of Lie's breath as he waited for a response. If they really do commit suicide, he thought, then I am the only prosecutor Lie will ever face. He made a note to use the line in the piece he would be writing. He began mentally building the prospective piece of writing around it. Still no answer from Lie. Suddenly Nielsen had an image of him standing in that empty house, the black mouthpiece still held to his lantern jaw and the eyes open but vacant, as though he had fallen asleep on his feet. When no answer came, he looked down at his notebook and read out his next question:

'I want to ask you a direct question; is that alright?'

'That depends. What is the question?'

'How does Lie see this ending? For all of you?'

'You can say that we have no intention of allowing ourselves to be taken alive under the prevailing and demeaning circumstances. We will not allow ourselves to be taken to Møllergate 19. All three of us are well aware that our cause is lost. You can say we are prepared to take the consequences of that realisation.'

With one hand the journalist scribbled down Lie's answer, thankful that Lie already spoke in quotes, a legacy of his career as a literary celebrity.

'I'd like to come up to the house and take some photographs for my readers. Would that be acceptable to Lie?'

'By all means. On your own head be it.'

There was a click followed by the continuous buzz of the unoccupied line. Lie was gone.

Wulfsberg was already losing patience with the distracting media circus that had built up around the siege operation and when Nielsen requested permission to approach the house to take photographs the request was summarily dismissed. Having discovered that the line to the farmhouse was still open, Wulfsberg then spent the next few minutes talking to the operator at the Stabekk Telephone Exchange, impressing on her again the importance of keeping the line closed; the operation was being led by D13, it was under his command and nobody – not even a chief of police from Oslo – had the authority to reopen it without his permission.

Hardly had he dealt with this new and unexpected complication than he received further proof of the bewildering tenacity of journalists. As he looked through the smudged windows of the Stabekk Youth Clubhouse in the direction of the car park where the media bus was parked, he saw a dark blue Buick begin moving towards the main gates to the estate. As the car passed outside the window he recognised Nielsen in the back seat. But what truly dismayed him was the sight of two men riding shotgun on the running boards on either side of the Buick, both with machine guns slung over their shoulders. Even as he watched he saw the car brake and skid to a halt as the two men guarding the main entrance to the estate trained their Sten guns on the approaching vehicle. There was a brief exchange of words between one of the guards and Nielsen in the back seat, then the Buick made a three-point turn and drove slowly back and pulled up outside the media bus.

Wulfsberg had already left the clubhouse, determined to find the identity of the two men Nielsen had paid to ride shotgun on his car and discipline them. Nielsen intercepted him. The journalist could hardly contain his rage as he spoke of the millions of dollars and readers he represented through his agency. Did Wulfsberg know that through his company's offices in New York he had access to over a hundred telephones manned twenty-four hours of every day and located in every corner of the world?

Wulfsberg heard him out patiently before replying.

'Listen, I don't care who you are or who you work for. It would make no difference to me if you worked for the *Asker og Bærum Budstikke* – you are not going in there.'

At Wulfsberg's little joke – the *Budstikke* was a small local newspaper with a weekly circulation of less than a thousand – the journalist finally lost all control.

'Do you realise what you are doing?' he raged. 'You are *helping* Quisling. All of you!' With a wild gesture in the direction of the clubhouse headquarters he turned on his heels and stamped away, disappearing up the steps of the press bus. Watching him, Wulfsberg had to smile; for perhaps the first time since the surrender of 7 May, the journalist's display of outraged entitlement and importance helped him realise that after five long years, things really were getting back to normal.

About half an hour after this a local man who had been out walking his dog in the woods surrounding the estate reported that he had come across a large hole cut in the wire fencing surrounding it. Given the tone of his exchange with Lie and Rogstad the preceding day Wulfsberg thought it highly unlikely that a man with Lie's exaggerated sense of personal honour would demean himself by wriggling his way to freedom through a hole in a fence. Nevertheless, he ordered one of his men to locate the opening and if possible ascertain whether Lie, Riisnæs and Rogstad were still at the farm.

Hans Aamodt was D13's photographer. When he set out to follow the dog-walker's directions he carried a camera as well as a pair of binoculars slung around his neck. On the forested, western side of the estate he presently located the hole cut in the barbed-wire fencing and carried out a search of the immediately surrounding area. Not far from the ragged hole, behind a group of laburnum bushes, he came across a mound of freshly disturbed dirt. Snapping a branch from a nearby tree he squatted and began poking into the mound. The cuff of the sleeve of a uniform jacket appeared. He stood up and stepped back, briefly certain he was about to unearth a dead body. He'd never seen one before. For all the training and the weapon exercises, during the time he'd been with D13.313 the group had never fired a shot in anger. For him personally the war in these final stages had been something going on at a distance. Yes, there was the constant and real uncertainty about the precise fashion in which it would end, but with the assassination of Karl Marthinsen, Terboven's suicide and most recently Quisling's surrender, the fear of some awful final bloodbath had receded.

Well, if this was to be his first dead body, so be it. He squatted down and continued to scoop and scrape away the piled earth. Very soon he was contemplating not one but three complete sets of police uniforms. They must, he thought, be associated with developments at the farmhouse at around midnight of the Monday/Tuesday, following Lie's announcement that anyone who wanted to leave was now free to do so. Some had been arrested as they left the following morning after they had telephoned Møllergata for a car to come and pick them up. Others, like these three, had preferred to take their chances alone.

Acting on impulse Aamodt now ducked in through the hole and began cautiously padding his way through the trees in the direction of the white farmhouse. As he neared the edge of the wood and the open area surrounding the farm buildings he could hear the distressed lowing of cows. It must have been days since they were milked.

At the edge of the wood he stopped, lifted his binoculars and peered across the fields at the farmhouse, looking and listening for any sign of life. And hoping for it too: the last thing any of them in D13.313 wanted was to lose three such prominent Nazis in the very first hours following the liberation. The world's press was now focused not only on the siege but on the whole of the Norwegian resistance organisation. It was a matter of pride for them to bring the operation to a successful and safe conclusion, and to do it on their own. Aamodt knew that Wulfsberg and their own expert had already spoken to the commander of the German forces at Lorangejordet, the site of Grossbatterie Stabekk, the Germans' largest anti-aircraft station in the Oslo region, about the 250 kilograms of plastic explosives stored in the west wing of the basement. He knew also of the observations made by D13.313 that led them to believe the depot could be detonated from Bunker No. 2, where the three Nazis seemed to spend so much of their time. One aim of the visit to Lorangejordet had been to try to persuade the Germans themselves to attack Skallum. The commander had refused, pointing out that the terms of the ceasefire ruled out any such attack, though in passing he made the technical point that if Lie, Riisnæs and Rogstad were to open fire on D13.313 then the ceasefire agreement would entitle them to return fire. Wulfsberg's proposal to the Germans had initially puzzled others in the group besides Aamodt, until someone pointed out the thinking behind it: if Lie, Rogstad and Riisnæs wanted to go out in a blaze of glory that might leave them martyrs to the national socialist cause, then what better way to prevent this than to have them shot by their own German teachers?

But it was not to be. And as much as people had come to hate Lie and the two others and to want to see them dead, there was a strong desire to bring it about as the result of a legal process. From every point of view the worst outcome of the standoff would be the detonation of the store of plastic explosives. The Germans' explosive expert at Lorangejordet had estimated that the explosion would destroy everything within a hundred metres' radius of the site. Buildings for 700 metres around would suffer catastrophic damage. Aamodt lowered his binoculars and looked around, trying to envisage the physical reality behind these figures. He heard a hoarse panting close behind him and whirled round. A pair of large black Alsatians not two metres away were lunging towards him, upper lips drawn back and gums foaming as they strained to get at him. Behind them, struggling to hold in one hand the short leather leashes that were stretched almost to breaking point, stood Jonas Lie. With his other he held a submachine gun aimed at Aamodt.

'Down! Down!' he roared at the frantically barking dogs. 'Get down!'

The dogs calmed down and stood panting, one on each side of the former minister. Moments later he was joined by Riisnæs and Rogstad.

'And who the hell are you?' he demanded, the gun still pointing at Aamodt. Then, with a slight note of incredulity: 'Is that a *camera* hanging round your neck?'

Aamodt instinctively raised his hand and touched it. Even before he could respond Lie had lowered the gun until it dangled by his side.

'You journalists really are something,' he said drily. 'You're always there where it happens. It never seems to occur to you that you just might get a bullet up your own arse.'

Aamodt nodded in relief. He put it together at once. Lie had mistaken him for the Reuters journalist he had spoken to earlier in the day, the one who had asked permission to take photographs of the three men at the house and been turned back as he tried to crash the site in a Buick.

He played along. Rogstad insisted it wasn't safe to stay where they were and led the way via a shortcut through the farm buildings back to the main house. They posed for him willingly, in retrospect he was almost inclined to use the word *cheerfully*. They seemed relaxed and friendly, making an effort to charm him as people do with journalists whom they hope will write kindly about them in their newspapers. He took two group pictures and individual portraits of the three of them. He kept up the pretence of being a journalist. Was it warm enough in the house? Did they have enough to eat? No, he couldn't give them any information about their families, though he was able to tell Lie that his wife had been released after being held for just twenty-four hours and was back home again. Lie took the news with almost palpable relief. And as Aamodt was getting ready to leave Lie impulsively took him by the shoulder and asked him to pass on a greeting to his wife. Rogstad, too, asked to be remembered to his parents, and to Ilse, the German wife he had married four days earlier, who had just given birth to their child. Only Riisnæs remained aloof from this strange and sorrowing intimacy. He stood off to one side, alternately glaring at Aamodt and addressing inaudible remarks to the dogs. There was something about him Aamodt couldn't quite put his finger on. It was as though he, unlike Lie and Rogstad, was having difficulty in coming to terms with the finality of the defeat of his party and the certainty of his imminent death.

Heading back along the same shortcut through the woods that would take him to the hole in the fencing, Aamodt reflected on the strangeness of the encounter. There had been something – what was the word – something peculiarly *Norwegian* about it. Four men meeting in the middle of a springtime forest. They looked so normal. Yes, all three were in uniform, Lie in his general major's outfit and Rogstad in his full-length coat. Riisnæs wore

the insignia of *Germanske SS Norge*, but his cap was slanted at what could only be described as a jaunty angle. All three needed a shave. They smelled of stale alcohol and tobacco and just for an instant he saw them simply as Norwegians *dressed up as soldiers and policemen* and exchanging news in a language understood by few others in the world. In one sense the whole country was like one large family. Aamodt was still only in his early twenties, and for perhaps the first time he felt a simple sadness at the tragedy of what could be described in so many ways as the civil war of the past five years. How could the divisions between their two sides have become so great? He found himself almost having to admit that he had quite *liked* the meeting, he had quite *enjoyed* the meeting.

But then he recalled the answer Lie had given to his final question when he asked if any of them had regrets. Rogstad and Riisnæs had simply looked the other way. Lie, after a moment's hesitation, admitted to a regret that they had 'backed the wrong horse'. His exact words. As though the ideological differences that had caused so much pain and distress had ultimately been of little significance when all that mattered, all he regretted, was the bad luck of the choices he had made. He'd offered the confession with the affable and melancholic charm for which he had been famous and even loved in the days of his literary celebrity; but then his voice changed as, in a seemingly unconscious moment, he rested the palm of his right hand on the butt of the holstered revolver he wore on his belt and added: 'But Germany's defeat will lead to only one thing; the Bolsheviks and the Jews will take over all of Europe. Mark my words.' And as Aamodt struggled with the confusing sameness of the interior of a trackless pine forest to find the exact location of that hole in the fence he had ducked through about an hour earlier, he found Lie's words echoing through his head. He tried to imagine what it felt like to believe such a thing. He couldn't do it. It made no sense to him.

Friday 11 May was the final day of the siege. About mid-morning Wulfsberg telephoned the house and told Rogstad, who answered the call, that the terms they had discussed on Wednesday were still being considered and that some kind of compromise was not out of the question. At 5 p.m. he telephoned the house again to tell Rogstad there had been no further developments, and that their offer was still being discussed. He noted that Rogstad sounded depressed at the lack of progress. He complained that he thought they were taking a long time to come up with their response.

Just over an hour later, at 6.15, Wulfsberg was called to the Stabekk clubhouse once more. It was at once apparent that things were happening. Lars L'Abée-Lund was there, the newly appointed Chief of Police for a liberated Oslo and the man whose failed attempt to persuade Lie to surrender had left the line open for the farcical interlude with the Danish Reuters journalist. He recognised Max Manus too, along with three or four other members of the Oslo Gang. His immediate assumption was that someone higher up the chain of command was considering a commando raid on the farm rather than the direct military confrontation Lie and Rogstad wanted. Then he was called to join the discussions and within minutes a final plan of action had been agreed on. At 7.15 p.m. he telephoned the house again. Rogstad took the call and Wulfsberg delivered the ultimatum in the form agreed on at the clubhouse meeting:

'Here is the response of the Norwegian authorities. The cease-fire is now over. You will all be arrested and you will be dealt with in accordance with Norwegian law. There are no conditions involved. However, you are all guaranteed proper treatment and a fair trial.'

Wulfsberg was by this time used to Rogstad's way of waiting a long time before responding. This time the wait seemed abnormally long and as he listened to Rogstad's slow breathing he found himself wondering why Lie seemed to have given up his role as the group's leader. Finally, with a shuddering intake of breath, Rogstad spoke:

'Alright then,' he said. 'Thank you for this time.'

The line went dead, leaving Wulfsberg to wonder exactly what it was Rogstad meant; was he referring to the truce? Or the promise of the twenty-minute respite before a final attack? It didn't matter. He telephoned the clubhouse and gave orders that the twenty-five men posted strategically around the house remain under cover but with rifles primed. He then made a call to the substation at Glommen Tresliperi and ordered that the electricity supply to the farmhouse be cut off. He also arranged for the mains water supply to be turned off.

Ten minutes after his call to Rogstad, at 7.25 p.m., Wulfsberg left operational headquarters and began an inspection round of the sentry posts. As his car approached the post guarding the main entrance to the driveway, he was greatly surprised to see a man walking up it towards him.

He ordered his driver to stop and stepped out.

The man held his hands high above his head. In one of them a dirty white handkerchief fluttered slightly in the evening breeze. Four of D13's sentries walked behind him, rifles trained on him. As the man approached the stone gate posts Wulfsberg recognised Sverre Riisnæs, the former Minister for Justice. Understanding that he was in the presence of authority, Riisnæs halted between the gateposts and stood to attention, arms to his sides, the handkerchief dangling. In a slightly mechanical voice he said:

'Jonas Lie died an hour ago. Rogstad has just shot himself. I have decided to take responsibility and accept the consequences of my actions.'

'A wise decision,' replied Wulfsberg.

Opened in 1928 and originally a youth centre used by the local scout troop and other youth groups, the Stabbek clubhouse had been requisitioned by National Unity during the occupation as a venue for the party's youth wing, the *Ungdomsfylking*. When D13 moved in and made it the group's operational headquarters seventy-two hours earlier they had found the walls plastered with propaganda posters, most of them by Damsleth, urging Norway's young people to join the occupying force in the national socialist struggle against revolutionary communism. Within a half hour of the group moving in all of them had been taken down.

As he waited for police transport to arrive that would take Riisnæs to join Quisling and the rest of his cabinet in Møllergata, Wulfsberg conducted an informal interrogation of the former Minister for Justice in a first-floor room of the clubhouse and heard Riisnæs' own account of what had taken place during the last few hours at Skallum. Wulfsberg sat him in a wooden chair and before he could even formally tell Riisnæs who he was, the former minister asked for a drink of water. He filled a white enamel pitcher from the tap in the corner of the small utilities room and was surprised to see Riisnæs empty it almost at one draft. The prisoner exuded despair rather than desperation and Wulfsberg did not think it necessary to handcuff him, though for the sake of form he stationed two sentries on the landing outside the door. Riisnæs appeared sober, but his eyes were bloodshot from the cumulative effects of a hangover and lack of sleep.

He took a second long gulp of water before composing himself in his chair. He looked expectantly at Wulfsberg.

'You say that Lie and Rogstad are dead; tell me what happened.'

'Both dead. Jonas Lie had one of his bouts of malarial fever this morning. He had them frequently. Couldn't get up. Couldn't eat. As the morning wore on he got worse. He was lying on a mattress. On the floor. Place was the most appalling mess.'

Riisnæs paused and looked distractedly up at the bare lightbulb, its light so weak it hardly penetrated to the corners of the small room. He rubbed his forehead with the knuckles of his left hand. It was clear he was close to exhaustion.

'Go on,' said Wulfsberg.

'At about ten o'clock he tried to get up. He was in dreadful pain. Face was swollen, red. Drenched in sweat. A journalist telephoned. Someone he used to know in his youth. Tried to get him to give himself up. Jonas wouldn't hear of it. Said there was no way he would ever get a fair hearing. The conversation seemed to drain him completely and he staggered back to his mattress and lay down again.'

Riisnæs ran his tongue over his lips several times, blinked up at the lightbulb again. Suddenly he slid his hand into the left pocket of his jacket, pinched something and put it into his mouth. Wulfsberg shouted, the door crashed open, the sentries rushed in and within seconds Riisnæs was on the floor. His *hird* cap came off as he writhed about beneath the knees of the guards. Wulfsberg bent over him and prised open his teeth, certain he had taken a suicide pill. Riisnæs turned his head to one side and spat onto the floorboards. Wulfsberg stooped to examine it.

'Tobacco,' he grunted, rubbing it into the floorboard with the toe of his boot. 'Let him up.'

The guards stood up, Riisnæs got to his feet, righted his chair and sat down again.

Wulfsberg wasn't a smoker himself. 'Either of you two got a cigarette?' he asked. The second guard pulled a packet from his jacket pocket, opened it, lit a cigarette and handed it to the former Minister of Justice. Riisnæs took it with a nod of thanks and inhaled as though his life depended on it.

Wulfsberg resumed his questioning: 'Where was this mattress?'

'In the main living room. Off the hallway. First door on the left. Anyway, young Rogstad and I were talking in the kitchen, wondering what to do about him. He was suffering. In great pain. And then suddenly there he was, standing in the doorway, a grenade in his hand. He was raging at us. In German. He was hallucinating. He started raving about Trotsky. Why, *why* wouldn't Trotsky shake his knee? Who is that talking to Frida Kahlo? That sort of thing.'

Wulfsberg had been standing peering from the window for any sign of the police car to take Riisnæs to Møllergata 19. Now he turned round.

'Why wouldn't *who* shake his knee?' he asked with a perplexed frown.

'Trotsky. Leon Trotsky. When the government expelled Trotsky in 1936, withdrew his asylum, Jonas was the government's official representative, accompanied him on the voyage to Mexico. There was some Christmas party. Some onboard party. One of the crewmembers there played the musical saw. He tried to persuade Trotsky to have a go. Trotsky was game enough. But he wouldn't shake his knee. You have to shake your knee. So that was the end of that.'

Wulfsberg peered intently at Riisnæs.

'What is the significance of all this?' he said.

'I'm telling you... I'm describing to you... Lie was hallucinating. He thought he saw Frida Kahlo talking to someone he knew on the quayside.'

'Quayside where?'

'In Mexico.'

'Who is Frida Kahlo?'

'The mistress of Diego Rivera. The painter. Friends of Trotsky.'

'I don't understand. Why are you telling me all this?'

Riisnæs leaned forward in his seat. 'You asked me what happened, I'm trying to tell you. Jonas was hallucinating. He had a grenade in his hand. He thought he was back in the trenches.'

'What happened?'

'He pulled the pin. But instead of throwing it he placed it on the floor. Like a pineapple. Very carefully. Rogstad stood up, he'd been sitting down. I think he intended to do something with the grenade. Throw it outside perhaps. But then Jonas drew his pistol and pointed it straight at Rogstad.'

Gripped by his own account, Riisnæs held out his right hand and stared at it.

'He pulled the trigger.'

Riisnæs mimed the action, jerking his middle finger upward. He seemed momentarily transfixed by the sight of the cigarette held between his fingers.

'Click. Nothing. Then he aimed it at me.'

Riisnæs jerked his wrist until he was pointing at Wulfsberg.

'Same thing. *Click*. Nothing happened. Then we both jumped on him and took the gun away. He had no idea where he was or what he was doing. We cleared a room of weapons and locked him inside. Then we walked over to Bunker No. 2.'

'So you were still considering resisting?'

Riisnæs laughed mirthlessly. 'No. It was something to do, somewhere to go. When we got back – this was late afternoon – I went in to Jonas to see how he was. He was lying on the floor. Not breathing. I touched his hand and it was cold. I called out to Rogstad to come quickly and we lifted him onto the mattress and left him there. My old friend. And then, not long afterwards, you telephoned. Rogstad took the call. Well, of course, you know that. And there was no agreement. So that was that. We had half an hour.'

His hands were back in his lap. The cigarette, held with a strange delicacy between index finger and thumb, was pointing upwards.

'Rogstad said we had two choices. One was to attack, shoot at you and compel you to return fire and kill us. The other was to take our own lives. I reminded him that we had a third option, which was to hand ourselves over to the authorities. I pointed out that there was very little he had done that would render him liable to punishment.'

'So you didn't really know too much about him?' Wulfsberg said drily. As on the earlier occasion of his meeting with Lie and Rogstad he immediately regretted allowing himself to be provoked. Rogstad's role in drawing up the list of the eleven loyalist hostages who were executed on Terboven's orders during the Trondheim State of Civilian Emergency in 1942 was well known. That alone would have guaranteed him a death sentence. Not for the first time during the interrogation he found himself wondering about Riisnæs' grasp of reality.

But Riisnæs appeared not to have registered the irony in Wulfsberg's remark and gave a straight answer: 'No, not until recently. Until we gave him command of the State Police. To replace Søvik.'

'But he wasn't interested in surrendering?' said Wulfsberg.

'No, he wasn't. And he said that if I wasn't prepared to die fighting with him then suicide was his only option. I didn't try to talk him out of it. But he was afraid he might somehow make a mess of it and not manage to kill himself. So he got me to promise that once he'd put a bullet through his temple I would put a second bullet through him. To make sure.'

Riisnæs fell silent again. He sighed deeply, dropped his cigarette to the floor and extinguished it with the toe of his boot.

'Which I did,' he resumed. 'So he is dead.' He silently held up a hand towards the sentry who had provided him with the cigarette earlier. The sentry looked at Wulfsberg. Wulfsberg nodded and the guard stepped forward and repeated the ritual of lighting and handing the cigarette to Riisnæs. Riisnæs this time twisted his lips in a small gesture of distaste and made a show of drying the end of the cigarette on his sleeve before placing it between his lips.

'So there you have it,' he went on. 'That left just me. I fully intended to honour the bond we three had made never to surrender. There's a note we signed, all three of us, you'll find it up at the house. So what did I do then? I went to my rucksack to find the pills Dr Eng had given us. A hundred of them. I don't know what was in them but, according to Jonas, Eng said they would put you to sleep more or less immediately. Might cause some vomiting but absolutely lethal. I couldn't find them. I went through every pocket of the rucksack three or four times and they weren't there.'

'Did Lie take one? Is that what killed him?'

'I don't know what killed him. Heavy smoker. Heavy drinker. A weak heart. Disappointment. Despair. I don't know. Anyway, I couldn't find them. Yes, it did occur to me that Jonas might have taken them. But then I remembered that, apart from that telephone conversation with his old friend, he had spent the whole day on the mattress, hardly able to move. So I decided to kill myself. I held the pistol to my head—' he mimed the action, middle finger of his left hand pressing into his left temple. 'And just as I was about to pull the trigger, God spoke to me. God told me to hand myself over and accept the consequences of my action. So here I am.'

He slumped in his chair, eyes closed, jaw hanging open. For a moment Wulfsberg thought he might have passed out. Then he suddenly looked up and said, with great clarity: 'Will I be shot tonight?'

Before Wulfsberg could reply there was a knock at the door. With a signal to the sentries to keep an eye on the prisoner, he got up and opened it. Hans Aamodt was standing there. In an urgent whisper he informed his chief that a member of the public had just telephoned the *Ungdomshus* and reported seeing two people up at the farmhouse. Wulfsberg groaned: had they been caught out by some elaborate ruse? Had the former Minister of Justice tricked them with this bizarre and self-sacrificing performance? He turned and shouted instructions to the two men guarding Riisnæs to handcuff him, and then ran down the stairs, shouting for his adjutant Sandberg and his driver as he ran out the front door and towards his staff car.

The large white timber building with its imposing first-floor balcony looked deserted as Wulfsberg and Sandberg opened the car doors and stepped out. Crouching, Sten guns at the ready, they split up and ran towards the wall, one on either side of the steps up to the double front door. The doors were closed. All six ground-floor windows were shuttered. After a few moments listening out for sounds from the interior and hearing nothing, Wulfsberg turned to the window behind him, wedged his fingers beneath the bottom of the shutter and jerked hard on it. The shutter swung open. He ducked down and stayed down for several long moments, listening out, still hearing nothing. Cautiously he stood up and pressed his face close to the window, cupping his forehead between his hands.

He was looking into a large room that appeared to extend to the entire width of the house. There was a window at the back but it was blanked out by a shutter too and it took several moments for his vision to adapt to the dim light inside what he could now see was a living room. His first impression was of a twisted mass of strewn and scattered clothing, briefcases, empty rucksacks, sheets of newspapers and empty bottles littering the floor. Further into the room, pushed up against the rear wall, he could make out a large dark shape on the floor. His first thought was that it might be an upended side table. He turned and waved to Sandberg to join him.

'What's that?'

For a few moments they stood side by side, peering into the darkened room. Sandberg had the better eyesight.

'It's a man,' he said presently. The figure lay quite motionless. 'I'm not certain but I think it might be Lie.' In silence they peered through the glass at the body on the floor. And as their eyes adapted further to the dimness inside they realised there could be no doubt about it: they were looking at the dead body of Jonas Lie.

He was lying fully clothed on a white mattress on the bare floorboards, eyes open and rolled to the top of his head, his mouth open as if gasping for one last breath.

'He wanted an honourable death,' Wulfsberg said at last, his voice soft and wondering. 'And look, his flies are undone.'

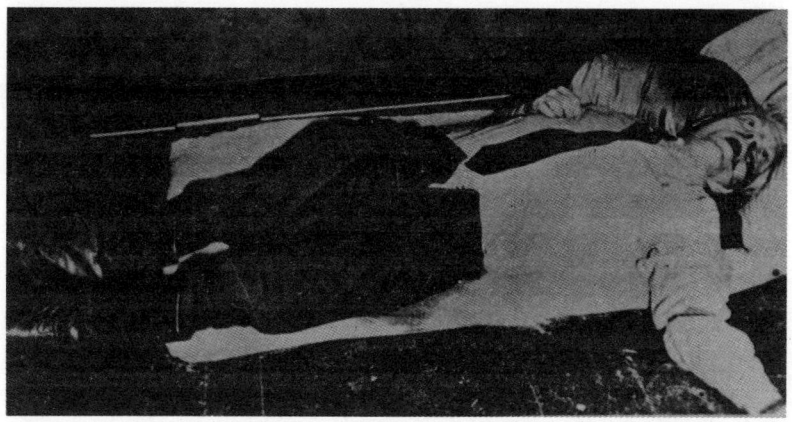

They stepped back from the window and walked around the front steps to the one on the other side. This was likewise shuttered. Using the same technique Wulfsberg jerked it open. There was a small round table next to the window and on one side of it. There was a black telephone on the table, with the receiver resting in the cradle. A small travelling clock stood next to it, opened inside its hard shell. The hands had stopped at ten minutes to five.

'There's the other one,' said Sandberg. 'I can see just half of him.'

'Is it him?'

'Yes. It's Rogstad.'

As they continued to peer into the room an Alsatian appeared in view from the left. The dog approached the body on the floor, sniffed at it, then began to lick at the coagulated blood that had formed in a stiff pool next to the dead man's head. Sandberg rapped heavily on the window with his knuckles and they stepped back.

'For God's sake,' said Sandberg. 'We have to get that dog out of there.'

He moved towards the double front doors.

'Stop,' said Wulfsberg. 'We can't go in.'

'Why not?'

Wulfsberg looked at his adjutant: 'Because this is a crime scene,' he said. 'We wait. We've done our job. Now the police take over. The war is over, remember?'

Even as he spoke they could hear the wailing sirens of approaching police cars.

Skallum remained closed while a team that included detectives, crime-scene technicians, the pathologist from Ullevål Hospital, Georg Waaler, as well as a dog handler went about their business. Georg Waaler formally pronounced both Lie and Rogstad dead before arranging to have them transported to the *Rettsmedisinskinstutt* for full autopsies at his coroner's lab. It would be a last trip with a certain irony for both of the dead men, since Georg Waaler's pathology lab had for much of the occupation doubled as one of Milorg's most important hiding places and a collection centre for information on everything from lists of informers and intended hostages to full-scale reports on German troop movements in Norway, secret transportations by train and the arrivals and departures of German ships. Waaler's informal diagnosis, given to Wulfsberg as they watched the ambulances drive away, was that the former Minister for Policing had died of chronic alcoholism and chain-smoking, combined possibly with the effects of the pills from Dr Eng, though his initial guess was that it was doubtful whether the pills really were fatal. The two bullet holes in Rogstad's head confirmed the story Riisnæs had told. The dog handler, meanwhile, subdued the Alsatian and gave it a side of ham to chew on. At the request of several members of D13.313 who wanted to keep the dog as a kind of pet it was left on the farm, attached to a running line that was already in place between the house and a slender birch growing on the lawn. Riisnæs had been transferred to Møllergata 19, still expecting to be summarily shot later in the evening.

Only then, once all these matters had been taken care of, did the twenty-five men of D13.313 take up residence at the farmhouse. They tidied up the clutter on the floors, cleaned the kitchen and the bathroom, bagged and threw out the rubbish and spent the next fourteen days on a rest and recreation furlough. There were training exercises, competitions involving the speed-stripping and assembly of assorted firearms, instructions in how to throw a hand grenade, running races and field sports. The plan to adopt the Alsatian as some kind of mascot didn't work out. The bewildered and frightened animal had to be kept fastened to the running line. One day it bit the nurse who went to feed it and after a brief discussion it was shot. As the group's joker pointed out, it was actually D13.313's first kill, not to mention the first time anyone in the group had fired a shot in anger. Three days later the manager at Skallum was allowed back on the farm to start his *våronna* – the annual ritual of ploughing and harrowing and fertilising the soil, sewing the crops and letting the cows out from their winter confinement to graze in the open fields – all the countless everyday things that had to be done now the war was over and spring had come.

15

The Legal Reckoning

The events at Skallum were already history by the time Haakon VII returned to Norway on 7 June, five years to the day since his flight to the United Kingdom and just over three weeks after the arrival on 13 May of Crown Prince Olav and the British general Andrew Thorne. For the next four weeks Thorne was the official ruler of Norway, with responsibility for disarming the 351,000 German military and police personnel in the country. With a force less than a tenth the size he had to rely on the assistance of the 40,000 members of Milorg and the 13,000 Norwegian refugees who had crossed the border into Sweden and been trained as an auxiliary police force specifically to deal with the pressures and dangers of the coming liberation. Given the disparity in size between the two parties to the process, the fraught moment of disarmament went off with remarkably little incident. Norwegian historians attribute this not least to the maintenance of discipline among the Germans, and to the conduct of Terboven's successor General Böhme, at his headquarters in Lillehammer. Böhme followed to the letter the instructions received from Hitler's successor Admiral Karl Dönitz, that the surrender be carried out without violence, and without further destruction. Logistical problems, exacerbated by the ruination of their own country, meant that the last of the occupying German soldiers and officials did not finally leave until 1947. Despite some initial anticipation of 'three lawless days' during which a lot of old scores would be settled once the Nazi regime had been overturned, the predominant mood during the first May days of freedom was one of intoxicated relief and celebration rather than vengefulness and violence. The Oslo offices and display cabinets of *Germaneren* (The Germanist), the Norwegian-language weekly that had been the main propaganda outlet for the Pan-Germanists in National Unity, were destroyed and there was a general tearing down of Damsleth's ubiquitous propaganda posters – a punishable offence during the occupation – and of the many photographs and busts of Vidkun Quisling in public places that had been part of the attempt to revolutionise Norwegian consciousness. But there were few instances of violent personal retribution, and nothing on the level seen in France, where estimates of the numbers put up against a wall and shot range from ten to fifty thousand. In Norway perhaps as many as a thousand women had their heads shaved by mobs for having had sexual or even simply friendly relations with members of the occupying force.[76] But in the main Norwegians were content to leave the matter of punishment and retribution to the justice system and the democratically elected authorities.

General Thorne remained officially in charge of the country until 7 June, at which point sovereignty was returned to King Haakon VII. Under pressure from Milorg leaders, Johan Nygaardsvold's London government had resigned on 26 June and a coalition government administered the country until 8 October, when the first general election for five years was held. It resulted in a large overall majority in the Storting for the Labour Party. The Communist Party did particularly well, garnering nearly 12 per cent of the votes, most of them from voters in the north who remained grateful and impressed by the Russians who had liberated them in 1944. Einar Gerhardsen took office as the country's first post-war prime minister on 5 November.

*

It might be useful to rehearse certain ways in which Norway's situation during the years of the occupation was distinct from that of the other occupied countries most natural to compare it to, in particular its Scandinavian neighbour Denmark. As noted earlier, the flight of the king and government had left Norwegians in limbo and brought a crude veneer of necessity to Quisling's actions on the evening of the first full day of the invasion. Ignored even by some of those he had nominated to serve in his 'cabinet' as ministers, his coup lasted only a few days. For the rest of the spring and summer the responsibility for negotiating with the occupiers was handled by the Administrative Council. During the weeks and months of negotiations with Terboven over its status and competence, the Administrative Council, and the collegium of the three parliamentary presidents that succeeded it at the negotiating table after the Norwegian surrender of 19 June 1940, had shown itself capable of some desperate accommodations with the demands of the Reichskommissar. These included a willingness, supported by a majority of members of parliament, to revoke recognition of the so-called *Elverumfullmaktet* (Elverum Decree) of 9 April 1940 which had empowered the Nygaardsvold government to legislate on behalf of parliament during its flight and subsequent exile, a formal request delivered to King Haakon VII to abdicate, and an undertaking to legally depose him should he decline to do, which he did. These unhappy negotiations dragged on until they became academic with Terboven's speech of 25 September and his appointment of Norwegian acting ministers as Norway's civil administration.

Quisling was not among these acting ministers but, as leader of National Unity and in obedience to the Führer principle on which all national socialist parties were founded, he was their *de facto* head. The primary concern of this administration, intensified after the State Act of 1 February 1942, was to bring about a revolution in the consciousness of Norwegian youth and in due course turn the country into an exemplary national socialist state. It was this campaign which sparked the counter-revolutionary Conscience Struggle that united the schools, the universities, the church, pupils, parents, priests and teachers in a campaign of dogged and ultimately triumphant resistance to the attempted Nazification of the crucial institutions of education and religion that marked the greatest achievement of Norwegian resistance to the occupation.

The inevitable result of this struggle for the soul of the people was to give the occupation of Norway many of the characteristics of a war within the war. The degree of hostility and loathing felt towards a collaborationist regime that went so far beyond simply trying to keep the wheels of normal life turning through tough times exceeded by some measure the anger felt for the German occupiers beneath whose protective and violent arm this regime was able to pursue its unpopular ends. By comparison the situation in Denmark could not have been more different. There the king and government remained at their posts and for the first three years of the occupation, until 1943, acted to protect the people from any attempt to carry out a similar campaign of Nazification in the country. Remarkably, a free general election was even permitted. Held in March 1943 with a turnout of almost 90 per cent, 95 per cent of the votes cast went to the democratic parties operating as the country's coalition cabinet and just over 2 per cent to the Danish Nazi Party, giving it roughly the same derisory share as National Unity had achieved in Norway in the two general elections in which it participated in the 1930s. The corrupt and illusory power wielded by National Unity in Norway and their persistent attempt to Nazify the country's political, social, educational, legal and clerical structures created passions and pressures close to those associated with a state of civil war. In contemplating the draconian nature of the legal process that now got under way in the Norwegian courts this particular feature of the occupation needs to be borne in mind.

The most dramatic and, in due course, legally contentious issues arose from two so-called *provisoriske anordninger* (Provisional

Laws) introduced by the London government under the terms of the Elverum Decree. The first involved alterations in the law regarding the death penalty. Spurred by the summary executions of the strike leaders Wickstrøm and Hansteen by the Germans on 10 September 1941, the London government passed two decrees on 3 October 1941. A law of 1902 had abolished the death penalty except in cases of treason involving the military, and even then only in time of war. The law of 3 October 1941 amended this to allow it to apply to civilians as well as the military. It also legalised its use once the war was over. A further amendment of 22 January 1942 made the death penalty available in cases where the use of torture could be proven. A second series of Provisional Laws opened with a decree of 22 January 1942 that made it illegal to be a member of National Unity, the *hird*, or of 'any other organisation materially assisting the enemy'. A further decree of 15 December 1944 made it a crime to have been a party member from the day of the invasion onward. The same legislation held party members legally responsible for the economic damage done to the country in supporting the occupying power. Between them the decrees introduced a new crime to the statute book. Termed *landssvik* ('betrayal of one's country'), it replaced earlier definitions of *forræderi* ('treason') and *høyforræederi* ('high treason') and formed the basis for the *rettsoppgjør* ('legal reckoning') once the occupation was over.

An influential voice in favour of this policy of collective guilt for National Unity party members was that of Eivind Berggrav, Bishop of Oslo. In a sermon preached on 17 May 1945 at Akershus Fortress, Berggrav reminded the congregation of how each of them had had to resort to cunning and deception in the face of the enemy's violence and power. 'We had to hide the truth. We did not owe the truth to men of treachery and lies.' All unconsciously he was echoing one of the central tenets of the *Hávamál* (The Sayings of the High One), a Viking Age wisdom poem attributed to Odin. In doing so he perhaps also revealed the degree to which his own faith had been tested by the war years. Berggrav had spent the last few weeks of his house-arrest writing *Folkedommen over Nasjonal Samling. Menneskelig og Moralsk. Hva vil være rett av oss?* (The People's Verdict on National Unity. Human and Moral Aspects. What Is the Right Way Forward?). Published in the year's first edition of the church magazine *Kirke og kultur* (Church and Culture), the essay also appeared as an offprint and was distributed and read widely. The general consensus was that it was exactly what it claimed to be in its title: the judgement of the people on the Norwegian Nazi Party. Berggrav was dramatically unequivocal in his demands; every member of the party must share in the blame for the wretchedness and pains of the preceding five years, every member should be subject to the collective punishment available to the state under the wartime laws. Only then could the process of forgiveness commence. In a pithy phrase he summarised his position: *Først rett, så godhet* – first justice, then kindness.

Most of the country's leading legal minds were of the same opinion. Sven Arntzen, a High Court judge and a leader of the resistance, was appointed attorney general and became one of the chief architects of the legal reckoning. On 4 June 1945 Arntzen held a course at Oslo University for the public prosecutors who would be handling the *landssvik* cases and for the lawyers of the newly created *Erstatningsdirektoratet* (Directorate of Reparations), whose job it was to track down and secure assets that could be confiscated to recover fines levied by the courts, to make claims for compensation and confiscation, and to manage the funds that came in. At several points in the course of his guidance Arntzen quoted from Berggrav's essay and commended the bishop's analysis to his audience: 'The more appalling the crime is, the less does the thought behind it matter… the whole party involved a conspiracy against the Norwegian people […] All members of National Unity are guilty. Each individual shares in the corporate guilt as guarantors in the business of violence.' Some of those who had doubted Berggrav's analysis found themselves swayed by Arntzen's enthusiasm, a hint that the bishop's essay may have shaped the public's verdict on National Unity rather than simply reflected it. Among the countries occupied by Nazi Germany, Norway was unique in criminalising membership of National Unity rather than simply reflected it. The Danish Nazi Party was not banned and the only Danes prosecuted for membership after the war were senior civil service bureaucrats who had actively supported the occupiers. A similar position was taken in Holland and Belgium.

What Berggrav did in his essay, and what Arntzen's legal mind went along with, was to take the principle of communal solidarity that had been followed so courageously and to such good effect in the 1942 campaign against the Nazification of Norwegian society, and to apply it to National Unity party members, thereby holding them collectively responsible for the damage done to the country. On a human level this attitude was understandable, from a legal point of view less so. Dissenting voices – a few, but much respected – were raised by Norway's leading experts on criminal law, notably Jon Skeie and Johs. Andenæs. To the objection to collective guilt they added the undeniable fact that the legislation involved was retroactive and as such in direct breach of paragraph 100 of the constitution, in which this was expressly prohibited.

These contrasting attitudes soon coalesced into two opposing 'fronts', the *isfront* and the *silkefront*, the 'ice front' and the 'silk front'. The former were in favour of the death penalty and severe in their demands for punishment for those found guilty of collaboration and worse. They drew the line, however, at an idea much discussed in the early stages of the sentencing process which would have involved traitors being deported to the remote island of Bjørnøya in the Svalbard archipelago, another echo of the pre-Christian idea of justice in the Viking north, when banishment from the country was a standard punishment for the most serious crimes. The much smaller *silkefront* faction urged from the start compassion and forgiveness. They were, of course, opposed to the use of the death sentence. As was only to be expected, in the early stages of the judicial response it was the *isfront* that dominated. The principle of collective guilt was accepted by the courts, despite legal objections. As Berggrav had maintained in his essay, all members of National Unity shared in the corporate guilt: they were all guarantors in the business of violence.

A worldly and sophisticated servant of the church, Eivind Berggrav had been one of the founders of the Administrative Council in April 1940. In those early stages he had also, in an initiative that would haunt his later reputation as a resistance hero without ever obscuring it, taken a megaphone into the trees at Krokskogen in the *marka*, the forested and hilly area around Norway's capital city, and urged Norwegian partisans hiding out in the trees to lay down their arms and accept the German invasion as a *fait accompli*. He was also later confronted with the response he had given in October 1940 to priests who had asked for guidance on whether or not it was right for them to join National Unity. Rather than rule it out he had responded that this was a matter for their consciences alone, this was all that counted. This evasive answer may well have been what lay behind his pointed reference in the war sermon at Akershus Fortress to the obligation they had all been under to lie to their opponents or at least offer them less than the truth. Quisling feared Berggrav more than any other Norwegian opponent, realising that he combined the instincts of a politician with those of a bishop. He had never forgiven him for his role in bringing down his first abortive coup government of 9 April and at one point considered putting him on trial for treason. In the event he simply unfrocked Berggrav early in 1942 and confined him to house arrest at his country cabin, where he remained for the duration of the war.

Despite his opposition to the death penalty Berggrav was widely seen as the voice of the *isfront*. The loyalist credentials of Kristian Ljostveit, one of his most trenchant theological opponents on the *silkefront*, were free of some of these debateable complexities that hovered on the fringe of Berggrav's reputation. Once National Unity had become the only legal political party in Norway in the autumn of 1940 attempts were made to replace the priests already contracted to preach the Sunday sermons broadcast by NRK with the few priests who were actually party members. Ljostveit, a relatively obscure parish priest from Larvik, had been scheduled to broadcast one of these Sunday sermons, but with the dawning of the 'new time' was informed that his name had been removed from the list.

The church protested. The two ministers responsible for this early salvo in the culture wars, Ragnar Skancke, at the Ministry for Education and Religious Affairs, and the Minister for Culture, Gulbrand Lunde, were not prepared to take on the institutional church at this early stage of the national socialist revolution and retreated. Ljostveit's name was returned to the list and on 16 February 1941 he delivered a sermon based on Luke chapter 8, verses 4 to 15, concerning the good seed and the bad seed:

> Of God's word come people who will please God and will serve Him with all their might. For this reason they will be among society's best. These are the ones who make a society. And how much this tells us about a time as evil as ours, where so much of what grows inside us does not come from the seed of God's word: I mean the bad faith, the broken promises, the lies, hatred, violence, the pain repaid with more pain, the suppression of truth, and a sexual immorality so blatant that it shames all Norwegians on behalf of their fellow countrymen. The word of God is disobeyed. A fatal sickness has taken hold of our people.[77]

Under normal circumstances few would have regarded this as politically charged; but in the paranoid climate of the times the National Unity authorities identified each word as a criticism aimed directly at them and Ljostveit's sermon brought their tolerance of the Lutheran Church to an end. Ljostveit himself was questioned several times by the Gestapo in Larvik and interrogated by the head of Sipo in Oslo. Urged to give an undertaking to avoid any 'political' comment in future sermons he declined, saying that he was under an obligation 'to preach in the way the word of God instructed him to'. The result was that censorship was introduced forthwith, and from Ljostveit's sermon onwards the only priests who accepted invitations to broadcast were those few who were National Unity members and sympathisers. People stopped tuning in to NRK (although once the general confiscation of radio sets came into force it no longer mattered anyway). But Ljostveit's uncompromisingly Christian sermon had made him one of the many heroes of the Conscience Struggle against the Nazification of public life in Norway.

With the coming of peace there was therefore an attractive symmetry in the invitation NRK extended to him to deliver the first uncensored broadcast sermon in peacetime once the regular slot was reintroduced to the corporation's programming. He began his sermon from Larvik church on 24 February 1946 with a reading from Matthew chapter 9, in which Jesus urges his disciples to offer help to the lost sheep. This led him quickly onto the theme of total forgiveness and a direct attack on the extent and severity of the ongoing *rettsoppgjør*. Many of his turns of phrase amounted to a direct rebuttal of what Berggrav had written in *Folkedommen mot Nasjonal Samling*, including the specific statement that 'if we allow mercy to take precedence over justice then we are in harmony with the way God treats us'. He stressed that with forgiveness the sin is wiped out. 'Go to our lost sheep,' he told his congregation in the church and his radio listeners up and down the country, 'go to our traitors and our outcasts.' We have not been good enough shepherds, he told them. We had a God-given opportunity to return them to the fold, and we lost it. And in what was probably the most shocking moment of the whole sermon he offered his own explanation for the ferocity of the *rettsoppgjør* – 'So smitten have we been by the spirit of Nazism that we have responded to those ranged against us with harshness.'

Ljostveit had nothing like the authority or status of Eivind Berggrav, but his sermon was recognised as an intervention that began the process of reminding people, after five years in hell, of something many had feared had been almost forgotten: the resonance of the Christian message. Immediately following the broadcast the telephones at NRK's headquarters at Marienlyst began ringing. Most of the callers were outraged listeners so inured to the idea of censorship that, with a tragically unconscious irony, they demanded to know why the sermon had not been cleared by the authorities before being broadcast.

The press treated the event as a major story. Incredulous journalists asked Ljostveit to confirm that he had indeed been defending traitors in his sermon. Ljostveit's response was that the question betrayed a complete misunderstanding of what he had said. All he had tried to do was urge forgiveness as a way of returning 'lost sheep' to the mainstream of Norwegian society. As far as he was concerned his sermon had nothing at all to do with politics. And without going into detail about their contents he referred to the hundreds of letters he had received following the broadcast. Some were from 'good nationalists', relatives of people who had suffered unimaginable distress at the hands of German and Norwegian Nazis, condemning Ljostveit as being not far off a traitor himself. But other 'good nationalists' who had suffered in the same way wrote to express their relief and gratitude that at last the Christian message of forgiveness had been voiced. The great majority of the letters came from former members of National Unity who had been arrested, or were related to someone who had been. In the context of the time, they were outcasts bewildered at the fury vented on them for having been, as they saw it, on the losing side in a legitimate struggle. They were desperately grateful to Ljostveit for daring to say what he had said.

Broadcast in February 1946, Ljostveit's sermon came too early to affect the progress of the *rettsoppgjør*, and Bishop Berggrav's mantra 'first justice, then kindness' remained the guiding principle behind the first two years of the legal response to the occupation. On opposite sides in the matter of punishment, the two churchmen were nevertheless linked by the powerful intrusion of personal experience into their respective positions. One of the crudest responses to Ljostveit's sermon came from a journalist in *Dagbladet*, a mass-circulation daily that had quickly established itself as the voice of the *isfront*. This individual, aiming to weaken Ljostveit's moral authority by suggesting that personal interest lay behind his message of forgiveness, referred to rumours circulating in late 1944 that Ljostveit's daughter Hanna, twenty years old at the time, had been one of a group of young people known to have socialised with German soldiers stationed in Larvik. A few days before Christmas of that year she was spirited out of the country and into Sweden by the resistance for her own protection. Having helped to arrange his daughter's escape Ljostveit was arrested on 15 January 1945 and spent the rest of the war in Grini as a hostage for his own daughter.

But history is not an exact science, and even if personal circumstances shaped Ljostveit's passionately Christian response to the moral questions raised by the *rettsoppgjør* they did not create it. In similar fashion, Eivind Berggrav's harsher and more rationally argued response was probably influenced by something that happened to his own son. At almost the same time as Hanna Ljostveit was being taken over into Sweden, Dag Berggrav was being held at Akershus Fortress and subjected to a torture session that lasted some thirteen hours. In post-war trials the names of two Norwegians who had participated in his torment emerged. One was a twenty-six-year-old Stavanger man named Reidar Haaland who worked for the Gestapo as a translator and investigator. Found guilty of having tortured at least nine other Norwegian prisoners, Haaland was sentenced to death on 16 July 1945. His appeal for clemency was turned down, and he was shot by a firing squad at Akershus Fortress on 17 August.

Haaland's trial, sentencing and death made him the first man to be legally executed in Norway since 1887. With hindsight the sentence seems to have been carried out as a necessary prelude to the trial of Vidkun Quisling, which opened three days later. All of the major legal hurdles facing the passing of a death sentence in a Norwegian peacetime court had been addressed and cleared in the course of Haaland's trial: the arguments offered by his defence included a claim that the king and the government-in-exile had no constitutional right to pass a law introducing the death penalty; and that the law itself was invalid since it had not been published in the prescribed fashion in *Lovtidende* (The Legal Gazette). The court's response to this was that the decrees of October 1941 had attained the status of law in virtue of their being broadcast by the BBC in their Norwegian language service from London. This ignored the mass confiscation of radios by the Germans in the same year, which could have justified the argument that Haaland did not know that what he was engaged in was a punishable offence.

Both legal objections were dismissed by the court. In the interim between the sentencing and the hearing of the appeal Jon Skeie, published arguments against all of the London government's Provisional Laws on the grounds that they were unconstitutional. Skeie also argued that since the High Court judges presiding over Haaland's case, Erik Solem and Paal Berg, had been involved in drafting the legal details of the *rettsoppgjør* while members of the wartime resistance, this should debar them from sitting in trials involving that legislation. These arguments were raised by the defence at the Appeal Court hearing but dismissed and Haaland's death sentence was confirmed. With these precedents established the way was now clear to proceed with the trial of Vidkun Quisling, a man whose name had long since become a widely used synonym for a 'traitor'.

Quisling's trial before the *Eidsivating lagmannsrett* (Eidsivating Court of Appeal)* opened on 20 August 1945 with a statement by the prosecuting counsel, Annaeus Schjødt, summarising many of the details of the prisoner's background – his association

---

* One of Norway's courts of appeal, located in the city of Hamar, with jurisdiction over the Eidsivating judicial district.

with Fridtjof Nansen, his membership of Peder Kolstad and Jens Hundseid's cabinets in the early 1930s, and his founding of National Unity in 1933. Schjødt himself was a former member of the resistance in the 2A group which had been involved in the killing of the informer Raymond Colberg at the Cheval Animal Hospital back in 1942, and the judge was once again Erik Solem. Despite the evident conflicts of interest, it was accepted that, under the circumstances, a genuinely independent judge in the trial of Vidkun Quisling would be impossible to find.

Schjødt outlined the case against Quisling and proceeded to go into some detail about the degree of Quisling's personal involvement in the invasion of 9 April 1940. From 1936 onwards, he told the court, Quisling had cultivated a friendship with Alfred Rosenberg, one of German national socialism's leading ideologists. Regarding a meeting between Quisling and Rosenberg on 11 December 1939, Schjødt could quote from Rosenberg's own diary entry: 'He once again put forward the definite idea of preparing a German landing at the invitation of a new government which would fight its way to prominence.' This and other similar initiatives were of paramount importance in the state's efforts to establish Quisling's direct collusion in the invasion of Norway. Then there was the matter of Quisling's response to the actual invasion. Though the state conceded that Quisling had not been informed of the exact date of the invasion of 9 April – not even the German Foreign Minister, Ribbentrop, had been informed until thirty-six hours before the actual event – Schjødt argued that Quisling had been expecting the invasion, and that his attempt to seize power by a coup on its very first day made this clear. He quoted Quisling's broadcast on the evening of 9 April in which he announced himself as Norway's new prime minister and read out the list of names of his cabinet, knowing as he did so that King Haakon VII and Nygaardsvold's legally elected government were still in office and still in the country. Among the many statements uttered by Quisling during the six days of his coup that Schjødt could quote to demonstrate his treachery, perhaps the most blatant was this:

... any opposition to the Germans is not only futile but in point of fact tantamount to the criminal destruction of life and property. Every civil servant and every public service employee and in particular all of our nation's army, navy, coastal defence and air force personnel have a duty to obey directives from the new national government. Any failure to do so will entrain the most serious personal consequences for those involved.

In effect, he was attempting to overrule the order to mobilise issued by the legitimate government. These numerous instances of collusion and active encouragement of a German invasion formed one of the two most serious charges brought against Quisling. The second involved his activities after Terboven had been installed as Norway's Reichskommissar and, in his notorious speech of 25 September 1940, banned all political parties save National Unity. Subsequently to this, Quisling was accused on numerous counts of attempting to subvert the constitution of 1814 by introducing an entirely new form of government to Norway: the dictatorship of the one-party state.

A vital sub-section of this class of charges related to the setting up of the Norwegian State Police's Special Court, initially for the express purpose of trying and executing Inspector Gunnar Eilifsen for insubordination, and subsequently for the trials and executions of another fourteen Norwegian patriots for various acts of opposition to the National Unity authorities. Quisling's formal recognition of the retroactive legislation under which Eilifsen was shot, as well as his failure to exercise the prerogative of mercy which the new legislation allowed him, resulted in his being charged with being an accessory to the murder of all fourteen victims of the Police Special Court. A further example of his interferences in the constitution was the reintroduction of the paragraph, removed in 1842, that once again made the presence of Jews in the kingdom illegal and so justified the subsequent deportation of all Jews living in Norway to the death camps in Poland and to the appropriation of their assets in the name of the state.

His subsequent responsibility for what would later be termed the holocaust in Norway was limited to a charge of *uaktsomt drap* (manslaughter) regarding the Jews deported from Norway in 1942 and 1943, and he remained the only Norwegian prosecuted for this offence in relation to the attempted annihilation of the Jews. The court's justification for the reduced charge was that Quisling 'was not fully aware that, as a result of the action he instigated, the Jews would lose their lives, since at the time knowledge of the existence of the gas chambers was not widespread'.

A final group of charges reduced Quisling's attempts to live in a style appropriate to the *fører* of the Norwegian people to the behaviour of a common thief. The constitutional changes of the State Act of February 1942 vested in Quisling as *fører* all the powers of the king and the government, and he subsequently turned the royal palace into his place of work and took up residence at a sumptuous mansion – Villa Grande – on the Bygdøy peninsula.

In keeping with his wish to distinguish his fascism from the Italian version he named his new home 'Gimlé', in Viking Age mythology a palatial home in Asgard reserved for dead warriors. He was accused of the theft of dizzying sums of money – including 10 million kroner stolen from the Order of Freemasons following its dissolution – and of property, among the more curious being the 'gift' to himself of the rectory estate at Fyresdal, neighbour to his own, smaller family estate. It was to this living he had hoped to retire once his dream of an independent Norway within a Pan-Germanic union began to disintegrate.

Quisling's defence was conducted by Henrik Bergh, a man appointed to the task by the state since most of the lawyers who might have had sympathy with Quisling's political views were themselves under arrest and investigation. Bergh made what is generally regarded as a good job of the near-impossible task assigned to him. He made no attempt to justify Quisling's actions politically. Instead, he concentrated on convincing the court of the degree to which Quisling believed himself to have been acting from motives of the most profound patriotism. He portrayed

Quisling as an enigmatic and mysterious person, hinting that he could scarcely be considered a normal person at all, but insisting that he had acted at all times out of the highest notions of self-sacrifice and patriotism. The proceedings were even halted at a certain point to allow Quisling to be medically examined for the possibility that a tumour on his brain may have brought about a change in his personality that would have allowed the defence that he was unfit to stand trial. Nothing was found, however, and the trial continued.

Quisling took the stand and delivered a series of what were essentially extended political lectures. These so tried the patience of Judge Erik Solem that at times he was seen to bury his face in his hands. Over and over again Quisling had to be asked to speak up, because the court couldn't hear him. The rationalisations and explanations he offered for his conduct over the five years of the German occupation seemed to the court like the ramblings of a man entirely divorced from reality. Wholly different understandings of what had happened in the world faced each other across the courtroom floor, but in the end, there could be only one outcome: on 10 September the court found Major Vidkun Abraham Laurits Quisling guilty of entering into a conspiracy against his country with Adolf Hitler that began in December 1939; of an attempted coup d'etat on 9 April 1940; of rescinding the legal government's mobilisation orders issued during the first few hours of the occupation; of illegally forming a National Unity government and appointing himself minister-president of the country on 1 February 1942; of actively pursuing the arrest and deportation of Norway's population of Jews; and of failing to exercise his prerogative as minister-president to prevent the execution of fifteen named victims executed by the Police Special Court, including Inspector Gunnar Eilifsen and the border guide Knut Mathiesen.

Judge Solem informed Quisling that he had been sentenced to death. He asked the prisoner if he had understood the sentence. Quisling replied that he had. Solem then added that, if Quisling found the sentence too severe or took exception to certain aspects of the conduct of the case, he had a right of appeal to the High Court. He was offered time to consider his decision but after a brief conference with his lawyer he replied that he would appeal.

On 9 October the High Court, sitting under Paal Berg and four other judges, considered the appeal. Quisling spoke again in his defence, but he seemed resigned to failure and the certainty of his death. He commended to the court his response to the victory of his opponents in May 1945 in surrendering and ordering his supporters to refrain from violence and contrasted it with the flight of the king and government five years previously. He had arrived at an understanding of himself as a prophet without honour in his own land. In the weeks spent waiting for his appeal he had spent much of his time organising notes he had been making sporadically over the years for a book which would articulate his visionary understanding of life in the form of a doctrine which he called Universalism. Universalism resembled other syncretic systems such as those of Madame Blavatsky and Rudolf Steiner in combining eastern philosophies and religious beliefs with aspects of Christianity, the insights of western philosophers such as Schopenhauer and Kant, and contemporary theories in the fields of science and astronomy. As he neared the end of his speech Quisling provided the court with a taste of his lonely and rambling quest for universal truth. He told the judges he had had two motives for his actions:

> One was to serve my Norwegian people, the other was to serve what I call the will of God. Politics is a means in the service of a higher end, that of History, that of God. Such has been my belief these last twenty years. And this I can say now, now that I have officially been declared sane. We are in the midst of an epochal time in which the kingdom of God is becoming manifest on earth. They say the kingdom of God is another world. But a kingdom of God is already being built here on earth. Marxism speaks of a kingdom of heaven on earth. But that is a kingdom of materialism. The kingdom I am speaking of is a spiritual kingdom of love

and brotherhood between people of all nations and all races. I once told Himmler that the German national socialist state was materialistic. But my faith is that I have worked towards the end of a spiritual kingdom of God.[78]

He concluded by saying that his execution – should it come to that – would remain a permanent badge of shame for Norwegians. He also offered a heartfelt condemnation of what he saw as the source of all his present troubles, the failure of the Nygaardsvold government adequately to understand the threat facing Norway's neutrality in the fraught political climate of the 1930s, and to fund and realistically equip Norway to defend itself militarily against an invasion.

Following the rejection in the Court of Appeal on 13 October, Quisling petitioned the king in council for clemency. This was rejected unanimously on 23 October and at 7 p.m. Pastor Carl Traaen visited the former minister-president to break the news to him, and to inform him that he would be executed later that same evening. The execution was scheduled for five minutes past midnight but had to be put back some two hours while they waited for the arrival of the Danish Chief of Police, who had requested permission to attend in order to prepare for the executions that were shortly to take place in his own country. Fog at Færder meant that his flight had to be diverted to the airport at Kristiansand, imposing a two-hour delay on his arrival.

When at last he arrived, Quisling was taken from his cell in Møllergata 19 at 2.30 a.m. and driven in convoy to Akershus Fortress. There, in a specially constructed theatre lit by two floodlights in front of the *kruttårnet* (gunpowder tower) he was held to a backboard by two straps, one around his waist and the other around his chest. His hands were crossed in front of his groin and his wrists tied together. His ankles were secured. In spite of his protests, he was blindfolded. A piece of paper was pinned to his pullover marking the approximate location of his heart, and at 2.40 a.m. he was shot by a firing squad of eleven men who stood six metres away from him. He slumped forward in his bindings and the officer in charge of the squad stepped forward and fired a final shot through his temple.

Over the years a number of authorities have suggested there were better reasons to have Quisling subjected to psychiatric examination to determine his fitness to stand trial than there ever were in the case of Norway's Nobel Prize-winning novelist Knut Hamsun, who *was* subjected to such an examination. Gabriel Langfeldt was one of the most prominent of several high-status forensic psychiatrists whose reports could materially affect who was and who was not fit to stand trial in the *rettsoppgjør* and, ultimately, who would end up before a firing squad and who wouldn't. In 1960 he published a short book in which he used Bergh's courtroom description of Quisling as an enigma (*gåte*) to express his view that Quisling had indeed been unfit to stand trial. But to promote such a notion in 1945 would have provoked an outcry similar to that which greeted the first forensic psychiatric report on the Utøya terrorist and mass murderer Anders Behring Breivik, which found him criminally insane and therefore unfit to stand trial, and which had to be replaced by a second report that came to the opposite conclusion.

Uniquely among cases in which a death sentence was passed, even the *silkefront* remained silent in Quisling's case. In a book written after the liberation, Eivind Berggrav provided a surprisingly sympathetic portrait of the 'enigma' of Vidkun Quisling.* He recalled a meeting to which he had been summoned at the royal palace early in 1942 to discuss the government's

---

* On 16 October Berggrav visited him in cell 34B, Møllergata 19. Quisling's biographer, Hans Fredrik Dahl, writes that the tone of the meeting was one of 'understanding, reconciliation, forgiveness'. Two days later, Berggrav wrote to the prime minister, Einar Gerhardsen, requesting that Quisling's life be spared, on the grounds that the state had no right to take a human life in peacetime.

alarm at the ferocity of the church's opposition to National Unity's policies. Jonas Lie was present, as was Albert Hagelin's deputy at the Ministry of the Interior, Thorleif Dahl:

> My impression after that meeting was one of surprise. They seemed like anything but statesmen. Undisciplined, unbalanced. Quisling was the most interesting. When he started on one of his long speeches he didn't look up, he spoke as though into a vacuum, not addressing anyone in particular. Suddenly he would become angry and lose control, both of his words and of his tone. Despite this, Quisling was the only person one felt an interest in. There was something helpless about him that was immediately appealing. He was devoid of any sense of humour and seemed inflexible. It was as though he was stuck in some kind of rut from which he could not escape. At times he simply seemed somehow absent. And yet there really was *something* about Quisling, something out of the ordinary.[79]

In her book *Eichmann in Jerusalem*, Hannah Arendt quotes lines from the judgement in the trial of Adolf Eichmann in 1963 on the 'banality of evil'. And there was indeed something banal about Quisling. There was something almost childlike, too, which is captured in Berggrav's description of him as someone trapped inside something from which he could not release himself. While awaiting trial he was taken from his cell in Oslo to witness the ghastly work of digging up the unmarked graves of the hundreds of Norwegians who had been shot and buried in Trandum Forest. He claimed to have been unaware that deaths had occurred on this scale, and one is inclined to believe him. He had never arrested anyone himself, far less tortured or killed anyone. It seems not to have occurred to him that in offering these disavowals of responsibility he was also betraying the Führer principle for which his entire war had been fought, seeking to evade an ultimate responsibility that was his and his alone. The words quoted

THE LEGAL RECKONING

by Hannah Arendt from Eichmann's trial could apply just as well to Quisling: 'the extent to which any one of the many criminals was close to or remote from the actual killer of the victim means nothing, as far as the measure of his responsibility is concerned. On the contrary, in general the degree of responsibility increases as we draw further away from the man who uses the fatal instrument in his own hands.'[80]

Quisling's last letter to his wife is a document of great tenderness. Though it cannot excuse the pain and torment caused by his conduct, and by the criminal arrogance that prevented him from realising how very few other Norwegians shared his beliefs, it reminds us that every monster is also a human being:

My beloved Maria,

I shall not have another chance to say goodbye to you, and so I send you here my last farewell and my heartfelt thanks for everything.

Thank you for your unbelievable loyalty and for your love for me. And not least for all you have meant to me during these last few difficult and heavy months. You have been wonderful.

My heart is filled with gratitude and love for you, and my deepest sorrow is that I must leave you, whom I love so greatly.

But I will always be close to you, and it is certain that we shall once again meet face to face.

May God give you strength and keep you in all things. Put your faith in him. Abandon yourself to him completely.

Believe in God and believe in me. Be strong and courageous.

Perhaps even this will turn out a blessing, and sorrow one day be turned to joy.

I bow to the will of God. For there must surely be some deeper meaning in this, both you and I must believe that, and find our comfort in that.

As agreed, I wish to be buried in Gjerpen churchyard. You

can arrange this with Hauge*, who I know will help you.

Do not, my beloved, be too downcast at this heavy blow. Try to find the light and the good sides. And keep all the good memories. How happy I am that we have found one another so completely and forgiven all!

Maria, I love you unto death and beyond. Remember the life we lived together, and that we shall meet again. Remember me. Thank you for everything.

Warm greetings to Jørgen and others.

God bless and keep you my darling.

Your Vidkun

My last thoughts are of you!

There was undeniably a sacrificial element to Quisling's death. Without it, it is hard to imagine how the trauma of the Nazi occupation and all its horrors would otherwise have begun to fade. Three days after Reidar Haaland's execution on 17 August, a demonstration organised by the Oslo and Akershus trade unions numbering some 30,000 was held in Youngstorget. The essence of the protest was that justice was taking too long and the opinions of the *silkefront* carrying too much weight. One banner carried the slogan 'Leniency to traitors betrays our country.' There could be little doubt the demonstration was intended as a signal to the judges at the start of Quisling's trial at 10 that same morning. Now, with the minister-president dead, a layer of the cold rage that had fuelled the *isfront* began to melt. But one more necessary death remained before the real thaw could begin.

Henry Oliver Rinnan, a small and slightly built man from Levanger, was twenty-five years old and working as a car salesman and lorry driver when the Germans arrived. He initially took part in what little formal military resistance Norway was able to offer before being arrested and imprisoned. Soon he began

---

* Dagfinn Hauge, the prison chaplain at Akershus Fortress.

working for the Germans, initially as an informer, then as head of Sonderabteilung Lola, a group of Norwegians dedicated to infiltrating and exposing the communist network in Norway following the German invasion of Russia in 1941. Rinnan himself, as undisputed head of the Rinnan Band, as the group was known, operated in what its leader euphemistically referred to as 'the negative sector'. His agents, posing as dedicated Milorg operatives, contrived to meet and gain the trust of as many genuine resistance groups as they could and then betrayed them to the Germans. Rinnan, a frighteningly resolute and intelligent man, was a wholly credible performer in this role, a sort of Gunnar Waaler in reverse. He inflicted terrible damage on resistance groups in the Trøndelag region where he was based. At his trial in the winter of 1946 evidence showed that he was responsible for the deaths of at least eighty Norwegians and the arrests of over a thousand men and women. Hundreds of those arrested by Sonderabteilung Lola under SS-Untersturmführer Rinnan were subjected to unimaginably cruel extremes of torture. A particular horror of some of the extended torture sessions examined at Rinnan's trial was that they seemed to lack even the basic justifying veneer of a search for information, descending swiftly into the pursuit of sadistic gratification for its own sake, with breaks for aquavit and sandwiches. One man had his genitals whipped with a cat-o'-nine-tails studded with shards of glass. Another, Einar Thorberg Svendsen, arrested by the group in October 1943, was stripped naked, whipped and beaten continuously for six hours. When he passed out his tormentors revived him by tapping his nose or eyes with the tips of their burning cigarettes. Eventually tiring of this method, Rinnan ordered that Svendsen be suspended from a ceiling beam by his thumbs. With his legs dangling freely he was then whipped for several more hours.

Rinnan's psychopathic personality compelled a terrified obedience. Marie Arentz and her lover Bjørn Bjørnebo, two of his own group members, were so disgusted by his activities they tried to flee to England. They were captured and taken to Rinnan's home at

Jonsvannsveien 46 in Trondheim, where the basement had been converted to serve as a combined bar, prison and torture chamber. Arentz was stripped and hung from a beam in the ceiling and her dead body lain on the floor. Bjørnebo was brought in and offered the choice of being hung himself or chloroformed and shot. He chose the latter and was told to lie down next to her before being chloroformed and shot through the head.

Milorg operatives tried to kill Rinnan on several occasions. One extraordinary story the court heard was Ørnulf Egge's account of a long conversation he had in 1942 with a man named Olav Wisth. Egge was a senior member of the Norwegian Communist Party and had been informed by reliable sources that Wisth was an important Milorg leader in the Trondheim area. He told his quick-witted and personable companion that on several occasions he had asked party members in the region to get rid of Rinnan as a matter of urgency. Wisth confirmed that they had indeed made several attempts on Rinnan's life but that he had survived them all through cunning and good luck. Only later did Egge learn that his sympathetic fellow traveller Olav Wisth was the very man they had been talking about liquidating, Henry Oliver Rinnan himself.

The Rinnan Band was tried in two groups, the first in the autumn of 1946, the second in the spring of 1947. Rinnan himself was tried in the first pool and found guilty of thirteen murders and sentenced to death. Eleven members of his group were also given death sentences. If Quisling's 'enigma' cast a persistent moral shadow over his execution in some liberal quarters in Norway, no such shadow complicated the response to Rinnan's wartime activities. That he was a psychopath seems obvious, though that term conveys nothing but the bewildered defeat of the diagnostic art. Like Quisling, he inhabited a different planet from most of the rest of us. His defence attorney, Thorvald Wiig, was with him the evening before his execution, which was scheduled for 4 a.m. on 1 February 1947. As Wiig later told his son, Rinnan showed few signs of being a man whose life was about to end in a few hours. He spoke about a time before the war, when he had been working as a petrol pump attendant and Wiig had pulled into the station one day to fill up his tank. Rinnan remembered the occasion well and had wanted to reminisce about it.

Rinnan was accompanied to the place of execution at Kristiansten Fortress in Trondheim by the prison chaplain Lars Tangvik Ofstad after taking a last – as well as probably a first – Holy Communion. He asked Ofstad to stay with him to the very end and the chaplain promised he would. Rinnan was then bound and blindfolded and the white target circle pinned to his jacket above his heart as Ofstad intoned Jesus' words to the thief beside him on the cross: *verily I say unto thee, today shalt thou be with me in paradise*. Rinnan seems almost to have taken this literally, as though he thought Oftstad was some kind of ticket that would keep him out of Hell. 'Are you still there, Lars?' he asked once the preparations were complete. 'Yes, still here,' came the reply. The signal to take aim and fire – arm raised, then dropped – was wordless. Intending to occupy Rinnan's mind at the critical moment, the chaplain improvised: as the squad commander's arm went up, he asked Rinnan, 'Is there any special person you would like to be remembered to?' before jumping aside. And as Rinnan was considering this, down came the arm and ten shots rang out.

Under the new laws, almost 93,000 cases of potential *landssvik* were investigated by the returning authorities. This was just over 3 per cent of the population in 1945 and affected approximately one in seven Norwegian households. The figures were greatly in excess of what the London government had anticipated when passing the emergency legislation and put a huge strain on the newly restored legal system. As many as 1,375 were tried and found not guilty; 17,000 received prison sentences; while 3,450 were found guilty and given some other form of sentencing. Three thousand, one hundred and twenty were offered a fine or a prison sentence and chose the fine. Another 25,180 paid a fine in place of some form of punishment other than imprisonment, and 37,150 cases were *henlagt etter bevisets stilling*, a verdict similar to the now obsolete Scottish verdict of 'not proven', implying that the prosecution believed a crime had been committed but that it did not have enough evidence to prove it in court. A further 5,500 other cases resulted in *påtaleunnlatelse*, a 'waiver of prosecution' applied when the prosecution believed it did indeed have enough evidence to proceed and get a conviction, but for a variety of reasons – perhaps the age of the defendant, or the unlikelihood of there being any repeat of the offence – decided not to. Both of these seemingly innocuous verdicts could lead to the loss of social privileges such as the right to vote and to hold public office. Both carried a significant social stigma.

Thirty Norwegians were sentenced to death. Four had their sentences commuted to imprisonment, including an informer named Aud Maggi Andersen who was spared on the grounds that she was a woman. One man died before his sentence could be carried out. Another fifteen, mostly Germans, were sentenced to death for war crimes. Two had their sentences commuted. Dagfinn Hauge, the prison chaplain at Akershus Fortress who during the years of occupation had ministered to so many Norwegians on the last night of their lives, made a forlorn attempt to keep the promise made to one of the first groups of condemned prisoners he had to minister to, five men who ran an escape route from Ålesund across the North Sea to the British Isles. On 11 November 1941, the eve of their execution, the group's leader, a thirty-seven-year-old lawyer named Harald Torsvik, approached Hauge: 'There's one thing we'd like to ask of you,' he said. 'Once things have returned to normal in Norway we would like you to do everything in your power to prevent the death penalty being used. We don't want anyone to face this punishment – not even our enemies among our own countrymen.'

'Do you mean everyone, from the highest to the lowest?'

All gave this their assent. Yes.

'We hope that you can make this known at the highest level.'

Another of the group, Rolv Lea, added: 'It's the innocent left behind who suffer most from the death penalty. It should never be used.'[81]

Hauge gave them his word and on an unspecified occasion early in the post-war legal process passed the request on to Prime Minister Einar Gerhardsen. As a political and moral realist Gerhardsen knew it was impossible to comply: the expiatory process had to run its course. Two more of Quisling's ministers were tried, sentenced to death and executed. The first was Albert Hagelin, one of Quisling's closest associates and a man intimately involved in the events leading up to the invasion itself and the abortive coup of the first week. As Minister of the Interior in Terboven's Reichskommissariat following the abolition of democracy in September 1940, Hagelin was responsible for the Nazification of local government, a task he continued in the government set up by Quisling in 1942. Hagelin was executed on 25 May 1946.

Hagelin, like so many other members of Quisling's cabinets, came from a family with deep social and cultural roots in Germany. Ragnar Skancke, the third and last National Unity politician to be executed, was a member of National Unity since its inception in 1933, and served as Minister for Education and Church Affairs in both of Quisling's regimes. This placed him in the forefront of National Unity's attempts to abolish democracy in Norway and replace it with the principles of national socialism. Skancke was not the most active and passionate advocate of the many fundamental changes this revolution demanded, but as head of the department involved he became the symbolic target against which the remarkable campaign of civil disobedience by the country's teachers, priests and parents in 1942 was directed, and as such his fate was sealed. After a trial lasting less than two weeks before the Eidsivating Court of Appeal, he was found guilty of high treason and diverse breaches of financial trust and sentenced to death on 21 May 1946. The sentence was confirmed on appeal on 27 March the following year, despite a petition calling for clemency signed by over 600 priests and a number of former professional colleagues.

On 27 August 1948, Skancke made an appeal to the king in council for mercy. It was his last option and it was rejected. By this time the mood in the country had turned so far against the death penalty that it seems even members of the firing squad were so affected by Skancke's distress as he was brought before them on the morning of 28 August that they refused to carry out the execution. There was a telephone call to the Minister of Justice O.C. Gundersen, who was told he might have to come to the fortress and carry out the shooting himself. Gundersen duly arrived, but it was only to quell the near mutiny by reminding the men of their obligations as police officers. Skancke was then shot.

Skancke was the last man to be legally executed in Norway. Almost as rapidly and fiercely as it had flared up, the desire to punish died down. By 1948 all prisoners with sentences of less than ten years had been released with time half-served, and by 1956 the last of those jailed in connection with the *rettsoppgjør* were free.

EPILOGUE

Requiem for a Border Guide
Knut Mathiesen
(31 March 1921 – 6 May 1944)

Gunnar Waaler and Knut Mathiesen
11.45 a.m., Thursday 4 May 1944, Grubbegata, Oslo[82]

It was the third time the Police Special Court had been in session since its establishment in August of the previous year. The defendant this time was Knut Mathiesen, a twenty-two-year-old *grenselos* (border guide) who had shot and killed a policeman who stopped the car he was travelling in with his driver and three refugees from Kristiansand. The killing took place at Damholt farm, some five kilometres from the Swedish border on the Norwegian side. The refugees and the driver escaped, Mathiesen got caught. As a State Police inspector grade 1, a career policeman since graduating from college in 1935 and a man known to be so strongly committed to the Germanist cause that he could bore even his own colleagues with extempore lectures and analyses of the virtues and proper application of national socialism, it had been a simple matter for Gunnar Waaler to obtain permission to attend from the lead judge at the trial, Carl Ludvig von Elverfeldt Stephanson.

He entered the courthouse shortly before 12 p.m. and took a seat on the left-hand side of the large courtroom. The prosecuting counsel, Ole Olsen Landerud, impeccable in his sharply pressed green police uniform, was already in place over on the right side of the court, left leg crossed over his right, glossy black jackboot bouncing rhythmically as he leafed through his papers. He looked up only briefly as the side door to the courtroom opened again and Mathiesen's lawyer, a man named Bergsjø, entered the courtroom with the defendant behind him. Mathiesen was handcuffed between two Stapo men wearing civilian clothes. It wasn't official policy, but rank-and-file Stapo men usually wore plain clothes when on duty. It made it easier for them to mingle with a crowd without attracting attention, to monitor changes in the atmosphere at a public gathering. If intervention became necessary it gave them the benefit of surprise.

Bergsjø led his client to a seat in the front row, directly in front of the judges' table and a little to the right of Waaler. As the little party sat down a third policeman closed the door behind them and then positioned himself in front of it, legs stiffly apart, hands crossed below his crotch.

Waaler leaned forward slightly and studied the prisoner. He did not look good. After thirteen days of solitary confinement in a cell in Akershus Fortress the boy's dark hair was spiky and unkempt and there were haemorrhagic bruises around both eyes, a clear sign that he'd been choked as part of his interrogation. Beneath a battledress jacket he was wearing what appeared to be a faded, blue-striped nightshirt. Waaler already knew that Per Willars Nilsen, the Red Cross official responsible for allowing the organisation's staff and ambulance and radiography vehicles to be used for the transport of refugees, had been alerted to the fact of Mathiesen's arrest and was already in neutral Sweden. The police had raided a number of homes in the Oslo area but some of the drivers involved in the transport of refugees had also managed to escape and were hiding out in the dense pine forests surrounding Oslo until things quietened down. But arrests had been made, and Waaler knew the Red Cross route over the Swedish border wouldn't be in use for some time to come.

Mathiesen had talked. No surprise there. Sooner or later everyone does. No one can endure torture. The most a prisoner could hope for was to hold out long enough for news of his arrest to get out and give his contacts time to go into hiding or, like Willars Nilsen, cross the border into Sweden.

At 12 p.m. precisely the large double doors at the front of the courtroom opened and the three judges entered the hall. Each one stopped briefly on entering and saluted stiffly with the right arm before moving forward towards the high table in front of them. Waaler jumped to his feet and responded in kind. The only other spectator in the courtroom was the pathologist, a professor from Ullevål hospital whose name was also Waaler, Georg Waaler. As he sat down again Waaler made a mental note to change the professor's name when writing his account of the trial later on that evening, to avoid the confusion of having two people with the same name. Then he reminded himself it was a report he would be writing, not a piece of fiction. With the natural curiosity one feels when encountering a namesake he glanced over at the professor. He noticed that he had failed to salute when the judges entered the courtroom. He was writing something on the notepad balanced on his knee and did not appear to have noticed their entry at all. Waaler wondered briefly what he was writing; notes from the autopsy, perhaps, for when he was called to give evidence.

Waaler watched as all three judges, following Stephanson's example, removed the bandoliers slung sash-style over their shoulders and hung them over the projecting spikes on the chair backs before sitting down at the long oak table. All wore green uniforms, the joint innovation some months previously of two members of Vidkun Quisling's cabinet, Jonas Lie, the Minister for Policing, and his Minister of Justice, Sverre Riisnæs, as part of an ongoing attempt to militarise the Norwegian police. All wore the same highly polished black jackboots, and as each one individually settled at the table, fidgeting, looking round, straightening papers, Stephanson removing and polishing his glasses, holding them up to the light that flooded in from the tall, street-facing windows, Waaler studied them, committing the details of the various insignias and badges of rank, party membership and service decorations worn by each man for when he came to write his report. Stephanson wore the distinctions of a lieutenant colonel, Skjønhaug a captain and Ekeland a junior officer. How would he sum them up for his report? Stephanson, a thirty-two-year-old police commander in Oslo, was the only one of the three with any legal training at all and a former adjutant for Jonas Lie. Rolf Skjønhaug was a career policeman who had risen under the new regime to the level of Stapo section leader. Harald Ekeland was a former salesman who had joined the force after the outbreak of war and rapidly advanced from constable to sergeant. Of the three, Skjønhaug was the only one Waaler knew well and socialised with. Indeed, he had reason to be grateful to him: when the Germans began requisitioning pet dogs for use on the Eastern Front it was Skjønhaug who had come to his rescue, saving his dog Varja by officially enrolling the Alsatian in the State Police's own canine unit.

Stephanson raised his right hand, rapped once on the tabletop with his gavel which, Waaler noted, was silver and shaped like a Thor's hammer. He announced that the court was in session and at once read out the charges: Knut Mathiesen of Number 2 Magnus Bergs gate Oslo, a driver and technical assistant employed in the state's Radiography Department, born 31 March 1921, is hereby summoned to appear before the Police Special Court for Southern Norway charged with crimes committed in contravention of statute 233, under military law paragraphs such and such, *cf* the Quisling Law regarding Special Courts of 16 August 1943. That the defendant did, on the 20th of April this year, at approximately twenty-two hundred hours, in the kitchen of the Damholt farm in Øymark, fire a number of shots into the chest and stomach of border police officer Harald Haugland, injuring him. And that subsequent to this, the victim having managed to crawl out into the yard, the defendant did pursue and kill Haugland by shooting him through the back of his head. Signed, Jonas Lie, Minister of Police.

★

EPILOGUE

Stephanson looked down at the defendant, placed the sheet of paper back on the table. He kept his head bowed for a few moments as though to let the gravity of the occasion sink in. Then he looked up and with a slight nod indicated to Ole Landerud, the officer prosecuting the case, that he might proceed. Landerud got to his feet. He moved his hand down across his tie as he walked forward into the space below the judges' table. Waaler heard a slight but regular scuffing noise, as though a gravel chip had become wedged in the sole of his boot.

Landerud turned round. Fixing his gaze unwaveringly on Mathiesen, he went on to describe the sequence of events that had led to the murder of Haugland; how Mathiesen's employment as a driver and assistant radiographer was a position of trust, vested in him as a servant of the state to safeguard the lives and health of decent, law-abiding Norwegian citizens, and as such in possession of formal permission to drive his screening truck freely throughout the eastern border region. It was, said Landerud, a trust Mathiesen had betrayed. He had done so in order to help criminals and other enemies of the state attempting illegally to cross the border into Sweden. By the defendant's own account, over the previous two months he had participated on several occasions in the transport of groups of people to the border regions of Halden, Rakkestad and Askim, also acting as their guide for the final stage of the flight to Sweden on foot.

As Waaler listened to Landerud's account of the infamies perpetrated by the defendant, his voice now and then quivering with a practised anger, he ran over in his mind what he already knew of the man, and how he would describe him in his report: Ole Olsen Landerud, acting inspector in the State Police force, born 1907 and so three years Waaler's junior; took his ex.art med TF in 1927 and after five years study became a *cand.mag.jur* with a good degree, *Står til Laud*. It indicated a degree of intelligence that Waaler, for a reason he couldn't quite fathom but which was perhaps connected to the sight of him in green police uniform and glossy black boots, found depressing.

Attentive to Landerud's narrative, Waaler learned that Mathiesen had joined a car containing a driver and the three fugitives at the junction of Nordraaks gate and Munthes gate, opposite the main entrance to Frogner Park and just a five-minute walk from his home in Magnus Bergs vei. The driver's name was Rolf Leisner. Leisner held a permit that allowed him to travel in the eastern region to gather kindling to fuel the *knottgenerator* (wood gas generator) mounted on the roof of his truck. The vehicle had left Oslo at 6 on the evening of 20 April. As it approached the farm at Damholt in Øymark, Leisner was waved to the side of the road by two border guards, Haugland and his partner, John Bergmann. Some minutes earlier Haugland had received a telephone call at the station at Ørje alerting them to the presence in the region of what the caller described as a 'suspicious vehicle'. He and Bergmann had cycled to the farm at Damholt and positioned themselves around a bend on a corner of the narrow road, and when Leisner's car came into sight they waved it down and ordered the occupants to produce their ID cards. Mathiesen's and Leisner's were scrutinised briefly before being slipped into the chest pocket of Haugland's shirt. The cards shown to him by the two men and the woman seated in the back failed to convince him, however, and he ordered them all out of the car and into the Damholt farmhouse.

Landerud paused at this point. He cleared his throat, turned his head and scanned the almost deserted courtroom. For one unnerving moment he seemed to be looking directly at and even *through* Waaler before resuming, now with his back to the defendant and addressing the bench. When he resumed he pitched his voice very slightly higher, the better to convey his sense of outrage and sorrow as he went on to describe in detail the subsequent series of events in the farmhouse kitchen briefly outlined in Lie's charge sheet. Haugland, as the senior man, had ordered Bergmann to stand guard at the kitchen doorway as he began a weapons search of the group. One of the three, a small man with a bandaged arm, reacted with barely concealed hostility as Haugland frisked him.

EPILOGUE

The two others turned out to be a man and the woman, a married couple from Kristiansand named Moy. Fru Moy was heavily pregnant and Haugland scarcely touched her before going on to her husband. As he raised his hands to pat Mathiesen's pockets, Mathiesen pulled a pistol from his jacket pocket and fired a shot. At that same instant the driver of the car, Leisner, gave Bergmann a violent push in the chest that sent him tumbling backwards into the large open fireplace while he and the three refugees ran from the kitchen, with Bergmann in pursuit.

Mathiesen's must have been a warning shot for it turned out that this first bullet buried itself harmlessly in the thick timbers of the kitchen wall behind Haugland. Haugland then drew his own Gluck and the two men engaged in a furious grappling match. Mathiesen clamped his left hand around Haugland's right wrist while Haugland clamped his left around Mathiesen's right. At thirty-five, Haugland was the older man and the more experienced in the use of force, but Mathiesen was young and strong and their desperate grunting waltz around the kitchen floor went on for two or three minutes before Mathiesen finally managed to turn his gun-holding hand down sufficiently to get off a shot and hit Haugland in the left side of his chest. Haugland's reaction was to drop his own gun and press his left hand to the wound. Mathiesen fired several more shots. Haugland staggered out the kitchen door and into the yard. Mathiesen picked up the Gluck and followed him out, still shooting. Two bullets struck Haugland in the left buttock and he stumbled into an empty milk churn and sent it rolling across the farmyard.

Farmer Damholt and one of his sons were watching from the kitchen as Mathiesen then walked up to the wounded man, bent over him and fired a bullet through the back of his head. He looked around. There was no sign of the bandaged man nor the couple from Kristiansand. Nor the driver Rolf Leisner. He heard movement from a copse over to his right, the cracking of a twig. In the gathering gloom he thought he could make out a face behind a bush, parting the branches slightly with his fingers.

He fired a shot and heard footsteps as someone ran off through the trees. Only at this point did Mathiesen realise he had been shot himself, a flesh wound on the inside of his left thigh. Possibly from his own weapon. From talking to colleagues discussing the case at Stapo headquarters on Kronprinsens gate Waaler knew what had happened next; Mathiesen had spent the rest of the night in the forest and in the morning made his way to the small village of Rakkestad, where he booked a room at the Centrall Hotel. He made a call from the phone in the lobby to Willars Nilsen in Oslo, telling him he needed urgently to be picked up, then went upstairs to his room.

Unfortunately for Mathiesen, his arrival at the hotel had been observed by a Rakkestad resident named Bjørn Rakestad (one 'k'). A keen member of National Unity, Rakestad's favoured contribution to the national socialist cause was to prevent as many refugees as possible from crossing into Sweden. He had at once telephoned the sheriff's office to report the sighting of a suspiciously wounded man booking in at the Centrall. From the ID cards found in Haugland's shirt pocket, police already knew who they were looking for as Mathiesen's photograph had been wired to stations across the region. Mathiesen's father Eystein, who ran a tobacco shop in Magnus Bergs gate, had been arrested earlier in the morning and was being held hostage pending the arrest of his son.

The sheriff at Rakkestad was another good national socialist. He knew the boy Mathiesen from his work in the region with the radiography unit and with two armed border guards as backup he arrived at the hotel and showed Mathiesen's photograph to the receptionist. Realising there was no point in denying anything, she had given them the room number. Mathiesen had been in the act of cleaning his wound at the small washbasin in the corner of the room when the knock came.

'You better give up, Mathiesen,' the sheriff shouted through the door. 'We've got your father.'

*

EPILOGUE

With a last glare at the accused, Landerud then walked back to his seat three rows in front of Waaler. Now it was Mathiesen's turn to give his version of events. He made his way to the witness box, limping slightly from his wound, and as Bergsjø put his questions to him Waaler took the opportunity to study the young face. Large, fleshy nose. What people called a 'generous' mouth. Eyes a deep and startling blue. With his dishevelled hair and bruised and dirt-stained face the boy looked like a tramp. Waaler didn't doubt for an instant that his appearance was a true reflection of the treatment he had been subjected to while under arrest and awaiting trial, and that his jailers at Akershus Fortress intended to make him look as much as possible like a common criminal. As he had done throughout the proceedings so far, Waaler struggled to make Mathiesen add up: that broken and pitiful lamb sitting there between the two Stapo guards had killed a man? How? Waaler had never killed anyone. He hoped to God he would never have to.

Like every other official present in the court, Mathiesen's defence lawyer Gulbrand Bergsjø was a member of National Unity. Waaler knew him quite well. Occasionally they shared a cup of coffee together in the canteen at Stapo headquarters on Kronprinsens gate or here at the justice building on Akersgate. It was Bergsjø who had introduced Waaler to Stephanson and obtained the judge's permission for him to attend the trial. Bergsjø was affable enough but Waaler found him hollow, a clever and charming man who stood for nothing. He went through the impossible task of defending Mathiesen well enough. There was no denying the facts of the case and his initial cross-examination of Mathiesen sought only to portray him in as sympathetic a light as possible, a deluded pawn in a game of which he understood nothing. Through this sympathetic line of questioning Waaler learned that Mathiesen's education was limited to secondary school; that as well as being a driver on the Red Cross radiology trucks he was a technical assistant able to operate the X-ray cameras; and that his fate had been sealed the day the transport manager at the Red Cross had invited him to his home for dinner and in the course of the meal broached the subject of whether he was willing to use his knowledge of the border regions and his travel permit to help transport Norwegian refugees across the border.

Mathiesen had agreed. He told the court he had made three such trips. The first in mid-March, the second just before Easter, and the third on the night of 20 April. Each time, he said, he had taken the same route, driving via Askim, Rakkestad and Halden. For the third trip he had been told to be at the junction of Nordraaks gate and Munthes gate at 6 p.m. He would find a blue car parked there. He was to knock on the window and ask if the driver knew where Jens Jensen lived. Everything had gone smoothly until they reached Øymark, where the car was flagged down by the two border policemen. What happened thereafter was already known to the court.

Bergsjø thanked him and sat down. Stephanson leaned forward, causing the dangling bandolier and holstered gun to thud against the back of his chair. He planted his elbows on the table in front of him, laced his fingers and asked the accused what his plans had been after shooting Haugland: had he been intending to make his way to Sweden?

Mathiesen answered no, that thought hadn't occurred to him, not then.

Stephanson raised his eyebrows in supercilious doubt and shook his head. *Bærumsgutt*. West End boy, thought Waaler. Thirty-two years old and the power of life and death in his hands. Carl Ludvig von Elverfeldt Stephanson. He silently enunciated each of the nine syllables in a slow trudge through the name. Each one would go into his report.

Stephanson sighed theatrically: did Mathiesen not then have any plans at all?

Waaler kept his eyes on Mathiesen. For a long time the boy said nothing. He turned his head and made a slight lifting gesture of the manacled hands resting on the edge of the witness box as though to scratch his neck before realising it wasn't possible. Presently he

EPILOGUE

told the court in a low monotone that after resting at the hotel in Rakkestad he had intended to make his way back to Oslo.

'Where presumably you would once again volunteer your services for the illegal transport of criminals and fugitives?'

Mathiesen shook his head but didn't speak.

'Then to do what, once you returned to Oslo?' asked Skjønhaug, joining in the judicial bullying with a note of exasperation in his voice.

Waaler noted again the lifting of Mathiesen's manacled hands, their brief forlorn flight and fall.

'I was going to ask my parents whether I should turn myself in or try to get across into Sweden.'

'You had just killed a man in cold blood, and you were going to ask your parents whether or not you should turn yourself in?' Stephanson echoed in disbelief.

'Or go to Sweden,' Mathiesen said weakly.

Skjønhaug let out a loud bray of laughter. He turned to share the moment with Ekdal, and Ekdal did share it. After the briefest of pauses he closed his eyes. He shook his head several times and then wrote something down. Wasn't listening, thought Waaler. Bored.

'Well I never,' said Stephanson, slapping the table loudly with the palm of his hand to emphasise his astonishment at Mathiesen's response. Yet there was something about the boy, a persistent air of innocence, that inclined Waaler to think he was probably telling the truth. No need for them to ask why he hadn't followed either alternative, he said to himself. Not when the police were holding his father as a hostage.

Now it was the turn of Bergmann, the second *Grepo* man, to give his testimony. He took the single step up into the witness box, jerked his chin in and raised his right arm in a vigorous salute. The one who ran off, thought Waaler. This should be interesting.

In answer to a question from Stephanson, Bergmann repeated the story about the telephone call to the post at Ørje regarding the suspicious vehicle seen heading their way. Stephanson at once interrupted, demanding to know the nature of the suspicion and urging the witness to be precise in his evidence. The tone of his voice was hostile.

Bergmann blinked.

'We thought it might be the Modum bank robbers. We had a tipoff they might be trying to cross the border with the money,' he said.

'With a pregnant woman among them?' Skjønhaug asked sarcastically.

Bergmann moved his fingers back and forth along the top of the witness box but said nothing.

'Please continue,' said Stephanson.

Waaler listened as Bergmann offered his description of what had happened. His account differed in certain details from Mathiesen's. According to him he had been guarding the kitchen door when the fight broke out between Haugland and Mathiesen. One of the suspects – the driver, he thought – pushed him violently in the back and ran out past him into the farmyard. The three passengers also ran out as well. He followed them into the yard but by then they had almost reached the forest. He fired a shot at them but missed, and then the fugitives were lost to sight among the trees. He stopped, uncertain whether to follow or stay close to the farmhouse in case Haugland needed help. He had heard shooting from inside the house but assumed the shots came from Haugland's gun. The suspects' blue car was still standing down by the roadside where they had stopped it, on a bend some 40 metres away. Suspecting the fugitives might try to make their way back to the car he decided to stay where he was in the yard, in a position in which he could keep an eye on both the car and the kitchen door.

By now it was 10 p.m. and dark. This was how he explained the fact that he had not seen Haugland come stumbling out of the kitchen door and collapsing in the yard, nor the accused either as Mathiesen bent over him and shot him through the back of the head. It was only a few moments later, when Mathiesen switched on a torch and shone it about inside the car, looking for something inside the car, that Bergmann realised he was still there. He said he

EPILOGUE

shouted a warning to Mathiesen to put down his gun. Mathiesen turned and fired two shots in his direction. Bergmann had then taken cover among the trees surrounding the farmyard.

'You mean, you ran off?' Stephanson interrupted.

Bergmann didn't respond and Stephanson told him to step down from the witness box and come forward to the bench. Bergmann did so. Stephanson then made a great show of leaning forward and examining the decorations on Bergmann's chest.

'I see you're a veteran of the Norwegian Legion, Number One Company. There's the Eastern Front medal. That I think is the Wounded Veterans Medal, and if I'm not mistaken that one there on your right shoulder is the Storm Medal for bravery. Tell me, Officer Bergmann,' he said, sitting back in his chair. 'Were you running away in the opposite direction the day you won your Storm Medal too?'

Bergmann didn't answer, but this time Stephanson insisted, and after a firmly shouted 'No sir,' Stephanson seemed to take pity on him. He asked Bergmann how long he'd been serving with the *Grepo* and learned that he had started on 16 February, less than three months previously. No, he had had no training. No, he had never received any training in the correct procedures to be followed during hold and search operations that involved stopping cars and fugitives.

'No, I thought not,' said Stephanson quietly. 'Thank you, Officer Bergmann. There will be further questions. You may step down.'

Stephanson straightened up, saluted with a click of the heels and returned to his seat.

The next witness was the proprietor of the farm at Damholt, a seventy-year-old man named Holt; Waaler didn't catch the first name. He retold the story the court had already heard several times by now, the only discrepancy being that in his version, when the first shot was fired it acted like a signal for everyone in the kitchen to make a rush for the door, Bergmann and himself included. Waaler assumed the slight contradiction could probably be explained by Bergmann's desire to cast his own response in a slightly better light.

Skjønhaug was in the process of taking the old farmer up on this when the side door opened and in walked the minister himself,

Jonas Lie, uniformed and chest ablaze with ribbons, medals, decorations and the insignia of general major, a newly created rank in the Norwegian State Police force held exclusively by himself and Karl Marthinsen, the force's operational head. An Iron Cross clinked against the buckle of a leather belt that cinched his pot belly. His adjutant fussed around him, now behind him, now in front, an insufferable man, '-haug'-something, Waaler couldn't quite bring the name to mind.

At the Minister's entry all present, Waaler and the judges included, leapt to their feet and saluted, lustily barking a *heil og sæl!* before sitting down again – Lie and Riisnæs had made the National Unity greeting mandatory among their officers and Waaler, consummate actor that he had become, was among its keenest users.

Lie and his adjutant took their seats on the right side of the courtroom. As soon as he had settled in his chair Lie lit a cigarette and began glaring, now at Mathiesen and now at Bergmann. As though he wants to eat them alive, thought Waaler.

Watching the intensity of that gaze, feeling the almost palpable hostility with which it charged the courtroom air, Waaler found himself recalling the opening paragraph of one of Lie's own books, *I Fred og ufred* (Days of Peace, Days of Turmoil). It was the last book Lie had written before the occupation, the last one Waaler had read and, as he knew by now, the last one he would ever read. The lines he was remembering were a clever but whimsical account of the time when Lie himself had been sentenced to death. It was in a field somewhere in France. Facing the firing squad he had been asked if he had any last requests. Yes, he had replied; since he was dressed all in white, would the executioners allow him to take one step forward, so that on falling he would not land in the pool of cow muck at his feet and dirty his clothes? Request granted. Lie stepped forward, stood to attention and closed his eyes. The firing squad raised their rifles to their shoulders, there was a loud shout of 'Bang!' and down he went, the thing was over. He was four years old at the time and on holiday with his family. The rifles, of course, were made of wood. On first reading Waaler had been charmed by the account. Now something about it chilled him. *So you did fall in that shit after all*, he heard himself say, so clearly that for an instant he looked up in alarm, certain he must have said it aloud.

After some forty minutes of theatrical presence Lie rose to his feet and departed as abruptly as he had come, to the accompaniment of another round of fervent saluting, adjutant darting ahead to open the door and then falling into place at his heels as the door closed behind them and they disappeared from sight, their footsteps echoing down the stone corridor. Cut off by that closing door, it seemed to Waaler momentarily that he could hear the muted sounds of a woman sobbing.

The court next heard from the officer in charge of the case, a man named Tjørn whom Waaler knew of but had never met. Then it was the turn of the pathologist, Waaler's namesake Georg. He told the court he was a professor in forensic medicine at the University of Oslo and went on to detail the various bullet wounds on Haugland's body. There were several to the chest and stomach, two in the left buttock with exit wounds at the front of the thigh, in addition to the shot through the back of the head that caused his instant death. Haugland would have died within minutes anyway, he added: a bullet on the left side had penetrated both chambers of the heart and entered the lungs, flooding them with a large quantity of blood. Professor Waaler finished giving evidence and Stephanson announced a half-hour recess. The judges rose, pushed back their chairs and filed out through the double doors behind them, not forgetting to shoulder their bandoleers as they departed.

Gunnar Waaler made his way out into the corridor to stretch his legs, keeping his eyes open for anything or anyone else involved in these proceedings, any name, any face, that belonged in the report he would write once he got home. For over two years now he had been submitting such reports and 'Nordtorp', his contact in the resistance, had once mentioned that his reports were *admired* for their literary qualities. The praise had left Waaler feeling a little uneasy. It seemed to imply that he derived a certain illicit enjoyment from situations such as this involving Mathiesen and viewed them as *literary material* as well as tragedies.

He was aware too that following 'Nordtorp's' comment his writing, his *style*, had become more self-conscious. Two or three times he had caught himself thinking that when it was all over he might write a book about his experiences. Write about Jonas Lie, for example. Ask himself why Lie fascinated him so much, and why it was more natural for him to see Lie as an enigma rather than simply an object of hatred and contempt. Was it because he admired writers so much, and Lie was such a good writer? Before the war Waaler had been an avid reader of the crime novels Lie published under the pen name 'Max Mauser'. The books had made him like the author in a very personal way that he recognised as irrational but nevertheless real. A kind of reader's gratitude, was how he thought of it; an author, a person unknown to you, becomes in an unguarded moment the companion of your solitude. For hours on end the voice of this stranger sounds inside your head. And you talk back to it, you discuss things with it.

It was an extraordinary intimacy. Lie/Mauser was not just an ordinary crime novelist content to supply a crime, a detective and a solution. The characters he created were more than simply puppets that kept his plot moving along. They had a recognisable everyday credibility to them. Moving through situations that were manifestly unreal, they nevertheless struck you as being real human beings. And he wasn't alone in his admiration: critics and readers were agreed that the psychological penetration of Lie's novels set them apart from those of the average crime writer. His most recent crime novel, *En hai følger båten* (A Shark Follows the Ship), submitted anonymously as one of 400 entries for Gyldendal's Best Crime Fiction competition in 1939, had won first prize.

Waaler realised later that Lie must have written most of it during the idle on-board hours when he had been assigned to accompany the communist Leon Trotsky on the six-week voyage from Norway to Mexico after Trotsky's refugee status had been

EPILOGUE

withdrawn; Lie had written about the trip at length in *I fred og ufred*, and shown a degree of respect and even an impersonal liking for Trotsky despite his distaste for the Russian's political beliefs. What had happened to that subjective tolerance, Waaler wondered. Where did it come from, that fanatical intolerance of the communists and the Jews – and as Waaler knew, for most National Unity members the terms were interchangeable. What had happened? War, that was all. War had happened. The occupation had happened. Minds had polarised into crude simplicities.

Or if not a book, then why not a doctoral thesis, he thought as he embarked, hands clasped behind his back, on a slow circuit of the large ground-floor vestibule. The idea of writing a *thesis* made the enterprise sound more respectable. It implied an excusable and even necessary scientific distance from the sufferings he would be writing about. He was still pondering this when, about halfway around the circuit, his thoughts were interrupted by the sounds coming from a group of four people sitting on chairs pushed back against the wall. Two were women. Both were in tears and he identified them as the source of the sobbing he had heard earlier. They sat one on each side of the prisoner. The woman with grey hair was, he presumed, his mother. The younger one – he heard the whispered name 'Grethe' as he walked by – was either his sweetheart or his sister. The prisoner was sitting between them. Bergsjø must have obtained permission for the meeting.

The mother's head was resting on the prisoner's shoulder, and she was holding on to his upper arm with both hands. The sister or girlfriend on the other side held his right hand between both of hers. The two Stapo guards sat some two metres away at a low, circular and highly polished table, submachine guns cradled in their laps as they chatted quietly to each other. The fourth member of Mathiesen's party, sitting on the chair beyond Grethe, was Dagfinn Hauge, the prison chaplain at Akershus Fortress. Their eyes met as Waaler passed by the group and the priest gave a slight nod, which Waaler returned.

On his second circuit Waaler saw that from somewhere the

priest had obtained a plate of sandwiches for Mathiesen. The boy, who had probably been starved during his time in custody, was holding it so tightly his knuckles were visibly white. As though the bread he was eating were his life, thought Waaler in a self-consciously literary moment, and Mathiesen could feel some overpowering force in the act of stealing it from him. The crying had stopped by this time.

As Waaler was midway through a third circuit of the vestibule the courtroom doors were opened again and he saw Bergsjø approaching the little family group, holding the flap of his dangling black cloak to one side as he apologetically broke up the gathering. Mathiesen stood up, his guards with him, and Waaler followed them back into the courtroom.

Now it was the prosecution's turn to present its case. Landerud appeared to have spent the recess working himself up into a state of sustained rage. Pacing back and forth across the brightly polished parquet floor, the little piece of gravel still wedged to the sole of one black boot and giving off a faint 'click' each time he moved, he gave the court yet another brief resumé of the facts of the case before going on to make a number of absurd quasi-legal observations on the unimpeachable validity of Minister-President Quisling's legislation of the previous autumn that had brought the Special Court into being, its function and scope and unique power to pass the death penalty. Mathiesen's guilt in the case being conceded on both sides, Landerud told the court he would move directly to the matter of an appropriate sentence for someone who had murdered a police officer in the execution of his duty.

From somewhere in the city, through the net curtains covering the high windows, the sound of a passing fire engine or police siren briefly entered the room. Landerud used the interruption to stop his pacing. He glared at the prisoner.

'As I shall show,' he said, 'there are a number of aggravating factors to this outrage that the court must take into account when considering the appropriate sentence to pass. In the first place,' he went on, raising his index finger and keeping it raised, 'in the first place the prisoner wantonly abused the trust placed in him by the authorities in issuing him with a pass to travel in these border regions.'

Up went a second finger: 'Two: At the time of his arrest the prisoner was illegally in possession of not just one but *two* pistols. And for that alone,' he continued, turning his back on Mathiesen and addressing the judges, 'for that alone, the penalty should be death. Because for what other purpose might that have been but to shoot and kill an innocent policeman who was simply doing his duty? Three.'

Up went the third finger: 'The prisoner has assisted people in the illegal enterprise of crossing the border into Sweden, our neutral neighbour Sweden. And what manner of people did he assist? Saboteurs. Murderers. Scoundrels determined to avoid their just deserts. At any cost. This heinous trafficking in known and wanted criminals is not the least of the many, many, many aggravating factors the court must consider in this case.'

As though stunned by the depravities of what he was describing he fell silent. The hand with its three rigid fingers sank to his side. Slowly he shook his head, as though he were struggling to come to terms with the sheer iniquity of the whole dreadful tale.

'And finally!' he roared, eyes opening, turning on his heels and pointing his finger directly at the prisoner, 'By his own account, the defendant is guilty of the crime of treason. As the law of 16th August 1943 makes crystal clear, this country is at war. It is at war with England, the United States and the Soviet Union, and it is allied with Germany in the pursuit of their certain defeat.'

'England, the United States, and the Soviet Union,' he repeated for emphasis, his voice slightly calmer now. 'Our enemies. The very people whom this man intended to help by smuggling Norwegians out of this country for the express purpose of travelling to England and joining our enemies. Or else,' he went on, lowering his voice still further, 'to remain in Sweden and undergo military training there with the ultimate goal of invading this country at some future date.'

Long pause.

'Treason, gentlemen,' Landerud resumed. 'Who does not recoil in revulsion from the very word? Who is not brought to nausea at the mere *thought* of the word? Who does not feel, who does not *know* in his heart of hearts that there is no lower depth to which a man can sink than to the betrayal of his own country? And *that* is what *this* man is guilty of: treason. And for the crime of treason there can be only one sentence: death.'

Treason? So bizarre was the introduction of this idea in this particular context that Waaler had to suppress the urge to burst out laughing. So many times during the course of the past four years he had felt like pinching himself to make sure he hadn't wandered into a rehearsal for the lunatic asylum scene in Ibsen's *Peer Gynt*, he hadn't entered a world in which ordinary commonsense had expired at precisely 9.32 p.m. on the evening of 9 April 1940, when Vidkun Quisling, Norway's head lunatic, had sat down in front of the microphone at the State Broadcasting studio in Roald Amundsen's gate in central Oslo and introduced himself to listening Norwegians as their new prime minister.

Landerud was finished. Now it was Bergsjø's turn. He stood up, freeing a wing of black cape that had somehow got trapped in his trouser pocket. With his owlish spectacles and monkish rim of white hair he looked like some kindly old schoolmaster about to plead for leniency for a boy caught smoking behind the bicycle sheds. As the *solkors* pinned to his gown indicated he was, of course, also a member of National Unity. Like Landerud, Bergsjø wasted no time on his client's guilt but proceeded straight to the matter of sentencing. He asked the court to look on Mathiesen as a misguided innocent, corrupted and led astray by cynical adults who should have known better. The real villain in this case was Willars Nilsen, chief financial officer at the Red Cross and the man in charge of the organisation's fleet of vans and lorries. It was he who bore the ultimate responsibility for Officer Haugland's death by his actions in enrolling the defendant in his criminal enterprise. He was the one who should be standing in the dock today: but where was he?

He turned slowly and gestured towards Mathiesen, his palms

EPILOGUE

open in a show of sorrowful dismay: gone. Vanished. Took to his heels the moment he realised his plans had been foiled, leaving this pawn, this boy, to pay the price. Surely, he pleaded, police time would have been better spent tracking down and arresting the puppet masters behind such activities.

'My colleague asks for the death sentence,' he said, shrugging the cape back up onto his right shoulder. 'I ask the court, what useful purpose could be served by taking the life of this misguided boy? A prison sentence – a lengthy one, to be sure, for he has taken a human life – but a prison sentence would give him the opportunity to reflect on what he has done and to consider the error of his ways. In all humility, and aware of the gravity of the crime, I nevertheless ask the court to show leniency.'

He took off his spectacles, wiped his forehead with the back of his wrist and sat down with a brief glance at his wristwatch. Landerud got to his feet and offered a short rejoinder: 'On one point, and on one point only, I am in agreement with my learned friend: yes, I would like to see each and every one of these puppet masters, as he calls them, standing here before us in court. And I would personally like to take each one of them by the hand and lead them to the gallows.'

Landerud sat down again. Stephanson, who had been sitting with his hammer-gavel raised and suspended throughout Landerud's brief response, now brought it down on the table and announced that the judges would retire to consider their verdict.

It was 2 a.m.

The height of the farce, Waaler whispered to himself, and wondered whether to include the line in his report to D13: '*The farce reached its height as the three lunatics retired to consider their verdict.*' Or was that too literary? As he stood up to stretch his legs he was surprised to find himself blushing slightly.

Bergsjø stepped out through a side door and moments later re-appeared accompanied by Mathiesen's mother and sister. He ushered them, along with Mathiesen, to a bench along one of the side walls then joined Landerud in the well of the courtroom.

Shortly afterwards General Major Egil Olbjørn came in, accompanied by Jørgen Nordvik, the regime's public prosecutor and Waaler's immediate superior. Nordvik appeared surprised to see his own departmental prosecutor standing there and on his way to join the two chatting lawyers halted briefly and raised his eyebrows quizzically at Waaler before moving on. Waaler dipped his head in acknowledgement, knowing that the ideological answer he would later give when his chief brought up the subject was there, fully formed in his head. It would be the same as the one he had presented to Stephanson the previous day when requesting permission to attend this trial: that the success of the national socialist revolution in Norway depended on an unwavering commitment to the forces of law and order; that the Special Court with its powers to pass the death sentence was a regrettable necessity; that for the murder of a serving policeman in the line of duty there could only be one punishment; and that as the public prosecutor's legal adviser it was his professional as well as his political obligation to acquaint himself with the workings of the new court.

The farce reaches its height. He said the words again inside his head. The word 'farce' gave him distance from the proceedings. It was a distance he felt in need of. Because in another part of himself he sensed the presence of something darker than the simple outraged pity he felt for the boy on trial. It flowed from those three judges at their high table, a dark, almost tangible, almost pornographic miasma: three insignificant bullies, their leader not much more than a boy himself, playing God with a pale, helpless child. No doubt there was a bottle of brandy or a good aquavit on the table in front of them to help them over the more difficult moments of their deliberations. Waaler did not doubt that one of the three (although he couldn't guess which one) would be assuming the role of the decent humanitarian who would need to be persuaded of the need for a death sentence.

He looked up and saw Olbjørn leave the little group of chatting men and make his way over to where the three members of the Mathiesen family sat. He said something to them, beckoned to

EPILOGUE

a guard and then opened the door of a small private room off the back of the courtroom and ushered them inside, closing the door behind them. The guard took up his position outside, legs apart, and Olbjørn then rejoined his colleagues. Waaler felt an instinctive admiration for the gesture that allowed son, mother and sister to spend what would certainly be their last moments together in privacy, but then found his admiration replaced by the suspicion that Olbjørn had done as he did because he found the sights and sounds of the sobbing distressing. That was what the occupation did to you, thought Waaler. It made you suspect the motives of everyone, it made you deny even these misguided monsters any shred of decency.

After three quarters of an hour the double doors behind the high table opened briefly and then closed again. Discreet signals were passed between two of the guards and the one outside the Mathiesens' door opened it and said something to the occupants. A few moments later the mother and sister appeared and made make their way around the edge of the courtroom and out of the door into the vestibule as a handcuffed Mathiesen was returned to his seat on the front bench between his guards. Now the double doors opened wide and Stephanson, Skjønhaug and Ekeland entered and took their seats at the high table. They didn't speak. Ekeland dropped a sheet of paper on the floor and Waaler watched as he tried, with foolish stabs of his hand, to catch it as it swayed lightly to the ground, and then bent to retrieve it from its resting place beneath his chair. The prisoner was told to stand. Stephanson cleared his throat and delivered the verdict. The pretence of legitimacy was maintained throughout. There was a repetition of the charges. The court found this proven, it found that proven. The verdict of the court: guilty as charged.

Stephanson turned to the matter of the sentencing. The court had some sympathy with the defence's claim that the greater responsibility for the murder of border policeman Haugland lay with others regrettably not present before them today. The court nevertheless found itself in agreement with the prosecution's assessment of the aggravating circumstances of the murder, including the illegal possession of firearms; the defendant's misuse of his travel documents and the betrayal of trust involved; and most damningly of all, the court agreed that the activity in which the defendant was involved at the time of Officer Haugland's murder was treasonable. Taking all this into account, there was only one sentence the court could hand down.

Waaler had his eyes on Mathiesen throughout Stephanson's announcement of the verdict. During the first hour or so of his trial the boy had been able to maintain a certain jauntiness to his manner. Perhaps he'd been able to convince himself he had a sporting chance of emerging from the process still alive, perhaps with a prison sentence of decades that the inevitable Allied victory would turn into months. But as the day dragged by whatever optimism the boy had been able to maintain had evaporated and for much of the past hour or so since the adjournment and the meeting with his mother and sister and pastor Hauge he had been visibly close to tears. Now, pulled to his feet for the sentencing, his face was white and his eyes shut tight. As the death sentence was passed he swayed so wildly the guard on his right side had to reach out a hand and steady himself on the back of his chair to stop them both overbalancing.

The judges stood up and unhooked the bandoliers from the high chair-backs. Stephanson got his caught fast on the tall spike and Ekeland and Skjønhaug both waited for him, bandoliers already slung across their shoulders, and then the three men passed in single file through the double doors and were gone from sight. Mathiesen was marched into the vestibule. Through the open door Waaler saw the mother and the sister get up from their chairs. Pastor Hauge was still with them; he must have waited outside while the judges were considering their verdict. Mathiesen's mother said something to one of the guards and the group stopped. The guard crossed to Olbjørn, who was standing a few metres away talking to Jonas Lie. He said something to Olbjørn and Olbjørn nodded: it was in order for the family to follow the prisoner out to the car that was waiting by the kerbside in Grubbegata and watch as it drove the prisoner the short distance to Akershus Fortress.

EPILOGUE

★

Once he had made up his mind to do something, Gunnar Waaler committed himself to it wholeheartedly. It was a quality he had inherited from his father, M.A. Waaler, a parish priest in Lillesand. And having decided to report on the workings of the Special Court he realised, as he sat at his window desk in the small apartment in which he lived alone at Bygdøy allé 109, where he had just typed and date-stamped his report of the day's proceedings for D13, that he was under an obligation to see the thing through to its completion: he needed to be there when Mathiesen was executed. The next morning – a Friday – he called at Kronprinsens gate 10 on his way in to work and knocked on the door of Oberst Søvik, the State Police's second-in-command after Karl Marthinsen, to obtain permission to attend.

Waaler knew Søvik. They had been students at the military academy together, with Waaler a year ahead of Søvik. The slight status this conferred on Waaler subtly evened out the fact that Søvik outranked him and left him usually well disposed towards Waaler. Søvik rose from behind his desk to greet Waaler as he stepped inside the large and well-lit office and the first thing Waaler noticed in the room was the long line of framed photographs of *Grepo* men on the wall behind him, with the legend above it in large lettering *Faldt på sin post* ('Killed in the line of duty'). Søvik greeted him warmly and introduced him to a second officer who was sitting on the sofa, Captain Vagn Knudsen. They hadn't met before but the name was familiar to Waaler. Vagn Knudsen was a member of a commission set up by National Unity a year earlier with a brief to find evidence for the persistent rumour that Crown Prince Olav was not the son of King Haakon and Queen Maud but the illegitimate child of a union between one of Maud's sisters and a young British army officer who had committed suicide in the wake of the scandal. It was one of the party's more bizarre propaganda initiatives and intended to destroy Haakon as the symbol of unity and hope he had become for Norwegians. The commission seemed to have made little progress in the year it had been sitting, and whether there was any truth in the rumours or not Waaler found the whole enterprise vulgar and hoped it had simply run out of steam. He certainly didn't intend to bring up the subject with Vagn Knudsen.

Søvik offered Waaler a cigarette from the mahogany box on his desktop and invited him to take a seat on the sofa; what was on his mind? To pave the way for the request he intended to put to Søvik, Waaler first brought up the subject of the trial of Knut Mathiesen, which he had attended the previous day. He expressed outrage at the brutal murder of Harald Haugland. Mathiesen fully deserved the death penalty handed down by the court, and was now perhaps the time to review the unnecessarily considerate and courteous routines demanded of these border policemen as they carried out their always difficult and dangerous and necessary task?

Søvik, sitting behind his mahogany desk, having looked around for his ashtray and finding he had lent it to Waaler on the sofa, tapped a long ash from his cigarette into the palm of his hand.

'You've read my mind,' he said. 'We're dealing with people who don't obey the rules. From now on it's "Hands up" and a full weapons search first thing. Hands up and faces to the wall. We can't afford to lose any more men of the calibre of officer Haugland.'

He turned to look at the gallery behind him as though wondering where to place Haugland's portrait. It looked to Waaler as though he might actually have to start a second row.

'Indeed not,' Vagn Knudsen interjected. 'I was talking to Lie before the trial and he told me Haugland had applied to join *Germanske SS Norge* just a couple of months ago. A good Germanist. The whole family good Germanists. A perfect candidate. But he had to say no, because men of Haugland's calibre are exactly what we need in the border police.'

They spoke briefly of the need in the border force for men for whom the uniform meant so much more than just a job, for whom it was a calling, a way of life in the momentous struggle against the expansionist and murderous Bolsheviks and their Jewish leaders and ideologists. Good Germanists were what the force needed. Men who understood they were in the midst of a revolution in which the very survival of the race was at stake. With the conversation now safely ensconced in sound ideological territory, Waaler took advantage of the entry of a blonde secretary with a document for Søvik to sign to raise the real purpose of his visit.

'I gather the sentence against Mathiesen is to be carried out this Saturday morning,' he said once the secretary had closed the door behind her and they could hear her footsteps moving away down the corridor.

Søvik hesitated before confirming this with a nod. 'A number of Haugland's colleagues have requested permission to attend,' he said.

'Quite understandable,' said Vagn Knudsen. 'Justice must not only be done, it must be seen to be done.'

'You gave them permission?' Waaler continued.

Søvik nodded again. 'I did. The whole business is a matter of the utmost secrecy. And naturally, they will be asked to sign a declaration to that effect. But yes, I felt I could hardly refuse, though the fewer people who know anything about it at all, the better.'

Waaler cleared his throat. 'Well, I hope you won't be too put out if I tell you that I'm here to request permission to attend as well,' he said.

Søvik looked up at him in surprise.

'You? Did you know Haugland?'

'I feel I know the man without ever having met him,' said Waaler. 'He's fully deserving of a place of honour in that gallery of yours. But no, I didn't know him personally. But as Special Police Prosecutor it's my professional obligation to familiarise myself with every aspect of the workings of any new court established to try cases brought under it, and to confirm the legality of the sentence as it is carried out.'

He saw the half-smile that crossed Søvik's face as he said this. He knew of his reputation among National Unity colleagues as a stickler for the legality of its activities. It was a reputation he cultivated. He had come to realise that there lay a great and unexpected security in assuming the role of the 'good' Nazi, the good conscience of National Unity. It was made easier by the widespread corruption at all levels of the party which he encountered on a daily basis in his work as Special Police Prosecutor.

His job was to decide which cases were potentially political, but he had long ago lost track of how often he had been asked and sometimes pressed to accept cases of violent and thieving behaviour involving members of Quisling's *hird* as having this dimension. To go along with the legal sleight of hand invariably meant the case would be dismissed by his boss Nordvik, a good party man.

Yet he persistently sent the more egregious examples back to Nordvik's office with the recommendation that they be tried as ordinary crimes or misdemeanours by the *Folkerett* (People's Court). The chances of automatic acquittal were much thinner there, for in spite of the fact that it was a National Unity innovation it had shown little inclination to go easy on the party members or *hird* thugs who appeared before it. By carefully balancing an apparent legal pedantry that often worked against party interests with a willingness to lecture colleagues on the finer points of true national socialism, Waaler had succeeded in creating the image of himself as someone who took it very seriously indeed and tried to follow its precepts with an uncomfortably puritanical fervour. The role came so naturally to him that there were times when he wondered whether he was really acting at all and had to reassure himself that he had merely inherited from his father a priestly temperament operating in a world in which corruption was endemic.

'I understand, of course,' said Søvik, already starting to write the brief authorisation. A few moments later he held the sheet of paper out across the desk and Waaler stood up and took it from him.

'Assemble here at three fifteen tomorrow morning. If there isn't room for you in one of the cars I'm afraid you'll have to stay behind. I hope you understand.'

Waaler nodded his acceptance of the condition and Søvik handed round the cigarettes again, American Lucky Strikes, not the homegrown Norwegian brands people in the streets were smoking. Vagn Knudsen was prompted to bring up the subject of 'Osvald' and his gang of communist saboteurs, bank robbers and killers and the theft a couple of weeks earlier of 600 kilograms of tobacco from Langaard's tobacco factory in Theresesgate. They were getting to be a real thorn in the side of the State Police. And as yet there was still no sign of the massive haul from the robbery at Modum Sparebank. So the atmosphere in Søvik's office had turned gloomy as Waaler took leave of his colleagues. His hand was already on the doorknob when, giving in to a sudden whim, he turned round:

'I almost forgot,' he said, his face breaking into an apologetic smile. 'I have a cabin out at Bjerkelangen. It's been in our family for decades. I gather from my neighbour that my roof is leaking badly and I'm going to need to replace it. And of course, that means being stopped and turned back either by German patrols or by our own border police. They're only doing their job, of course, but if I had a permanent travel pass for the region it would make it so much easier for everyone.'

Søvik, relieved to be ending the meeting on a light and domestic note, duly scribbled his personal endorsement on a travel pass he took from a desk drawer and with a warm smile handed it over to Waaler.

Outside Waaler headed back up Kronprinsens gate and then down Stortingsgate in the direction of his office in Akersgate. As he crossed Roald Amundsen he glanced over to his right, towards the fjord and the gaunt skeleton of Oslo's new Town Hall. Work had stopped as soon as the Germans arrived. Through the scaffolding in the bright May sunlight he saw the massive grey walls of the Akershus Fortress prison. For an instant he saw again the boy as he was at the moment of his death sentence. The blood-drained face, the eyes tight shut. The way his legs failed, the way he would have fallen to the floor had he not been handcuffed on both sides. Today was his last day. As he turned down Karl Johans gate he wondered if the boy had been told yet.

Dagfinn Hauge and Knut Mathiesen
7.00 p.m. Friday 5 May, Kronprinsens Gate

Hauge cycled to work as often as he could. Even on the twice weekly round trip of 24 kilometres from the church in Sagene out through Røa to the countryside and the camp at Grini to visit the Norwegian prisoners he liked to use his bicycle. Those visits weren't especially disheartening. None of the prisoners there were under sentence of death and conditions at Grini were relatively good. The inmates even produced their own newspaper with the blessing of the German prison authorities. Once over the crossroads at Røa, he was into five kilometres of unspoiled and rolling countryside, a part of the ride that always emptied his mind of the troubled sadness he lived with each day as part of his work.

But trips to Akershus and to Kronprinsens gate, such as this one, were different. His job was to guide a twenty-three-year-old boy through his final hours. Instinct told him he didn't want to

be alone with his mind for the ride into town from Sagene, and there was anyway the practical problem of the small black case of Holy Communion requisites he always carried with him on these special visits. Instead he took a taxi into Oslo, telling the driver to drop him off in the city centre, outside the Storting. He wanted to walk the rest of the way up Karl Johans gate and use the walk to make his spirit calm and strong so that by the time he met the boy he would be able to help him.

At 7 p.m. precisely he presented himself at the desk at Number 10. He was told an interview room had been put at his disposal and a uniformed Stapo man emerged from the corridor behind the counter to show him the way. Before he left the reception area he was told he had three hours. He was also told he must inform the prisoner that the plea for clemency had been turned down and the sentence would be carried out in the early hours of Saturday morning. Hauge nodded his acceptance of these conditions and followed the uniformed policeman down the dimly lit corridor and into the heart of the building. They passed several offices, most of them with doors closed. From one he heard someone speaking angrily into the telephone and then the sound of the receiver being slammed down into its cradle. By the last door in the corridor, just before a staircase leading down to the basement, the guard stopped, took a quick glance at the note in his hand and then opened the door and ushered Hauge inside.

The small room was at the back of the building, and the first thing Hauge noticed was the white, rectangular iron bars on the frosted window on the rear wall. The room was sparsely furnished – deliberately so, he presumed. In the middle was a wooden desk with legs secured to the floor by metal brackets. Two plain wooden chairs were pushed back against the side wall on the right-hand side, and a third against the wall directly inside the door. As Hauge stood taking this in the guard walked past him and, as though he were a landlord showing a property to a prospective tenant, opened the door wide and stepped inside still holding onto the handle. Hauge, accepting the unspoken invitation to look, saw that it opened onto a smaller room. A dark green couch occupied about half the space.

'If the prisoner wants to sleep he can sleep here,' the guard said.

Briefly disorientated, Hauge stared at the couch and then at the guard. Sleep? he thought. Why would he want to sleep? He'll be dead in a few hours' time.

'Thank you,' he said. 'That's very thoughtful.'

'I'll go and get him.'

Hauge nodded.

The guard slowly crossed the floor, opened the door and went out into the corridor. Hauge listened to the hollow ring of footsteps descending the metal staircase at the end of the corridor, and when he could no longer hear them he sat down on the chair by the door, crossed his legs and for several minutes stared with a vacant intensity at the filament of the pale yellow lightbulb dangling from its twisted purple cord in the centre of the ceiling.

A few minutes later he heard the double tramp of approaching footsteps and got to his feet. Obeying some obscure instinct, he walked around the desk so that he was behind it and facing the door. When the guard and the prisoner entered the room, he leaned slightly forward and rested the tips of fingers on the tabletop. Without a word the guard turned the chair by the door sideways on to the room and sat down. He folded his arms and closed his eyes.

Mathiesen remained standing where he was, handcuffed in the middle of the room beneath the lightbulb. Hauge knew the rules and there was no need for the guard to repeat them: prisoner to be handcuffed at all times; no reference to the crime; nothing political to be discussed. Hauge observed them scrupulously. He knew his position as a pastor who was not a party member was always precarious. Two years earlier the Nazified Department of Education and Religious Affairs under the minister Ragnar Skancke had done its best to have him removed and replaced with a Norwegian priest who was a party member; to Hauge's enduring surprise there were a handful of these.

Mathiesen looked better than he had done in court. He had

been allowed to shave and comb his hair. In place of the battle-dress top and nightshirt he was wearing a cream shirt a little too large for him around the collar and a threadbare tartan tie. On the left lapel of his dark blue sports jacket he was wearing a small round shield badge showing a red Greek cross over a white background. Hauge recognised it as a Red Cross badge. He smiled. He was about to say hello and offer his hand and suggest they pull the two vacant chairs up to the desk, but it was Mathiesen who spoke first:

'What do you think of me?' he said.

He spoke with such strange and searching intensity that for several moments Hauge wondered what the boy could mean. Then he had it.

'You mean, what does God think of you? What does God think of the thing you did?'

Mathiesen nodded, eyes still fixed on the priest, and in that revelatory moment Hauge understood it all. For the past fourteen days, ever since his arrest, this boy had been alone in a cell and tormenting himself with but a single thought: that he had taken a human life. He was in visible torment and Hauge knew he had to answer quickly and be as categorical as possible. And he knew he had to choose the words carefully and not risk upsetting the guard.

'I'm not familiar with all the details of your case,' he began cautiously. 'But what I can say is this: the thing that you did cannot be looked at the same way in a time of war as it would be in a time of peace.'

As soon as he spoke Hauge instinctively glanced over at the guard by the door. He was sitting half-slumped in the wooden chair, the fingers of his hands now interlaced in his lap. His eyes were still closed. Hauge decided to keep going.

'You were a soldier, Knut. The man you met was a soldier too. And this is something you can go before God with. As we may go before God with anything. With everything.'

He stopped and waited, holding the boy's blue eyes, steeling himself to hold onto the light he could feel shining through his own eyes, even though it pained him like a migraine. And as he waited he saw the desperation drain from the boy's eyes and he knew that he could do it, that he could take this boy all the way to the end.

The guard cleared his throat and bounced his crossed right leg slightly. He blinked twice in rapid succession but left his eyes shut and Hauge realised they had been lucky; their guard was a half-decent man who would not make things difficult for them this evening. He relaxed, pulled the two chairs up to the table and he and Knut Mathiesen sat down and started talking.

In all of the last nights he had spent with the young Norwegians awaiting execution, Hauge never lost sight of the fact that he was not there as an individual. He was there because he represented something. And what he represented was the Christian way of dealing with death. As far as he was concerned, the only way. And though he was not there as a friend he had already experienced many times the intimacy that could arise in the conversations of these final moments. Within an hour he felt as though he had known Knut Mathiesen for most of his short life. In terms of adventures, activities, jobs, love affairs, the boy hadn't done much – there hadn't been time – but there was a powerful decency about him that moved Hauge. There would be time later to get to the purpose of his visit this evening, but to begin with he deliberately kept their conversation on everyday matters and on Knut's family life. At one point he asked how the family had spent the last Christmas, and that got Knut onto the subject of the explosion in the Filipstad docks on the 19th, the Sunday before Christmas, when ammunition from a ship being unloaded blew up and started a series of secondary explosions and fires that had destroyed hundreds of city centre buildings and, Hauge had read in his newspaper, broken the windows of the tourist cabin at Skjennungstua 12 kilometres away from Oslo. As an active member of the Red Cross Knut had spent much of the Christmas week helping out some of the hundreds of homeless families who were being temporarily sheltered at the Hartvig Nilsen school five minutes up the road from Magnus Bergs' gate, where the family lived. He liked to help people. His hobby was first aid and he spent many of his free weekends at the Red Cross first-aid stations in the Oslo *nordmarka*.

'I go with my father,' he said. 'Have you heard any news of him?'

Hauge knew that Eystein Mathiesen had been arrested as a hostage the morning after the incident at the Damholt farm.

'He's still being held in Åkerbergveien.'

'Does he know what's happened to me?'

'I don't think so, no.'

'Why are they keeping him?' Mathiesen flared up. 'They have me. They could have let him go as soon as they arrested me. Why do they do these pointless things?'

Hauge glanced over at the guard again. He had stopped pretending to be asleep. Chewing on the end of a red pencil he now appeared to be struggling with a newspaper crossword puzzle and seemed oblivious to their presence.

'I wish I could talk to him,' Mathiesen continued. 'There are so many things I'd like to say to him. Explain to him. Now it's too late.'

'Write to him,' said Hauge. 'You can say anything you want to say in a letter. As long as there's nothing political in it. Guard?'

The guard looked up and Hauge got permission for Mathiesen's handcuffs to be removed so that he could write his last letters. Hauge then picked up the black leather attaché case from beside his chair and, balancing it on his lap, unbuckled the flap and took out the pen and writing pad he always took with him on these prison visits and placed them on the desk in front of Mathiesen. The guard went back to his crossword puzzle and Hauge glanced at his watch. It was almost nine. He had one more hour. Dipping into his bag again he pulled out his Bible, opened it and began to plan how they would spend it.

He had already performed this service for men condemned to death over thirty times and inevitably a degree of routine had crept into his preparations. For the last supper they would always read together Luke chapter 22, verses 14 to 19, then Hebrews chapter 9, verse 12, John, Isaiah and perhaps Corinthians. For reassurance on eternal life he usually returned to John and to the Book of Revelations. Then – always – Psalm 23, 'The Lord is my Shepherd', and finally Holy Communion, if the prisoner wanted it. Only a few had declined.

From past experience he knew how hungry a condemned man could be and once Knut had finished writing the letters, one to his father, one to his mother and another to his sister, Hauge picked up his black bag and, dipping inside it again, pulled out the jar of fresh milk and the sandwiches Lully had prepared.

'I expect you're hungry, Knut. My wife made these for you.'

Having cleared it with the guard he set the milk and sandwiches down in front of Mathiesen. The boy's round blue eyes stared at the food.

'Is this fresh milk?' he exclaimed. And without waiting for an answer he unwrapped the sandwiches and began to eat, attacking the food with the same savagery Hauge had noted earlier in the day during the break in his trial. There was something so terrible in the sight that instinctively he averted his eyes and for the next few minutes tried to immerse himself in his Bible. The rough and bestial sounds of the boy's eating and drinking proved a major distraction. He found it hard to concentrate. His thoughts wandered. *The Bible is the mind of God*, he heard. It was a phrase from a Gideons Bible he'd found in the drawer of the bedside table in his hotel room some months earlier on an overnight trip to Risør. He'd never come across it before and for some reason the phrase haunted him. He couldn't understand why it didn't say 'the Bible is the *word* of God', and he couldn't understand why he cared. *In a matter of hours*, he heard himself think, *Knut will be dead. But he's hungry, so he eats. He's thirsty, so he drinks.* It didn't make sense if you wanted it to make sense. It only made sense if you didn't want it to make sense.

Hauge put the Bible down, leaned forward, picked up the three envelopes Knut had placed on the tabletop and slipped them into his bag. He heard the scratch of a match as the guard lit a cigarette and the sound made him jump. He picked up the Bible again and opened it at random but all he heard was a voice inside his head repeating over and over the same few words: *in a few hours from now he will be dead. He thinks he deserves to die.* All his previous experience seemed to count for nothing as for some reason this boy's sense of his own guilt threatened to bring on what felt like an almost catastrophic destabilisation. Fearing that he might topple and fall from his chair, he put the Bible down on the table and with his left hand held on hard to the seat.

From the corridor outside came the sound of footsteps. The guard hurriedly pinched out the cigarette between his fingers and slipped the butt into his pocket. The footsteps passed and with a slight sigh of annoyance the guard pulled the butt out and relit it.

Mathiesen had finished eating. He wiped milk from his upper lip with the tip of his finger and looked at Hauge as though wondering what to do now. He looked almost bored. Hauge asked if had he any favourite hymns. Knut recalled a childhood favourite *Så ta da mine hender* (Then take my hands). They sang it together. The boy remembered another, *Jesus det eneste* (Jesus the only one) and again their voices were raised in a lusty rendition, Knut singing his heart out, as people say. Hauge had experienced it before, the way singing brought release from the darkness of the moment. He remembered a condemned man telling him once he wished he could die to the sound of a child singing.

'I like that tune so much,' said Knut once they'd sung it through. 'We learned it at school and we sang it at my Confirmation.' The boy then asked if he could borrow the priest's Bible, and as Hauge handed it over he sneaked a look at his wristwatch. The guard caught the look and gave an almost imperceptible nod of affirmation. It was almost ten. The three hours were up. 'Knut,' he said. 'Do you want to take Holy Communion?'

The boy looked up at him wide-eyed: 'You mean I can? Even now?'

'Especially now, Knut. Remember: *Den som kommer til meg, vil jeg ingenlunde støte ut.* (All that the Father giveth me shall come to me; and him that cometh to me I will in no wise cast out).'

Again the priest lifted the leather bag onto his lap and opened it. From within it, in a routine that often struck him as being like a conjuror at a children's party, he produced a white serviette, a cup and a dish made so that the dish sat over the chalice like a lid. Two thin white candles were carefully fitted into small silver candlesticks and arranged centrally on the desk. Hauge struck a match and lit them. Then, aware that time was running short, he began to read, much quicker than he would have liked to, from John chapter 10, on Jesus the good shepherd. After this they put their hands together and chanted the confessional prayer from the First Book of Corinthians chapter 11, verse 26: *For as often as ye eat this bread, and drink this cup, ye do shew the Lord's death till he come.* Then they ate the bread and drank the wine. One of us for the strength to die, Hauge thought, the other for the strength to go on living. Without further ceremony Hauge then placed his hand on the boy's head and in the name of the Father, the Son and the Holy Ghost absolved him of all sins.

From the adjacent office came the noisy whir of a floor clock followed by its tinny chiming. The hour had come to tell him.

He took a deep breath: 'I don't know how much longer you have to live, Knut,' he said. 'Maybe just a few hours.'

The boy looked at him and almost smiled.

'It doesn't matter,' he said. 'Really. It feels so strange, to have known a night such as this. It makes up for so many things. And I've been lucky. So many people die these days. Not all of them get the chance to... I feel safe. It's so strange, I almost feel happy.'

He asked if he could read Psalm 23 again and Hauge found the page and handed the Bible across to him. Hauge's bladder was aching and he had to excuse himself for a few moments. The toilet was one flight up at the end of the second-floor corridor. On his way back down the stairs he caught sight of Oberkriegsgerichtstrat Dobinski about to enter one of the ground-floor offices. Dobinski was the Wehrmacht commander at Akershus and the man who had given him permission to begin visiting Norwegians being held in the fortress prison awaiting either execution or deportation to a camp in Germany. He knew Dobinski had supported him in defiance of the wishes of both the Gestapo and of Ragnar Skancke, and in his encounters with the commandant he had found him an honourable and decent soldier who respected the rules of war. Briefly he wondered what Dobinski was doing in Kronprinsens gate: was he part of the execution arrangements? But then he realised that couldn't be, the Special Court was a Norwegians-only affair. On impulse he called out to him.

'Major Dobinski!'

The major turned.

'Pastor Hauge, good evening. You have business here?'

'Yes, I do. The boy in there is to be executed tonight.' He pointed to the closed door a few metres further down the corridor. 'Do I have your permission to stay with him a little longer? It's ten o'clock now. The execution won't be for some hours yet.'

It was worth a try. Officially at least the major had no authority in Kronprinsens gate, but as a high-ranking officer in the German military command Dobinski would expect any order he gave to be obeyed by rank-and-file members of the Norwegian State Police.

'What's his name?' Dobinski asked.

'Knut Mathiesen.'

'The man who killed the border guard?'

'Yes.'

Dobinski shook his head sadly. 'You know, Father, you Norwegians made a big mistake. You should have done as the Danes did and surrendered with dignity. They still have their own king, their own elected government. All they notice of the occupation there is the presence of German troops in the streets. The Führer wanted the same thing here. You should not have resisted.'

Hauge couldn't let this pass: 'Didn't Adolf Hitler himself once say that a people that would not defend itself had no right to live?'

'Yes, but your situation here was hopeless. Your king and

government should have stayed in the country once the fighting was over. You should have done as the Danes did.'

'That may be so,' Hauge responded cautiously, anxious not to antagonise him. 'But Denmark didn't have a Quisling.'

Dobinski gave a small, tired smile and shook his head: '*Davon dürfen wir nicht sprechen* (The less said about that the better). Yes, I'm sure that'll be alright.' Abruptly ending the conversation, he turned on his heels and pushed open the door to the room where Mathiesen was being held. Hauge waited in the corridor and after thirty seconds Dobinski re-emerged.

'You can stay until three,' he said, without looking at him, and walked away down the corridor.

Mathiesen looked up from the Bible as Hauge returned to the room and gave him the good news. In Hauge's absence Mathiesen's mind had been wandering over his short life and had arrived at the memory of his old scout master, Einar Jensen. 'Please will you visit Jensen,' he said. 'Tell him I remember with gratitude every one of his sermons and every word he ever said to me. Jensen was a true Christian in everything he said and did. I realise that now. And ask him to remember me to everybody else in my troop. Troop 9.' Hauge promised to do so and while Mathiesen went back to his Bible-reading Hauge wrote down two texts the boy had especially asked him for, explaining that he wanted to have them on his person when the time came for him to leave. Hauge knew the texts by heart and had no need to consult the Bible as he opened his notebook on the table, leaned forward and wrote

them out with a stub of pencil. Afterwards he tore the leaf from his notebook and read them over to himself:

Se det Guds lam som bærer verdens synd
(Behold the lamb of God, which taketh away the sin of the world).
Den som kommer til meg, vil jeg ingenlunde støte ut
(All that the Father giveth to me shall come to me. And him that cometh to me I will in no wise cast out).

Staring at the words, he was suddenly convinced that his handwriting was illegible and Mathiesen wouldn't be able to read it. He froze, appalled, and was wondering whether to screw the paper into a ball and throw it away and write the lines out again when the boy interrupted with a wild shout:

'Haugland's wife! His sons!'

Hauge jumped. Mathiesen was staring at him, the fingers of both hands buried in his long black hair. Suddenly he was once more that panicked figure he had seen emerging from the courtroom earlier in the day. He realised immediately that the whole edifice of acceptance they had together managed to build over the previous two hours was seconds away from devastation. In the three years in which he had been performing this terrible service for the walking dead he had seen such collapses twice before. Both times the men involved had been arrested, tried and sentenced alone. Men sentenced as part of a saboteur or smuggling group were able to derive strength from the presence of the others and the knowledge that these others would die with them and for the same reason. It was almost, he sometimes thought, as though they were all passengers about to board the same train.

But for someone who had to take the journey alone the pressures could become unendurable. A collapse was a nightmarish experience. In the grip of it one terrible night a prisoner had tried to kill himself by repeatedly running head-first into the stone wall of his cell in the Akershus Fortress. Hauge had tried to restrain him, but the man was possessed of a demonic strength and in the end he needed to call for assistance. It took three guards to stop him in his bloodied, groggy tracks. Nightmarish in a different way was the feeling of total impotence in himself as an observer when it struck. Hauge dreaded its return. At all costs he mustn't lose the boy. If that were to happen then God alone knew if he would be able to get him back.

'I think we must pray for them, Knut,' he said with all the calm authority he could muster, holding the boy's eyes with his own as he silently commanded him to close them, and felt again the sharp, migraine-like stab in his forehead. Knut's eyes flickered shut and Hauge led them in a prayer in which they asked God to give Haugland's widow and his four sons the strength to carry on without a husband and father.

They both opened their eyes and Hauge could see that he had done it; the crisis was over.

'Pastor Hauge, please,' Knut said, reaching out and holding onto the sleeve of Hauge's jacket. 'Please will you visit Haugland's family and tell them how sorry I am for what I did? I don't understand how I could have done it. A sort of mist came over me.'

He let go of the priest's jacket. 'I don't want them to hate me,' he said in a whisper.

A promise made to a condemned man would be hard to break, but he knew this one would be difficult to keep. Any message from the killer of the family's husband and father would most likely be rejected. But he told Mathiesen he would do what he could, and in the privacy of his mind told himself he meant it.

At about 1 a.m. Hauge suggested to the prisoner that he try to get some sleep. The guard opened the door to the adjoining room and Mathiesen lay down in darkness on the green velour couch. His wrists had once again been handcuffed. There was no chair in the room and the priest sat on the small coffee table next to the couch.

EPILOGUE

He had run out of significant things to say and for some minutes talked quietly about his own life, his wife Lully and their baby boy Dag Olav, and how they'd recently celebrated his first birthday, until presently Knut fell into a fitful sleep. Fearing that the faint tremoring of his limbs and almost inaudible cries from deep in his throat were perhaps the reduced translation of ear-splitting cries of distress in the dreamer's world, Hauge  wondered whether sleep had been a good idea after all and thought of waking the boy up again. Perhaps anything would be better than a nightmare.

But as suddenly as it had started the fitful struggling stopped. In the shaft of the light passing through the open door – the guard was now occupying one of the seats next to the table in the other room so that he could continue to monitor the two of them – he studied the face. The boyishness of it. The full, sensual lips. The fleshy nose and firm chin, a boxer's chin. His ears were large. Mathiesen had told him earlier in the evening that he was sensitive about the size of them, it was why he wore his hair long. He was lying still and silent now, the only sign of life the slight rise and fall of the badge pinned to his lapel. As he told the priest, he had been given permission to wear it all the way.

At 2.30 a.m., half an hour before he would have to leave, Hauge leaned over and gently shook the boy's shoulder.

'Knut, wake up.'

Mathiesen's eyes opened immediately. He stared up at the ceiling.

'In an hour's time, Knut, you will know eternal rest. You will be with God in heaven. Are you afraid?'

'No,' the boy answered.

He sat up and swung his legs over the side of the couch. With difficulty he raised his manacled hands and scratched the side of his face.

'It's just so strange to think about it: an hour's time.'

They walked back into the office. The guard had discreetly returned to his seat by the door but neither Mathiesen nor Hauge felt any inclination to sit anymore.

'Shall we recite Psalm 23 together again?' Hauge suggested.

'Yes.'

'As loud as you can, Knut!'

'Right.'

They began together:

The Lord is my shepherd; I shall not want. He maketh me to lie down in green pastures: he leadeth me beside the still waters...

Mathiesen's voice faltered as his memory of the lines failed him. Hauge picked up the Bible and, leaning into him until their bodies touched, he held the Bible open for him while they chanted the rest of the psalm together:

He restoreth my soul: he leadeth me in the paths of righteousness for his name's sake. Yea, though I walk through the valley of the shadow of death, I will fear no evil: for thou art with me; thy rod and thy staff they comfort me. Thou preparest a table before me in the presence of mine enemies: thou anointest my head with oil; my cup runneth over. Surely goodness and mercy shall follow me all the days of my life: and I will dwell in the house of the Lord for ever.

The priest closed the Bible and laid it on the table.

'I can't be with you all the way, Knut,' he said. 'I wish I could.'

'I wish you could too. I know it would help me. But I won't be alone. Jesus will be with me. I have these.' He patted his breast pocket and then, as though Hauge might not know what he

EPILOGUE

was talking about, pulled out the slip of paper Hauge had given him and read both verses fluently and without a moment's hesitation:

Se det Guds lam som bærer verdens synd.
Den som kommer til meg, vil jeg ingenlunde støte ut.

He pushed the note back down into the pocket. They could hear footsteps approaching along the corridor. From his chair by the doorway the guard cleared his throat and got to his feet. Mathiesen reached out with his manacled hands and took hold of one of the priest's hands. He opened his mouth as if to speak but nothing came out. He cleared his throat and after a few seconds the words came:

'You know in the Bible, when Jesus says, Father forgive them, for they know not what they do?'

Hauge nodded and wondered what was coming next. He prayed it wouldn't be a collapse.

'Does it mean Father, forgive them, because they didn't know Jesus was the Saviour? Or does it mean, forgive them because even if he wasn't, they still shouldn't be doing it?'

The boy looked so calm as he waited for the priest to answer. Hauge stared down at the floor. In all his years as a priest the question had never arisen and at that exact moment he had no idea how to answer. For several moments he simply stood there, his mind a blank.

'I don't like to interrupt but you must finish up now,' the guard said, rescuing him.

Hauge stepped back, raised his hand and made the sign of the cross over Mathiesen's head.

'Now you must be a good, strong, Norwegian Christian boy, Knut. All the way to the end.'

'I'll try,' Mathiesen said. 'I feel much better now.'

'Try to think of the one who walked the same path as the path you are about to take.'

'I will.'

Mathiesen lifted his manacled hands and fastened the top button of his jacket.

The footsteps in the corridor came to a halt outside the door. Hauge reached out and rather awkwardly clasped both of Mathiesen's manacled hands in his and gave them a firm squeeze. *Til lykke og salighet* (God bless and keep you), he said. Then turned and walked quickly towards the door. The guard opened it for him and stood aside as he walked out into the corridor.

Waaler and Mathiesen
02.30 a.m. Saturday 6 May 1944

At 2.30 on the morning of Saturday 6 May Gunnar Waaler emerged from his flat, locked the door behind him, quietly descended the two flights of stairs and left the art deco building at Bygdøy allé 109 and began walking towards the centre of town. A full-moon lit his way, cold and white. He allowed a half-hour for the walk to Stapo headquarters at Kronprinsens gate 10 and on impulse chose the route via Drammensveien. It was marginally longer than Bygdøy allé but he preferred its sights and its architecture. He was also aware of responding to unease at the notion of what the night held in store for him and that he was perhaps seeking to delay his arrival in this slight way.

After completing his report of the proceedings of the Special Court, to which he had added a brief note on how he had obtained permission to attend the execution, he had delivered it to 'Nordtorp' at the caretaker's flat at the arts and crafts school at the junction of St Olavs gate and Ullevålsveien. 'Nordtorp' was head of the D13 Milorg group that covered Oslo, Aker, Bærum and Asker. Waaler never wrote these reports in his office on Akersgate, nor kept anything there that might incriminate him should his luck run out and the office be searched. And he always tried to deliver them as soon as possible after writing them. Afterwards

EPILOGUE

he'd taken a drink with the major and spent an hour exchanging news before taking the tram back to Bygdøy allé at about ten.

He'd tried to sleep but it hadn't worked and instead he'd taken Varja out for a walk around Bygdøylokket, getting back home at about midnight. He made no further attempt to sleep but set his alarm for 2.15 a.m. and, in an attempt to override the persistent hum of dread and unease at the thought of what lay ahead of him, settled in his armchair to read *De dødes tjern* (The Lake of the Dead), a crime novel published two years earlier by Bernhard Borge, which Waaler knew to be an alias for André Bjerke. Bjerke was still only in his mid-twenties but already he wrote with the same kind of psychological insight that had made Jonas Lie a household name, until Lie's political choices had made him impossible to read any longer. The diversionary tactic worked and the fierce ringing of the alarm startled Waaler away from Bjerke's sinister lake in the depths of the Østerdalen forest.

It was eerie to walk that long, quiet, blacked-out thoroughfare with the moon as his only light, the sound of his footsteps the only sound. By the time he reached Solli plass and the university library he still hadn't met a soul. In his full Stapo uniform he hadn't expected to either; anyone out delivering illegal newspapers to letterboxes and postboxes would be sure to keep out of sight as soon as they saw and heard him approaching. At the junction of Parkveien and Løkkeveien he heard the drone of an approaching vehicle. He turned and saw a green flatbed truck with a tarpaulin flapping on the back. He watched it head down in the direction of the National Theatre, suspecting it might be connected with the night's activities. Sure enough, he heard the grind of the gears as it slowed a couple of hundred metres further down the road and then made the right turn into Kronprinsens gate.

It was standing parked outside Number 10 by the time he arrived a few minutes later. It was just after 3 a.m. The driver, hurriedly attempting to hide the cigarette he was smoking, offered a clumsy salute as Waaler passed him and entered the building. At the reception desk the duty officer detailed someone to accompany him up the stairs to the second-floor office of the man in charge of the execution, Inspector Gunnar Lindvig. Entering the room amid the subdued hum of voices, Waaler found a number of familiar faces already present. Lindvig he knew by sight, a man about his own age with dark wavy hair and a rather sulky face. Ragnvald Kranz was there too, in conversation with two of Waaler's fellow police prosecutors, Gottfried Skule and Sverre Thorhus. In another corner Gulbrand Bergsjø, Mathiesen's defence lawyer at the trial, was talking to a man with a monk's tonsure and watchful, intense eyes. Bergsjø waved him over and introduced him to Dr Hans Eng. They shook hands. Eng was wearing a baggy grey suit that looked as if he'd been sleeping in it. He and Bergsjø, now without his cloak, were the only two in civilian clothes. Everyone else wore the green uniform and polished jackboots of Jonas Lie's State Police force.

Waaler had heard a lot about Dr Eng. Among other things he knew that he was the youngest PhD in Norwegian academic history, awarded his doctorate in 1938 for a thesis written when he was just thirty-one years old. As well as being Stapo's own doctor he was Vidkun Quisling's private physician, a largely honorific title since it was well known that Quisling was never ill. After the introduction Eng resumed the account he had been giving Bergsjø of a dramatic episode in which he had been personally involved two days earlier. Waaler immediately and thankfully fell into the role of interested listener.

'Anyway – it was past seven o'clock by the time I got back home after seeing my patient. I walked up from the station at Majorstua and turned into the entrance to my block, at Kirkeveien 90. As I did so I passed a young man about seventeen or eighteen lounging against the wall with one hand wedged rather forcefully in his pocket. I didn't recognise him, and he pointedly looked the other way as I passed him, but I had the distinct impression he was *monitoring* my arrival. I suspected at once it was a gun he was holding in his pocket.

'As I was about to unlock the door to my stairwell I noticed, at the far end of the block, a second young man lounging against the fence on the far side of Harald Hårfagres gate in the same apparently casual manner. Hand in his pocket, flat hat, cigarette. All of this struck me as so unnatural I carried on past the door to my stairwell and then turned left, and left again, into Åsaveien, where there are two more entrances to the block. And what do I see there? Two more young men. Well. All of this was extremely alarming. I walked back out onto Kirkeveien turned back into the yard, past the first young man, let myself in and went up the stairs to my flat and...'

Gottfried Skule had joined them by now and was following Eng's story. 'Why did you find it alarming?' he said abruptly.

Eng made no attempt to hide his annoyance at the interruption and glared at Skule before replying.

'I was *alarmed*', he said slowly, as though explaining to a child, 'because I thought they might be going to kill me. Or kidnap me. I'm on their list,' he said. 'Two years ago someone put a bullet through my kitchen window. Kranz and I—' he looked up and nodded in the direction of Kranz, who had also now joined the group of listeners, 'Kranz and I are both on their list.'

'At least you have good all-round visibility from your flat,' said Kranz. He was a friend of Eng's and a frequent visitor to his home.

'I expect that's why he bought it,' someone else said, trying to lighten the atmosphere in the room. They were still waiting for Jonas Lie to arrive to get the proceedings under way.

Eng resumed his narrative. He told them how he had walked through his corner flat to the window that looked down onto the crossroads with Suhms gate and watched as the first young man strolled up to the corner of the junction and looked up and down in all four directions before sauntering back to his post outside the arched entrance to the block. By now, he said, he was certain he was under surveillance and that something was about to happen. He let half an hour pass and then took his dog Dux out for a short walk. The same four boys were still loitering outside when he returned twenty minutes later.

'Were your family at home?' asked Bergsjø.

'My wife was. The boys were staying with their Great-Aunt Helga.' He glanced around Lindvig's office in search of an ashtray, spotted one set into the top of a narrow wooden pedestal next to a set of filing cabinets, stepped over and tapped the ash from his cigarette into it. 'So when I got back inside I telephoned Inspector Skjønhaug at Majorstua,' he said, resuming his tale.

Waaler looked at his watch. It was almost 3.25 a.m. Where was Lie? Without him there would be no execution. Eng was still telling his story, but Waaler's attention had wandered. He had taken an instinctive dislike to Eng. As a double-agent, a trusted and high-ranked Stapo officer with access to some of the Quisling regime's most confidential documents and discussions who also kept the resistance informed of significant developments affecting themselves and their own plans, Waaler had few difficulties in dealing with the conflict of personal loyalties this could give rise to. There were several members of the State Police whose politics he detested but whose company he was able to tolerate and even enjoy – Skjønhaug was one – even as he made mental notes of information gleaned from them that would be passed on to his contacts. In the same way there were some among his resistance contacts whom he agreed with politically and yet whose personalities he could scarcely endure.

Waaler knew more about the threat to Eng's life than Eng did himself. He knew that the gunman who had fired at him through his kitchen window on that earlier occasion had been the legendary communist 'Osvald'. He also already knew where Eng's story was going. Had he not known better, he might have thought the story illustrated the doctor's obviously considerable personal vanity, because as things turned out he was mistaken. He had not, after all, been the target of the Milorg operation at Kirkeveien 90 two nights earlier. Waaler knew this because after he had delivered his report on Mathiesen's trial to 'Nordtorp', the major had given him an account of what had really been going on. One of the primary aims of the Quisling regime was to establish a Norwegian version of the Hitler *jugend* that had proved such an efficient way of indoctrinating young men and women into the national socialist way of thinking in Germany. To this end a comprehensive card index had been built up containing personal details of all young Norwegians aged 18 to 23 eligible for conscription to an *Arbeidstjeneste* (Work Service) that would be a vital step in the process.

Aware of this ulterior motive for what National Unity tried to pass off as a period of patriotic work service, Milorg had made the destruction of these records a priority. They had learned that they were stored in the flat of one of the men in charge of the plan, Major Jan Kielland, who lived in the same complex as Eng but on the opposite wing. The young men whom Eng had spotted were indeed sentries posted at the entrances to the complex, but their task was to warn three comrades engaged in destroying the records up in the major's top floor flat of any sign of trouble. None of those involved had any idea that Dr Eng lived in the same complex. The way things turned out, Eng's misreading of the situation turned out to be just a case of very bad luck indeed.

Three of Milorg's best operatives had carried out the raid on Kielland's flat: Max Manus, Gregers Gram and Edvard Tallaksen. Manus had established from a reconnaissance trip the previous week that the major used a security chain once he was home for the night, and they had considered the possibility of getting onto the roof of the block and lowering themselves onto his open balcony and entering his flat via the bedroom window. Once it became clear Kielland slept with his windows closed at night they had to abandon the idea.

In the end they concluded they had no option but to ring on the doorbell and use the element of surprise to overpower and subdue the major. They had obtained a key to the main entrance to the block and at 7.15 p.m. had let themselves in and taken the lift up. Tallaksen packed a length of parachute cord in his rucksack with which to tie the major up. In case the AT cards were kept locked in a safe he also brought along plastic explosives and a metal saw, as well as firebombs if all else failed and they had to burn the whole place down. All three carried handguns and grenades. The leader, Max Manus, also carried a Sten gun. Max forgot to pack the breach, 'Nordtorp' had told Waaler, but he didn't think it would matter that much if he had to use it.

As the lift rose Manus went over the plan again; Gregers, wearing an outrageously large *solkors* on the lapel of his jacket, was to knock on Kielland's door and say he had an important message for the major. If Kielland smelt a rat and refused to open up, Gram would fasten plastic explosives to the door, light the fuse and take cover. Once inside they would shoot to kill if they encountered any resistance.

The lift stopped on the sixth floor. Manus and Tallaksen stepped out; the doors slid shut on Gram and they listened as it made the short jerky climb to the top floor and stopped with a dull thud. They heard the doors open. Gram's footsteps across the tiled floor. His heavy, confident knock on the door. A woman's voice asking who was there. Gram said his rehearsed sentence: an important message for the major, must be delivered in person, for his ears only. And then the sound of the door opening, and the muffled scream of a woman. At that Manus and Tallaksen sprinted up the last flight of stairs and saw the door open and Gram just inside it holding a young woman's head down to the hallway carpet. They ran past Gram. A quick sweep of the flat told them that they had been astonishingly lucky: Kielland wasn't home. It was empty save for this young woman. Max reminded them all to put on the masks that covered the lower parts of their faces and while Tallaksen and Gram began the searching for the filing cards Max tried to calm the terrified young woman.

As yet they had no idea who she was or what she was doing in Kielland's flat. But once she realised he had no intention of harming her she answered Max's questions. The major was out at a National Unity meeting, she said, and she wasn't expecting him back until late. She was just the lodger. Hadn't been able to find anywhere else to live. Swore she wasn't a Nazi and Max swore he believed her. Realising that Kielland would certainly throw her out for having

EPILOGUE

let them in, he dug into his back pocket, pulled out his wallet and counted out 300 kroner which he gave to her – at least it would help her find another flat. He also told her to be as exact as she liked in giving their descriptions to the Stapo when they arrived, and to tell the whole truth about how they had tricked their way in, knowing as he did that she had never seen their faces.

Eng was still holding forth with his own version of the events at Kirkeveien 90 as Waaler looked at his watch again. Already he could feel a sick excitement gnawing at the pit of his stomach. There was a brief interruption as a group of four men entered. One of them passed on the news that Lie was in the building. Waaler realised this must be Lie's driver and that there wasn't long to go now.

The four were all drivers and they gathered in a small group of their own. He recognised the driver of the green lorry with the tarpaulin over the flatbed that had driven past earlier. He was talking to Lie's new driver. The story of what happened to his previous driver, Henrik Hebo, had already done the rounds in resistance circles. Hebo had been temporarily posted to the job when Lie's regular driver was off sick, it seems that Lie had taken a personal liking to him and insisted on keeping him on as his official driver, despite the fact that Hebo was not a member of National Unity. He even turned a blind eye to Hebo's using the ministerial car in the evenings in the belief that Hebo was doing it to impress his girlfriend. In fact, Jonas Lie's driver was utilising the ministerial car to take refugees over the border into Sweden. With Hebo in full Stapo uniform and behind the wheel of the minister's very own Cadillac, it was a brave *Grepo* man who would have dared question the reason for his frequent presence in the border region at all sorts of odd hours of the night. It seems that, while out buying shoes in Bogstadveien with Jonas Lie's daughter, he had been warned that the Germans were onto him and after driving the girl home he had coolly driven himself to safety across the border.[83]

Hebo's duplicity struck Waaler as close to his own, and though he'd never met Hebo he felt a connection to him. A strange postscript to the story was that Lie preferred not to believe what he was told about Hebo and instead attributed the driver's flight to pressure amounting to persecution from both Riisnæs and Olbjørn, who found it intolerable that Hebo was not a party member. Lie had even written to Hebo in Stockholm, urging him to return and promising to sort things out with the Germans.

Hebo preferred not to accept the invitation, but for Waaler it was yet another aspect of the enigma attaching to Quisling's Minister for Policing. Because, although he did his best to disguise the fact, Lie's contempt for Quisling and most of the National Unity leadership was evident. Once, when Waaler's work as a Special Police Prosecutor took him to Lie's offices in the Storting, he had been present when Lie's friend Bjørn Bjørnson paid a social call to the minister. As the two passed a clerk with an open copy of the party newspaper *Fritt Folk* (Free People) on the desk in front of him, Bjørnson had harrumphed loudly and made a sarcastic reference to *Dritt Folk* (Shit People). Waaler had heard Lie's snorted chuckle of enjoyment at the observation. The man remained a dark mystery to him.

Eng had reached the point in his narrative at which he made the emergency call for help to Inspector Kranz down the road at Kirkeveien 23 and Kranz had despatched two cars with four armed Stapo officers in each. Waaler knew that the goal of destroying the AT filing cards and at least seriously delaying the conscription of Norway's young men and women had been successful. 'Nordtorp' had told him so. In every other respect, however, from the resistance point of view it had been a tragedy and a disaster. The arrival of Stapo had taken the young sentries by surprise and a gun battle ensued. The two boys watching the entrances on Åsaveien had both been arrested. The gunshots from outside had alerted Max Manus and the others up on the seventh floor and they had raced down the stairs as fast as they could and out into the yard. Max had his Sten gun ready and almost peppered a figure he saw crouching behind the bushes 10 metres from the door but just in time recognised his own sentry. Tallaksen, Gregers Gram and the sentry ran for the nearest exit into Harald

EPILOGUE

Hårfargres vei and then up and left along Suhms gate, past the big German naval warehouse. Manus made for the Kirkeveien exit, cursing himself as he struggled to hold the gun steady for not having bothered to fit the stock onto it.

By the time he reached the Kirkeveien exit, the boy posted to keep watch there and whose presence had originally alerted Dr Eng was already gone. Two Stapo men had taken him by surprise. Approaching with pistols drawn, they had ordered him to put his hands up. With great coolness he had done so, raising his left above his head at the same time as he pulled the pistol from his right pocket and fired at the police. He'd been hit twice but managed to stagger round the corner into Suhms gate and hide among the bushes that lined the wall of the complex. He remained in hiding until all was quiet then crawled from the bushes and walked out onto Kirkeveien. As he passed the bus stop 50 metres away from the scene of the evening's drama, a bus stopped and a middle-aged couple got off. Noticing he was in a bad way, the woman stopped and asked if he was alright, did he need help? He took an enormous chance and told them yes he did, he'd been shot, he did need help. His luck was in. They turned up to be a *jøssing* couple on their way home after a visit to the Eldorado cinema. They helped him to their flat on Trudvangveien just five minutes away, where he was able to spend the night before being picked up the next day by a member of the resistance.

Max Manus meanwhile, emerging onto Kirkeveien through the covered exit, found himself confronted by the two Stapo men still reloading their weapons after the gunfight with the lookout. He swore at them – in English, for some reason, he had told 'Nordtorp' – and ordered them down on the ground. Sprinting across Kirkeveien, he pulled out a grenade, removed the pin and was about to throw it into a group of Stapo men who had set up a post on the far side of the crossroads. By this time the gunfight had attracted a crowd of onlookers, some standing so close to the Stapo position that he realised it would kill many of them too if he were to throw it. He'd already pulled the pin and now had to fumblingly unscrew the base and remove the detonator before throwing it into the gutter. Firing wildly from the hip with the Sten gun, he had no control over where the bullets went but kept up a steady spray anyway as he ran off down the road in the direction of Majorstua.

Midway between Åsaveien and Hammerstads gate, just before Schønings gate, he spotted a man in a raincoat standing and holding his bicycle by its leather saddle. 'Your bike or your life,' he roared as he pointed the Sten gun at him, then grabbed the bike and pedalled as hard as he could down Kirkeveien in the direction of the T-bane station. At the foot of the station steps he tossed the bike aside and bounded up the steps and through a narrow passageway onto the platform bridge from where he had a view of both platforms. A westbound train was just pulling in and, dropping the Sten gun onto the tracks below, he turned and raced down the slope and jumped on board just as the doors were closing. A quick survey of the carriage told him there were no Germans on board and he slumped down into a seat. His collar felt wet and when he checked with his fingers and looked, he saw the blood and realised he'd been hit.

Later, at a safe house, he realised he'd been lucky and it was just a graze. Not so the lookouts who had been arrested. They'd be tortured, give up names, and be dead within a week. The third sentry who'd got away with Gregers Gram and Tallaksen had stayed out all night and called home in the morning. A voice he didn't recognise picked up the phone and he put it down and knew he could never go home again. His worst fears were confirmed later the same day when information reached 'Nordtorp' that the boy's older brother had been arrested as a hostage. The mission itself had been a success, said 'Nordtorp'. But in every other way the night had been a tragedy.[84]

At 3.35 a.m. the door opened and Jonas Lie entered the room, followed by Olbjørn. As though the appearances were orchestrated, a side door to the office that Waaler had presumed to be some kind

EPILOGUE

of storage cupboard opened and a group of about ten men marched in, in uniform and all with rifles slung over their shoulders in the German manner. Lindvig positioned himself in front of his desk, clapped his hands and called for silence. He then explained the purpose of the gathering. As he did so Waaler realised that those ten men, the men Lindvig had picked to be Mathiesen's executioners, had no idea what the night held in store for them. They had simply been told to report for night duty. It wasn't unusual. There was no reason for them to suspect they would be involved in anything other than a routine sweep and arrest operation. Waaler watched their faces and as soon as they realised he saw their distress. Several of them openly protested. The oldest among them, Sandberg – he heard someone say the name – objected vigorously.

'This isn't police work, sir. This is soldiers' work.'

'This is police work, Sandberg, and you will obey orders. All of you. Or you will find yourself in front of the Special Court facing the harshest penalty the law will allow.'

'Soldiers' work,' Sandberg muttered contemptuously. Waaler heard three or four others repeat the phrase. Lindvig called for silence but didn't get it. The muttering continued and showed no sign of stopping. Waaler could see that Lindvig was about to explode; but instead his tone changed, and he began a justification of the necessity of the task ahead of them.

'The man whom you are to shoot tonight', he said, 'killed one of your own. In cold blood. It could have been any one of you. Officer Haugland was obeying orders; this man killed him for it.'

Now he had everyone's attention.

'Sergeant Haugland was shot five times and executed in brutal fashion. His killer stood over him as he lay wounded on the ground and—' Lindvig paused, looked intently down at the floor and with two fingers of his right hand extended suddenly jerked his arm upwards '—put a bullet through his head. So when you carry out this order – and you *will* carry out this order – remember why you are doing it. Remember what this man did to one of your own: he shot him in cold blood. Like a dog.'

He stared at Sandberg. No doubt on account of his greying hair Sandberg seemed to have become the conscience of the group. This time there was no response from him. Lindvig allowed the silence to persist until all traces of protest had faded and then continued. He stressed the need for complete secrecy surrounding every aspect of what was about to take place. This applied to the site of execution; the routes taken there and back; the names of all those involved and in particular the names of members of the firing squad – everything, everyone.

And to stress the seriousness of what he had been saying Lindvig then asked them all to come forward to his desk and sign the declaration he had drafted for the occasion. He read it out:

> I declare on my honour and on my conscience that I will never reveal to anyone what happens in connection with the special orders I have been given this evening nor make any reference to the occasion at all.
>
> I understand that if I break this promise in any way I will face the ultimate penalty.
>
> ...... (Signature)

Lindvig positioned himself behind the leather-topped desk and with a slight nod of the head indicated to each man in turn to come forward and sign the document. When it was Waaler's turn to step forward he did so firmly. After signing he stood up, looked Lindvig straight in the eye and gave him a particularly vigorous Nazi salute. Lindvig returned the salute and as Waaler turned away he told himself that the wording of the secret document was something he would include in his report to 'Nordtorp', but that this last detail was something he might or might not add. His role-playing as the 'good conscience' of the Norwegian Nazi Party meant he was grudgingly admired by many of his Stapo colleagues, who were not blind to the thuggish nature of most of the young men who had joined Quisling's *hird*, and to the corruption and favouritism that were generally accepted as unfortunate consequences of the difficult road they were travelling along on national socialism's way towards the 'glorious new future', and they admired Waaler's refusal to turn a legal blind eye to crimes involving National Unity members.

Waaler was able to balance any potential hostility and suspicion his strict interpreting of the law might give rise to by these routinely exaggerated displays of ideological enthusiasm for national socialism. He was pleased to note that he was the only one present so far who had saluted in such an enthusiastic fashion after signing Lindvig's form, but as he returned to his place next to Bergsjø he felt an uneasy chill in his stomach. This role-playing as an enthusiastic Nazi was the most frightening part of the double game he was playing. His survival depended on his extreme caution, and the role of devout Nazi wasn't something he could take off once he got home in the same way he took off his uniform. His neighbours in Bygdøy allé took it for granted that he was the Nazi his uniform proclaimed him to be. Most tried to avoid him if they saw him in the street. If they met him on the stairs inside the building they hurried past without looking at him. The sole exception was the caretaker of the block, a middle-aged man with soft grey hair and watery blue eyes who made a point of greeting him effusively no matter how far apart the two of them were. Waaler didn't trust him. He was *stripete*, striped, meaning an unprincipled opportunist who backed both sides. Waaler didn't fear him. His real fear was the one every Stapo member entertained to a greater or lesser degree, that of being shot on his way to work one morning by a member of the resistance. The almost hysterical atmosphere of secrecy surrounding the trial and execution of Knut Mathiesen was a manifestation of this fear. And though he tried hard not to think about it, in the context of his double role as high-ranking State Police officer and patriot supplying classified information to the resistance, Waaler knew he ran the risk of being shot by both sides.

Once everyone had signed Lindvig gathered up the pile of documents and locked them in the small safe standing by the floor behind him. He then read out a list of who would be travelling with who in which car, and the order in which the cars were to line up for the drive. The drivers were told it was essential for them to stay as a group at all times. As he went through the list people left the office one by one and made their way down to Kronprinsens gate.

When there were no more than four or five left in the office Lindvig stopped reading and looked up from his list in dismay: Dr Eng was still standing in front of him. He had not yet been assigned a place. Somehow or other his name had been left off the list. In political terms Eng was not an important man in the party, but he was a reliable source of essentials such as cod liver oil and vaccines and his status as Quisling's own doctor was high. Lindvig was mortified. He began to stammer an apology at the same time as he studied the list to see where there were still any vacant seats. Waaler began to fear that his participation in the execution hung in the balance and felt an uneasy pang of disappointment.

Realising the nature of the problem, the self-assured doctor came to the rescue.

'*Jeg får vel kjøre med liket jeg da*' ('Well then I suppose I'll just have to drive with the corpse'), he said, sparing Lindvig's blushes. He had apparently worked out on his own that the passenger seat in the car in which Mathiesen would be travelling in the back seat between his two guards was still vacant. With relief Lindvig noted that this was correct: there was indeed a vacant seat there. And Waaler's own fears were laid to rest as he and Bergsjø were assigned the last two available seats. Led by Lindvig, the final group then walked in silence down the spiral staircase to the ground floor and out into the pre-dawn chill of Kronprinsens gate.

As the column of six or seven vehicles pulled away from Number 10 and down the slope from Victoria terrasse they followed the road as it swung left opposite the Østbanen railway station and followed the curve of the harbour front. Several small fishing vessels were already starting up their engines for the day. They drove

EPILOGUE

past three solitary individuals headed for the row of warehouses and the gaunt, stark cranes and hoists that lined the waterfront stretching out towards the Bygdøy peninsula. Shadowy figures could be seen making their way across the waterfront, probably shift workers heading for the Akers Mek. shipyard.

The car carrying Waaler and Bergsjø brought up the rear of the column and Waaler spent the first couple of minutes of the drive trying to work out the order of the cars in front of him. Lie and Police Major General Olbjørn were first. Then came the car – a taxi – carrying Mathiesen. While leaving the building in Kronprinsens gate he had caught a glimpse of him in the back seat between his guards, and Dr Eng in the front seat, staring straight ahead through the windscreen. As the column followed the curve of the fjord he noted, behind Mathiesen's car, the long dark shape of the green bus carrying the ten policemen appointed to carry out his execution. In the two taxis behind the bus sat colleagues of the dead *Grepo* man Haugland, who had expressed a personal wish to be present at the execution of their friend's killer. Immediately ahead of Waaler and Bergsjø's car was the small flatbed truck Waaler had seen earlier in the morning. Beneath the tarpaulin he now clearly saw the outlines of a coffin.

Away from the hum of conversation and even occasional eruptions of laughter in Lindvig's office, usually at something said by Dr Eng, Waaler and Bergsjø spent the first few minutes of the journey each in their own private world. Waaler, sitting on the right side, looked through the window at the still waters of the fjord illuminated by the almost full moon. It shone in a solid column of light, like a path of light you could walk along. It reminded Waaler of Munch's painting.

Lost in contemplation of the melancholy beauty of the scene, he did not immediately become aware that Bergsjø was talking to him, or rather *at* him, since he knew Bergsjø to be a man who talked regardless of whether anyone was listening to him or not. Latching briefly onto the monologue, he gathered it was about his frequent experiences as defence advocate in German *krigsretter*, and how German naval and military courts were notably more lenient in their sentencing than Norwegian courts. The SS, on the other hand…

Still absorbed in the oriental stillness of the moonlit scene he was surprised to hear himself interrupt Bergsjø:

'You can't help wondering what thoughts and feelings are going though that poor boy's head right now.'

Bergsjø stopped speaking in mid-sentence and Waaler felt himself being scrutinised.

'Well yes,' Bergsjø finally responded with a shrug. 'But remember what he did.'

The exchange was followed by silence in the back seat for a minute or so. Then, as though Waaler's spontaneous expression of what could only be seen as pity required something more substantial than a brief rejoinder, Bergsjø went on to deliver an ideological attack on the subject of pity.

'Pity is understandable in circumstances like this,' he began. 'But that doesn't make it right. Friedrich Nietzsche saw this very clearly. According to Nietzsche, the whole evolutionary process has consisted of the strong eliminating the weak, those who can eliminating those who can't, the clever eliminating the stupid, and so on. And it's only because these processes have been going on unbrokenly over millions of years that civilisation has developed at all. These processes have created everything of value we possess. But then along came the ancient Greeks – and the Jews – the so-called moralists who taught that these processes were immoral, they were in fact wicked. Now the strong were to humble themselves. They were to shelter the weak and the meek, to submit themselves to the rule of law. The clever were to help the stupid, those who were able fight for the rights of those who were not able. Etcetera etcetera. But had we always done that, said Nietzsche, then we should never have emerged from the pre-human state. Surely what we ought to be doing, he said, is to continue with – or return to – the values and standards that have created humanity and civilisation.'

EPILOGUE

He gave Waaler a reproachful look: 'Not put those standards into reverse. You of all people, Waaler, I would have expected to know this.'

Still shocked at having revealed himself as he had done, Waaler nodded several times as though chastened by Bergsjø's lecture. He knew his Nietzsche well enough, and Bergsjø's mention of the name reminded him also of an aphorism with which he sometimes tormented himself: that when a man goes out to fight monsters he must guard against becoming monstrous himself. Gaze long enough into the abyss, said Nietzsche, and it will gaze back at you. That gaze returned was something Waaler feared almost as much as he did liquidation or betrayal.

After Holmlia he lost track of the way as the lead car with Lie and Olbjørn made several changes of direction that took them along country lanes. He guessed it was part of the plan to keep everything connected to the morning's business as secretive as possible. Finally, after they'd been driving about three quarters of an hour, the procession pulled over to the side of the road. Waaler opened the car door and looked around. They were in a narrow, dark, featureless stretch of road with dense forest on both sides.

'Know where we are?' he asked. 'I lost track after we left the fjord.'

Bergsjø had grown up in the capital and knew the suburbs and countryside around Oslo well. 'Enebakkveien,' he said. He gestured vaguely towards the trees. 'There's an open-air dance floor over there somewhere,' he said. 'I took a girl there once.'

Together they walked briskly up the line of parked vehicles as the shrill of the dawn chorus was punctuated by the slamming of car doors as the passengers stepped out. In the faint grey light Waaler saw Lindvig already making his way through the trees and up a grassy path that sloped up at a forty-five-degree angle onto a semi-circular plateau. It was bounded on its western side by a clearly defined arc of rock about six metres high, a strange and striking feature with dense forest stretching away on its two other sides. Peering upwards, Waaler saw a tall pine tree standing almost centrally in front of the wall and realised at once that this must be the place.

In almost complete silence the party of onlookers now began to arrange themselves in a loose group around the edge of the plateau and facing the wall of rock. Lindvig had returned to the road and Waaler heard him posting sentries by the roadside to keep away any curious early morning farmworker cycling on his way to work. He heard a last car door open and close and looking down the slope saw the prisoner standing outside the car. He remained standing there for a few moments while one of the guards fastened a large white blindfold over his eyes. Then the little group began making their way up the slippery grass slope.

Waaler watched. He registered the boy's complete submission to his fate. The way he responded to each directing touch on the shoulders and arms from his two guards as they gently helped him up the slope. He noted the tenderness with which the guard on his left reached out to support him as his foot caught on a root at one point and he stumbled and almost fell. Then they were up on the plateau and passed so close by Waaler that in the first rays of sunlight beginning to filter through the trees he was able to identify the small round badge the boy was wearing on the lapel of his dark sports jacket as a Red Cross badge. He even heard him breathing as he passed.

The guards stopped at the tree in front of the wall of rock and turned the prisoner round, and while one held a hand against his chest the other began to secure him to the tree with a broad brown leather strap he had been carrying. As he watched Waaler found the boy's absolute passivity maddening. He felt almost angry with him. What was the matter with him? Why didn't he shout? Why didn't he struggle?

He caught a waft of tobacco and stale alcohol in the crisp air as Jonas Lie and Olbjørn strode by and took up a position some five metres away from the prisoner. Lie stood with hands behind his back, as always with the long black cigarette holder jutting from his square jaw. Olbjørn had a fixed sneer on his face as he stood staring up into the trees and drawing deep breaths as though trying to fill his lungs through his nostrils alone. Haugland's *Grepo*

EPILOGUE

colleagues were gathered in a group on the far side of the clearing. They stood close together, waiting in silence, smoking. They were like men who didn't know each other at all and had simply found themselves standing there together by chance.

Now the firing squad of ten climbed down the steps from the police bus and followed Lindvig in straggling single file up the grassy slope. At the top they formed a line in front of the prisoner bound to the tree. At Lindvig's crisp command they turned with their backs to him and stood to attention. Lindvig walked on a few paces and stood off to one side.

'About turn!'

The ten men turned. Lindvig raised his right arm as a signal for the squad to take aim. Then he dropped the arm in a swift downward chop:

'F-i-r-e!'

The volley sounded like a single shot. For a few seconds all birdsong stopped. Mathiesen slumped forward and swayed like a doll in the cradle of the leather strap. A stain the size of a rose appeared on the blindfold next to his right ear. No jerking, no tremors, no signs of life at all.

At a command from Lindvig the ten members of the firing squad then shouldered their rifles and marched back down the slope to the bus. Two men carrying the coffin from the flatbed truck stood to one side to let them pass. Two others walked behind them. Waaler watched as they made their way over to the tree and lowered the coffin to the ground and stood, panting slightly from their exertions, while the two others cut through the strap that held Mathiesen to the tree and eased the corpse onto the grass.

As they were preparing to lift him up to put him in the coffin, Dr Eng stepped forward and motioned them to stand aside. He took a small revolver from his pocket, bent down, removed the blindfold and fired a single bullet through Mathiesen's temple. He then straightened up, slipped the revolver back into his pocket and with a nod to the two men walked away. All four men of the coffin detail then lifted the body up and with some difficulty placed him inside the coffin. Waaler was standing so close he could see the white paper sheet lining the box instantly turn dark. The boy's eyes were still open and he had to quell a sudden urge to step forward and close them. Then the coffin lid was being screwed on and the coffin carried down to the waiting lorry where it was shoved and manhandled from the sides until it rested flush against the back of the cab. On went the tarp, up went the tailgate with a rusty shriek and then one man alone went around and swiftly secured the eyeholes in the tarp to the fixed pins that lined the sides and the tailgate.

It was almost over. Lie walked over to Lindvig with his hand outstretched and congratulated him on a job well done. In a rather distracted way Lie then began shaking hands with anyone else who happened to be standing close. Presently it was Waaler's turn. Faithful to his mission, loathing himself, Waaler took the proffered hand. He shook it firmly, looking deeply into those alcohol-glazed eyes that seemed hardly to register whose hand he was shaking.

On the drive back to Oslo the cortege took a different route, and as they entered the suburbs the cars split up. The lorry carrying Mathiesen's coffin drove to the crematorium at Vestre cemetery, about ten minutes' walk away through Frogner Park from where Mathiesen used to live, and the taxis and private cars took the passengers home to their respective destinations.

'I got back home at five thirty, three hours after I'd left there,' Waaler wrote in his report later that morning. 'Three truly eventful hours. I had hoped to sleep, but sleep wasn't possible. And when I got up in the morning the events of the night seemed unreal, like a bad dream.'

Echoes and Afterlives

Norway

In February 1948 the Soviet Union sponsored a coup in Czechoslovakia and handed power to the Czech Communist Party. With preposterous irony the party then abolished democracy in the country. Stalin followed this up with a blockade of all road and river routes into West Berlin that lasted from 24 June 1948 to 12 May 1949 and obliged the Western allies to come to the city's rescue with a massive airlift. These further steps in the direction of what was already being referred to as the 'Cold War' sent shock waves through Europe and precipitated a political crisis in Norway.

While neutrality had proved a successful policy for Sweden in 1940, it had failed for both Norway and Denmark. It was obvious that in any future conflict between the United States and Soviet Russia the Scandinavian peninsula would again become a centre of violent confrontation over matters in which neither Norway, Sweden nor Denmark had any direct interest. The idea of a Pan-Scandinavian union that had been so much discussed in the region in the 1850s and 1860s now made a brief reappearance. The Swedes, on the basis of a policy that had stood them in good stead since the end of the Napoleonic Wars in 1814, urged both Denmark and Norway to face the future in a new and formalised neutrality pact. As far as Sweden was concerned the alternative, which was membership of a transatlantic pact in which the United States and Great Britain were ranged against the Soviet Union, constituted a dangerous provocation of its powerful neighbour in the east. But when the time for decision came the Norwegians were no longer willing or able to believe that the great powers would respect any declaration of neutrality. Hitler's violence against his European neighbours had been made possible by the lack of a united military front to oppose it and the Norwegian government came to the conclusion that what the country needed for its future peace of mind was the certainty of military support in the event of an invasion.

In March 1948 Great Britain, France, Belgium, the Netherlands and Luxembourg had signed the Treaty of Brussels, which guaranteed that in the event of any one of these countries being attacked the others would come to its assistance. The following year, after extensive negotiations which saw the end of the United States' long-standing policy of non-involvement in affairs outside its own direct sphere of influence, the Brussels Treaty was redrafted and the North Atlantic Treaty Organisation (NATO) came into being. The signatories in Washington on 4 April 1949 were the Foreign Ministers of the United States, Great Britain, Canada, France, Italy, Luxemburg, the Netherlands, Belgium, Denmark, Iceland and Norway.[85]

Dr Hans Eng

Following the end of the *rettsoppgjør*, the need to get on with the reconstruction of Norway took precedence over all else. Extraordinary paradoxes ensued. Dr Hans Eng, Quisling's personal physician, the man who put the final bullets through the heads of many of those condemned to death by the Police Special Court, who had prepared and distributed suicide pills for Lie, Rogstad and Riisnæs at Skallum, had been sentenced to seven years' imprisonment at his trial in 1948. Historians of the period generally agree that had he been tried earlier he would undoubtedly have faced the death penalty. In the event, time served since his arrest in 1945 saw him released with immediate effect after the trial.

Eng's licence to practice as a doctor was among the social privileges he was now denied and for the next year he worked as a furniture upholsterer. Then, in 1950, the state made him an offer he could not refuse: his licence would be returned to him on condition that he agreed to practise up in Kvænangen, a sparsely populated county in the remote north of Norway. The far north had always suffered from a lack of doctors (and of priests), for most of whom it was simply too far from Oslo. Eng agreed. He got his licence back and he travelled north.

He was understandably nervous about the sort of reception he would get on his arrival.[86] It was, after all, his side, in the person of Jonas Lie, that had made more than 45,000 northerners homeless as a result of the scorched-earth policy just six years earlier. But beggars can't be choosers and the need for a doctor turned out to trump any desire the people of Kvænangen might have felt to reject Eng's posting on principle. And Quisling's doctor was to show selfless devotion to his new patients. Making frequent short and often stormy sea voyages to visit patients in their remote island homes, and car journeys over distances so vast that he had to keep a sleeping bag in the back of his car, he rapidly became a respected member of the community. Over time he became active in local politics and was credited with almost single-handedly creating a functioning health service in the region. But tempting as it might be to see in Eng's story the example of a man who had seen the error of his ways and was determined to make amends, this was not the case. Tracked down by an intrepid reporter from *Vi Menn* (We Men) magazine in 1978, Hans Eng reluctantly gave an interview in which he made it clear that, under similar circumstances, he would respond in exactly the same way as he had done in 1940. His respect for Vidkun Quisling remained undiminished and he allowed himself to be photographed posing next to a bronze relief of the former *fører* that hung on the wall of his home.[87] Such are the enigmas of the human spirit. Eng retired in 1985 but stayed on in Kvænangen until his death in 1995 at the age of eighty-eight.

Ingrid Bjerkås

A more edifying figure who benefited from the unwillingness of professional Norwegians to seek work in the far north of the country was Ingrid Bjerkås, the housewife and mother who had heckled the speaker at Terboven's first, triumphant assembly in the square outside the royal palace in Oslo in 1940, and later rebuked Quisling, in letters and subsequently to his face, as a concerned mother of two children and an inspirational figure in the Conscience Struggle of 1942. It was Bjerkås' letters to Quisling that inspired Dr Eng to create his wilfully absurd diagnosis of her as suffering from *jøssingismus anglemanicus paranoidformis* (psychopathic English sickness – Jøssingism with persecution mania).

The war had changed Bjerkås from an agnostic into a passionate Christian. Driven by the urge to do something meaningful and useful with what remained of her life, she enrolled at the Theological Institute in Oslo in 1951 with the aim of becoming a Lutheran priest. The extraordinary nature of this decision, at a time in which there were no female priests and active opposition to the very idea, was compounded by the fact that she was now fifty years old. The course itself was weighted towards academic theology and included three years of compulsory classes in Latin, Hebrew and Greek. She stuck at it, scraped through the exams and became a *cand.theol* (BA in theology) in 1958. In 1961 she was ordained by a sympathetic and liberal bishop and began her search for a living.[88] Persisting in the face of hostility from the conservative wing of the church, she applied for several vacant posts in the south of the country, only to find a large number of other, male applicants, better qualified and with longer seniority than her, unexpectedly taking an interest in the same posts. The phenomenon repeated itself until one day she applied for the vacant post on the island of Senja, in what is now the county of Troms, in the far north of Norway. The job had been advertised three times but no male priest had applied. This turned out to be the chance Ingrid had been waiting for. She applied, was accepted and on 14 April 1961 the king in council formally appointed her to the parish of Berg and Torsken. Despite her sex and her sixty years, she overcame her doubters and became a much-loved figure in her community, braving many of the same practical difficulties in the pursuit of her ministry across her rugged island parish as Dr Eng faced in neighbouring Kvænangen. The loss of her husband Sigurd in May 1965 left her unable to continue and a month later she applied to be relieved of her post. She returned to her home district of Bærum and was appointed priest at the Martine Hansen Hospital, remaining there until she reached retirement age in 1971. Bjerkås died in 1980, fondly remembered as both a hero of the non-violent resistance and as Norway's first female priest.

Sverre Riisnæs

A curious fate was reserved for Sverre Riisnæs, the former Minister of Justice to whom God – perhaps even the same God – had spoken at Skallum. Riisnæs was more deeply implicated than most in some of the worst crimes committed by the National Unity regime. He had been one of the party's main ideologists and leader of the Norwegian branch of the SS known as *Germanske SS Norge* and an avid promoter and defender of the young Norwegian Front Fighters. From the start of the occupation he was active in pursuing the Nazification of Norwegian society. Among his first acts on taking office under Terboven was the introduction of a reform that lowered the compulsory retiring age for members of the High Court so that several were immediately excluded and the posts 'legally' filled with his own nominees. Riisnæs was behind the creation of the State Police's own Special Court and the reintroduction of the paragraph in the 1814 constitution that forbade the presence of Jews in Norway. Following the assassination on 8 February 1945 of Karl A. Marthinsen, Riisnæs joined the firing squad at the shooting of one group of the twenty-nine executed at Akershus Fortress in reprisal. By his own account he was very drunk at the time, but sober enough to avoid firing his service pistol directly at any of the men standing in front of him.

For these crimes alone Riisnæs faced the death sentence several times over when his trial began on 3 June 1947. Less than a week later it had to be abandoned as a result of his bizarre behaviour in the courtroom, at times shouting, laughing, howling, abusing and threatening the judge and at other times appearing sane and quite capable of defending himself against the charges. He claimed Norway was controlled from Moscow and that he had seen Stalin outside the door of his prison cell in Møllergata 19. Later attempts to resume the trial failed for the same reasons, and on the instructions of forensic psychiatrists Riisnæs was declared unfit to stand trial and committed to Reitgjerdet mental hospital.

Here was a man, like many another, one supposes, who would do and say anything just to go on living. He had vowed to avenge his dead friend Marthinsen by joining the firing squad and then, by his own account, skewed his aim. At Skallum, where the three desperadoes had written and signed a joint suicide note, Lie and Rogstad had suspected Riisnæs was not a man who would take his own life and written a second note signed only by the two of them which they hid from him. And sure enough, Riisnæs didn't take his own life. It was not long afterwards he arrived at the gate of the Skallum estate waving his white handkerchief and telling Jens Wulfsberg he was ready to face the consequences of his own actions.

But if the consequences meant death then he most certainly wasn't ready. Instead he used a knowledge of the antics of the insane he had picked up as a district attorney in the 1930s, when criminal insanity had been a professional interest of his, to put on the performance of a lifetime for which he was rewarded with another forty years of life. He remained a patient at Reitgjerdet until 1958, when he was allowed out to live and work on a smallholding at Fosen, in Trøndelag. In due course he was transferred to another smallholding at Solør, where he remained until 1973. By this time the case against him had passed the statute of limitations. His social privileges were returned, as was his passport, and the following year he used it to travel to Sicily, where he converted to Roman Catholicism and for the next year lived in a monastery. The attractions of this otherwise unusual destination probably included the genetic presence in Sicily of 'Nordic' blood left behind by the Norman conquests in southern Italy between 999 and 1139. In 1975 Riisnæs travelled to Austria and for the next ten years lived in Vienna with the widow of an old friend. In 1985 he returned to Norway, spending the last three years of his life at a care home in Hovseter and dying there in 1988 at the age of ninety.

Johannes Andersen ('Gulosten')

Some two months after the liberation of Norway, on the night of 13 July 1945, Gulosten got extremely drunk. He had recently learned of the execution of his wife Ruth by the Germans, in the person of Albert Wiener, for her complicity in the murder of the informer Raymond Colberg – it seems she had been at the animal hospital on the night of the killing but failed to report it to the police. Inevitably, an informant had sealed her fate. Brooding on the news of her death and fuelling his anger with fantasies of the torture she may have endured prior to it, he broke into a cell where two German prisoners of war were being held. He made some impossible demand of them to provide him with more alcohol, and when they pointed out the absurdity of it he opened fire with a machine gun, killing them both. The ensuing legal proceedings were a cause of controversy even at the time. Amid rumours of a royal intervention, no charges were ever brought against Andersen for the murders of the two men. In due course he started his own timber business, according to some sources with the financial support of the king. But old habits died hard and at intervals throughout the remainder of his life, until his death in 1970 at the age of seventy-two, Andersen appeared in court on charges as banal as the theft of building materials and the illegal sale of methylated spirits. His unorthodox and amoral personality remains the catalyst that dissolved the barriers of decent and civilised behaviour among ordinary Norwegians and forced them to see the dreadful necessity of killing those whose activities as informers were responsible for the imprisonment, torture and execution of literally hundreds of loyal Norwegians.

Asbjørn Sunde ('Osvald')

With the liberation of June 1945 came a desire to hail the heroes of the resistance. There is a famous photograph of the Milorg saboteur Max Manus riding shotgun for the newly returned Crown Prince Olav, eyes scanning the crowd as he holds his Sten gun at the ready while the crown prince's open car passes Oslo Town Hall. Another iconic photograph, showing Gunnar Sønsteby, one foot resting on the pedal of his bicycle as he insouciantly watches the columns of German soldiers marching down Karl Johans gate on 9 April 1940, became the model for the sculpture of one of Milorg's most resourceful and daring heroes that now stands in the shade of the trees behind the Oslo National Theatre. These and other Milorg men and women were rightly fêted

and decorated as national heroes. The more celebrated among them became the companions of Norwegian royalty and remained idols for generations of young Norwegians decades after the war was over.

No such recognition was afforded Asbjørn Sunde and his Osvald Group. The great problem was the known close association between the group and Moscow, and a lingering sense of discomfort at how it had not seen fit to begin resistance activities until 1941 and the end of the Nazi–Soviet non-aggression pact. In 1947 Sunde wrote and published a superbly laconic account of his group's activities, *Menn i mørket* (Men in the Dark), in which he scarcely mentions that what had inspired him was the protection and promotion of the communist ideology rather than a simple and unalloyed Norwegian patriotism. In 1954 Sunde was arrested and tried on charges of spying for the Soviet Union. Caught up in the violent polarisations of the Cold War, it seems he anticipated the outbreak of open warfare between Russia and the United States and had convinced himself that Norway would be occupied by the Americans. Following a trial that was described in the press as the most spectacular in Norway since Vidkun Quisling's, Asbjørn Sunde was sentenced to eight years' imprisonment, of which he served five before his release in 1959. He lost the right to vote for ten years and was obliged to spend the rest of his life labelled a traitor to his country.[89] He remained a deeply uncomfortable reminder of the roots of the Norwegian Labour Party's social democracy in the revolutionary communism of the early twentieth century. In the end this became too much even for the Norwegian Communist Party, which expelled Sunde in 1970. He died in Oslo on 23 April 1985 at the age of seventy-six. The Osvald Group was belatedly honoured by the unveiling in 2015 of a monument on the forecourt outside the Østbanen (Central Railway Station) depicting a large silver hammer crushing a swastika. On the side of the monument are the names of the thirty-five members of Sunde's group killed in the struggle.

Jonas Lie

The best of Jonas Lie's crime novels from the 1930s, written under the name 'Max Mauser', appeared in new editions in 2011. Contemporary reviewers had little difficulty in separating the crime novelist from the Nazi politician and confirmed the judgement of a previous generation of critics that these were outstanding examples of the genre.

Gunnar Waaler, Hellmuth Reinhard and Albert Weiner

The legal pursuit of members of National Unity inevitably involved those, like Gunnar Waaler, whose double life as a Stapo officer reporting to the resistance required both party membership and a credible performance as a devoted Nazi for the benefit of his colleagues. The folders relating to his activities in the National Archives at Sognsvann contain dozens of documents Waaler had to solicit from those he had helped as proof of where his true loyalties lay. They included testimonials from the refugees he had guided over into Sweden and from Ole Hallesby, one of the leaders of the secret Church Group that was formed following the mass resignations of the bishops and priests in 1942. They also included letters of trenchant and even outraged support from Major Langeland, head of Milorg group D13 in Oslo,  to whom Waaler reported, and from Jens Christian Hauge, head of the whole Milorg organisation. In the event no case was ever brought against him. In 1948 Waaler was employed as a legal adviser in cases arising out of legislation on prices, rationing and supply. In 1949 he was a witness in the *landssvik* trial of his old boss Jørgen Nordvik that resulted in a sentence of fourteen years' forced labour for Quisling's former public prosecutor. Shortly afterwards, Waaler was appointed district attorney in the Troms and Finnmark region in the far north of Norway. In 1952 he married his secretary, Rannveig Sigmundsdatter Einarson, twenty years his junior. In 1967 he was given special leave to attend the trial of the former head of the Gestapo in Norway, Hellmuth Reinhard. There in the Baden-Baden courtroom he heard a tale unfold that in its strangeness almost rivals the miserable odyssey of Sverre Riisnæs. It seems that in the very early days of the war Reinhard had changed his surname from Patzschke to the more Germanic-sounding Reinhard and in 1940, as Hellmuth Reinhard, married Gunhild Röschmann. In the chaos following the German surrender in May 1945 Reinhard managed to disappear by reverting to his pre-war name and tweaking the spelling slightly to become Hellmuth

Patschke. By 1948 he was on the staff of a weekly magazine, the *Betriebsberater*, and in December 1951 managed the extraordinary feat of marrying his own widow, Gunhild having registered her husband Hellmuth Reinhard as 'presumed dead' earlier in the year.

In due course Reinhard/Patschke started a publishing house in Baden-Baden and lived a quiet and industrious life until some sharp-eyed bureaucrat in the department investigating war crimes noted the oddity of a widow marrying a man with almost exactly the same name as her own former husband. Investigations were made and Reinhard's true identity and significance emerged. He was arrested in 1964 and held in custody pending trial on charges of war crimes. Found guilty, he was sentenced in June 1967 to five years' forced labour and three years' loss of social privileges as an accessory in four of the *Blumenpflücken* murders carried out on the orders of his housemate, Albert Weiner. He was also found guilty of the murder of a resistance man named Olav Sanden during a raid in Hokksund, and for the 'unlawful deprivation of liberty' of Norwegian Jews that ushered in the Norwegian holocaust. The statute of limitations for crimes of this nature was set at fifteen years; too many years had passed since their commission and no sentence was ever imposed on the charge. Reinhard was released from jail in 1970 and died in 2002 at the age of ninety-one.

Another among the small party of Norwegians who attended Reinhard's trial in 1967 was Knut Kleve, one of the young Norwegians held at Grini whom Reinhard had started to befriend towards the end of the occupation. By the 1960s the adult Kleve had embarked on an academic career as a classical philologist, in the course of which he developed a new method for the restoration of carbonised papyrus fragments that led to the reconstruction of lost works by the Roman writers Lucretius and Ennius. Rather nobly, Kleve had agreed to appear as a sort of character witness for Reinhard, though he refused all of Reinhard's subsequent attempts to continue what the former Gestapo leader clearly thought of as a normal friendship.

Albert Weiner was not as lucky as Reinhard. He too changed

his name following the German surrender and acquired forged documents that identified him as a Czech citizen named Hans Zrenner. However, Major W.D. Roberts, head of the British intelligence agency responsible for tracking down and capturing wanted German Nazis in Norway, was able to expose his true identity and he was arrested and held under armed guard at Akershus Fortress. There, on 4 December, Weiner provided a statement corroborating in every detail the account Gunnar Waaler had given of the nature of the relationship between Weiner and himself during the final months of the war. Weiner's statement proved to be of immense value to Waaler. After reading it he felt compelled to say that, in spite of the many terrible things he now knew Weiner to have been guilty of, he nevertheless owed his life to him and was grateful. Two weeks later, on 17 December 1945, in circumstances that remain unclear, Weiner managed to overpower the guard outside his prison cell and seize his gun. He then killed his cell-mate Erich Lorenz – either because he believed Lorenz to be a stool pigeon planted on him by the British or because Lorenz had been ordered to prevent him from committing suicide and had tried to do so – before turning the gun on himself.

A few weeks after he returned from Reinhard's trial in Baden-Baden, Waaler was appointed district attorney for Trondheim, a post in which he remained until his retirement in 1974. In a valedictory note, the Trondheim daily newspaper *Adressavisen* praised this enigmatic man for the 'thoroughness' of his work. His wife Rannveig died on 7 May 1980 at the age of fifty-five. Waaler survived until March 1987. The couple had no children.

Reparations to the Norwegian Jews

Of the hundreds of Jewish men, women and children who had their property confiscated before being deported from Norway and killed in concentration and extermination camps in Germany and occupied Poland, only twenty-nine returned. For several decades the fate of the Norwegian Jews remained a nightmare within a greater nightmare and the material losses involved regarded almost an act of God. The special magnitude of the injustice was not fully realised until the appearance of the second volume of Oskar Mendelsohn's monumental *Jødenes historie i Norge gjennom 300 år* (Three Hundred Years of Jewish History in Norway) in 1987, with its detailed account of a process in which 230 complete families of Norwegian Jews had been wiped out. When Kai Feinberg's *Prisoner Number 79108 Returns* was published in 1995, this memoir of Feinberg's time as a prisoner and slave and of his return to Norway and his exhausted arrival at the old family home on Jonas Reins gate 9 gave a face and a narrative to the suffering. In the same year the journalist Bjørn Westlie took up the matter of financial restitution – or the lack of it – in a series of articles in *Dagens Næringsliv* (The Business Daily). In March 1966 the government appointed a committee to look into the situation. Following its report, the Norwegian Storting voted in March 1999 to pay restitution to the Norwegian Jewish community of 340 million kroner, a sum worth 58 million US dollars at the time, in today's values just over 105 million US dollars. A small part of the grant went towards the conversion of the Villa Grande mansion on the Bygdøy peninsula into a Centre for Studies of the Holocaust and Religious Minorities. It was an apt fate for a building that had been, for much of the war, the home of the Norwegian Führer Vidkun Quisling.

Chronology

1940

9 April: Norway is invaded and occupied by German troops. The king and government flee the capital and begin a journey northwards through the country. In an attempted coup that lasts just a few days, Vidkun Quisling declares himself prime minister of Norway.

18 April: *Nortraship* is established by an emergency decree of the Norwegian government. All Norwegian ships over 500 metric tons not already sailing for the British, Norwegian or French governments are placed at the government's disposal.

24 April: Hitler appoints Josef Terboven his Reichskommissar in Norway.

10 May: Winston Churchill succeeds Neville Chamberlain as British prime minister. German troops attack France, Belgium, the Netherlands and Luxembourg.

10 May: On German orders, radios belonging to Norwegian Jews are confiscated by the Norwegian police.

12 May: Norwegian POWs captured in southern Norway are released. Professional soldiers are required to pledge not to take up arms again.

7 June: King Haakon VII and his Norwegian government escape to England.

10 June: Norway surrenders. The military campaign ends.

22 June: France is occupied and divided. The Germans occupy the north of the country, while a collaborationist regime under Pétain is established in the south.

10 July–31 October: Battle of Britain, the battle for air supremacy over the British Isles.

22 August: At a price of NOK 100 each, a Gjøvik car mechanic buys several British planes destroyed by the Germans in Gudbrandsdalen.

27 August: A man found guilty of stealing a bicycle in Hokksund is sentenced to ten months in prison and ten-year loss of civil rights.

25 September: Terboven bans all political parties in Norway except Quisling's *Nasjonal Samling* (NS). He appoints an advisory cabinet of Norwegian NS members.

27 September: Germany, Italy and Japan sign the Tripartite Pact of alliance.

21 December: The Norwegian Supreme Court resigns from office.

1941

29 January: Heinrich Himmler arrives in Norway. He spends three weeks travelling through the country.

March: The American President Franklin D. Roosevelt signs the Lend-Lease Agreement enabling the Allies to obtain American-produced weapons and military equipment.

21 March: An Oslo shoe shop is closed down and the owner accused of selling shoes to the value of NOK 940,000 without coupons and at a markup of 79 per cent.

26 March: Five men accused of the theft and sale of spare tyres from German lorries are sentenced by a German military court to four years in a house of correction. Three men who bought the stolen goods, including a policeman, are sentenced to two years in jail.

April: German troops occupy the Greek capital, Athens.

22 June: Barbarossa, the German invasion of the Soviet Union, marks the end of the non-aggression pact between the two countries.

30 June: *Landsorganisasjon* (LO, Norwegian Confederation of Trade Unions) delivers a formal protest against arrests and assaults and threatens strike action.

20 July: The communist-led Osvald Group begins its campaign of sabotage following the end of the Nazi–Soviet non-aggression pact.

10 September: Terboven responds to the so-called 'Milk Strike' by declaring a Civilian State of Emergency. Two union members, Viggo Hansteen and Rolf Wickstrøm, are arrested, tried and executed.

29 October: Supplies of original brands of whisky, cognac and French liqueur run out at the *Vinmonopolet* (state-run off-licence).

10 November: A National Unity member is appointed new leader of the Norwegian LO.

6 December: The German attack on Moscow is repelled.

7 December: The Japanese attack the American fleet in Pearl Harbor and invade Burma and the Philippines.

8 December: The United States declares war on Japan.

11 December: Germany declares war on the United States.

1942

22 January: Norwegian Jews are ordered to have their passports and ID cards stamped with a 'J'.

1 February: Vidkun Quisling becomes minister-president of Norway under the so-called *Statsakt* (State Act) and attempts to impose a national socialist revolution on Norway. The *holdningskamp* (Conscience Struggle) begins in earnest, pitting the church, the schools and the parents against the Quisling administration.

15 February: The Japanese occupy Singapore.

14 March: 14,000 teachers refuse to join *Lærersambandet*, the new Nazi teachers' union.

20 March: 1,100 teachers are arrested; 647 are sent as slave labour to Kirkenes, on the border with Russia in the far north of Norway.

15 April: The Norwegian government in exile issues the so-called 'Bigamy Law' in London. This amendment to the Marriage Act makes it possible for one party unilaterally to terminate a marriage when the couple involved have no contact due to the state of war.

30 April: The village of Telavåg is burned to the ground following the killing of two German policemen. Eighteen prisoners are executed in reprisal.

27 May: A leading figure in the SS, Reinhard Heydrich, is attacked by members of the Czech resistance in Prague. Heydrich is mortally wounded and dies on 4 June.

1 June: Tobacco rationing is introduced.

June: American victory in the Battle of Midway, with decisive consequences for the war in the Pacific.

6 June: Shoes and gloves made of fish skin begin to appear on the market.

10 June: Four men die in Trondheim after drinking *tresprit* (methanol).

28 June–September: Second German offensive against the Soviet Union. German troops reach Stalingrad and occupy the Crimean Peninsula.

August: Hairdressers begin sending cut hair to a felt factory in Flekkefjord where it is processed for use in chairs, under rugs, as insoles for shoes, etc.

28 August: Arrest of three Oslo men for impersonating Norwegian State Police officers and threatening to arrest a businessman and his wife and have them transported to Germany for selling goods without a ration card.

1 September: Potato rationing is introduced.

16 September: Dentists report that schoolchildren's teeth have never been healthier. This is attributed to the shortage of sweets and sugar products and bread made of whole-wheat flour, eaten dry.

25 September: Four De Havilland Mosquito aircraft attack the Gestapo headquarters at Victoria terrasse in Oslo, killing eighty civilians.

6 October: Civilian State of Emergency declared in Trondheim.

25 October: All male Jews are arrested.

23–24 October: British victory over German and Italian forces at El Alamein in Egypt.

30 October: The entire tobacco quota for November is stolen from Tiedemann's tobacco factory in Grimstad.

21 November: A spate of thefts from boats in Bergen for the alcohol in the ships' spirit compasses occurs.

28 November: Fifteen centres are established in northern Norway and eleven in the south for the collection of fish skin for use in tanning.

25 November: All remaining Jews are arrested and transported on the SS *Donau* to Auschwitz and other death camps for liquidation or slave labour.

November: The Germans occupy the south of France, which has been administered since June 1940 by Marshal Pétain's collaborationist regime.

19 December: Major General Carl Gustav Fleischer, who led the field campaign in northern Norway and coordinated Norwegian, French, Polish and British forces in the recapture of Narvik on 28 May 1940, commits suicide in Ottawa, Canada.

1943

18 January: Forty thousand cigarettes as well as large amounts of snuff and chewing tobacco are stolen from Langaard's tobacco factory in Bergen.

26 January: The Norwegian tanker *Nortind* with its cargo of petrol is torpedoed and sunk south of Iceland. All thirty-four Norwegian and seven British crew members perish.

4 February: Minister-President Quisling orders public mourning following the German defeat at Stalingrad. All places of entertainment are to be closed for four days.

15 February: Three men claiming to be Sipo investigators visit a woman in Amtmann Meinichs gate. They confiscate her bottles of spirit and tobacco and hand her a receipt before disappearing.

26 February: Organising or taking part in public dances are forbidden by the Ministry of Policing.

28 February: Norwegian saboteurs trained in England sabotage the German heavy water plant at Rjukan in Telemark.

3 March: Ten British Mosquito planes attack the Molybdenum mining operations at Knaben in Vest-Agder, with widespread material damage to the site. Seventeen civilians killed.

15 March: Fifty workers at Kalhovde, near Rjukan, are taken ill after drinking methanal intended for use as anti-freeze. Six die, the remainder recover.

19 April–16 May: The Warsaw Ghetto uprising in Poland is quashed. Thirteen thousand Jews are killed.

20 April: The Osvald Group starts the campaign against *Arbeidstjenesten* (AT, National Work Service) by blowing up the service's offices at Pilestredet 31 in central Oslo.

10 May: Tobacco rationing is again reduced. For men the ration per clip on a rationing card is now 100 grams of tobacco or eighty cigarettes and for women twenty cigarettes over a thirty-eight-day period.

21 June: A group of around twenty armed young men raid a factory in Oslo's Skjoldgata that produces ersatz coffee. They steal thirty sacks of raw coffee and twenty sacks of sugar, locking up the workers before driving away.

24 June: The novelist Knut Hamsun's speech to the International Journalists Convention in Vienna is delivered in German by an interpreter. In it Hamsun claims that 'Sympathy for England is a fatal affliction for the human race. England must be brought to its knees before there can be peace on earth.'

5 July: The Soviet Union repels the Germans at a battle near Kursk.

23 July: The Norwegian tanker *Alcides* is torpedoed by a Japanese U-boat in the Indian Ocean en route from Abadan to Australia. Two lifeboats are launched and the captain, wireless operator and mate taken on board the U-boat. Still on the lifeboats, the remaining fifty-two survivors from the *Alcides* are killed by rifle and machine-gun fire.

16 August: Police officer Gunnar Eilifsen is arrested for insubordination, tried by the Police Special Court and executed the following day.

18 August: Mainline railways in southern Norway are sabotaged in a series of attacks.

August: Allied forces occupy Sicily.

9 September: Allied troops land at Salerno in south-western Italy.

6 November: Soviet troops liberate Kiev.

19 December: Ammunition being off-loaded from a German ship docked at Filipstad in Oslo explodes. It starts a chain reaction of explosions that kills seventy-five Germans and thirty-eight Norwegians. Damage to property is extensive and hundreds are left homeless in central Oslo.

1944

22 January–5 June: Allied troops land near Anzio, south of Rome, and defeat German and Italian forces.

19 February: The Tinnsjø ferry carrying heavy water processed at the Rjukan plant and destined for Germany is sabotaged and the ferry sinks. Fourteen Norwegian civilians lose their lives.

4 March: Requisitioning of pet dogs in Norway for use on the Eastern Front. All dogs are to be registered with name, breed and estimated age. Of specific interest to the German military are Alsatians, Great Danes, Dobermans, Airedales, Boxers, St Bernards and Giant Schnauzers. Paragraph 4 of the ordinance prohibits any attempt to evade its terms by killing the dog, selling it or in any other way attempting to avoid the order on pain of a prison sentence of up to three years' hard labour.

4 June: Allied forces enter Rome.

6 June: D-Day, the Allied landings in Normandy in northern France.

1 August–2 October: The Warsaw Uprising: the Polish underground attempts and fails to liberate Warsaw from German occupation.

25 August: Allied forces enter Paris.

September: Allied forces mass on the German border.

4 September: The Continuation War between Finland and the Soviet Union ends. The Finns agree to expel German forces from their territory.

17–25 September: Operation Market Garden – the Allied attempt to create an invasion route into northern Germany by taking a number of Rhine bridges ends in failure.

4 October: Allied planes bomb the German U-boat bunker at Laksevåg near Bergen. A school is hit as well as other civilian buildings; 193 Norwegians die.

25 October: Russian troops liberate Kirkenes on Norway's northern border.

28 October: Hitler orders a scorched-earth policy in Finnmark in the north of Norway. Sixty thousand people are forcibly evacuated south. Another 25,000 take refuge in the surrounding countryside.

16 December–25 January 1945: German troops mount the Ardennes Offensive against the Allies. The offensive fails.

31 December: Twelve RAF De Havilland Mosquitos attempting to bomb Gestapo headquarters in central Oslo hit a crowded tram passing the National Theatre. Eighty-seven people are killed and more than 1,000 rendered homeless.

December: France, most of Belgium and part of the southern Netherlands are liberated.

1945

12 January: Soviet forces liberate Krakow and Warsaw.

27 January: Auschwitz, Nazi extermination camp in occupied Poland, is liberated by the Red Army.

8 February: Killing of the head of the Norwegian State Police, Karl A. Marthinsen. Twenty-nine prisoners are executed in reprisal.

13–15 February: 800 British and 400 American planes bomb and largely destroy the German city of Dresden. Estimates put the number of civilians dead at between twenty-five and thirty-five thousand.

March: Widespread sabotage of the rail network in Norway in order to prevent German troops from being transported to mainland Europe to join the fighting on Germany's borders.

10 April: American forces liberate Buchenwald concentration camp near Weimar and free the prisoners.

13 April: Soviet troops enter Vienna.

15 April: British troops enter Bergen-Belsen concentration camp at Celle in Germany and free the prisoners.

30 April: Adolf Hitler and his wife Eva Braun commit suicide. The bodies are burned.

8 May: The war in Norway ends as the German High Command in Norway surrenders to the British at Lillehammer.

9 May: Vidkun Quisling and his ministers are arrested pending trial for treason.

7 June: King Haakon VII returns, five years to the day since his departure for England. General Andrew Thorne, in charge of the British forces in Norway and *de facto* head of the government following the German capitulation, formally returns control of the country to the king. The occupation of Norway is over.

6 July: Norway declares that it has been at war with Japan since 7 December 1941. This is to facilitate the claim for reparations for the 900 Norwegians, mostly missionaries and seamen, held in Japanese prison camps during the war.

6–9 August: American planes drop atom bombs on Hiroshima and Nagasaki.

15 August: The Japanese Emperor Hirohito surrenders. The Second World War is over.

Endnotes

1. Online resource (in Norwegian) at: www.arkivverket.no/utforsk-arkivene/andre-verdenskrig/krigen-bryter-ut/adolf-hitler-pa-visitt-i-sognefjorden
2. Berit Nøkleby, *Hitlers Norge. Okkupasjonsmakten 1940–1945* (Oslo: Cappelen Damm, 2016), p. 16.
3. Robert Ferguson, 'Nikolai Astrup and the Creation of a Norwegian National Identity', in MaryAnne Stevens (ed.), *Nikolai Astrup: Visions of Norway* (New Haven and London: Yale University Press, 2021), pp. 24–30.
4. Robert Ferguson, *Henrik Ibsen: A New Biography* (London: Richard Cohen Books, 1996), p. 204.
5. Robert Ferguson, *Enigma: The Life of Knut Hamsun* (London: Hutchinson, 1987), p. 143.
6. Robert Ferguson, *The Cabin in the Mountains: A Norwegian Odyssey* (London: Head of Zeus, 2019), p. 131.
7. Robert Ferguson, *Scandinavians: In Search of the Soul of the North* (London: Head of Zeus, 2017), p. 302.
8. Hilde Harbo (ed.), *Min 9. april. Øyenvitne forteller* (Oslo: Vigmostad and Bjørke, 2016), p. 56.
9. Ibid. p. 67.
10. Ingrid Bjerkås, *Mitt kall* (Oslo: Cappelen, 1966), p. 12.
11. Nils Petter Thuesen, *Oslo under andre verdenskrig* (Oslo: Historie & Kulture, 2015), p. 44.

12. Jan Christensen and Moland Arnfinn, *Myter om krigen i Norge 1940–1945* (Oslo: Nova, 2011), p. 25.
13. Dag O. Bruknapp and Thomas Nilsen *Vidkun Quisling. Fra Fedrelandselsker til Landssviker* (Skallestad: Ares forlag, 2019), p. 99.
14. Hans Fredrik Dahl, *En kort historie om rettsoppgjøret etter krigen* (Oslo: Pax, 2018), p. 8.
15. John Grehan and Martin Mace, *The Battle for Norway 1940–1942* (Barnsley: Pen and Sword Military, 2015), p. viii.
16. Per Jahr *Tre skritt bak: mennesker og opplevelser som Quislings unge adjutant så dem* (Oslo: Historisk forlag, 2002), p. 20.
17. Berit Nøkleby *Det Tyske Okkupasjonsstyret i Norge* (Oslo: Norges Hjemmefrontmuseum, 2002), p. 16.
18. Odd Hølaas (ed.), *Norge under Haakon VII* (Oslo: J.W. Cappelens forlag, 1946), p. 432.
19. Heather Pringle, 'Fra forfedrenes rom til «Ahnenerbe»: Himmlers forskningsinstitutt'. In Terje Emberland and Sem Jorunn Fure (eds.), *Jakten på Germania* (Oslo: Humanist forlag, 2009), p. 132.
20. Online resource: www.the-orb.arlima.net/orb_done/dudo/11-conquest
21. Terje Emberland and Matthew Kott, *Himmlers Norge. Nordmenn I Det Storgermanske Prosjekt* (Oslo: Aschehoug, 2012), p. 80.
22. Pål A. Berg, *Kirke i Krig. Den norske kirke under 2. Verdenskrig 1940–45* (Oslo: Genesis, 1999), p. 203.
23. Eivind Berggrav, *Da kampen kom* (Oslo: Land og kirke, 1945), pp. 166–179.
24. Per Voskø (ed.), *Krigens Dagbok Norge 1940–1945* (Oslo: Det Beste, 1984), p. 136.
25. Harald Berntsen, *To Liv – Én Skjebne. Viggo Hansteen. Rolf Wickstrøm* (Oslo: Aschehoug, 1995), p. 8.
26. Ibid. p. 155.
27. Ibid. p. 9.
28. *Aftenposten*, 53, 2 February 1942. pp. 10–13.
29. Henrik Ibsen to Georg Brandes, 17 February 1871. Online resource at: www.ibsen.uio.no/BREV_1844-1871ht%7CB18710217GB.xhtml
30. Per Voksø (ed.), *Krigens Dagbok* (Oslo: Forlaget Det Beste, 1984), p. 204.
31. Ibid.
32. Hans Fredrik Dahl et al., *Norsk Krigsleksikon 1940–45* (Oslo: J.W. Cappelens forlag, 1995), p. 129.
33. Pål A. Berg, *Kirke i Krig* (Kjeller: Genesis forlag, 1999), p. 209.
34. Online resource at: www.norgeshistorie.no/kilder/andre-

verdenskrig/K1726-kirkens-grunn.html
35. Nicola Karcher *Kampen om skolen. Nazifisering og lærernes motstand i det okkuperte Norge* (Oslo: Dreyers forlag, 2018), p. 155.
36. *Adressavisen*, 20 March 2017. Online resource at: www.adressa.no/midtnorskdebatt/i/y72a8R/slik-var-laerernes-kamp-mot-naziskolen
37. Vegard Kvam, *Skolefronten. Einar Høigård i norsk skole, pedagogikk og samfunnsliv* (Oslo: Scandinavian Academic Press, 2013), pp. 264–268.
38. Ibid. pp. 259–260.
39. Luke chapter 12, verses 4–5.
40. Ingrid Bjerkås, *Mitt kall* (Oslo: Cappelen, 1966), p. 21.
41. Aud Valborg Tønnessen, *Ingrid Bjerkås. Motstandskvinnen som ble vår første kvinnelige prest* (Oslo: Pax, 2014), p. 52.
42. Bjarte Bruland, *Holocaust i Norge. Registrering. Deportasjon. Tilintetgjørelse* (Oslo: Dreyers forlag, 2017), p. 187.
43. Ibid. p. 17.
44. Nils Petter Thuesen, *Oslo under andre verdenskrig* (Oslo: Historie & Kulture, 2015), p. 237.
45. Ragnar Ulstein, *Svensketraffiken I. Flyktningar til Sverige 1940–43* (Oslo: Det Norske Samlaget, 1974), p. 225.
46. Sigrid Helliesen Lund, *Alltid underveis* (Oslo: Tiden, 1981), p. 99.
47. Kai Feinberg and Arnt Stefansen, *Fange nr 79108 vender tilbake* (Oslo: Cappelen, 1995), p. 57.
48. Ibid. p. 27.
49. Myrtle Wright, *Norwegian Diary 1940–1945* (London: Friends Peace International Committee, 1974), p. 170.
50. Arnfinn Moland, *Over Grensen. Hjemmefrontens likvidasjoner under tyske okkupasjonen av Norge 1940–1945* (Oslo: Orion, 1999), p. 49.
51. Asbjørn Sunde, *Menn i Mørket* (Oslo: Spartacus, 2010), pp. 103–107.
52. *Store norske leksikon*. Online resource at: snl.no/Asbj%C3%B8rn_Sunde
53. no.wikipedia.org/wiki/Lars_Roar_Langslet
54. Thoralf Berg, *Henry Gleditsch. Skuespiller. Teatergründer. Motstandsmann* (Trondheim: Communicatio forlag, 2007), p. 60.
55. Ibid. p. 67.
56. Ibid. pp. 110–112.
57. This and all subsequent material relating to Gunnar Waaler are from the Gunnar Waaler archives. Riksarkivet (National Archives and

Regional State Archives of Oslo), RA/s – 3138 – 01/D/De/L 0061.
58. Sverre Rødder, *Min Ære er Troskap. Om politiminister Jonas Lie* (Oslo: Aschehoug, 1990), p. 157.
59. Takala, Hannu, and Tham, Henrik (eds.), *Krig og moral. Kriminalitet og kontroll i Norden under andre verdenskrig* (Oslo: Universitets forlag, 1987), pp. 165–166.
60. Knut Kleve in *Levende Historie*, 1 (2003), pp. 33–35.
61. Ibid. pp. 33–35.
62. Arnfinn Moland, *Over Grensen? Hjemmfrontens likvidasjoner under den tyske okkupasjonen av Norge 1940–1945* (Oslo: Orion forlag, 1999), p. 153.
63. *Nå* magazine, 21 (1962), p. 2.
64. Bernt Rougthvedt, *Med Penn og Pistol. Om politimesteren Jonas Lie* (Oslo: Cappelen Damm, 2011), p. 307.
65. Alf R. Jacobsen, *Skjebnehøst. Nord-Norge 1944* (Oslo: Vega forlag, 2017), p. 242.
66. Per Voksø (ed.), *Krigens Dagbok* (Oslo: Forlaget Det Beste, 1984), p. 466.
67. Ibid. p. 464.
68. Arne Fjellbu, *Minner fra krigsårene* (Oslo: Land og kirke, 1946), p. 183.
69. Arnfinn Moland, *Over Grensen. Hjemmefrontens likvidasjoner under tyske okkupasjonen av Norge 1940–1945* (Oslo: Orion, 1999), p. 166.
70. Nils Johan Ringdal, *Gal mann til rett tid. NS-minister Sverre Riisnæs. En psykobiografi* (Oslo: Aschehoug Profiler, 2004), pp. 131–132.
71. Nils Petter Thuesen, *Oslo under Andre Verdenskrig* (Oslo: Historie og Kulture, 2015), p. 536.
72. Article by Alf R. Jacobsen at: www.klikk.no/historie/josef-terbovens-siste-timer-6809726
73. Berit Nøkleby, *Josef Terboven. Hitlers mann i Norge* (Oslo: Gyldendal Norsk forlag, 1992), p. 298.
74. Bernt Rougthvedt, *Med Penn og Pistol. Om politimesteren Jonas Lie* (Oslo: Cappelen Damm, 2011), p. 342.
75. This account is based on contemporary newspaper reports of the siege at Skallum that also contained interviews with Riisnæs, Lie and Rogstad: *Asker og Bærums Budstikke*, Friday 11 May 1945; *Dagbladet*, Monday 14 May 1945; on the account in *Morgenbladet*, Friday 2 December 1983; and on Jens Wulfsberg and Per O. Andresen, *Milorg 13313 – Gruppens Historie og opplevelser* (Oslo:

Ch. Dybwads Bokhandel 1948), pp. 89–106.
76. Hans Fredrik Dahl, *En kort historie om rettsoppgjøret etter krigen* (Oslo: Pax, 2018), p. 43.
77. Sjur Isaaksen, *Ulykkelig fred. I frigjøringens skygger* (Oslo: Vårt Lands forlag, 2020), p. 37.
78. Peter Lykke-Seest, *Omkring Quisling-Prosessen* (Oslo: Cammermeyers Boghandel, 1945), pp. 134–135.
79. Eivnd Berggrav, *Front – Fangenskap – Flukt 1942–45* (Oslo: Forlaget Land og Kirke, 1966), pp. 30–36.
80. Hannah Arendt, *Eichmann in Jerusalem. A Report on the Banality of Evil* (London: Penguin, 2006), p. 247.
81. Dagfinn Hauge, *Slik dør menn* (Oslo: Lutherstiftelsens forlag, 1947), p. 27.
82. The main sources for the Epilogue are Gunnar Waaler's two short accounts of the trial and execution of Knut Mathiesen delivered to his Milorg contact on 6 May 1944 (Gunnar Waaler, 'Særdomstolen I arbeid: Saken mot grensepolitibetjent Hauglands drapsmann, chauffør Mathisen', 4 May 1944 (copy), HLS Oslo); and Dagfinn Hauge's account of Knut Mathiesen's final night, 'En kveld i Kronprinsens gate', pp. 108–118 of *Slik Dør Menn*.
83. Terje Valvatne Foss, 'Henrik Hebo – Politimester Jonas Lie's (… og mange flyktningers…) sjåfør', Politihøgskolen (April 2003).
84. Max Manus, *Det blir alvor* (Oslo: Essforlagene, 1953), pp. 30–34.
85. Jakob Sverdrup, 'Veien til Atlanterhavspakten 9. april 1940 – 4. april 1949', in John Kristen Skogan (ed.), *I frigjøringens spor. Artikler i anledning frigjøringsjubileet 1995* (Oslo: Universitetsforlaget, 1995), pp. 35–54.
86. Brita Garden, *– Ikke et ondt ord om han dr. Eng! Lege for Quisling og Kvænangen* (Oslo: Styrk, 2016), pp. 161–170.
87. Helge Åmotsbakken, 'Quislings livlege – fortsatt nazist', in *Vi Menn* (1 August 1978), pp. 2–4. As online resource at: http://www.sno.no/db/index/page:288/sort:dok_dato/direction:desc/q:Folk%20og%20Land
88. Aud Valborg Tønnessen, *Ingrid Bjerkås. Moststandskvinnen som ble vår første kvinnelige prest* (Oslo: Pax forlag, 2014), pp. 81–103.
89. Morten Conradi and Alf Skjeseth, *Osvald. Storsabotøren Asbjørn Sunde* (Oslo: Spartacus forlag, 2016), pp. 261–262.

Bibliography

Andenæs, Johs., *Det vanskelige oppgjøret. Rettsoppgjøret etter okkupasjonen* (Oslo: Tanum-Norli, 1979).
Arendt, Hanna, *Eichmann in Jerusalem. A Report on the Banality of Evil* (London: Penguin, 2006).
Berentsen, Aksel, *Ola Fritzner. En norsk kapteins kamp før og etter frigjøringen* (Oslo: Arne Gimnes forlag, 1949).
Berg, Pål A., *Kirke i krig. Den norske kirke under 2. Verdenskrig 1940–45* (Kjeller: Genesis forlag, 1999).
Berg, Thoralf, *Henry Gleditsch. Skuespiller, teatergründer, motstandsmann* (Trondheim: Communicatio forlag, 2007).
Bergfald, Odd, *Hellmuth Reinhard. Soldat eller morder* (Oslo: Schibsteds forlag, 1967).
Berggrav, Eivind, *Da kampen kom. Noen blad fra startåret* (Oslo: Land og Kirke, 1945).
—, *Folkedommen over NS. Hva vil være rett av oss?* (Oslo: Land og Kirke, 1945).
Berntsen, Harald, *To liv – én skjebne. Viggo Hansteen og Rolf Wickstrøm* (Oslo: Aschehoug, 1995).
Beslaglagte bøker. Liste over de bøker, forfattere og forlag som var forbudt under krigen (Oslo: Biblioteksentralen, 1995).
Bjerkås, Ingrid, *Mitt kall* (Oslo: J.W. Cappelens forlag, 1966).
Bruknapp, Dag O., and Nilsen, Thomas, *Vidkun Quisling. Fra Fedrelandselsker til Landssviker* (Skallestad: Ares forlag, 2019).
Bruland, Bjarte, *Øyenvitner. Rapport etter norske jøders hjemkomst fra*

konsentrasjonsleirene (Oslo: Dinamo forlag, 2012).
—, *Holocaust i Norge. Registrering, deportasjon, tilintetgjørelse* (Oslo: Dreyers forlag, 2017).
Carruthers, Bob, *Hitler's Wartime Orders. The Complete Führer Directives 1939-1945* (Barnsley: Pen and Sword Military, 2018).
Christensen, Jan, *Oslogjengen. Europas beste sabotørgruppe* (Oslo: Orion forlag, 2005).
—, *Myter om krigen i Norge 1940-1945* (Oslo: Nova forlag, 2011).
Conradi, Morten, and Skjeseth, Alf, *Osvald. Storsabotøren Asbjørn Sunde* (Oslo: Spartacus forlag, 2016).
Dahl, Hans Fredrik, *Vidkun Quisling. En fører for fall* (Oslo: Aschehoug, 1992).
—, *En kort historie om rettsoppgjøret etter krigen* (Oslo: Pax forlag, 2018).
— (ed.), *Krigen i Norge* (Oslo: Pax forlag, 1974).
—, Hagtvet, Bernt, and Hjeltnes, Guri, *Den norske nasjonalsosialismen. Nasjonal samling 1933-1945 i tekst og bilder* (Oslo: Pax forlag, 1982).
—, et al. (eds.), *Norsk krigsleksikon. 1940-1945* (Oslo: J.W. Cappelens forlag, 1995).
Dahl, Willy, *Max Mauser - men Jonas Lie. Ein studie i dikt og liv* (Bergen: Eide forlag, 1990).
Diesen, Gerd Øfwerman, *Dagbok fra andre verdenskrig 1939-1945. En ung oslokvinnes beretning* (Oslo: Kolofon forlag, 2019).
Dybvig, Kjersti, *Jøder og politi i Stavanger* (Oslo: Pax forlag, 2012).
Eggen, Eystein, *Gutten fra Gimle: et NS-barns beretning* (Oslo: Aschehoug, 1993).
Emberland, Terje, *Religion og rase. Nyhedenskap og Nazisme i Norge 1933 - 1945* (Oslo: Humanist forlag, 2003).
—, and Kott, Matthew, *Himmlers Norge. Nordmenn i Det storgermanske prosjekt* (Oslo: Aschehoug, 2012).
—, and Fure, Jorunn Sem (eds.), *Jakten på Germania. Fra nordensvermeri til SS-arkeologi* (Oslo: Humanist forlag, 2009).
Esborg, Line (ed.), *Krigshverdag. Oslo-kvinner forteller* (Oslo: Norsk folkemuseum, 1995).
Fanebust, Frode, *Krigshistorien TM. Toralv Fanebust og sannheten* (Oslo: Pax forlag, 2009).
Feinberg, Kai, and Stefansen, Arnt, *Fange nr. 79108 vender tilbake* (Oslo: J.W. Cappelens forlag, 1995).
Ferguson, Robert, *Enigma: The Life of Knut Hamsun* (New York: Farrar, Straus & Giroux, 1988).
—, *Henrik Ibsen: A New Biography* (New York: Dorset Press, 2001).

—, *The Hammer and the Cross: A New History of the Vikings* (London: Penguin, 2010).
—, *Scandinavians: In Search of the Soul of the North* (London: Head of Zeus, 2017).
—, *The Cabin in the Mountains: A Norwegian Odyssey* (London: Head of Zeus, 2019).
Fyrst, Walter, *Min sti* (Oslo: Eget forlag, 1981).
Gallagher, Thomas, *Assault in Norway: Sabotaging the Nazi Nuclear Program* (Connecticut: Lyons Press, 2002).
Garden, Brita, – *Ikke et ondt ord om han Dr Eng. Lege for Quisling – og Kvænangen* (Oslo: Styrk, 2016).
Godøy, Bjørn Are, *Okkupert. En oppdatert historie om andre verdenskrig i Norge* (Bergen: Vigmostad og Bjørke, 2018).
Grehan, John, and Mace, Martin, (eds.), *The Battle for Norway 1940–1942* (Barnsley: Pen and Sword Military, 2015).
Grimnes, Ole Kristian, *Norge under andre verdenskrig 1939–1945* (Oslo: Aschehoug, 2018).
Grüner-Hegge, Rolf, *Gestapo henter deg om natten* (Oslo: Gyldendal Norsk forlag, 1990).
Grünfeld, Nina F., *Ninas barn. Fortellingen om det jødiske barnehjemmet i Oslo* (Oslo: Kagge forlag, 2015).
Guhnfeldt, Cato, *Bomb gestapo-hovedkvarteret!* (Oslo: Wings, 1995).
Gylseth, Hals Christopher, *Operasjon Blumenpflücken. Gestapos hemmelige terrorplan* (Oslo: Aschehoug, 2013).
Halleraker, Tormod, *Gulosten. Kjeltring, motstandsmann og kongevenn. En biografi om Johannes S. Andersen* (Oslo: Juritzen forlag, 2015).
Halse, Steinar (ed.), *Humøret kan ingen ta fra oss. Vitser, anekdoter og sanger fra okkupasjonen 1940–45* (Oslo: Grøndahl Dreyer, 1993).
Hamsun, Tore, *Efter år og dag. Selvbiografi* (Oslo: Gyldendal norsk forlag, 1990).
Harbo, Hilde (ed.), *Min 9. april. Øyenvitne Forteller* (Bergen: Vigmostad og Bjørke, 2016).
Hauge, Dagfinn, *Slik dør menn* (Oslo: Lutherstiftelsens forlag, 1947).
Hellesen, Gunnar, *Benådet* (Oslo: Tiden Nork forlag, 1968).
Hem, Per E., *Mannen fra underverdenen. Gulosten – et forbryterliv* (Oslo: Aschehoug, 2017).
Hjeltnes, Guri (ed.), *Krigshverdag. Bilder fra norske familiealbumer 1940–45* (Oslo: Schibsted, 1990).
Hjeltnes, Guri (ed.), *Norge i krig. Bind 5. Hverdagsliv* (Oslo: Aschehoug, 1986).

Holst, Jan Erik (ed.) *To liv – Zwei Leben* (Tvedestrand: Bokbyen forlag, 2019).
Høidal, Oddvar, *Trotskij i Norge, et sår som aldri gror* (Oslo: Spartacus forlag, 2009).
Hølaas, Odd (ed.), *Norge under Haakon VII* (Oslo: J.W. Cappelens forlag, 1946).
Ilner, Kristian, *De tyske soldatene på Alfaset. Fra heltedyrkelse til forsoning* (Norderstedt: Books on Demand, 2021).
Isaksen, Sjur, *Ulykkelig Fred. I frigjøringens skygger* (Oslo: Vårt Land forlag, 2020).
Jacobsen, Alf R., *Skjebnehøst. Nord-Norge 1944* (Oslo: Vega forlag, 2017).
Jensen, Finn Robert, *Gunnar 'Kjakan' Sønsteby. Om samhold og innsatsvilje* (Oslo: Pantagruel forlag, 2009).
Johansen, Per Ole, *Den illegale spriten. Fra forbudstid til polstreik* (Oslo: Unipub, 2004).
— (ed.), *På siden av rettsoppgjøret* (Oslo: Unipub, 2006).
Johnson, Alex, *Eivind Berggrav. Spenningens mann* (Oslo: Land og Kirke, 1959).
Jonassen, Mari, *De overlevende. 19 Norske kvinner og menn forteller om sine liv i Hitlers fangeleirer* (Oslo: Damm & Søn, 2006).
—, *Norske kvinner i krig 1939–1945* (Oslo: Aschehoug, 2020).
Karcher, Nicola, *Kampen om skolen. Nazifisering og lærernes motstand i det okkuperte Norge* (Oslo: Dreyers forlag, 2018).
Kersaudy, Francois, *Vi stoler på England, 1939–1949* (Oslo: J.W. Cappelens forlag, 1991).
Kofstad, Hege, *Grenselosene* (Oslo: Pax forlag, 2019).
Kroglund, Nina Drolsum, *Hitlers norske hjelpere. Nordmenns samarbeid med Tyskland 1940–45* (Oslo: Forlaget Historie og kultur, 2010).
Kvam, Vegard, *Skolefronten. Einar Høigård og norske læreres kamp mot nazismen* (Oslo: Scandinavian Academic Press, 2013).
Langeland, Major O.H., *– Forat I ikke skal dømmes* (Oslo: Familieforlaget as, 2010).
—, *Dømmer ikke* (Oslo: Familieforlaget as, 2010).
Langfeldt, Gabriel, and Ødegård, Ørnulv, *Den rettspsykiatriske erklæring om Knut Hamsun* (Oslo: Gyldendal, 1978).
Lauritzen, Per Roger, *Claus Helberg. Veiviser i krig og fred* (Oslo: DNT Boksenteret forlag, 1999).
Lewis, Sinclair, *Det kan aldri hende her*, trans. C.J. Hambro (Oslo: Gyldendal, 1936).
Lie, Jonas, *I 'fred' og ufred* (Oslo: Steenske forlag, 1940).

(pseud) Mauser, Max, *En hai følger båten* (Oslo: J.W. Cappelens forlag, 1992).
—, *Natten til fandens geburtsdag* (Oslo: Kurér forlag, 2011).
—, *Rittet fra Olesko* (Oslo: Kurér forlag, 2012).
Lillegaard, Leif Bryde, *Filipstad i flammer 1943. Et 40 års-minne* (Oslo: Ernst G. Mortensen forlag, 1983).
Lund, Diderich H., *Fra Norges fjell til fjerne kyster* (Oslo: Aschehoug, 1972).
Lund, Sigrid Helliesen, *Alltid underveis* (Oslo: Tiden forlag, 1981).
Lykke-Seest, Peter, *Omkring Quisling-prosessen. Iakttagelser og inntrykk* (Oslo: Cammermeyers Boghandel, 1945).
Lynau, Kjell, *De gav sitt liv. Minneskrift over falne i Nordstrand sogn under krigen 1940–45* (Oslo: Nordstrand, 1945).
Lyngvi, Arne, *Bomber over Laksevåg. 4.oktober 1944 og tiden som fulgte* (Bergen: Alma Mater forlag, 1991).
Løken, Roar, *The Race for the Atom Bomb – Was It Decided in Telemark?* (Forsvaret, 2015).
Manus, Max *Det blir alvor* (Oslo: Essforlagene, 1953).
—, *Rottejegeren* (Oslo: Kagge forlag, 2020).
Mendelsohn, Oskar, *Jødenes historie i Norte gjennom 300 år. B1 og 2* (Oslo: Universitetsforlag, 1986).
Michelet, Marte, *Hva visste hjemmefronten? Holocaust i Norge, varslene, unnvikelsene, hemmeligholdhet* (Oslo: Gyldendal, 2020).
Moland, Arnfinn, *Over Grensen? Hjemmefrontens likvidasjoner under den tyske okkupasjonen av Norge 1940–1954* (Oslo: Orion forlag, 1999).
Mollø-Christensen, Helga, *Mat i krigstid* (Oslo: Aschehoug, 1942).
News of Norway (Washington Royal Norwegian Information Service, 1941–1942, 1944–1945).
Njølstad, Olav, *Jens Chr. Hauge, Fullt og helt* (Oslo: Aschehoug. 2008).
Nøkleby, Berit, *Josef Terboven. Hitlers mann i Norge* (Oslo: Gyldendal Norsk forlag, 1992).
—, *Gestapo. Tysk politi i Norge* (Oslo: Aschehoug, 2003).
—, and Ellingsen, Ane Langballe (eds.), *Norge i krig i bilder* (Oslo: Aschehoug, 2009).
Olsen, Per Kristian, *Jevnet med Jorden. Brenningen av Finnmark og Nord-Troms 1944* (Oslo: Aschehoug, 2020).
Olstad, Finn, *Den store forsoningen. Norsk historie 1905–1945* (Oslo: Dreyers forlag, 2019).
Owen, James, *Nuremberg. Evil on Trial* (London: Headline Review, 2006).

Øyen, Odd *et al.*, *Milorg D13 i kamp* (Oslo: Nova forlag, 2011).
Pollan, Brita, *Ritualer for menns ærefulle død. Selvofler og livsmening* (Oslo: Emilia, 2003).
Prøis, Arne, *I samtale med Dagfinn Hauge* (Oslo: Lunde forlag, 1986).
Rapport fra Den militære undersøkelseskommisjon av 1946 (Oslo: Forlaget Oktober, 1978).
Ringdal, Nils Johan, *Mellom barken og veden. Politiet under Okkupasjonen* (Oslo: Aschehoug, 1987).
—, *Ordenes pris. Den norske forfatterforening 1893–1993* (Oslo: Aschehoug, 1993).
—, *Gal mann til rett tid. NS-minister Sverre Riisnæs. En psykobiografi* (Oslo: Aschehoug, 2004).
Rolfsen, Wilhelm Münter, *Usynlige veier. Fra Edderkoppens og flyktningeksportens historie* (Oslo: Jacob Dybwads forlag, 1946).
Rougthvedt, Bernt, *Med Penn og Pistol. Om politimesteren Jonas Lie* (Oslo: Cappelen Damm, 2011).
—, *Norges verste nazister. Nordmenn og tyskere i Hitlers tjeneste 1940–45* (Oslo: Spartacus forlag, 2016).
Rødder, Sverre, *Min ære er troskap. Om politimesteren Jonas Lie* (Oslo: Aschehoug, 1990).
Rydmark, Dag. 'Aksjonen i Kirkeveien 90'. In *St Hallvard*, 2 (Oslo, 2021).
Samuelsen, Ottar, *Det var her det skjedde* (Dinamo forlag, Oslo 2010).
Sass, Ann (ed.), *Jewish Life and Culture in Norway: Wergeland's Legacy* (New York: Abel Abrahamsen, 2003).
Sivertsen, Aage G., *9. april 1940. Et varslet overfall* (Oslo: Fønix forlag, 2020).
Skjeseth, Alf, *Nordens Casablanca. Nordmenn i Stockhom under krigen* (Oslo: Spartacus, 2020).
Skogan, John Kristen (ed.), *I frigjøringens spor. Artikler i anledning frigjøringsjubileet 1995* (Oslo: Universitetsforlaget, 1995).
Solbrekken, Ingeborg, *Landssvikoppgjørets hemmelige historie* (Oslo: Opera forlag, 2015).
Steinsvik, Marta, *Frimodige ytringer* (Oslo: Eget forlag, 1946).
Stratigakos, Despina, *Hitlers norske drøm. Nazismens ariske utstillingsvindu* (Oslo: Vega, 2021).
Stray, Sigrid, *Min klient Knut Hamsun* (Oslo: Aschehoug, 1979).
Sunde, Asbjørn, *Menn i mørket* (Oslo: Spartacus forlag, 2010).
Sæther, Orvar, *Hirdboken. Hirdens historie og oppgaver* (Oslo: J.M. Stenersens forlag, 1941).
Sønsteby, Gunnar, *Report from No. 24* (London: Fontana Books, 1973).

Takala, Hannu, and Tham, Henrik (eds.), *Krig og moral. Kriminalitet og kontroll i Norden under andre verdenskrig* (Oslo: Universitets forlag, 1987).
Thoresen, Jan Erik, *Mørket er min venn. En grenselos forteller* (Oslo: Spartacus forlag, 2008).
Thorsdahl, Geir, *Quislings biskoper. En norsk kirke i nazismens tjeneste* (Oslo: Kagge forlag, 2017).
Thuesen, Nils Petter, *Oslo under Andre Verdenskrig* (Oslo: Historie og Kulture, 2015).
Tofte, Rolf, *Med hånden på plogen. Om biskop Dagfinn Hauge* (Oslo: Luther forlag, 2002).
Tønnessen, Aud Valborg, *Ingrid Bjerkås. Motstandskvinnen som ble vår første kvinnelige prest* (Oslo: Pax forlag, 2014).
Ueland, Asgeir, *Tungtvannsaksjonen, historien om den største sabotasjeoperasjonen på norsk jord* (Oslo: Gyldendal, 2013).
Ulstein, Ragnar, *Etterretningstjenesten i Norge 1940–1945. B.1. Amatørenes tid* (Oslo: J.W. Cappelens forlag, 2008).
—, *Etterretningstjenesten i Norge 1940–1945. B.2. Harde år* (Oslo: J.W. Cappelens forlag, 2008).
—, *Etterretningstjenesten i Norge 1940–1945. B.3. Nettet strammes* (Oslo: J.W. Cappelens forlag, 2008).
Vaale, Lars-Erik, *Dommen til døden. Dødsstraffen I Norge 1945–50* (Oslo: Pax forlag, 2004).
Vesaas, Hilde, *Carl Fredriksens transport. Den ukjente historien om krigens største heltedåd* (Oslo: Kagge forlag, 2017).
Veum, Erik, *Nådeløse nordmenn. Statspolitiet 1941–1945* (Oslo: Kagge forlag, 2012).
—, *De kalte dem Rottejegere* (Oslo: Kagge forlag, 2022).
—, and Dalen, Torgeir Lindtvedt, *De døde for Norge. Nordmenn som ga sitt liv i allierte krigstjeneste 1940–45* (Oslo: Kagge forlag, 2019).
Voksø, Per (ed.), *Krigens Dagbok. Norge 1940–1945* (Oslo: Forlaget Det Beste, 1984).
Vollestad, Per, *Livet på Grini under annen verdenskrig* (Oslo: Kagge forlag, 2020).
Walle, Olaf R., *Norsk politi bak piggtråd. Stutthofpolitiets historie* (Kragerø: Naper boktrykkeri, 1947).
Wiesener, Albert, *Nordmenn for tysk krigsrett 1940–1942* (Oslo: Dreyer, 1954).
—, *Seierherrens justis* (Oslo: Dreyers forlag, 1964).
—, *Lys over landssvik oppgjøret* (Oslo: Dreyer, 1985).

Wright, Myrtle, *Norwegian Diary 1940–1945* (London: Friends Peace and International Relations Committee, 1974).

Wulfsberg, Jens, and Andresen, Per O., *Milorg 13313 – Gruppens Historie og opplevelser* (Oslo: Ch. Dybwads Bokhandel, 1948).

Films and radio

Jorfald, Knut W. (dir.), *M/S Donau* (Lanterna Magica, 1998).

Kvamme, Elsa (dir.), *Tysklandsstudenter. Students at War*, DVD (Alert Film/FRM/NRK, 1997).

Moland, Arnfinn (script), *Gunnar 'Kjakan' Sønsteby. Rapport fra 'Nr.24'*, DVD (Forsvaret mediesenteret, NRK, NFI, 2009).

Netland, Tore Severin (dir.), *Offer eller spion? Om Asbjørn Sunde*, DVD (Fiksjon & Fakta as, 2015)

Nordisk Film Distribusjon AS, *Nordmennenes egen historie fra krigen 1–4*, 4 DVDs (Nordisk Film Distribusjon AS, 2008).

Rakkanes, Øystein (dir.), *Brødre i krig*, DVD (Norsk Filminstitutt, 2011).

Rikli, Martin, and Buhle, Werner (eds.), *Kampf um Norwegen. Feldzug 1940*, DVD (Norsk Filminstitutt, 2007).

Stokkan, Torill, and Bjerketvedt, Gunnar, *Kvinner i krig. Women at War*, DVD (Karivold Film AS, 2015).

Svensson, Eirik (dir.), *Den største forbrytelsen (Betrayed)*, DVD (Nordisk Film Distribusjon, 2020).

Image Credits

p. 2 Photo: Heinrich Hoffmann / Courtesy of Christopher John Harris and John Asmussen

p. 15 Unknown author / Wikimedia Commons

p. 32 Bettmann / Getty Images

p. 46 Bundesarchiv, Bild 183-1990-0518-028 /photographer: Bernd Settnik

p. 68 Riksarkivet (National Archives of Norway)

p. 74 NTB / Alamy Stock Photo

p. 81 NTB / Alamy Stock Photo

p. 88 Private collection / NRK

p. 92 okkupasjonen.no

p. 98 Author's collection

p. 106 ARKIVET / Artist: Kaare Sørum

p. 113 TT News Agency / Alamy Stock Photo

p. 122 By kind permission of the family of Sigrid Helliesen Lund

p. 125 Oslo Jewish Museum / snublestein.no

p. 136 Klongn / Wikimedia Commons

p. 152 The National Archives of Norway

p. 175 NTNU University Library / Ukjent, Victor Huseby Giver

p. 216 Author's collection

p. 259 NTB / Alamy Stock Photo

p. 287 Budstikka.no

p. 297 National Library of Norway

p. 358 Author's collection

p. 368 Gunnar01 / Norsk Speidermuseum

p. 371 Author's collection

p. 393 Author's collection

p. 400 NTB / Alamy Stock Photo

p. 405 NTB / Alamy Stock Photo

p. 407 National Library of Norway

IMAGE CREDITS

Plate Section

1. TT News Agency / Alamy Stock Photo
2. Varden / Wikimedia Commons
3. Photo: Ukjent / Kunnskapsforlagets archive
4. Av Ukjent/NTB Scanpix
5. NTB / Wikimedia Commons
6. Unknown photographer / NTB
7. Arbeidernes Leksikon, Oslo 1933 / Wikimedia Commons
8. NTB Scanpix / Arkivverket / Flickr
9. Av Ukjent fotograf/Riksarkivet
10. Av Anders Beer Wilse (1865–1949) / Galleri Nor
11. Arkivverket / Flickr
12. Okkupasjonen.no
13. Hjemmefrontmuseet Rakkestad
14. Krg / Wikimedia Commons
15. Unknown / Lokalhistoriewiki
16. Photo: The Narvik Centre Archive
17. Heispe / Wikimedia Commons
18. NTB
19. Oslo Byarkiv / Wikimedia Commons
20. Municipal Archives of Trondheim / Photo: R. Kamrath-Lied / Flickr
21. Photo: J. Utheim/ The Norwegian Museum Of Science And Technology
22. Arkivverket / Photo: Ole Friele Backer / Flickr
23. AFP / Staff / Getty Images
24. Arkivverket / Flickr
25. Photo: Johannes Stage
26. Atle Råsberg / Wikimedia Commons
27. Author's collection
28. Photo: Rude, Ernest / Oslo Museum

Acknowledgements

My thanks to Guri Hjeltnes, director of the Centre for Studies of the Holocaust and Religious Minorities in Oslo, who facilitated contact with Terje Emberland, senior researcher at the Centre, who then gave me access to his archive of documents relating to Gunnar Waaler, who features so extensively in this book. Thanks also to Jan Alexander Svoboda Brustad, historian and archivist at the centre.

Thank you to my friend Jan Erik Holst, former director of the Norwegian Film Institute in Oslo, who generously lent me books and films on the subject of the occupation from his own personal library.

My thanks to Sjur Isaksen, priest to the Norwegian Storting, parish priest at Uranienborg Church in Oslo and author of *Ulykkelig fred* (Unhappy peace), for sharing some of his thoughts on the Norwegian *rettsoppgjøret* with me.

My thanks also to Olav Dag Hauge for kindly providing me with a copy of the journal kept by his father, Dagfinn Hauge, while serving as prison chaplain at Akershus fortress during the occupation.

Thank you Richard Milbank, editor at Head of Zeus, whose knowledge of and fondness for Norway and its culture has been a source of encouragement as well as relief to me throughout the writing of this book.

My thanks to Petter Næss, former executive director at the USA-Norway Fulbright Foundation, who was a consistent source of help and support.

Thank you to Lena Pasternak and the taxpayers of Visby for the offer of hospitality at the Baltic Centre for Writers and Translators on the island of Gotland, where parts of this book were written.

For the past three years I have enjoyed the luxury of a researcher's seat at the National Library of Norway in Drammensveien and access to the library's collection of Norwegian newspapers, magazines and books. I must also thank the staff at the Norwegian National Archives and at the Majorstua branch of the Deichmanske Public Library.

A special thank you to my father-in-law Rolf Sverre Normann. Rolf's father, Sverre Vidar Normann, was chief engineer on board the MS *Ronda*, which sailed into a minefield off the coast of Holland on 13 September 1939 and sank, drowning him and fifteen other crew members, the first Norwegian fatalities of the war. Rolf was nine at the time, ten when the occupation started. Now ninety-four, he retains vivid memories of the atmosphere in the Oslo streets during those five years.

And as ever, particular thanks to my dear wife Nina Elisabeth Normann Ferguson, for her patience, support and conversation.

Index

Aamodt, Hans
  and the Skallum Manor siege 283–8, 295
Administrajonsråd (Administrative Council) 27–8, 30–1, 33, 51, 302
Admiral Graf Spee (battleship) 16
Aftenposten 64, 170–1
Ahnenerbe Institute, Germany 48–9
Akershus Fortress Prison 154, 224, 231, 307, 311, 402, 409
  Knut Mathiesen imprisoned in 352, 357
  Pastor Hauge's visit to 358–74
  Quisling's execution at 318–19
Allied forces
  Normandy landings 249
Altmark incident 16–17, 18
Andenæs, Johs. 306
Andersen, Aud Maggi 326
Andersen, Finn Roald 133
Andersen, Johannes (Gulosten, 'Yellow Cheese') 151–8, 403–4
  and Operation Bittern 156–8
Andersen, Ruth 234, 403–4
Anderson, Charles 133
Arbeidstjeneste (AT, Work Service) 143–5, 151, 204–5, 207, 213, 379, 382

Archer, William 7
Arctic Highway 255
Arendt, Hannah
  Eichmann in Jerusalem 320
Arentz, Maria 323–4
Arntzen, Sven 305–6
'Art and Non-Art' exhibition 169–71
Artists' Union 170
Aschehoug (publishers) 167
Ask, Øyvind 154–5
Askvig, Bernard 204–6, 211
Astrup, Nikolai 169
Auschwitz-Birkenau 124–6, 126–7
Austria 403

Backer, Harriet 169
bank robberies 147–50, 357
Barthel, Friedrich 263–5
Berg, Odd 236
Berg, Paal 27, 312, 317, 319
Berg prison camp 124
Bergen 44
  Reichskommissariat 39
  resistance fighters 139
  and the *Weserübung* operation 21, 28
Bergens Tidende (newspaper) 1–2

438

INDEX

Berggrav, Dag 311
Berggrav, Eivind, Bishop of Oslo 27,
  51–5, 58, 64, 68, 177, 246
  description of Quisling 319–20
  essay on collective guilt 304–7,
    309, 311
  house arrest of 80
  Kirkens Grunn (The Foundation
    of the Church) 79, 82
Bergh, Henrik 315–16
Bergmann, John 334–5, 339–41
Bergsjø, Gulbrand 330, 337–8, 34–6,
  349, 349–50, 376, 387, 388, 389–91
Berlin Blockade 397
Bjerkås, Ingrid 23–4, 91–103, 400–1
Bjerkås, Sigurd 97, 101–3, 401
Bjerke, André 375
Bjerkedal, Tor 235–6
Bjørnebo, Bjørn 323–4
Bjørnøya island 306
Bjørnson, Bjørnstjerne 6, 7, 382
Black Hand, the 146–7
Blessing-Dahle, Peder 74–6, 77
Blücher
  and the *Weserübung* operation
    19–21, 25, 132
Blumenpflücken campaign 233–4,
  237, 408
Böhme, General Franz 262, 300
Bojer, Johan 166
Bondepartiet (Farmers Party) 10
books, censorship of 166–9
Bøtker, Henning 58
Boyle, Admiral 29
Brandes, Georg 70
Bräuer, Curt 27–8
Brecht, Bertolt 167–8
Bredtveit Prison, Oslo 88–9, 124,
  205
Breivik, Anders Behring 319
Brenno, Ole 46, 48, 55
Brinchmann, Alex 166
Britain
  and the *Altmark* incident 16
  breach of neutrality 16–18
  First World War 13–14
  Helberg's flight to 162–3
  and Nortraship 26
  and Norwegian culture 8–9

Norwegian refugees in 29
  and the Norwegian resistance
    134, 135, 151, 156–7
  and the occupation of Norway
    29
  Operation Claymore 76
  Operation Grouse 159–61
  Operation Gunnerside 159–61
  Operation Sunshine 163
  Special Operations Executive
    (SOE) 156–7
Brochmann, Georg 166
Brussels, Treaty of (1948) 398
Bruun, Johan Petter 146–7
Bygdøy peninsula 389
  Himmler's visit to 45–7
  Villa Grande mansion 272, 315,
    410

Cappelen, August 169
Céline, Louis-Ferdinand 167
Charles the Simple, French king 50
Cheval Animal Hospital 154–5,
  234, 313
children, Norwegian-German 165
Christianity
  and Ingrid Bjerkås 91–3
  see also Lutheran Church
Churchill, Winston 117
Civilian State of Emergency (CSE)
  59–60, 62–3, 65, 178
Colberg, Raymond 154–7, 234, 313,
  403
Cold War 397–8, 405–6
collective guilt 304–7
Comintern 9
communism 9, 56, 61, 68, 76, 149,
  167, 194, 290, 406
  and Sonderabteilung Lola 323–4
  and trade union activists 61
Communist Party, Norwegian
  (NKP) 9, 11, 33, 137, 301
  and the Osvald Group 147–50,
    357, 378, 405–6
Conscience Struggle 73–90, 91–104,
  143, 164–5, 193, 203–4, 234, 303
  and the church 74–82, 327
  Ingrid Bjerkås 91–103
  and *Sivorg* 134

439

teachers 73–4, 82–90, 98–102, 327
Constitution of Norway 73
Continuation War 18
Cossack, HMS 16
culture 164–81
  'Art and Non-Art' exhibition 169–71
  books 166–9
  films 179–81
  national socialistic German culture 44
  theatre 171–9
Czechoslovakia 122, 260, 262, 397

Dagbladet newspaper 44, 311
Dagens Næringsliv (Business Daily) 410
Dagestad, Nils 188–9
Dahl, Hans Fredrik 319
Dahl, J.C. 6, 169, 236
Dahl, Thorleif 320
Damholt Farm 329, 332, 334–6, 340–2
Damsleth, Harald 12–13, 290, 301
Dasposten 175
death penalty 119, 204, 304, 311, 326–8
  and the People's Court 201–3
  and the Police Special Court 205–14, 280
  post-war trials and executions 324–8
  Quisling 311–12, 316–19
  and Riisnæs 402
  and Rinnan 324–5
Degrelle, Leon 262, 263
Dellbrügge, Dr Hans 30–1, 33
Denmark
  and the Cold War 397, 398
  German occupation of 18, 31, 39, 192, 302, 367–8
  and the Lapland Army 250
  Nazi Party 306
  neutrality policy 13
  and Norway 5–6
Deutschland (later the *Lützow*) 1, 19
Dobinski, Oberkriegsgerichtstrat 366–7

Dönitz, Admiral Karl 262, 300
Dønnum, Einar 226, 230
Drøbak 20, 25
drumhead courts (*standrett*) 59–60
Dudo of St Quentin 50
Dühringen, Oberfeldwebel 262–3

Eastern Europe 41, 49
Egedius, Halfdan 169
Egge, Ørnulf 324
Eichmann, Adolf 320
Eidsvoll constitution 5–6, 31
Eilifsen, Gunnar
  trial and execution 204–12, 215, 225, 276, 314, 316
Einarson, Rannveig Sigmundsdatter 407, 409
Einsatztab Wegener 36
Ekeland, Harald 332, 351, 352
Elverum Decree (*Elverumsfullmakten*) 26–7, 29, 33, 302, 304
Eng, Dr Hans 95–6, 97–8, 123, 140, 210, 268, 298, 376–9, 381–3, 398–400
  and Knut Mathiesen's execution 388–9, 394
  and Quisling 376–7, 399–400
  trial of 398–9
Engelbrecht, General Erwin 25
Engeseth, Ludwig 214
Eriksen, Håkon 142

Falkenberg, Arvid 145, 147
Falkenhorst, General Nikolaus von 18, 92
Farmers Party 10–11
Fatherland League 9
Fehlis, Heinrich 41, 106–7, 260, 262
Fehmer, Siegfrid 229–30, 240
Fein, Nathan 123–4, 126–7
Feinberg, Elias 124, 125
Feinberg, Kai 124–7, 410
Feldmann, Herman 110–11
Feyling, Sigmund 73
Filipstad docks explosion 362–3
films 179–81
Finland
  Continuation War 249, 250

INDEX

Winter War 17–8, 35, 45, 61, 249
Finnmark 250–6, 276–7, 407
First World War 9, 13–14, 131
Fiveland, Arne 139
Fiveland, Mardon 139
Fjelbu, Arne 49, 74–9, 256
Fjell, Kai 170
Fleicher, General Gustav 22
Fokerett (People's Court) 195–202, 201–2, 203, 229, 356
food shortages 62
Fram expedition 7
Framnes concentration camp 136
France 29, 31
Freemasons, Order of 315
Fritt Folk (Free People) 51, 111, 153, 382
Fritzner, Ola 229–30
Frontkjempere (Front Fighters) 45
Fuglesang, Rolf 168–9
Furubotn, Peder 147–8

Gåsland, Ludvig 186
Geithus bridge explosion 148–9
Gerhardsen, Einar 301, 319, 327
Germany
    Ahnenerbe Institute 48–9
    Altmark incident 16–17, 18
    Berlin Blockade 397
    deportation of Jews to 112–13, 120
    First World War 14
    invasion of the Soviet Union (Operation Barbarossa) 45, 56, 58–9
    non-aggression pact with Soviet Russia 137
    and Norwegian culture 6–9, 165
    Norwegian surrender to 29–30
    and Norwegian theatre 172–3
    Pan-Germanism in Norway 7
    Sachsenhausen concentration camp 120, 132
    and the Second World War
        defeat 249, 260
        outbreak of 15
        surrender 261, 266, 300
    the SS 41, 390
    and the State Act in Norway 68–9
    Stutthof prison camp 212
    unification of (1871) 7
    Wehrmacht 40–1
    Weserübung operation (invasion) 2, 18–25, 28–30, 39, 92, 186–7, 313–14
    young people's movements in Nazi Germany 72
    see also Hitler, Adolf; national socialism
Gestapo 41–2, 63, 140, 186
    and Ingrid Bjerkås 93
    interrogation of Fjelbu 75–6
    and Norwegian resistance fighters 138
    see also Sipo (*Sikkerhetspolitiet*); Stapo (*Statspolitiet*); Weiner, Albert
Gleditsch, Henry 171–4, 175–8, 233, 267
Goebbels, Joseph 43, 165
Gram, Gregers 245, 379–81, 382–3, 384
Grensepolitiet (Grepo, border police force) 110, 111, 227, 244, 339, 341, 353, 381, 389, 392
Grieg, Edvard 6, 7
Grini prison camp 42, 102–3, 111, 118, 166, 179, 280
    internment of Jews 117, 120, 123
    Jugendabteilung 234–6
    Kullman in 132
    Pastor Hauge's visits to 358
    punishment exercises 103–4
    schoolteachers in 85
    Waaler in 243–4, 259
Grüner-Hegg, Rolf 235–6
Gude, Hans 169
Gulosten see Andersen, Johannes (Gulosten, 'Yellow Cheese')
Gundersen, O.C. 328
Gyldendal (publishers) 167, 344

Haakon VII, King of Norway 8–9, 22, 27, 29, 31–3, 42, 80, 313, 353
    and 'Carl Fredriksens Transport' 113

and Gulosten 156
request and refusal to abdicate
   31–2, 75
return to Norway 300–1
Haaland, Reidar 311–12, 322
Hærland, Einar 233–4
Hagelin, Albert 34, 42–3, 58–9, 320, 327
Hallesby, Ole 407
Hamar, evacuation of the Storting to
   22–3, 25–6
Hambro, C.J. 22, 31, 168
Hammerfest,
   Reichskommissariat branch in 39
Hammerö, Sigrid 234
Hamsun, Knut 6, 166, 167, 170,
   221–2, 260, 319
   Mysteries 7
Hamsun, Tore 170–1
Hans, Oskar 178, 234
Hansen, Rigmor 143
Hansen, Sigurd 142
Hansteen, Aasta 60
Hansteen, Christopher 60
Hansteen, Viggo 59, 60–1, 63–4,
   134, 135, 177, 233, 304
Harald Hårfagre (Finehair) 12
hardingfele (hardanger fiddle) 46
Harstad,
   Reichskommissariat branch in 39
Hasvold, Nina 122–3
Hauge, Jens Christian 146, 216, 222, 229, 407
Hauge, Pastor Dagfinn, prison
   chaplain 154, 322, 326–7, 352
   and Knut Mathiesen 345, 358–74
Haugesund resistance fighters 138
Haugland, Harald 254, 332, 333,
   334–6, 340–2, 343, 351–2, 385, 389, 392–3
Hebo, Henrik 381–2
Helberg, Claus 160, 161–3, 245
Helle, Fredrik 186–7
Helliesen Lund, Sigrid 115–23, 134, 162–3
Hemingway, Ernest 168
Heroes of Telemark, The (film) 158
Hettich, Gerda 262

Heydrich, Reinhard 41, 60, 65, 136, 157, 188
   and Waaler 188, 190
Heyerdal, Hans 169
Himmler, Heinrich 33, 41, 64, 126, 246, 318
   and the Lebensborn project 164–5
   meeting with Berggrav 52–5
   and the Norwegians 49–51
   'racial safari' trip 44–9
   and the SS 188
   witness to mass executions 55–6
hird, the 12, 22, 193, 304, 386–7
   and Johannes Andersen 152–3
   and Rogstad 267
   and the State Act ceremony in
      Trondheim cathedral 76–7
   Viking Hird Training Centre 110
   violence in schools and colleges
      51–2, 53–5, 58, 246
   Waaler's prosecution cases and
      hird members 195–9
Hitler, Adolf 22, 48, 86, 147, 262, 278, 367
   on the *Deutschland* visiting the
      Norwegian fjords 1–2
   and the evacuation of north
      Norway 250, 252–3, 276
   and Heydrich 60
   Nazi Party 11
   and the Norwegian Work
      Movement 144–5
   and the occupation of Norway 30
   and Quisling 12, 26–7, 27–8,
      35–6, 49–50, 56, 71, 100, 261–2, 316
   and the SS 41, 188
   suicide 260–1, 261–2
   and Terboven 28
   and V2 missiles 160–1
   see also Germany
Hoel, Adolf 87
Hohenzollern (royal yacht) 1
Høigård, Einar 82–4, 87–90, 103,
   134–5, 177
   Pedagogical Studies 88
Høigård, Elfrida 89

INDEX

Holocaust, Norwegian *see under* Jews
Holtman, Reidar 147
Hornsrud, Christopher 10
Høyre (Right/the Conservatives) 11
Hügel, Friedrich von 119
Hundseid, Jens 11, 132, 313
Hungary 260
Hvam, Arne 110–11

Ibsen, Henrik 6–7, 70–1, 174, 180, 348
  The Wild Duck 175, 178
informers 133, 135–6, 139–40
Irgens, Otto 80–2
iron ore exports to Germany 17–18, 22, 83
isfront (ice front) 306–7, 311, 322
Italy 12, 205
Iversen, Norman 150

Jacobsen, Knut Riise 178–9
Jahr, Per 34–5
Jensen, Einar 368
Jensen, Jens 338
Jews 48, 60–1, 68, 402
  arrest and detention of 111–12
  deportation of to Auschwitz 112–13, 123–6
  escapes to Sweden 122
    attempted 107, 110–11
    'Carl Fredriksens Transport' 113–15, 123
  identity card stamping 106–7, 110–11, 112
  Jewish community in Trondheim 76
  the Norwegian Holocaust 105–27, 408
  and Quisling's trial 314–15, 316
  reparations to the Norwegian Jews 409–10
  rescue of, the *Sivorg* circle 115–23
  and the State Act 69–70
Jodl, General Alfred 261
Jørdstadmoen concentration camp 85

jøssing Norwegians 16–17, 33, 96, 110
  see also Conscience Struggle; resistance movement/fighters

Kant, Immanuel 317
Karlsen, Martin 1–2
Kiel, Treaty of 5
Kielland, Kitty 169
Kielland, Alexander 6
Kielland, Major Jan
  Milorg raid on flat of 379–81
Kierkegaard, Søren 236
Kirkenes 250, 251–2, 255–6
  banishment of teachers to 86–7
  mine-dwellers 254
  Reichskommissariat 39
Kirkeveien
  Milorg operation at 378–84
Kleve, Knut 235–6, 408
Knudsen, Captain Vagn 353–5, 357
Koht, Halvdan 14, 22–3, 25
Kolstad, Peder 313
  Bondepartiet government 10, 11
Komissar, Hirsch 110
Koordinasjonskomiteen (KK, the Coordinating Committee) 134–5
Koteng, Guttorm 139
Kranz, Ragnvald 95, 97, 376, 377, 382
Kretsen (the Circle/Group) 134
Kristiansand,
  Reichskommissariat branch in 39
Kristiansen, Alf 142
Krogh, Christian 169
Kullmann, Olaf 131–3
Kvænangen
  Dr Hans Eng in 399–401

L'Abée-Lund, Lars 288
labour force
  and the occupation 30
Labour Party 9–11, 13, 132
  and the general election (1945) 301
  Nygaardsvold government 13–15, 22, 24–5, 26, 27, 30, 33, 301
  published books 167
lakselords (salmon lords) 8
Landerud, Ole Olsen 329–30, 333–7, 346–8, 349

Landfeldt, Gabriel 319
landssvik cases, prosecution of 325–6
landsvakt (National Guard) 14
Langeland, Major Oliver 213–14, 216, 230, 245–6, 407
langeleik (droned zither) 46, 48, 55
Langen, Albert 7
Langslet, Lars Roar 165
Lapland Army 250
Larsen, Johannes 155–6
Lea, Rolv 327
League of Nations 14
Lebensborn programme 41, 164–5
Leisner, Rolf 334–6
Lewis, Sinclair
  It Can't Happen Here 22, 168
Liberal Party 14
Lie, Jonas 166, 228, 258
  appearance and character 33
  book on trip to Mexico with Trotsky 223
  crime novels as 'Max Mauser' 342, 344–5, 362–3, 375, 406
  death 290, 291–3, 296–8
  and the Department of Policing 33–4, 51, 53, 98, 186, 192–3, 331
  driver (Henrik Hebo) 381–2
  and the evacuation of northern Norway 250–2, 254–5, 256–7
  and Himmler's 'racial safari' trip 47
  and the Jews 106
  and Knut Mathiesen
    execution 377, 384, 389, 392, 394
    trial 331–2, 334, 342–3, 352
  and Marthinsen's assassination 260
  and Operation Bittern 157
  and the Police Special Court 204–7, 209, 211–12
  and Quisling 35, 50, 382
  and *Regiment Nordland* 45
  and Riisnæs 34
  and the Skallum Manor siege 267–99, 398–9, 402
Lie, Jonas Snr 6, 33, 166
Lindboe, Asbjørn 10

Lindvig, Gunnar 215–16, 233, 242, 376, 378, 385–6, 387–8, 391–2, 393
Linge, Martin 156
Lippestad, Andreas 251
Ljostveit, Hanna 311
Ljostveit, Kristian 307–11
Landorganisasjon (LO) *see* Norwegian Confederation of Trade Unions
Lofoten Islands 45, 76
London
  Norwegian government in 136, 301, 312
Lorangejordet 284–5
Lorenz, Erich 409
Løvenskiold, Herman 222–3, 230, 239–40
Løvestad, Karsten 110–11, 200–2
Lund, Bernt 115–16, 116–17, 118
Lund, Lars L'Abée 279–80
Lunde, Gulbrand 34, 165, 167–8, 174, 179, 308
Luther, Martin 78
Lutheran Church 27
  Church Free Leadership organisation 199–200, 246, 407
  and the Conscience Struggle 74–82
  Ingrid Bjerkås and the priesthood 400–1
  priests and National Unity membership 307–11
  see also Berggrav, Eivind, Bishop of Oslo

McCarthy, Senator Joseph 175
Majavatn resistance fighters 109, 178
Malaparte, Curzio 168
Manus, Max 245, 288, 379–81, 382–4
Marthinsen, Karl A. 140, 206–7, 208–9, 210, 342, 353
  assassination of 257–9, 267, 274, 283, 402
  and Waaler's interrogation 218–19, 220, 221, 228–9, 241
Marthinsen, Kjell Andreas 258
Marx, Karl

INDEX

Das Kapital 166
Mathiesen, Eystein 336, 363
Mathiesen, Gerhard 186–7
Mathiesen, Knut (border guide) 139, 316, 329–95
  death sentence 351–2, 357
  execution of 215–16, 242, 374–95, 388–95
  and Pastor Hauge (prison chaplain) 358–74
  torture of 330–1
  trial of 216–17, 242, 329–52
Maud, Queen of Norway 8–9
Mendelsohn, Oskar 410
Michelsen, Christian 9
Middelfart, Willi 170
milk strike 62, 63–4, 65
Miller, Arthur 175
Milorg (Military Resistance Organisation) 135–6, 139–40, 146, 147, 151, 157, 177, 252, 300
  assassination of Marthinsen 257–9
  attack on Norsk Hydro 158–61
  operation at Kirkeveien 378–84
  post-war celebration of 404–5
  and the Rinnan Band 323–4
  Skallum Manor delegation 268–78
  and Waaler 186, 213–14, 215–16, 222, 228, 239, 241–2, 244, 245–6, 374–5, 406–7
Ministry for Culture and Propaganda 34
Modum Sparebank robbery 147–50, 357
Moen, Olaf 212–13, 225, 276
Molde 27
Møllergata 19 prison 42, 62, 242, 269, 281, 284
Molotov, Vyacheslav 255–6
Mørk, Birger 62
Moscow, Treaty of 18
Mowinckel, Johan Ludwig 14
Moy, Arne and Ruth 139
MTB (Motor Torpedo Boats) 158
Muhle, Erik 190
Müller, G.W. 43–4

Müller-Scheld, Wilhelm 165
Munch, Edvard 6, 7, 169–71, 389
Munthe, Gerhard 169
music
  Norwegian folk music 47–9
  traditional musical instruments 46
Musil, Robert 168
Mussolini, Benito 11–12, 205

Nansen, Fridtjof 7, 9, 11, 50, 120, 313
Nansen, Odd 120
Napoleonic Wars 5, 13, 398
Narvik
  and Operation Avonmouth 17–18
  Reichskommissariat branch in 39
  and the *Weserübung* operation 21–2, 29–30
Nasjonal Samling see National Unity party
National Archive documents
  and Waaler's interrogation 240, 241, 242–4
national identity, Norwegian 6, 7
national socialism
  and art 169–71
  and Himmler's 'racial safari' 47–9
  and the Lutheran Church 75, 79–80
  Nazification of Norwegian society 42–4, 69–70, 72–3, 83, 302–3, 402
  and Norwegian culture 164–81
  propaganda films 181
  and Quisling 34, 36
  and Terboven 39
  and Waaler 194–5, 246
National Unity government 71–3, 302–3
  executions of members of 327–8
  and the Germans 236–8
  and the Jews 106–10, 111–12
  and Norwegian culture 164–81
  and the occupation 25, 33
  and Oslo University 87
  and the police 185–6, 192–3, 194–202

protests *see* Conscience Struggle Work Service   143–7, 151, 204–5, 207, 213, 379, 382
Youth Movement   71–3, 80, 82
see also Statsakt (State Act, 1942)
National Unity party   12–13
and the church   74, 307–11
and collective guilt   304–7
the *hird*   12–3
and Hitler   36
membership   72, 164
and national socialism   42–3
National Unity Office for Public Service Personnel (NSPOT)   57, 59
police membership   185–6
priests   81–2
and the *Reichskommissariat*   40
and the *Riksråd* (National Council)   31
and Terboven   34
Viking Age imagery   13
and violence by the *hird*   41
and the *Weserübung* operation   21–2
Youth Movement   12, 72
see also the *hird*; Quisling, Vidkun
National Work Service   71–3, 80, 82, 143–7, 151, 204, 205, 207, 213, 379, 382
NATO (North Atlantic Treaty Organisation)   398
neutrality policy   13–18, 131
the broken rifle symbol   15
newspapers, censorship of   43–4
Nielsen, Danish journalist at Skallum Manor   279–82
Nielsen, Rolf   87–9
Nietzsche, Friedrich   390–1
Nilsen, Per Willars   330–1, 336, 348
Nilssen, Marino   138–9
Nord-Troms
evacuation of   250–7
Nordvik, Jørgen   193, 195–6, 201, 350, 356, 407
Norges Kommunistiske Parti see Communist Party, Norwegian (NKP)

Norges Socialdemokratiske Arbeiderparti (Norwegian Social Democratic Labour Party)   9
Normandy landings   249
Normann, Axel Otto   172
Norsk Hydro, Milorg attack on   158–61
Norsk rikskringkasting (Norwegian State Radio, NRK)   23
*Norsk Telegrambur*å, Norwegian News Agency, NTB)   22–3
Nortraship   26
northern Norway
evacuation and scorched-earth policy in   250–7, 276–7, 399
Kvænangen   399–401
Senja   401
transport of schoolteachers to   85–6
Waaler in   407
Norway
culture   6–7
German invasion of
see Weserübung operation
and the Cold War   397–8
independence   5–6, 7–8, 9
neutrality policy   13–18
Norwegian Communist Party *see* Communist Party, Norwegian (NKP)
Norwegian Confederation of Trade Unions (*Landorganisasjon*, LO)   56–66
Norwegian Film Institute   180
Norwegian Society of Authors   166
Norwegian Teachers' Organisation   83–4
Nygaardsvold, Johan
government of   13–15, 22, 24, 26–7, 29, 33, 70, 313, 318
in London   136, 301
Ofstad, Lars Tangvik   325
Olav, Crown Prince   22, 26, 300, 353–4, 404
Olav Haraldsson, saint-king   12, 47, 67
Olbjørn, Egil   190, 205–7, 208, 210, 228, 350–2, 382, 384, 389, 392–3

INDEX

Onsager, Søren 169, 171
Operation Avonmouth 17–18
Operation Bittern 156–7
Operation Claymore 76
Operation Grouse 159–60, 161
Operation Gunnerside 159–60, 161
Operation Sunshine 163
Oscarsborg fortress 20–1, 132
Oslo
  Bredtveit Prison 88–9
  Cheval Animal Hospital 154–5, 234, 313
  Continental Hotel 24–5, 172
  Freemasons Lodge 126
  Himmler's visit to 44–7
  Jewish Children's Home 122
  marka 102
  Møllergata 19 prison 42, 62, 242, 269, 281, 284
  National Theatre 44, 172, 174, 404
  occupation of 23–5, 27, 28
  prisons 42
  railway station bombs (1942) 131, 136
  University 57, 87–8, 102
  Victoria terrasse 63, 89, 93, 166
Oslo Gang 260–1, 288
  assassination of Marthinsen 257–9
Oslofjord 18
  and the *Weserübung* operation 19–21
Østbye, Fru Halldis Neegaard 108
Osvald Group 138, 147–51, 177, 357, 378, 405
Øymoen, Thorleif 139

Pan-Germanism 7, 34, 168
Pedersen, August 193
People's Court (*Folkerett*) 195–202, 201–2, 203, 229, 356
Petersen, Ålvik 196, 198
Peterssen, Eilif 169
Pettersen, Alf 113–15
Poland
  German invasion of 15, 17
police
  Nazification of the police force 185–6, 192–3

Særdomstol (Police Special Court) 206–13, 206–14, 216, 228, 276, 314, 402
  see also Gestapo; Sipo (*Sikkerhetspolitiet*); Stapo (*Statspolitiet*); Waaler, Gunnar
prisoners of war
  Eastern Europeans 41
  in Grini prison 42
prisons 42
Prytz, Fredrik 166

Quisling, Jon Lauritz (Vidkun Quisling's father) 80
Quisling, Vidkun 10–12, 172, 301, 302–3
  and the Administrative Council 27–8
  and the Conscience Struggle, Ingrid Bjerkås's letter-writing 93–103
  and Dr Hans Eng 376, 377, 399–400
  and Eilifsen's trial 205, 206, 207
  and the evacuation of northern Norway 250–1
  execution 318–22, 324
  German contempt for 236
  and Hagelin 34
  and Himmler 47, 49, 56
  and Hitler 12, 26–7, 27–8, 35–6, 49–50, 56, 71, 100, 144, 261–2
  and Kullmann 132
  last letter to his wife 321–2
  and Lie 33, 280, 382
  as Minister-President
    and the Church 79, 80–2
  last days of the war 261–2, 267
  Law Concerning National Youth Service 71–3, 80, 82
  Law Concerning the Norwegian Teachers' Organisation 72–3
  and the Police Special Court 206, 209–10, 316
  and the State Act 67–71, 73, 76, 79, 136, 315
  and national socialism 34, 36

and the National Unity Party 12,
   35, 42, 44
and Norwegian culture 166, 168
radio broadcast and the
   Weserübung operation 24–5,
   39, 313–14, 348
and *Regiment Nordland* 44–5
and the resistance movement
   257–8
and the Stapo 228
surrender and detention of the
   Quisling cabinet 268–9, 272,
   283
and Terboven 30, 35–6
trial of 311–18, 322, 406
and the Trondheim Theatre
   Company 175–6
and Universalism 317
Villa Grande mansion 272, 315,
   410
and Waaler 200, 230, 246
see also National Unity
   government; National Unity
   party

radios 101, 105, 179, 252, 312
Rakestad, Bjørn 336
Ravner, Øystein 34–5
Rediess, Wilhelm 41, 47, 205, 233,
   264–5
Regiment Nordland 44–5, 49
Reichborn-Kjennerud, Egil
   206–9
Reichskommissariat 39–42, 327
   forordninger (Resolutions) 40
   and the Wehrmacht 40
Reimer (Terboven's butler) 264–5
Reinhard, Hellmuth 42, 112, 233,
   234–6
   trial of 407–8, 409
Reiss, Johan 124
Remarque, Erich Maria 168
resistance movement/fighters
   131–63
   attack on Stapo headquarters
      140–3
   and the *Blumenpflücken* campaign
      233–4
   fugitives 123

informers 133, 135–6, 139–40, 157
Majavatn 109
and the Norwegian Work Service
   143–7, 151
and Operation Bittern 156–7
Oslogjengen (the Oslo
   detachment) 245
Osvald Group 138, 147–51, 177,
   257–8
paroles 134–5, 204, 252
and the Rinnan Band 323–4
see also Andersen, Johannes
   (Gulosten, 'Yellow Cheese');
   Milorg (Military Resistance
   Organisation); *Sivorg* (Civil
   Organisation); Sunde, Asbjørn
Ribbentrop, Joachim von 65, 313
Riisnæs, Sverre 61, 166, 259–60, 382,
   401–3, 407
   and Eilifsen's trial 209–10
   and Himmler's 'racial safari'
      trip 47
   as Minister of Justice 34, 43, 51,
      97, 186, 192, 202, 331
      and Eilifsen 205–6, 206–7
      and the Jews in Norway
         108–9
      and *Regiment Nordland* 45
   in Sicily 403
   and the Skallum Manor siege
      267, 269–99, 399, 401, 402–3
      surrender 289–95, 298
   and Waaler 226
Rikshird (National Hird) 12
Riksråd (National Council) 31, 131
Ringerike 148
Rinnan, Henry Oliver 138–9, 322–5
Roberts, Major W.D. 409
Rogstad, Henrik 109–10, 175, 256
   and the Skallum Manor siege
      267, 269–99, 399, 402
Rollo, Viking leader 50
Røschmann, Gunhild 407–8
Rosenberg, Alfred 35, 313
Rosenlund, Georg 225
Røthe, Ole 23
rural life 6
Russia *see* Soviet Russia
Russian Revolution (1917) 9, 50

Sachsenhausen concentration camp 120, 132, 135
Særdomstol (Police Special Court) 206–13, 206–14, 216, 228, 276, 314, 402
Sæther, Ivar 64
Sæther, Orvar 13, 72, 84, 86
Samuel, Amos 121–2
Samuel, Isak Julius 121–2
Sandberg, adjutant to Wulfsberg 271, 275, 277–8, 297–8
Sandberg, police officer (firing squad) 385–6
Sanden, Olav 408
Saur, Helmut 264
Saxe-Meiningen, Duke Georg 6–7
Scandinavian neutrality 397–8
Schelderup, Harald 88
Schermann, Willy 110–11
Scheskat, Günter 149–51
Schjødt, Annæus 154, 156, 312–13
Schjødt, Hedevig 154–6
schools
 National Unity legislation on 72–3
 violence by *hird* members 51, 53
 see also teachers
Schopenhauer, Arthur 317
Seip, Didrik Arup 87
Senterpartiet (the Centre Party) 10
Sicily 403
silkefront (silk front) 306–7, 322
Sipo (Civilian Police) 41–2, 109, 140
 and the Jews 105
 release of Norwegian prisoners 261
Sivorg (Civil Organisation) 134–5
 the *Sivorg* circle 115–23, 162–3
Skallum Manor siege 266–99, 398–9, 402–3
 conditions for surrender 273–8
 journalists' reports on 278–82
Skancke, Ragnar 52, 84, 98, 100–1, 308, 327–8, 360, 367
Skeie, Jon 306, 312
Ski Hunters Company 268
Skjønhaug, Rolf 216–17, 220, 222–3, 227, 332, 339, 351–2, 378
Skule, Gottfried 89, 376, 377

slave labour
 banished schoolteachers as 86–7
Slingsby, William Cecil 8
Social Democratic Labour Party
 see Norges Socialdemokratiske Arbeiderparti
SOE (Special Operations Executive) 245
Sognefjord 1, 34
Sohlberg, Harald 169
Solem, Judge Erik 312–13, 316–17
Sonderabteilung Lola 323
Sønsteby, Gunnar 245, 257–8, 261, 404
Sønsterød, Harry 149–50, 150–1
Sørum, Kaare 105
Soviet Russia 68
 army in Norway 250, 255–6
 and the Cold War 397–8, 405–6
 German invasion of (Operation Barbarossa) 45, 56, 58–9
 and Kullmann 132
 liberation of Auschwitz-Birkenau 125–6
 non-aggression pact with Nazi Germany 137
 and Norway 9, 11
 Operation Bagration 240
 Russian prisoners of war 255
 Stalingrad 203
 war with Finland 17, 18, 35, 45, 61, 249, 250
Søvik, Erling 353–7
 interrogation of Waaler 216–24, 227, 229, 241
Spanish Civil War 137
Speer Organisation 144–5
SS (*Schutzstaffel*) 41, 44, 49, 402
 and Waaler 188–90
Stabell, Holgeir John 88
Stalin, Josef 397
Stalingrad 203
Stapo (*Statspolitiet*) 186, 226
 arrest and detention of Jews 111–12, 112–13
 and the Conscience Struggle 79–80, 93, 95
 oath of loyalty to 210–12, 216

and the Police Special Court 213
and resistance fighters 138, 140–3, 147
Waaler's interrogation 224–31
Waaler as police prosecutor 193–202, 246
see also Gestapo
Statsakt (State Act, 1942) 67–71, 73, 302–3
  celebrations 67–71, 76–9, 97–8, 176
  and the Norwegian Holocaust 105–6
  and Quisling's trial 315
  the state church and the Conscience Struggle 74–82
Stavanger 21, 39
Steen, Erling 58
Stein, Kristian 139
Steiner, Rudolf 168
Stephanson, Judge Carl Ludwig von 250, 329, 331–2, 337, 338–9, 349, 351–2
Stølen, Arne 155
Støren, Johan, Bishop of Trondheim 74–5, 77–9
Storting (Norwegian legislature) 10
  and the Administrative Council 31
  evacuation of members 22–3, 25–6
  general election (1945) 301
  Norway's declaration of independence 7–8
  Presidentskap (Presidential Council) 31–3
  reparations to the Norwegian Jews 410
  and the State Act 69–70
Straume, Birger 173
Straveseth, Charles 196
Streicher, Julius 232
strikes 10, 14, 56–8, 304
  milk strike 62, 63–4, 65
Sturluson, Snorri
  Saga of Harald Hårfagre 47
Stutthof prison camp 212
Sunde, Arnfinn 217, 218–20, 227, 244

Sunde, Asbjørn 136–51, 404–6
  bank robberies 147, 148–50
  and the Black Hand 146–7
  Menn i mørket (Men in Darkness) 140–3
Sunde, Haakon 145, 146
Sundlo, Konrad 21–2
Supreme Court 27, 51, 67, 134
Svendsen, Einar Thorberg 323
Svolvær 76
Sweden
  and the Cold War 397–8
  Jewish refugees in 107, 110–11, 122
  Jews and 'Carl Fredriksens Transport' 113–15
  Norway's independence from 5–6, 7–8
  Norwegian refugees 87–8, 139, 213, 300, 311, 337–8, 381, 407
  resistance fighters in 156, 157–8
  and Waaler 191–2, 214, 240
Sweden-Norway, Kingdom of 5–6
Sylten, Mikal 61

Tallaksen, Edvard 245, 379–81, 382–3, 384
Tangen, Jens 59
teachers
  and the Conscience Struggle 73–4, 82–7, 98–102
  National Unity legislation on 72–3
Telavåg
  resistance group in 135–6
Terboven, Josef
  and the *Blumenpflücken* campaign 233
  Civilian State of Emergency (CSE) 59–60, 62–3, 65, 109, 178
  and the Conscience Struggle 86
  and Eilifsen 205, 210
  and the evacuation of northern Norway 252–3
  and Helberg 161–2
  and Ingrid Bjerkås 91–3, 96, 102
  and Marthinsen's killing 260

INDEX

meeting with Berggrav 52–5
and the National Unity party 164
as Norway's *Reichskommissar*
  28–9, 30, 31, 33–6, 39–40,
  42–4, 58–9, 76
and Norwegian culture 165
and the Norwegian Work Service
  144
and the police force 185, 192
and Quisling 35–6, 314
and the State Act (1942) 67–8, 71,
  80, 185
suicide 262–4, 283
and trade union activism 57–60,
  65
and Weiner 236
Thaulow, Fritz 169
theatre 171–9
Thorhus, Sverre 22, 216–17, 223,
  24–3, 376
Thorne, General Andrew 300, 301
Thu, Arne 103–4
Tiden publishing house 166–7
Tiedemann, Adolf 169
Tinghus, Oslo 207
Tjørn, Johan 225–7, 230, 231
Tofteberg, Arne 142
Tønsberg 120
Torsvik, Harald 326–7
torture 42, 88–9, 139–40, 142–3, 280
  and the death penalty 304, 311
  Knut Mathiesen 330–1
  and the Police Special Court 213
  and the Rinnan Band 323–4
  and Waaler's interrogation
    226–8
Traaen, Pastor Carl 318
trade union activism 56–66, 135
Trandum Forest
  executions in 135, 142, 146–7,
    159, 320
Tranmæl, Martin 11
Tromsø 27, 29
  Reichskommissariat branch in 39
Trondheim
  Gestapo headquarters 75–6
  Kristiansten Fortress 325
  Nidaros Cathedral 47, 49, 74–9,
    256

Reichskommissariat branch in
  39
Students' Union 51
Trøndelag theatre company
  171–3, 174–7
Waaler as district attorney in
  409
and the *Weserübung* operation
  21, 28, 29
Trondheim Fjord 16
Trotsky, Leon 223, 277, 292, 344–5

Ulstein, Ragnar 138
Universalism 317
Upwall, Karl 225, 226, 231

Vigdis (film) 180–1
Vikersund
  Modum Sparebank robbery
    147–50
Vikings 48, 49, 50
Viksjold, Finn 23

Waal, Dr Nic 122–3
Waaler, Georg, pathologist 298,
  331, 343
Waaler, Gunnar 186–246, 406–7
  as district attorney for Trondheim
    409
  and Engeseth 214
  and the German invasion 186–8
  in Grini prison 243–4, 259
  and Jonas Lie 276
  and Knut Mathiesen
    trial of 329–57
    witness to execution of
      274–95
  as legal advisor to the public
    prosecutor 181, 214, 387
  as Milorg double agent 186,
    212, 213–14, 215–16, 228, 244,
    245–6, 374–5, 387, 406–7
  and National Archive documents
    240, 241–2
  National Unity membership 216
  in Nazi Germany 187–8
  and the occupation 191–3
  as police prosecutor in the
    Staspolitiet 192–202

and the Police Special Court 209, 212
release from prison 244–5
and the SS 188–90
Stapo interrogation of 216–31
and Weiner 231, 237–46, 249, 409
Wegener, Paul 36
Weiner, Albert 231–46, 408–9
background 232–3
Blumenpflücken campaign 233–4, 237, 408
and the *Jugendabteilung* 234–5
and Waaler 237–46, 249, 409
Werenskiold, Erik 169
Wergeland, Henrik 108
Weserübung operation (German invasion of Norway) 2, 18–25, 28–30, 39, 92, 186–7, 313–14
Wessel, Horst 71
Westlie, Bjørn 410
Weygand, Maxine 192
Wickstrøm, Rolf 61–2, 63–4, 135, 304
Wiers-Jenssen, Hans
Anne Pedersdotter 174–5
Wiesener, Albert 154–5, 181, 206, 208, 403
Wiig, Thorvald 324–5

Wilhelm II, Kaiser 1, 34
Willoch, Kåre 165
Wisth, Olav 324
Wold, Terje 256
Wolff, Karl 55
Wollweber Organisation 137–8
women
and the Conscience Struggle Ingrid Bjerkås 23–4, 91–103, 400–1
for schoolteachers 84–5, 86
mothers of Norwegian-German children 164–5
prisoners 42
the *Sivorg* circle 115–23
Work Service 71–3, 80, 82, 143–7, 151, 204–5, 207, 213, 379, 382
Wright, Myrtle 115–21, 133–4, 140, 162–3
Norwegian Diary 1940–1945 116
Wulfsberg, Jens
and the Skallum Manor siege 268–78, 279, 281–2, 284–5, 288–98, 403

young people
and Work Service 71–3, 80, 82, 143–7, 151, 204–5, 207, 213, 379, 382